The WINNERS! Handbook

A Closer Look at Judy Freeman's Top-Rated Children's Books of 2010

GRADES PreK-6

Judy Freeman

LIBRARIES UNLIMITED

AN IMPRINT OF ABC-CLIO, LLC
Santa Barbara, California • Denver, Colorado • Oxford, England

ISBN: 978–1–59884–977–6
EISBN: 978–1–59884–982–0

15 14 13 12 11   1 2 3 4 5

This book is also available on the World Wide Web as an eBook.
Visit www.abc-clio.com for details.

Libraries Unlimited
An Imprint of ABC-CLIO, LLC

ABC-CLIO, LLC
130 Cremona Drive, P.O. Box 1911
Santa Barbara, California 93116-1911

This book is printed on acid-free paper ∞
Manufactured in the United States of America

028.162

The WINNERS! Handbook
A CLOSER LOOK AT JUDY FREEMAN'S TOP-RATED CHILDREN'S BOOKS OF 2010
GRADES PreK-6

CONTENTS

CONTENTS, cont.

WHAT IS THE PURPOSE OF THIS PROGRAM?

Every year, well over 5,000 new books are published for children. In order to review and evaluate those new books properly, a conscientious book selector would have to read more than 13 books every day of the year. Most already-overworked librarians therefore depend on the book reviews in professional journals and online for guidance, but even a good review can be misleading.

Each year, several prestigious professional organizations and publications present their nominations for the "best" books of the year. Libraries with limited budgets may decide that the "best of the year" list is what they should buy, but even those critical lists frequently disagree with each other! So how do you decide which books you really need to buy for your classroom or library, and why?

In 1985, having been burned too often by inaccurate reviews and incomprehensible lists, I began, along with Alice Yucht, another children's books maven and New Jersey librarian, what became an annual project: to critically examine and compare all the books from four of those yearly lists: "Notable Children's Books" from the Association of Library Services to Children (ALSC), a division of the American Library Association; "Editor's Choice" from *Booklist*; "Fanfare" from *Horn Book*; and "Best of the Year" from *School Library Journal*.

Each year Alice and I found that many titles were on only one or two of the lists, that we were unimpressed (or even astonished) by some of the books chosen, and that some of the titles we considered outstanding had been ignored. That's why we began presenting **WINNERS!**, our own original all-day workshop for teachers, librarians, and other book-lovers, then sponsored by the Professional Development Studies Department of Rutgers University's School of Communication, Information, and Library Studies. After ten years, in 1994, Alice decided to bid a fond cheerio, and ever since, I've done the program on my own. After twenty years of Rutgers sponsorship, WINNERS! is now presented under the auspices of my publisher, Libraries Unlimited, which also publishes this spiffy handbook for the workshop.

As a Web-based children's book reviewer (for **NoveList**, the online database; *School Library Journal*'s **Curriculum Connections**; and author James Patterson's website, **www.READKIDDOREAD.com**); writer of professional books about children's literature; and a presenter of many workshops, seminars, and speeches throughout the U.S. and abroad, I read a lot. I spend much of my professional time each year evaluating and considering which books teachers, librarians, and parents would love to share with their kids. I search for memorable and exemplary books that are read-alouds, read-alones, and resources for the classroom and library. I look for a multicultural treatment of the world, and books that boys and girls will find unforgettable—an eclectic mixture of picture books, fiction, nonfiction, biography, poetry, and folklore, all with varied interest and reading levels, that you can use as welcome companions to your curriculum.

In order to share with you, my colleagues, what I've learned, I develop and present an all-new, all-day edition of **WINNERS!** each year, showing and telling my reactions to the past year's "best" books for pre-kindergarten through sixth grade. From the thousands of children's books I've read each year, I choose 100 or so titles, all published in the past year, pulling together my favorites on and off the major "Best of the Year" lists into my own personal list of significant, controversial, and/or award-winning books I feel teachers and librarians will want to know.

I'll give you my honest opinions and those of other professional book reviewers; then it's up to you to examine the books and decide what you think. After all, you are the one who makes the decision on what books you find to be the best to introduce to your children. I would never expect everyone to agree with all my choices, and relish discussing our differing opinions. May you find many of these books to be welcome companions to your students, your curriculum, and your life.

HOW IS "WINNERS!" PUT TOGETHER?

Although I read reviews and new books all year, the serious work for WINNERS! can't really begin until mid-December, when the first of the "year's best" lists come out. By then I have already started to predict much of what will be on the lists, and what will win major awards, but I am always surprised at some of the final choices. I read, and reread. As each list is published, I start to see the overlaps, disagreements, and gaps. I weed out titles that I don't consider especially noteworthy.

I compile my list of personal favorites and then consult the lists to fill in award-winners, significant, controversial, or provocative titles, and books I may have overlooked or not seen. I choose books I personally think no teacher or librarian should live without, most of which are glorious read-alouds, but also great read-alones, and if/when they come out in paperback, ideal for Book Clubs and discussion groups.

It's one thing for me to like a book, but until I've tried it out with the people for whom it is intended—actual children—I can't know for sure how it will go over. I field test as many books as possible with children, fellow librarians, and teachers, so each book can be judged both intrinsically, and in its targeted "user context." Since leaving my school library job in 2000, I have stayed current by visiting classes of children in grades kindergarten to six at several New Jersey schools. Several times a year, I visit these schools to work with the teachers, librarians, and children.

For each visit, I bring in a big box of my favorite new books to try out, and spend the day working with many classes of children and their wonderful teachers and librarians. I test out, read aloud, and booktalk a batch of books with each group. I give the teachers suggested lesson plans, detailing some ideas for making each book come alive through writing and discussion prompts, curricular and research projects, drama, music, art, movement, and games. The teachers use their knowledge of their kids, their innate creativity, and their sense of fun to do interesting, fulfilling, and often spectacular follow-ups with their classes, and give me samples to bring with me to my workshops.

I am indebted to all the wonderful educators and students at these schools. I give my heartfelt thanks to two special librarians this year—Maren Vitali, librarian at Milltown School in Bridgewater, NJ; and Loreli Stochaj, librarian at Franklin School in Summit, NJ—for their time, generosity, coordinating skills, ideas, innovative lesson plans, and friendship. You'll see some of their many projects in this handbook.

By February, my eyeballs are falling out, but I begin to see a pattern in the year's publishing, and that shapes the program I present to you. To the booktalks and show-and-tell descriptions, I add songs, chants, stories, related titles, curricular ideas I call "GERMS" that you can borrow and "germinate" as you see fit, and assorted fun but educationally relevant shtick that you can take back to try out on your own children.

In this handbook, you will find my annotated booklists of my 100+ favorite or noteworthy books of the past year, 2010. You'll find a list of the books I chose not to review during the workshop on page 64, and the list of young adult titles for grades seven and up that don't fit our grade PreK-6 audience on page 67.

Follett Library Resources, thanks to the efforts of the wonderful David Rothrock, has been kind enough, for the past many years, to support the WINNERS! Workshops. To make ordering easy, look for the annotated WINNERS! list on the Follett website. (Open your free TitleWave account at Follett's indispensable website at **www.titlewave.com**. You can even find, for easy ordering, all my best books lists there from last year's and this year's BER and WINNERS! conferences. After you log in, click on: **Essentials > Expert Picks > Judy Freeman > Judy Freeman/Drill Down**.) You'll also find this list on the Mackin site, at **www.mackin.com**.

ABOUT THE "WINNERS!" RATINGS

THE "BEST OF THE YEAR" LISTS

As you will see, the four following well-known and respected "Best of the Year" booklists often disagree with each other. In fact, each year very few titles make it onto all four lists! This year, out of a total of **158** books, *only 3* were on all four lists. (Look for *A|B|H|S|* to find them.) Only **6** were on three lists, **31** were on two lists, and a whopping **118** were on only one list. I also included **47** of my own additional choices to the list, for a **GRAND TOTAL of 205 titles**, out of which I chose **101** to cover in my program and in this handbook.

|A| *American Library Association's "ALSC's Notable Children's Books"*
Announced at the ALA Midwinter Conference, and published in *Booklist's* March 15th issue and *School Library Journal's* March issue. Compiled by the Notable Children's Books Committee (different members each year) of the Association for Library Service to Children, a division of ALA. Included are books for children up to age 14. **Go to:**
www.ala.org/ala/mgrps/divs/alsc/awardsgrants/childrensnotable/index.cfm

|B| *Booklist "Children's Editors' Choice"*
Published in the January issue. Selected by the Children's Books Editors as being examples of the year's most outstanding picture books, fiction, and nonfiction. These titles represent their best-of-the-year selections, based on literary and artistic quality, and on special appeal to older and middle readers and the young. **Go to: *www.booklistonline.com* and scroll way down to Awards on the left, where you'll see the link for "Booklist Editors' Choice."**

|H| *The Horn Book "Fanfare"*
Published in the January/February issue. Honor list of titles chosen by the editors.
Go to: *www.hbook.com/resources/books/fanfare/fanfare11_short.asp*

|S| *School Library Journal "Best Books of the Year"*
Published in the December issue. Selected by the SLJ book review editors as the best of the titles reviewed in the magazine that year. ". . . books . . . have been selected as the best among the year's output on the basis of their originality, quality of writing and art, presentation of material, and appeal to the intended audience." **Go to: *www.schoollibraryjournal.com* and type "Best Books 2010" in the search bar.**

ABOUT JUDY FREEMAN'S PERSONAL RATINGS

[J] Judy considers this book a winner. Included in this category are marvelous titles that you won't want to miss, including a good number of books all the other review journals and established lists overlooked, and which Judy felt deserved to be included.

[J*] Judy then starred those titles she considered to be the best of the best.

[j] Judy didn't consider this book to be one of her "best of the year" choices, but she liked it well enough to consider it worth buying.

[_] Judy felt that this book was not worth purchasing. Her opinion of this book ranges from mild indifference to strong dislike.

[X] Judy loathed this book, and/or vehemently disagreed with its inclusion on a "best books" list. (NOTE: There were no [X] books again this year. Judy must be getting mellower.)

WHAT HAPPENS AT THE WINNERS! WORKSHOP?

This program, which I create from scratch every year, my five-hour vaudeville act and passion play for all book-lovers, grades PreK-6, is set up like a school day: language arts in the morning, when we're fresh and ready to read, and a tour of the curriculum after lunch—math, science, social studies, and don't forget the special areas!—with an end-of-day cool down of folklore-based stories and fantasies. It is my aim to recommend stimulating, enticing, and practical ways to use these books with their intended audience—**children**.

During the **WINNERS! Workshop**, we examine each book's possible classroom and library connections, from story hour to school curriculum tie-ins, including writing and drawing prompts, lots of comprehension and critical thinking skills, songs, plenty of great across-the-curriculum poetry, creative drama and Reader's Theater, storytelling, and, of course, nonstop booktalking all day long.

All day I endeavor to model hundreds of useful strategies, ideas, activities, lessons, read-aloud techniques, writing prompts, and ways you can incorporate literature into every aspect of your day and your life. Many of my ideas are what I call "quick and dirty"—you hear it today, and take it back to inflict on your kids tomorrow. I'll show you what I've found really works with real kids.

My best advice: Read off your grade level! Enjoy fooling around with the books you might never get to see otherwise. The **WINNERS! Workshop** is a day for reveling, for wading, and for wallowing in print. It's a day for readers, but also a day for writers and artists. Over the course of the day, we'll model, appreciate, and emulate dozens of writing techniques, strategies, and styles to try out with your children. Keep an open mind as we look at this past year's treasures and trends. I love to bring in examples of children's work to showcase on the display tables and in my program. It's a highlight of the day for me. Quite a few examples are reproduced in this book.

Will every book or idea apply to your situation? Well, no, not every one. This is a PreK-6 workshop. It's always up to you to pick and choose those books and ideas you can use and develop, that you feel will work best with your kids, whether you're a teacher looking for classroom read-alouds, writing prompts, and curriculum tie-ins; a school librarian looking for library lesson ideas and books to recommend to staff and students; or a public librarian, who needs to be a reader's advisory expert in every aspect of children's lit, pre-birth to post-teen.

And once I finish presenting this year's best books program, there are already shelves and boxes bursting with the Spring, 2011 books waiting for me in my garret and stacked up in the basement so I can get started on next year's seminars. We're hoping to have the garage rebuilt this year, complete with floor-to-ceiling bookshelves so I can get organized for once. Want to come over and help me move everything?

ACKNOWLEDGMENTS

I GIVE GRATEFUL THANKS TO:

FOLLETT LIBRARY RESOURCES and my pal **DAVID ROTHROCK** for saving my bacon with **TitleWave.com** and providing the online order list for this program.

DEBBY LABOON for her support and her determined never-say-die, I-can-do-that attitude that keeps the WINNERS! Conference running every year.

EMMA BAILEY for being so patient and editing and preparing the WINNERS! Handbook on such a tight deadline.

THE STUDENTS AND STAFF AT MILLTOWN ELEMENTARY SCHOOL, BRIDGEWATER, NJ AND FRANKLIN SCHOOL, SUMMIT, NJ for helping me test out, evaluate, come up with wonderful ideas for, and fool around with so many new books.

A special thanks for their innovation and imagination in creating one-of-a-kind follow-up projects and lesson plans, to librarian **MAREN VITALI** at Milltown School and **LORELI STOCHAJ**, librarian at Franklin School, both of whom also devoted inordinate amounts of time and energy to coordinate my visits and/or inspire their students to turn out amazing responses to this year's WINNERS! books.

The following teachers generously gave of their time and expertise; their students once again created delightful and intriguing follow-up projects:

Milltown Elementary School, Bridgewater, NJ
GRADE 1:	**Esther Loor, Brittany Maple**
GRADE 2:	**Erin Hodgdon, Keri Peloso**
GRADE 4:	**Phoebe Hastings, Jamie Vinciguerra**
LIBRARY:	**Maren Vitali**

Franklin Elementary School, Summit, NJ:
GRADE 1:	**Amy Chambers**
LIBRARY:	**Loreli Stochaj**

Thanks to my wonderful brother **RICHARD FREEMAN** who volunteered once again to proofread everything without even complaining.

And, as always, to my best-in-the-world husband, **IZZY FELDMAN**, who puts up with way more than anyone should have to and is always ready to drag the Attic Girl out for a movie or a vacation.

Welcome to Judy Freeman's 27th Annual
WINNERS! CONFERENCE

A Closer Look at the 100+ Top-Rated
Children's Books of 2010

Presented April 26–April 29, 2011

HIGHLIGHTS OF TODAY'S SCHEDULE

8:30–10:00   **LANGUAGE ARTS**
 Books About Books
 School & Home Stories
 Reading & Writing & Wordplay

10:00–10:15   **BREAK (& BOOK LOOK)**

10:15–12:00   **MORE LANGUAGE ARTS**
 Writing & Reading & More Wordplay
 Poetry Break

12:00–1:00   **LUNCH (& BOOK LOOK)**

1:00–2:10   **BOOKS ACROSS THE CURRICULUM**
 The Arts, Sports, Math, Science

2:10–2:20   **BREAK (& BOOK LOOK)**

2:20–3:00   **BOOKS ACROSS THE CURRICULUM**
 Social Studies
 Memorable Folklore & Fantasy Books

WINNERS!

A Closer Look at the 100+ Top-Rated Children's Books of 2010
for Grades PreK-6

THE ANNOTATED BOOKLIST

Compiled and written by Judy Freeman, Spring, 2011

The following "WINNERS!" booklist, arranged in alphabetical order by title, contains 101 of the most memorable, interesting, distinguished, and award-winning titles published in 2010. The list is broken into four sections: Easy Fiction/Picture Books; Fiction Books; Nonfiction and Biography Books; and Poetry and Folklore Books. For easy access, refer to the Author and Title Index on page 200 and the Subject Index on page 208.

EACH BOOK ENTRY CONSISTS OF SIX PARTS:

1. **RATINGS:** You can compare each title to see if Judy Freeman, your seminar leader, adored it [**J***]; loved it [**J**]; liked it OK [**j**]; disliked it [**_**]; or truly loathed it [**X**], and see which of the review journals (**A** = ALA Notables List; **B** = Booklist; **H** = Horn Book; and **S** = School Library Journal) included it on their "Best of the Year" lists. A book on all four lists will look like this: |**A**|**B**|**H**|**S**|. A book that was not on any of the four lists looks like this: | | | | |. (These are books Judy nevertheless thought were "bests.")

2. **BIBLIOGRAPHIC INFO:** Includes title, author, illustrator, publisher and date, ISBN number, number of pages, call number (**E** = Easy Fiction/Picture Book; **FIC** = Fiction; **B** = Biography; **#** = Nonfiction), and suggested grade level range (though that is never set in stone; picture books so often can, should, must be used well beyond their intended grade levels—what I call Picture Books for All Ages).

3. **ANNOTATION:** To help you remember what the book is about, or to lure you into reading it.

4. **GERM:** A good, practical, do-able, useful, pithy idea; one or more ways to use the book for reading, writing, and illustrating prompts and other activities across the curriculum, and for story hour programs, including creative drama, Reader's Theater, storytelling, group discussion, booktalks, games, crafts, research, and problem-solving. Your mission is to take that *Germ* of an idea and "germinate" or synthesize it as you see fit: nurture it, grow it, expand upon it, and incorporate it into your own lessons, programs, and story hours to make them shine.

5. **RELATED TITLES LIST:** A carefully compiled list of exemplary books that share the same theme, subject, style, genre, or type of characters; are by the same author; or extend the reader's knowledge. The more than 900 related titles listed will give you a tour through the best children's books of the past many years. Use these for read-alouds, thematic units, story hour tie-ins, and booktalks; for Guided Reading, Literature Circles, or Book Clubs; and for Reader's Advisory to recommend to kids as wonderful follow-up reads.

6. **SUBJECTS:** Subject designations for each title so you can ascertain where the book might fit thematically into your curricular plan, literary program, or your life. You'll find all of these listed in the Subject Index on page 208.

WINNERS!:
100+ Best Children's Books of 2010

EASY FICTION / PICTURE BOOKS

[J*] | | | |S|
Animal Crackers Fly the Coop. O'Malley, Kevin. Illus. by the author. Walker, 2010. {ISBN-13: 978-0-8027-9837-4; 32p.} E (Gr. 1-4)

Hen loves to tell jokes and dreams of being a standup comedi-hen in a comedy club. (A sample of her material: Why did the chicken go to the library? To check out the *bawk, bawk, bawk.* For a story using this punch line, go to page 193 of this handbook.) Sick of working for chicken feed, she won't lay eggs, and the farmer is planning to turn her into chicken dinner come Fry-day. Instead, she flies the coop and takes to the road. She meets up with three other aspiring comics: a brown and white hound, a cat-erwauling gray cat, and an udderly miserable brown and white cow. When they come upon an old house and spy upon the three robbers inside who then head out to rob a bank, the four animals take over the place. Back come the robbers, greeted by the four animals, who tell them jokes and scare them silly. You know this story as "The Musicians of Bremen" by the Brothers Grimm. There's no singing in this version, just comedy. O'Malley's dedication says it all: "For my dad, who worried we'd grow up with no sense of humor." Fine black-lined inks, colored with Photoshop, look like old-time lithographs, but a lot funnier. The black and white eyes of those soulful-faced animals burn with intensity, determined as they are to fulfill their dream of opening their own animal comedy club.

GERM: The riddles begin on the endpapers, where the four animals tell and answer such truly kid-funny numbers as: What do cows do for entertainment? They rent mooovies! And: What was the name of the very intelligent monster? Frank Einstein. Continue with the similarly-punned companion book, *Gimme Cracked Corn and I Will Share,* and then have your punsters tell all the jokes they know. Get started with the riddles on page 181 of this handbook. Do read or tell the original folktale, reprinted on page 184 of this handbook, so children can understand the parody elements in O'Malley's version. For another spirited retelling, read aloud Jan Huling's deliciously down home *Ol' Bloo's Boogie-Woogie Band and Blues Ensemble,* set in the Louisiana woods.

RELATED TITLES: Emberley, Rebecca. *Three Cool Kids.* Little, Brown, 1995. / Grimm, Jacob, and Wilhelm Grimm. *The Bremen Town Musicians.* North-South, 1992. / Hawkins, Colin, and Jacqui Hawkins. *The Fairytale News.* Candlewick, 2004. / Huling, Jan. *Ol' Bloo's Boogie-Woogie Band and Blues Ensemble.* Peachtree, 2010. / Kimmel, Eric A. *The Three Little Tamales.* Marshall Cavendish, 2009. / O'Malley, Kevin. *Gimme Cracked Corn and I Will Share.* Walker, 2007. / O'Malley, Kevin. *Humpty Dumpty Egg-Splodes.* Walker, 2001. / O'Malley, Kevin. *Once Upon a Cool Motorcycle Dude.* Walker, 2005. / Paul, Ann Whitford. *Tortuga In Trouble.* Holiday House, 2009. / Plume, Ilse. *The Bremen-Town Musicians.* Bantam, 1980. / Scieszka, Jon. *The Stinky Cheese Man and Other Fairly Stupid Tales.* Viking, 1992. / Scieszka, Jon. *The True Story of the 3 Little Pigs.* Viking, 1989.

SUBJECTS: ANIMALS. CATS. CHICKENS. COMEDIANS. DOGS. HUMOROUS FICTION. JOKES. LANGUAGE ARTS. PARODIES. READER'S THEATER. RIDDLES. ROBBERS AND OUTLAWS. WORDPLAY.

EASY FICTION / PICTURE BOOKS, cont.

[J] |A| |H| |

April and Esme, Tooth Fairies. **Graham, Bob. Illus. by the author. Candlewick, 2010. {ISBN-13: 978-0-7636-4683-7; 40p.} E (Gr. PreK-2) 2011 Charlotte Zolotow Honor Book**

When seven-year-old tooth fairy, April Underhill, gets a call on her cell phone from a grandma asking for a tooth visit for her grandson, she and her little sister Esme start making plans to fly to Parkville that evening. Their mom and dad think the girls are far too young to go out on their own this first time, but they give their blessing and some advice. Dad says, "To Daniel, you are a . . . a . . . spirit of the air. You are magic. He must never see you." Mom gives them a string bag to hold the coin on the way out and the tooth on the way back. These tiny winged flying people have all the modern conveniences in their two-story thatched house nestled in a tree trunk near the busy highway: a bathtub made out of a cream pitcher, a sink made from a thimble, and even a little brown winged dog for a pet. Paneled ink and watercolor illustrations of the two tiny winged girls flying through the moonlit sky to Daniel's house are utterly believable. They crawl under the front door, and "THERE'S THE TOOTH!" Esme cries, shivering with excitement. Unfortunately, he's left it in a glass of water. April dives for it and brings it out just as Daniel wakes up. Together the sisters pull his eyes shut again, and then text Mommy for advice. (Who knew tooth fairies were so tech-y?) When they arrive back home with their first tooth, Mom and Dad hug them till their wings crackle and hang it with string from the rafters.

GERM: This charmer gives us a whole different perspective on the life and work of a tooth fairy. Expect a spirited discussion of loose and lost teeth and how tooth fairies operate. Meet a very different kind of tooth fairy in *Mabel the Tooth Fairy and How She Got Her Job* by Katie Davis.

RELATED TITLES: Bate, Lucy. *Little Rabbit's Loose Tooth.* Crown, 1975. / Beeler, Selby B. *Throw Your Tooth on the Roof: Tooth Traditions from Around the World.* Houghton Mifflin, 1998. / Birdseye, Tom. *Airmail to the Moon.* Holiday House, 1988. / Davis, Katie. *Mabel the Tooth Fairy and How She Got Her Job.* Harcourt, 2003. / Diakité, Penda. *I Lost My Tooth in Africa.* Scholastic, 2006. / Graham, Bob. *Dimity Dumpty: The Story of Humpty's Little Sister.* Candlewick, 2007. / Graham, Bob. *How to Heal a Broken Wing.* Candlewick, 2008. / Graham, Bob. *Max.* Candlewick, 2000. / Graham, Bob. *"Let's Get a Pup!" Said Kate.* Candlewick, 2001. / Keller, Laurie. *Open Wide: Tooth School Inside.* Henry Holt, 2000. / MacDonald, Amy. *Cousin Ruth's Tooth.* Houghton Mifflin, 1996. / McGhee, Alison. *Mrs. Watson Wants Your Teeth.* Harcourt, 2004. / Palatini, Margie. *Sweet Tooth.* Simon & Schuster, 2004. / Steig, William. *Doctor De Soto.* Farrar, 1982.

SUBJECTS: FAIRIES. FANTASY. RESPONSIBILITY. SISTERS. TEETH. TOOTH FAIRY.

[J*] | | | |S|

Art & Max. **Wiesner, David. Illus. by the author. Clarion, 2010. {ISBN-13: 978-0-618-75663-6; 32p.} E (Gr. PreK-6)**

Every time you think David Wiesner can't surpass his last award-winning picture book, he gobsmacks you anew with something astonishing. He's already won three Caldecott gold medals and two silvers. There might be another one in the wings for this imaginative romp about the power of art. Art and Max are two desert lizards who love to paint. Arthur, the establishment guy, is a slightly pompous brown horned lizard who paints serious portraits of other lizards. Little green Max is the goofy young upstart who insists he *can* paint, but doesn't know *what* to paint. Arthur says, "Well . . . you could paint me." Max takes him literally, covering Art's body in dripping blues, yellows and reds. That's when the book really goes haywire. "This is preposterous," Arthur exclaims. "Max!" he roars, causing the paint to literally explode from his body, leaving him with an undercoat of dusty rainbow colors. When he takes a drink of water, the color washes right off leaving only his outline. Max grabs hold of Art's tail, and the line collapses into a tangle, which Max then must reassemble and recolor, Jackson Pollock–style. Visually mind-blowing, this is an imaginative romp that defies logic but gets us all looking at Art (and Arthur) with fresh eyes.

GERM: Illustrations done in bright shades of acrylic, pastel, watercolor, and India ink will have young artists itching to fool around in mixed media. Break out the paints, though nix any thoughts of body painting. Ask an open-ended question to your kids: What is art? Have a Wiesner Fest of his many groundbreaking picture books.

RELATED TITLES: Bishop, Nic. *Nic Bishop Lizards.* Scholastic, 2010. / Hurd, Thacher. *Art Dog.* HarperCollins, 1996. / Juster, Norton. *The Dot and the Line: A Romance in Lower Mathematics.* Chronicle, 2000, c1963. / Laden, Nina. *When Pigasso Met Mootisse.* Chronicle, 1998. / LaMarche, Jim. *The Raft.* HarperCollins, 2000. / Lithgow, John. *Micawber.* Simon & Schuster, 2002. / Raczka, Bob. *Art Is . . .* Millbrook, 2003. / Reynolds, Peter H. *The Dot.* Candlewick, 2003. / Thomson, Bill. *Chalk.* Marshall Cavendish, 2010. / Wiesner, David. *Flotsam.* Clarion, 2006. / Wiesner, David. *Free Fall.* Lothrop, 1988. / Wiesner, David. *Sector 7.* Clarion, 1999. / Wiesner, David. *The Three Pigs.* Clarion, 2001. / Wiesner, David. *Tuesday.* Clarion, 1991.

SUBJECTS: ARTISTS. FRIENDSHIP. LIZARDS. PAINTING.

[J] | | | | |

Banana! **Vere, Ed. Illus. by the author. Henry Holt, 2010. {ISBN-13: 978-0-8050-9214-1; 32p.} E (Gr. PreK-1)**
How much emotion can you invest in the word "banana"? In this nearly wordless book, a googly-eyed, ropy-tailed, ebullient brown monkey in a red and white striped shirt pursues a monkey in a blue and white shirt, who is tossing a banana in the air. "Banana!" the first monkey shouts, while the other one holds the fruit covetously. The banana-deprived monkey demands, has a tantrum, cries piteously, and finally says, "Please" (the only other word in the text), before he gets to share that tantalizing piece of fruit. Illustrated against superbright monochrome backgrounds, the figures of the two monkeys look like they've been outlined by a toddler wielding an oversized black marker.
GERM: Toddlers on up will recognize the stages of grief the monkey experiences when he thinks he's not getting that banana, and can act out the whole story. Bring in bananas so you can have kids pair up and share. Teach them how equitable sharing works: one person divides the banana; the other person has first choice of the two pieces. Then go bananas with the "Go Bananas" chant in this handbook on page 178.
RELATED TITLES: Anholt, Catherine, and Laurence Anholt. *Chimp and Zee.* Putnam, 2001. / Christelow, Eileen. *Five Little Monkeys Jumping on the Bed.* Clarion, 1989. / Elliott, David. *Finn Throws a Fit.* Candlewick, 2009. / Freymann, Saxton. *Fast Food.* Arthur A. Levine/Scholastic, 2006. / Gravett, Emily. *Monkey and Me.* Simon & Schuster, 2008. / Gravett, Emily. *Orange Pear Apple Bear.* Simon & Schuster, 2007. / Raschka, Chris. *Yo! Yes?* Orchard, 1993. / Willems, Mo. *The Pigeon Finds a Hot Dog.* Hyperion, 2004. / Yolen, Jane. *How Do Dinosaurs Eat Their Food?* Scholastic/Blue Sky, 2005.
SUBJECTS: BANANAS. CREATIVE DRAMA. EASY READERS. LANGUAGE ARTS. MANNERS. MONKEYS. SHARING.

[J] | | | | |

A Bedtime for Bear. **Becker, Bonny. Illus. by Kady MacDonald Denton. Candlewick, 2010. {ISBN-13: 978-0-7636-4101-6; 32p.} E (Gr. PreK-2)**
Welcome to the sparkling third installment (following *A Visitor for Bear* and *A Birthday for Bear*) of the developing relationship between a gruff brown bear and his new mouse friend, small and gray and bright-eyed. Mouse appears at Bear's door one evening, clasping a tiny red suitcase in his paw, ready to spend the night. Bear has never had an overnight visitor before, and he is a fellow who requires absolute quiet when he sleeps. After a pleasant evening of checkers and warm cocoa, the two head off to bed. Mouse's bed is contained in a little drawer partially pulled out from Bear's night table and is made up with a blue blanket and tiny pillow. Mouse brushes his teeth and hums softly while donning his long white night shirt. Bear, in his multicolored nightcap grits his teeth and cries, "My ears are highly sensitive." To test this, Mouse hides in the farthest corner of the closet and uses his tiniest voice to see if Bear can still hear him. Irascible Bear wails, "Will this torment never cease!" When the two finally settle into bed, Bear is unnerved by noises he thinks he hears in the house, and wakes Mouse up to investigate. In a sweet turnaround, Mouse checks the house and allows Bear to tell him a bedtime story about the "Brave Strong Bear and the Very Frightened Little Mouse," though readers will recognize that Mouse is the fearless one. Denton's watercolor, ink and gouache illustrations capture perfectly the contrasting personalities of the large, lumpy, set-in-his ways Bear and tiny, insouciant, insightful Mouse.
GERM: Ask your listeners what they do each night to get ready for bed and the techniques they use to fall asleep. Hold a bedtime story hour for your own little mice. Go to page 150 for Judy Freeman's Reader's Theater script of the whole story.
RELATED TITLES: Becker, Bonny. *A Birthday for Bear.* Candlewick, 2009. / Becker, Bonny. *A Visitor for Bear.* Candlewick, 2008. / Murphy, Jill. *Peace at Last.* Dial, 1980. / Murray, Marjorie Dennis. *Don't Wake Up the Bear!* Cavendish, 2003. / Waber, Bernard. *Bearsie Bear and the Surprise Sleepover Party.* Houghton Mifflin, 1997. / Wilson, Karma. *Bear Snores On.* McElderry, 2002.
SUBJECTS: BEARS. BEDTIME. FRIENDSHIP. MICE. READER'S THEATER. SLEEP. SLEEPOVERS. VISITORS.

EASY FICTION / PICTURE BOOKS, cont.

[J*] |A|B| | |

Big Red Lollipop. Khan, Rukhsana. Illus. by Sophie Blackall. Viking, 2010. {ISBN-13: 978-0-670-06287-4; 32p.} E (Gr. K-4) 2011 Charlotte Zolotow Award (for outstanding writing in a picture book)

Rubina is elated when she is invited to a birthday party, her first ever. "What's a birthday party," Ami, her mother, asks, for in Pakistan, where they're from, children don't celebrate the day they are born. Hearing about the upcoming games, toys, cake, and ice cream, Rubina's little sister, Sana, screams, "I wanna go too!" Ami won't let Rubina go unless she takes Sana, even though she's not even invited. At the party, Rubina is embarrassed to be the only one with a tag-along, crying little sister. The next day, when she goes to retrieve the big red lollipop she has saved from her goodie bag, there's only a little triangle of lollipop left on the stick. Sana! "She ate my lollipop! The greedy thing! She ate it!" Rubina storms. Their mother sides with Sana: "For shame. Can't you share with your little sister?" Worse still, no one invites Rubina to parties anymore, knowing her little sister will have to tag along. The characters are painted in spare, delicate watercolors outlined in fine black line, with expressive faces.

GERM: The author blurb on the back flap reveals that this story is based on an incident from the author's childhood in Canada. Ask your listeners why the girls' mother wanted Rubina and Sana to take their sisters to a birthday party to which they had not been invited. Discussion Point: What other customs do we follow in North America that a new immigrant might find unfamiliar. (As an adult, you'll empathize with her mother, still wearing traditional Pakistani dress, raising three daughters in a new land.) When reading the story aloud, stop at the point where Ami tells Sana that she'll need to bring little Maryam to the party, and have children predict what they think Rubina will do. Older children can do this as a Quick Write or write a persuasive letter to Ami explaining why Maryam should stay home. See the "Lollipop Vignettes" writing lesson developed by Maren Vitali, librarian at Milltown School in Bridgewater, NJ on page 99 in this handbook. It's not easy fitting in to a new place, as you'll also learn in *One Green Apple* by Eve Bunting and *The Gold-Threaded Dress* by Carolyn Marsden.

RELATED TITLES: Aliki. *Marianthe's Story.* Greenwillow, 1998. / Amato, Mary. *The Chicken of the Family.* Putnam, 2008. / Blumenthal, Deborah. *Don't Let the Peas Touch!: And Other Stories.* Scholastic, 2004. / Bunting, Eve. *One Green Apple.* Clarion, 2006. / Choi, Sook Nyul. *Halmoni and the Picnic.* Houghton Mifflin, 1993. / Cohen, Barbara. *Molly's Pilgrim.* Lothrop, 1983. / Garland, Sherry. *The Lotus Seed.* Harcourt, 1993. / Khan, Rukhsana. *Ruler of the Courtyard.* Viking, 2003. / Kline, Suzy. *Song Lee in Room 2B.* Viking, 1993. / Levine, Ellen. *I Hate English!* Scholastic, 1989. / Lin, Grace. *Ling & Ting: Not Exactly the Same!* Little, Brown, 2010. / Marsden, Carolyn. *The Gold-Threaded Dress.* Candlewick, 2002. / Nagda, Ann Whitehead. *Dear Whiskers.* Holiday House, 2000. / Pomeranc, Marion Hess. *The American Wei.* Albert Whitman, 1998. / Potter, Giselle. *Chloë's Birthday . . . and Me.* Atheneum, 2004. / Recorvits, Helen. *My Name Is Yoon.* Farrar, 2003.

SUBJECTS: ARAB AMERICANS. BEHAVIOR. BIRTHDAYS. CONDUCT OF LIFE. IMMIGRATION AND EMIGRATION. LOLLIPOPS. MOTHERS. MULTICULTURAL BOOKS. PARTIES. SIBLING RIVALRY. SISTERS.

[J*] |A| | | |

Bink and Gollie. DiCamillo, Kate, and Alison McGhee. Illus. by Tony Fucile. Candlewick, 2010. {ISBN-13: 978-0-7636-3266-3; 96p.} E (Gr. PreK-2)

In three quirky, delicious short chapters that transcend or maybe redefine the easy to read genre, meet two best friends—spiky blonde-haired, round and diminutive Bink, and lanky, toothpick-legged, brown-haired Gollie. The two girls couldn't be more different. Gollie lives in a tree house up a long staircase atop an old tree in an angular house with retro-modern furniture. Bink lives in a little cottage at the base of the same tree. On a shopping excursion to Eccles' Empire of Enchantment, Bink burrows through the bin of sale socks and picks out a garish striped pair. Appalled, Gollie says, "…The brightness of those socks pains me. I beg you not to purchase them." Bink crows, "I can't wait to put them on," and does just that. Even though she is longing for a plate of Gollie's pancakes, Bink is unwilling to acquiesce to Gollie's one condition—to remove her new socks—though the two come to an acceptable compromise. In the next chapters, Gollie journeys forth on an imagined adventure climbing the Andes Mountains and Bink brings home a marvelous companion, a goldfish she names Fred. Melding with the effervescent text are the utterly marvelous illustrations of Tony Fucile who, in just a few fluid lines and touches of color, has breathed such momentous personality into the two gal pals.

GERM: Thinking it would be fun to collaborate on book, the two friends, authors DiCamillo and McGhee, came up with the idea of writing a story about a short girl and a tall girl, which is also a description of the two of them. Their next idea was to give the two characters a sock and see what would happen. (Speaking of socks, sing the song "Black Socks" in this handbook on page 179.) Have your students pair up to write a story together with themselves as the main characters. Hand each duo an item (a pencil, a flashlight, an apple—it can be the same for each pair, or just a random accumulation of stuff that will help you make use of all the junk in your room), which they must incorporate into their stories.

RELATED TITLES: DiCamillo, Kate. *Because of Winn-Dixie.* Candlewick, 2000. / DiCamillo, Kate. *Mercy Watson to the Rescue.* Candlewick, 2005. (And others in the Mercy Watson series.) / Frazee, Marla. *A Couple of Boys Have the Best Week Ever.* Harcourt, 2008. / Fucile, Tony. *Let's Do Nothing!* Candlewick, 2009. / Lin, Grace. *Ling & Ting: Not Exactly the Same!* Little, Brown, 2010. / McGhee, Alison. *A Very Brave Witch.* Simon & Schuster, 2006. / Perkins, Lynne Rae. *The Cardboard Piano.* Greenwillow, 2008.
SUBJECTS: ADVENTURE AND ADVENTURERS. BEST FRIENDS. CLOTHING AND DRESS. FRIENDSHIP. HUMOROUS FICTION. IMAGINATION. MOUNTAINEERING. PETS. SOCKS.

[J] | | | | |
Binky to the Rescue. **Spires, Ashley. Illus. by the author. Kids Can, 2010. {ISBN-13: 978-1-55453-502-6; 64p.}**
       741.5 (Gr. PreK-3)
In this farcical graphic novelette, Binky, a tubby, hind leg-walking black and white kitty shaped like a black and white egg, now an official certified space cat, spends his days protecting his space station (house) from an alien invasion (wasps). You may recall his adventures in *Binky in Space*, when he built a rocket ship in his litter box. This time, his relentless pursuit of aliens leads to his falling out of a first floor window (due to a loose screen) with his trusty copilot, his pink stuffed mouse, Ted. "HOLY FUZZBUTT! Binky is in OUTER SPACE!!!" For the first time ever, he finds himself outside of his space station. (You might recognize his new environment as the yard.) Binky worries he won't be able to breathe out there in such dangerous territory until he finds an "oxygen source" (a garden hose), tethers himself with rope to a garden gnome, and sets out to spy on the enemy. Binky's human comes across him in the nick of time, just as the cat is being ambushed by dozens of stinging, winged aliens, and brings him inside. It doesn't take Binky long to realize who is still out there: Ted! "MMMEEEEOOOOWWW!!!" he howls, knowing he must undertake a new mission to rescue his pal.
GERM: Beyond hilarious, the artwork—captioned panels in shades of gray and neutral colors with touches of green and pink—is "rendered in ink, watercolor, cat fur, and bits of kitty litter." More of a one-on-one or independent reading book, this would also make an interesting transition, if you have a document camera, to a large screen. One group of children could read aloud the captions and the other could do all the wonderful sound effects. They'll want to compare Binky's perceptions of what is happening to him with their more realistic take on his adventures. Start your cartoonists composing their own graphic stories about the weird things their pets do.
RELATED TITLES: Billingsley, Franny. *Big Bad Bunny.* Atheneum, 2008. / Bruel, Nick. *Bad Kitty.* Roaring Brook, 2005. / Bruel, Nick. *Bad Kitty Gets a Bath.* Roaring Brook, 2008. (And others in the Bad Kitty series.) / Calhoun, Mary. *Blue-Ribbon Henry.* Morrow, 1999. (And others in the Henry series.) / Collington, Peter. *Clever Cat.* Knopf, 2000. / Hicks, Barbara Jean. *The Secret Life of Walter Kitty.* Knopf, 2007. / Holm, Jennifer L., and Matthew Holm. *Babymouse: Our Hero.* Random House, 2005. (And others in the Babymouse series.) / Meddaugh, Susan. *Martha Speaks.* Houghton Mifflin, 1992. (And others in the Martha series.) / Rathmann, Peggy. *Officer Buckle and Gloria.* Putnam, 1995. / Watt, Melanie. *Chester.* Kids Can, 2007. (And others in the Chester series.) /
SUBJECTS: CARTOONS AND COMICS. CATS. FANTASY. GRAPHIC NOVELS. HUMOROUS FICTION. IMAGINATION. INSECTS. STUFFED ANIMALS. WASPS.

[J*] | | | |S|
The Boss Baby. **Frazee, Marla. Illus. by the author. Beech Lane, 2010. {ISBN-13: 978-1-44240-167-9; 40p.} E**
       (Gr. PreK-2)
"From the moment the baby arrived, it was obvious he was the boss." The bald, square-headed tot, dressed like a banker in a black Dr. Denton–style suit and striped tie, and toting a briefcase as big as he is, arrives by taxi at Mom and Dad's house. He sets up his office—a rolling green walker with a baby bottle and rattle on the tray—in the middle of the living room, and throws a fit if his "workers" (i.e., parents) don't attend to his every whim. Exhausted from the boss's nonstop demands, including holding meetings at his crib in the middle of the night, Mom and Dad collapse on the couch. What's a baby to do? The two-toothed tot comes up with a brand new tactic that recaptures their attention. Prismacolor pencil and gouache illustrations of the overwhelmed parents and their tyrant baby abound with sly humor as the baby throws his food, has a meltdown on the changing table, and runs his doting parents ragged.

GERM: The baby's fierce facial expressions are ripe for imitating as we try to recall what it was like to be a raging toddler. Before reading the ending aloud, ask your listeners what they think the baby can do to regain the attentions of his folks. For the youngest listeners, the tongue-in-cheek business analogies in the text will go over their heads, but they'll enjoy the broad humor regardless. Discussion Point: What does a boss do? Answers will surely vary, depending on what your kids have heard at home. Who is the boss of the school? Of the classroom or library? Check out Frazee's *Walk On!*, where a baby learns to stand on his own two feet. To hear more from the baby's point of view, read *A Teeny Tiny Baby* by Amy Schwartz and *Born Yesterday: The Diary of a Young Journalist* by James Solheim.

RELATED TITLES: Anholt, Catherine, and Laurence Anholt. *Catherine and Laurence Anholt's Big Book of Little Children.* Candlewick, 2003. / Appelt, Kathi. *Brand-New Baby Blues.* HarperCollins, 2010. / Ashman, Linda. *Babies on the Go.* Harcourt, 2003. / Bertrand, Lynne. *Granite Baby.* Farrar, 2005. / Frazee, Marla. *A Couple of Boys Have the Best Week Ever.* Harcourt, 2008. / Frazee, Marla. *Hush, Little Baby.* Harcourt, 1999. / Frazee, Marla. *Roller Coaster.* Harcourt, 2003. / Frazee, Marla. *Walk On!: A Guide for Babies of All Ages.* Harcourt, 2006. / Harris, Robie H. *Mail Harry to the Moon!* Little, Brown, 2008. / Keats, Ezra Jack. *Peter's Chair.* Viking, 1967. / Long, Melinda. *Pirates Don't Change Diapers.* Harcourt, 2007. / Regan, Dian Curtis. *Chance.* Philomel, 2003. / Root, Phyllis. *What Baby Wants.* Candlewick, 1998. / Schwartz, Amy. *A Teeny Tiny Baby.* Orchard, 1994. / Solheim, James. *Born Yesterday: The Diary of a Young Journalist.* Philomel, 2010.

SUBJECTS: BABIES. BOSSES. HUMOROUS FICTION. PARENTING. PICTURE BOOKS FOR ALL AGES.

[J] | | | | |

Bridget's Beret. **Lichtenheld, Tom. Illus. by the author. Henry Holt/Christy Ottaviano, 2010. {ISBN-13: 978-0-8050-8775-8; 32p.} E (Gr. PreK-2)**

"Bridget was drawn to drawing. She liked to draw as much as other kids liked ice cream." There she is, in her oversized black beret, crayoning page after page of flowers and nature scenes that cover her desk and walls. Outdoors is her favorite place to draw, though, even on sidewalks. She ascribes her talent to the beret, just like other great artists wore. (Note the self-portraits on her wall of beret-wearers Cezanne, Picasso, Rembrandt, and Monet.) When her beret blows away in the wind, she is sure she has lost her ability to draw. She tries out other hats—a cowboy hat, a fez, a coonskin cap, and even a pith helmet, but none have the desired effect. "I can't draw. I have artist's block," she tells her friend. (Note the sidebar gives four ways to cure this dilemma.) It's not until she is asked to make a sign for her little sister's lemonade stand that she gets back into the groove. (Note her lemonade signs, which are modeled on other masterpieces. See if your kids can identify them. If not, show reproductions of the originals: Warhol's soup cans, Van Gogh's "Starry Night," "Whistler's Mother," and even Uncle Sam in his "I Want You" pose.) With kid-friendly illustrations done in ink, colored pencil and watercolor, this will be ideal for getting your students thinking about art.

GERM: The final two pages contain eleven "Bridget-approved ideas for inspiring yourself," titled "How to Start Your Art," accompanying classic art reproductions of paintings and sculpture that your own Bridget-types will be itching to emulate. Compare Bridget's flowery chalk sidewalk murals with similar drawings that come to life in *Chalk* by Bill Thomson.

RELATED TITLES: Barton, Chris. *Shark Vs. Train.* Illus. by Tom Lichtenheld. Little, Brown, 2010. / DePaola, Tomie. *The Art Lesson.* Putnam, 1989. / Kroll, Steven. *Patches Lost and Found.* Winslow, 2001. / LaMarche, Jim. *The Raft.* HarperCollins, 2000. / Mills, Claudia. *Ziggy's Blue-Ribbon Day.* Farrar, 2005. / Reynolds, Peter. *The Dot.* Candlewick, 2003. / Reynolds, Peter. *Ish.* Candlewick, 2004. / Rosenthal, Amy Krouse. *Duck! Rabbit!* Illus. by Tom Lichtenheld. Chronicle, 2009. / Rosenthal, Amy Krouse. *Yes Day!* Illus. by Tom Lichtenheld. HarperCollins, 2009. / Schwartz, Amy. *Begin at the Beginning: A Little Artist Learns About Life.* HarperCollins, 2005.

SUBJECTS: ARTISTS. DRAWING. HATS. PAINTING. SELF-CONFIDENCE.

[J] | | | | |

Can I Play, Too? **(Elephant & Piggie series) Willems, Mo. Illus. by the author. Hyperion, 2010. {ISBN-13: 978-1-42311-991-3; 57p.} E (Gr. PreK-1)**

(SEE PAGE 11 FOR ANNOTATION)

EASY FICTION / PICTURE BOOKS, cont.

CAT THE CAT SERIES BY MO WILLEMS:

[J*] | | | | |

Cat the Cat, Who Is That? **(Cat the Cat series) Willems, Mo. Illus. by the author. Balzer + Bray, 2010. {ISBN-13: 978-0-06-172840-2; 24p.} E (Gr. PreK-1)**

And you thought the Elephant and Piggie series was easy to read, weighing in at an average of 60 words per story. Now Mo proves that he can tackle the easiest of the easies with the new "Cat the Cat" emergent reader series. The first four books range from 18 to 31 words, proving that you can indeed do more with less sometimes. More laughing, that is. Cat the Cat, the lead animal, a light brown cat with big, round eyes and wearing a purple shift, dances through all of the books on her two hind legs. An omniscient observer asks the title refrain: "Cat the Cat, who is that?" We see a gray mouse in a yellow shirt, bouncing a red ball. "It's Mouse the Mouse!" it says on the next page. In balloon dialogue, Cat the Cat greets him: "Hi, Mouse the Mouse." "Hello there!" Mouse the Mouse replies. Romping along the green strip that lines the bottom of each robin's-egg blue page, Cat the Cat sees a duck in a beanie with a blade on top. That's Duck the Duck of course, clutching his Pigeon doll. (You can always find Pigeon lurking somewhere in each Willems book.) "A pleasure as always," the Duck says. Then there's Fish the Fish, blowing bubbles, who salutes her with a "Hey, Dude." In each book of the series, there's a wacky ending, character, or situation that will crack readers up. In this case, it's an unidentifiable, yellow, monster-y creature with four arms and three legs. Who is that? "I have no idea," says Cat the Cat. "Blargie! Blargie!" says the creature, eager to become a new friend.

GERM: Continue the name game. Children can draw pictures of other animals and ask, "Cat the Cat, who is that?" for each one. Find supporting games, event kits, and activities for the Cat the Cat series at **www.gomo.net**. For more very simple reads with abundant humor, look for little sets in the Brand New Readers series published by Candlewick Press, with titles by established authors including Kathy Caple, Johanna Hurwitz, Michelle Knudson, and Phyllis Root.

RELATED TITLES: Arnold, Tedd. *Hi! Fly Guy*. Scholastic, 2005. / Caple, Kathy. *Well Done, Worm*. Candlewick, 2000. (And others in Candlewick's Brand New Readers series.) / Gravett, Emily. *Dogs*. Simon & Schuster, 2010. / Willems, Mo. *City Dog, Country Frog*. Hyperion, 2010. / Willems, Mo. *Don't Let the Pigeon Stay Up Late*. Hyperion, 2006. (And others in the Pigeon series.) / Willems, Mo. *Leonardo the Terrible Monster*. Hyperion, 2005. / Willems, Mo. *Let's Say Hi to Friends Who Fly!* Balzer + Bray, 2010. / Willems, Mo. *Time to Sleep, Sheep the Sheep*. Balzer + Bray, 2010. / Willems, Mo. *Today I Will Fly!* Hyperion, 2007. (And others in the Elephant & Piggie series.) / Willems, Mo. *What's Your Sound, Hound the Hound?* Balzer + Bray, 2010. (And others in the Cat the Cat series.)

SUBJECTS: ANIMALS. CATS. CHANTABLE REFRAIN. EASY READERS. FRIENDSHIP.

[J*] | | | | |

Let's Say Hi to Friends Who Fly! **(Cat the Cat series) Willems, Mo. Illus. by the author. Balzer + Bray, 2010. {ISBN-13: 978-0-06-172846-4; 24p.} E (Gr. PreK-1)**

"Can you fly, Bee the Bee?" Cat the Cat asks blue and yellow striped Bee the Bee, in his green baseball cap, sitting on a swing. "Watch me!" says Bee the Bee. On the next double page, Cat the Cat cheers him on—"Go, Bee the Bee!"—as he zooms and buzzes in circles across the page. Cat the Cat then watches Bird the Bird and Bat the Bat flap and flutter. "Who else can fly," asks the narrator, as the animals come upon Rhino the Rhino, bouncing on a Pigeon ride. "Watch me!" says Rhino the Rhino. How on earth can a rhinoceros fly? ZOOM! By airplane, of course.

GERM: Have kids draw other animals in flight and identify them. An easier-than-easy text, filled with repetition, encourages children to join right in. See what happens when Piggie tells Elephant she'd like to take to the air in *Today I Will Fly!*.

RELATED TITLES: Arnold, Tedd. *Hi! Fly Guy*. Scholastic, 2005. / Patricelli, Leslie. *Higher! Higher!* Candlewick, 2009. / Willems, Mo. *Cat the Cat, Who Is That?* Balzer + Bray, 2010. (And others in the Cat the Cat series.) / Willems, Mo. *City Dog, Country Frog*. Hyperion, 2010. / Willems, Mo. *Don't Let the Pigeon Stay Up Late*. Hyperion, 2006. (And others in the Pigeon series.) / Willems, Mo. *Today I Will Fly!* Hyperion, 2007. (And others in the Elephant & Piggie series.)

SUBJECTS: ANIMALS. CATS. CHANTABLE REFRAIN. EASY READERS. FLIGHT.

EASY FICTION / PICTURE BOOKS, cont.

CAT THE CAT SERIES BY MO WILLEMS, cont.:

[J*] | | | | |

Time to Sleep, Sheep the Sheep. **(Cat the Cat series) Willems, Mo. Illus. by the author. Balzer + Bray, 2010. {ISBN-13: 978-0-06-172847-1; 24p.} E (Gr. PreK-1)**

"It's late," says Cat the Cat, clutching her blanket and pillow, on the cover. She heads off to remind Sheep the Sheep, who is reading a book, what time it is and help the others with their bedtime preparations. She brings a towel to Pig the Pig, scrubbing in the tub; toothpaste to Giraffe the Giraffe who is holding a long-handled toothbrush; a glass of milk to Crab the Crab; and averts her eyes from Horse the Horse, sitting on the toilet. Approaching brown, wide-eyed Owl the Owl, she says, "Time to—Never mind . . ." Let your children explain the joke to you, with Owl the Owl watching from his perch as the other animals retire in a comfy-looking line of colorful sleeping bags. ("Checkers, anyone?" he asks on the last page.) The blue pages turn progressively darker as night comes on, until the final page, which is studded with white stars.

GERM: Willems has already tackled bedtime with *Don't Let the Pigeon Stay Up Late.* Read these two together and pantomime getting ready for bed with your sleepy crew. Borrowing the format of *Time to Sleep, Sheep the Sheep,* the first grade students in Esther Loor's class in Milltown School, Bridgewater, New Jersey wrote and illustrated their own book, *Time to Eat, Hippo the Hippo.* See an excerpt on page 92 in this handbook.

RELATED TITLES: Becker, Bonny. *A Bedtime for Bear.* Candlewick, 2010. / Christelow, Eileen. *Five Little Monkeys Jumping on the Bed.* Clarion, 1989. / Dewdney, Anna. *Llama Llama Red Pajama.* Viking, 2005. / Markes, Julie. *Shhhhh! Everybody's Sleeping.* HarperCollins, 2005. / Rathmann, Peggy. *Good Night, Gorilla.* Putnam, 1994. / Rathmann, Peggy. *10 Minutes Till Bedtime.* Putnam, 1998. / Shea, Bob. *Dinosaur vs. Bedtime.* Hyperion, 2008. / Waber, Bernard. *Bearsie Bear and the Surprise Sleepover Party.* Houghton Mifflin, Sky/Scholastic, 2000.

ANIMALS. BEDTIME. CATS. CHANTABLE REFRAIN. EASY READERS. SLEEP. SLEEPOVERS.

[J*] | | | | |

What's Your Sound, Hound the Hound? **(Cat the Cat series) Willems, Mo. Illus. by the author. Balzer + Bray, 2010. {ISBN-13: 978-0-06-172844-0; 24p.} E (Gr. PreK-1)**

What's Hound the Hound's sound? "Woof! Woof! Woof!" he says taking what looks like freshly baked bone cookies from the oven. Chick the Chick, brewing tea in a teapot, says, "Peep!" while Cow the Cow, taking a carton of milk from the fridge, says, "Mmmmmooooooooooooooo!" It's when Cat the Cat says to Bunny the Bunny, holding a tray of teacups, "What's your sound . . . ?" that a problem arises. Bunny wiggles his ears and utters a silent sound, bunnies not being known for their noisiness. Have children surmise what all the animals are doing together, and they'll predict the upcoming tea party.

GERM: Hold your own animal tea party with little cups of iced tea and crackers. Play the What's the Sound Game. Sit in a circle and start the sounds rolling. Say, "I'm a bee." The others have to say, "What's the sound, Bee the Bee?" and you respond with "Buzzzzz." Have them continue the fun, one at a time announcing their animals' identities in a call-and-response bit of public speaking (or, maybe, shrieking). After reading four Cat the Cat books with their repeated titles and reinforcement of oft-said words, watch your children's independent reading skills improve, as will their senses of humor. Graduate from these titles to the mayhem of the Elephant and Piggie books.

RELATED TITLES: Feiffer, Jules. *Bark, George.* HarperCollins, 1999. / Fleming, Denise. *The Cow Who Clucked.* Henry Holt, 2006. / Martin, Bill, Jr. *Polar Bear, Polar Bear, What Do You Hear?* Henry Holt, 1991. / Seeger, Laura Vaccaro. *Dog and Bear: Two Friends, Three Stories.* Roaring Brook, 2007. (And others in the Dog and Bear series.) / Shapiro, Arnold L. *Mice Squeak, We Speak.* Putnam, 1997. / Willems, Mo. *Cat the Cat, Who Is That?* Balzer + Bray, 2010. (And others in the Cat the Cat series.) / Willems, Mo. *Don't Let the Pigeon Stay Up Late.* Hyperion, 2006. (And others in the Pigeon series.)

SUBJECTS: ANIMAL SOUNDS. ANIMALS. CATS. CHANTABLE REFRAIN. EASY READERS.

[J*]　　|A| | | |

Chalk. Thomson, Bill. Illus. by the author. Marshall Cavendish, 2010. {ISBN-13: 978-0-7614-5526-4; 40p.} E
　　(Gr. PreK-3)

Walking through the park one stormy day, two girls and a boy in raingear come upon a big, green, plastic dinosaur on springs in the playground. Hanging from its open jaws are the corded handles of a gift bag decorated with yellow moons and stars. Looking inside the bag, the kids see nine thick pieces of colored chalk. One girl pulls out a yellow stick, and draws a sun on the blacktop. In a blinding flash, the bright sun rises from the image and appears in the sky. You can see the flash of recognition on the other girl's face as she pulls out another piece and begins drawing butterflies, which rise from the pavement as giant monarchs. Next, the boy, with a look of sly anticipation, pulls out a green piece and draws the outline of a dinosaur. The children scream and cover their eyes as a huge, green T-rex with gleaming claws and needle sharp teeth emerges from the macadam. They hide in the playground equipment, which shields them from the angry creature. Photorealistic paintings in acrylic and colored pencil show every bump on his scaly snout. Viewers may scream. Quickly, the boy draws a rain cloud on the inside of the plastic covered slide where he is hiding; the rain commences, and the dinosaur dissolves in the drops. What a relief, though the children look almost wistful as they look at the now dissolved green chalk and hang the bag back where they found it. In your mind's ear, you'll surely hear the children talking and yelling, and the dinosaur roaring, even though this is a wordless book, told entirely through the extraordinarily believable illustrations.

GERM: Children can add sound effects, and dialogue as you show the extraordinary pictures. Older children can write up the story in prose, adding dialogue and description. As in *Jumanji* by Chris Van Allsburg, and *Flotsam* by David Wiesner, readers will speculate what might happen to the next children who discover and use the chalk. Hand each child a piece of chalk so you can adjourn to the playground where they can draw the things they'd like to see come to life and act them out in pantomime. (Or just have them do their chalk drawings on black paper.)

RELATED TITLES: Ahlberg, Allan. *The Pencil.* Candlewick, 2008. / Banyai, Istvan. *Zoom.* Viking, 1995. / Johnson, Crockett. *Harold and the Purple Crayon.* HarperCollins, 1955. / Lehman, Barbara. *Rainstorm.* Houghton Mifflin, 2007. / Lehman, Barbara. *The Red Book.* Houghton Mifflin, 2004. / Nevius, Carol. *Baseball Hour.* Illus. by Bill Thomson. Marshall Cavendish, 2008. / Nevius, Carol. *Building with Dad.* Illus. by Bill Thomson. Marshall Cavendish, 2006. / Nevius, Carol. *Karate Hour.* Illus. by Bill Thomson. Marshall Cavendish, 2004. / Rohmann, Eric. *Clara and Asha.* Roaring Brook, 2005. / Rohmann, Eric. *Time Flies.* Crown, 1994. / Van Allsburg, Chris. *Jumanji.* Houghton Mifflin, 1981. / Wiesner, David. *Art and Max.* Clarion, 2010. / Wiesner, David. *Flotsam.* Clarion, 2006. / Wiesner, David. *Free Fall.* Lothrop, 1988. / Wiesner, David. *Sector 7.* Clarion, 1999. / Wiesner, David. *Tuesday.* Clarion, 1991. / Yoo, Taeeun. *The Little Red Fish.* Dial, 2007.

SUBJECTS: CREATIVE DRAMA. DINOSAURS. DRAWING. FANTASY. IMAGINATION. MULTICULTURAL BOOKS. PLAY. RAIN AND RAINFALL. STORIES WITHOUT WORDS.

[J*]　　|A|B| | |

City Dog, Country Frog. Willems, Mo. Illus. by Jon J Muth. Hyperion, 2010. {ISBN-13: 978-1-42310-300-4;
　　64p.} E (Gr. PreK-1) 2011 Charlotte Zolotow Honor Book; Judy Freeman's 2011 Best of the Best for
　　Easy Fiction/Picture Books

On his first day in the country, City Dog, a brown dog with white markings, runs far, fast, and without a leash. There, sitting on a rock is Country Frog. "What are you doing?" City Dog asks him, his long ropey tail wagging. "Waiting for a friend," Country Frog replies, "But you'll do." Together they play Country Frog games like jumping, and splashing, and croaking. In summer, City Dog returns, and this time, he teaches his friend games like sniffing, and fetching, and barking. In fall, Country Frog is tired, so they sit together on the rock, playing remembering games. City Dog naps, and County Frog reaches out to touch his friend, or perhaps bid him goodbye. On his winter visit, City Dog can't find Country Frog. (If you can look at this chapter without worrying or sniffling at the sight of solitary City Dog waiting forlornly but expectantly on their rock, you have a far stronger constitution than I do.) The final chapter, "spring again," is satisfyingly surprising, and not in the way readers will expect. Jon J Muth's soft, blurred watercolors, soulful and achingly real, introduce themes of joy, sorrow, friendship, death, grieving, and acceptance of change in a natural, understandable way.

GERM: The cycle of life question that will come up for discussion is "What happened to Country Frog?" Children will want to read this more than once to look for clues. See the podcast of Willems and Muth at **www.NYtimes.com/books**.

RELATED TITLES: Gravett, Emily. *Dogs.* Simon & Schuster, 2010. / Henkes, Kevin. *Old Bear.* Greenwillow, 2008. / Meschenmoser, Sebastian. *Waiting For Winter.* Kane Miller, 2009. / Muth, Jon J. *Zen Shorts.* Scholastic, 2005. / Nelson, Marilyn. *Snook Alone.* Candlewick, 2010. / Rohmann, Eric. *A Kitten Tale.* Knopf, 2008. / Willems, Mo. *There Is a Bird on Your Head!* Hyperion, 2007. (And others in the Elephant & Piggie series.) / Wilson, Karma. *A Frog in the Bog.* McElderry, 2003.

SUBJECTS: DEATH. DOGS. FRIENDSHIP. FROGS. LIFE CYCLES. PICTURE BOOKS FOR ALL AGES. SCIENCE. SEASONS.

[J] | |B| |S|

Clever Jack Takes the Cake. **Fleming, Candace. Illus. by G. Brian Karas. Schwartz & Wade, 2010. {ISBN-13: 978-0-375-84979-4; 32p.} E (Gr. PreK-3)**

When Jack, a poor boy, receives an invitation from His Majesty the King to attend the princess's tenth birthday party at the castle, he decides to make her a cake as his gift. He trades his axe for two bags of sugar and his quilt for a sack of flour. From his hen he gets two eggs, his cow gives him a pail of her sweetest milk, and he dips his own birthday candles. Finally, Jack finds the "reddest, juiciest, most succulent strawberry in the land." The enterprising young lad bakes a beautiful cake, topped with the strawberry. On his way to the castle, he is set upon by four and twenty blackbirds that snatch up the walnuts spelling "Happy Birthday Princess" atop the icing. A wild-haired troll demands half the cake for payment to cross his bridge, and a dancing bear named Samson gobbles up the other half. At the castle, the bored princess is receiving her fabulous gifts. ("More rubies? . . . How tiresome. Another tiara? How dull.") Before Jack can hand over what is left of his gift—the strawberry—a guard takes it and eats it, claiming the princess is allergic. All that is left to give her is the story of his adventure, which he tells to the delighted princess. Who doesn't love a good story?

GERM: Jack's tale, filled with Karas's familiar scrappy gouache and pencil full-page illustrations, employs common motifs from fairy tales, and ends up being all about the power of stories. On page 153 of this handbook, see Judy Freeman's Reader's Theater script of Jack's adventures. Neil Gaiman's picture book, *Instructions*, takes you on a journey that surveys the common quests and obstacles one must overcome in fairy tales.

RELATED TITLES: Bar-el, Dan. *Such a Prince.* Clarion, 2007. / DeFelice, Cynthia, and Mary DeMarsh. *Three Perfect Peaches: A French Folktale.* Orchard, 1995. / DeRegniers, Beatrice Schenk. *Little Sister and the Month Brothers.* Marshall Cavendish, 2009, c1976. / Fleming, Candace. *Muncha! Muncha! Muncha!* Simon & Schuster, 2002. / Fleming, Candace. *Sunny Boy!: The Life and Times of a Tortoise.* Farrar, 2005. / Fleming, Candace. *When Agnes Caws.* Atheneum, 1999. / Gaiman, Neil. *Instructions.* HarperCollins, 2010. / Taback, Simms. *Joseph Had a Little Overcoat.* Viking, 1999.

SUBJECTS: BIRTHDAYS. CAKES. GIFTS. PRINCES AND PRINCESSES. READER'S THEATER. STORIES TO TELL. STORYTELLING.

[J*] | | | |S|

Dust Devil. **Isaacs, Anne. Illus. by Paul O. Zelinsky. Schwartz & Wade, 2010. {ISBN-13: 978-0-375-86722-4; 48p.} E (Gr. K-4)**

The last time we saw Angelica Longrider was back in 1831, in the Caldecott Honor book, *Swamp Angel,* after the giantess defeated the bear, Thundering Tarnation, and moved to Montana. Now living with her little red dog in a log cabin, on land flatter than a frying pan, Angel is feeling a bit homesick for the trees and shade she left behind in Tennessee. So she plucks a batch of tall mountains from the Rockies and plants them on the prairie. "That's a beaut," she says each time she sets one down (which is why those flat-topped peaks all over Montana are now called buttes). The soil is so rich that the corn she plants at daybreak rockets to the sky by noon, taking along three cows, and it then rains milk all summer. In 1835, as the worst dust storm ever tears across the prairie, Angel mounts the howling whirlwind and rides it like a horse, creating the Grand Canyon when she digs in her heels. As it begins to rain and the dust is washed away, what is in the center of the whirlwind but a giant white horse she names Dust Devil. When Blackwood Bart and his Flying Desperadoes, astride ten-foot mosquitoes, ride into town, Swamp Angel offers to help Sheriff Napalot capture them, but he won't deputize her since she's not a man. Nevertheless, she sets out after the gold-stealing bandits, whose 2,000-pound leader is half rattlesnake, half badger, and half mad hornet. He also says and does everything backward. Angel shouts, "Fight to prepare or stolen, you've gold the back give, varmints!" Naturally, Bart is no match for Angel and Dust Devil. The tall tale prose is a dream to read aloud, and Zelinsky's folk art paintings done in oils on hardwood veneers are beyond spectacular.

GERM: Show books and photos of Montana today and of the landmarks Swamp Angel "creates" in the story, including buttes, the Sawtooth Range, and the Grand Canyon. Children can write a new tall tale adventure starring Angel, explaining how she created another national wonder. What would she do if she moved to your state or town? For more tall tale fun, try the "Create an Instant Tall Tale" activity in this handbook on page 132.

RELATED TITLES: Bertrand, Lynne. *Granite Baby.* Farrar, 2005. / Byrd, Robert. *Finn MacCoul and His Fearless Wife: A Giant of a Tale from Ireland.* Dutton, 1999. / Cuyler, Margery. *Big Friends.* Walker, 2004. / Dadey, Debbie. *Shooting Star: Annie Oakley, the Legend.* Walker, 1997 / DePaola, Tomie. *Fin M'Coul, the Giant of Knockmany Hill.* Holiday House, 1981. / Isaacs, Anne. *Pancakes for Supper.* Scholastic, 2006. / Isaacs, Anne. *Swamp Angel.* Dutton, 1994. / Kellogg, Steven. *Sally Ann Thunder Ann Whirlwind Crockett.* Morrow, 1995. / Klise, Kate. *Stand Straight, Ella Kate: The True Story of a Real Giant.* Dial, 2010. /McCully, Emily Arnold. *Wonder Horse: The True Story of the World's Smartest Horse.* Henry Holt, 2010. / Mora, Pat. *Doña Flor: A Tall Tale About a Giant Woman with a Great Big Heart.* Knopf, 2005. / Osborne, Mary Pope. *American Tall Tales.* Knopf, 1991. / Pinkney, Andrea Davis. *Peggony Po: A Whale of a Tale.* Hyperion, 2006. / San Souci, Robert D. *Larger Than Life: The Adventures of American Legendary Heroes.* Doubleday, 1991. / Schanzer, Rosalyn. *Davy Crockett Saves the World.* HarperCollins, 2001. / Walker, Paul Robert. *Big Men, Big Country: A Collection of American Tall Tales.* Harcourt, 1993. / Wood, Audrey. *The Bunyans.* Scholastic, 1996.

SUBJECTS: EXAGGERATION. FANTASY. FRONTIER AND PIONEER LIFE. GIANTS. HORSES. HUMOROUS FICTION. LANGUAGE ARTS. MONTANA. MOSQUITOES. PICTURE BOOKS FOR ALL AGES. ROBBERS AND OUTLAWS. SCIENCE. TALL TALES.

ELEPHANT & PIGGIE SERIES BY MO WILLEMS:

[J] | | | | |
Can I Play, Too? **(Elephant & Piggie series) Willems, Mo. Illus. by the author. Hyperion, 2010. {ISBN-13: 978-1-42311-991-3; 57p.} E (Gr. PreK-1)**

[J] | | | | |
I Am Going! **(Elephant & Piggie series) Willems, Mo. Illus. by the author. Hyperion, 2010. {ISBN-13: 978-1-42311-990-6; 57p.} E (Gr. PreK-1)**

[J*] |A| | |S|
We Are in a Book! **(Elephant & Piggie series) Willems, Mo. Illus. by the author. Hyperion, 2010. {ISBN-13: 978-1-42313-308-7; 64p.} E (Gr. PreK-1) 2011 Geisel Honor**

Elephant and Piggie books continue to break new ground in the emergent reader world, with the simplest 75-word repetitive texts that never fail to crack up readers. Here are three new stellar additions.

In *Can I Play Too?* the two friends are planning to play catch, when a grinning little green snake asks to join them. "We are playing catch," Piggy says. "With our arm," Elephant adds diplomatically. "So?" says the snake. "You do not have arms," Piggy says, while Elephant blushes apologetically. After a few false starts, the three come up with a working solution to that minor problem.

I Am Going! is what Piggie announces to Gerald, sending the elephant bud into a tailspin. "I WILL NOT LET YOU GO!!!" he roars, but she is adamant. Elephant runs through his always over the top display of emotions, before crying in despair, "Why?" "It is lunchtime, Gerald," she explains. Oh.

Talking with your kids about the importance of reading? *We Are in a Book!* looks at that from the inside out, literally. "I think someone is looking at us," Gerald whispers to Piggie. She walks toward us and looks out of the page. "A reader is *reading* us!" The two are elated to realize that they are in a book and the reader is reading their word bubbles. "THAT IS SO COOL!" trumpets Elephant. Piggie makes us say a word aloud and the word is "BANANA." This makes the two laugh like mad. When Elephant realizes, with great alarm, that the book will end on page 57, he is undone. "I just want to be read," he says plaintively. Piggie comes up with a good idea, which readers can try to guess before turning to the last page.

GERM: The important thing to remember when reading aloud an Elephant and Piggie book is that there are three components to each story: the words, the facial expressions, and the body language. Want your kids to learn to read with expression, comprehension, and fluency? No one does it better than Mo Willems. Do the "Go Bananas" chant on page 178 in this handbook. For another book within a book, see Mordicai Gerstein's *A Book.* Dive into Mo's activities-rich website, **www.pigeonpresents.com**, to play the Elephant & Piggie Dance Game and more.

RELATED TITLES: Catalanotto, Peter. *Ivan the Terrier.* Atheneum, 2007. / Drescher, Henrik. *Simon's Book.* Lothrop, 1983. / Gerstein, Mordicai. *A Book.* Roaring Brook, 2009. / Harris, Robie H. *Maybe a Bear Ate It!* Orchard, 2008. / Lies, Brian. *Bats at the Library.* Houghton Mifflin, 2008. / Lobel, Arnold. *Frog and Toad Together.* HarperCollins, 1972. (And others in the Frog and Toad series.) / Marshall, James. *George and Martha: The Complete Stories of Two Best Friends.* Houghton Mifflin, 1997. / Seeger, Laura Vaccaro. *Dog and Bear: Two Friends, Three Stories.* Roaring Brook, 2007. (And others in the Dog and Bear series.) / Smith, Lane. *It's a Book.* Roaring Brook, 2010. / Stein, David Ezra. *Interrupting Chicken.* Candlewick, 2010. / Willems, Mo. *Are You Ready to Play Outside?* Hyperion, 2008. / Willems, Mo. *Cat the Cat, Who Is That?* Balzer + Bray, 2010. (And others in the Cat the Cat series.) / Willems, Mo. *Don't Let the Pigeon Stay Up Late.* Hyperion, 2006. (And others in the Pigeon series.) / Willems, Mo. *Elephants Cannot Dance.* Hyperion, 2009. / Willems, Mo. *Today I Will Fly!* Hyperion, 2007. / Willems, Mo. *Watch Me Throw the Ball!* Hyperion, 2008. (And others in the Elephant & Piggie series.)
SUBJECTS: BEST FRIENDS. BOOKS AND READING. EASY READERS. ELEPHANTS. FRIENDSHIP. LANGUAGE ARTS. PIGS. PLAY. SNAKES.

[J] | | | | |
Even Monsters Need Haircuts. **McElligott, Matthew. Illus. by the author. Walker, 2010. {ISBN-13: 978-0-8027-8819-1; 32p.} E (Gr. PreK-2)**
As a young brown-haired boy explains in his matter-of-fact narrative, his dad is a barber and he likes to watch him work. Tonight is a full moon, though, so the child goes to bed early, waking at midnight when he hears Vlad, a bat, tapping on the bedroom window. Together, they cross the fields into town, with the full moon lighting their way. While the boy uses a skeleton key to unlock the back door to dad's shop, Vlad transforms into a purple-caped vampire. Once inside, the boy unpacks his supplies: rotting tonic, horn polish, stink wax, and, of course, the shamp-*ewww*, and stands on a high stool to give Vlad a trim. The slyly comical, sensible ink, pencil, and digital illustrations tell their own story throughout. Look in the mirror and you'll see the boy using his scissors, but there's no reflection of Vlad—just an empty chair. By one a.m., the shop is packed with monsters, and the boy, in his fuzzy green monster slippers, gives each creature an appropriate do. As the night ends, the monsters help him sweep up, trying to make sure they don't leave any of their supplies behind.
GERM: The final illustration contains a twist that will get listeners speculating on what will happen next. Kids can draw their own monsters and give them creative hairstyles.
RELATED TITLES: Emberley, Ed. *Go Away, Big Green Monster!* Little, Brown, 1993. / Park, Barbara. *Psssst! It's Me . . . the Bogeyman.* Atheneum, 1998. / Sierra, Judy. *Monster Goose.* Harcourt, 2001. / Silverman, Erica. *Big Pumpkin.* Macmillan, 1992. / Tarpley, Natasha Anastasia. *Bippity Bop Barbershop.* Little, Brown, 2002. / Viorst, Judith. *My Mama Says There Aren't Any Zombies, Ghosts, Vampires, Creatures, Demons, Monsters, Fiends, Goblins, or Things.* Atheneum, 1973. / Wheeler, Lisa. *Boogie Knights.* Atheneum, 2008. / Willems, Mo. *Leonardo the Terrible Monster.* Hyperion, 2005. / Yorinks, Arthur. *Mommy?* Scholastic, 2006.
SUBJECTS: BARBERSHOPS. FANTASY. FATHERS. HAIRCUTTING. HUMOROUS FICTION. MONSTERS. PERSONAL NARRATIVES. VAMPIRES.

[J] | | | | |
Everything But the Horse. **Hobbie, Holly. Illus. by the author. Little, Brown, 2010. {ISBN-13: 978-0-316-07019-5; 32p.} E (Gr. K-4)**
Growing up on Sunnyside Avenue, packed with kids and pets, Holly was scared at first when her parents bought an old farm in the country. There was no electricity, and the toilet was in an outhouse. She soon learned to love the outdoors, and, best of all, the animals: Buster, the dog; cats; ducks; "ornery geese"; chickens; and a Guernsey cow named Tinkerbell she learned to milk. Watching high schooler Sarah Wilcox riding by on her horse made Holly want a horse more than anything in the world. Already the best artist in her family and class at school, she covered her bedroom walls with drawings of horses. On her birthday, she hoped there would be a horse waiting for her in the barn. This autobiographical picture book, a remembrance by well-known artist, Holly Hobbie, is illustrated in delicate watercolor and pen and ink illustrations that capture the farm experience and the wistfulness of her younger self.
GERM: Before showing the last few pages, have children predict what her birthday present will be. A black and white photo on the back flap shows her with the chickens on her family's farm at age ten. As a writing prompt, have children write and illustrate a personal narrative about one of their best or worst birthdays.

RELATED TITLES: Brady, Irene. *Doodlebug.* Houghton Mifflin, 1977. / Diakité, Penda. *I Lost My Tooth in Africa.* Scholastic, 2006. / Haas, Jessie. *Runaway Radish.* Greenwillow, 2001. / Hobbie, Holly. *Annabelle.* Little, Brown, 2008. / Hobbie, Holly. *Toot & Puddle.* Little, Brown, 1997. (And others in the Toot & Puddle series.) / McCully, Emily Arnold. *Wonder Horse: The True Story of the World's Smartest Horse.* Henry Holt, 2010. / Polacco, Patricia. *Mrs. Mack.* Philomel, 1998.
SUBJECTS: AUTOBIOGRAPHY. BICYCLES. BIOGRAPHY. COUNTRY LIFE. FAMILY LIFE. FARM LIFE. HORSES. LANGUAGE ARTS. PERSONAL NARRATIVES.

[J*] | | | | |
How Rocket Learned to Read. **Hills, Tad. Illus. by the author. Schwartz & Wade, 2010. {ISBN-13: 978-0-375-85899-4; 32p.} E (Gr. PreK-1)**
Rocket, a winsome white dog with dark gray spots, is taking a snooze under his favorite tree when a little yellow bird alights on his head. "Aha! My first student! Wonderful!" she sings. Hanging from the tree is a little chalkboard that reads, "Class starts today." Between some trees, the bird hangs a banner of what she calls "the wondrous, mighty, gorgeous alphabet," and then perches on a branch and begins to read aloud from a book. Rocket is disturbed at first, but soon becomes caught up in the story about Buster, an unlucky dog who has lost his favorite bone. So begin Rocket's reading lessons. As the leaves change color and the fall winds blow colder, Rocket learns all his letters, and begins to sing and sound them out to form whole words. Each afternoon, the bird reads aloud another story. When the weather turns, she flies off for the season, calling, "Don't forget! Words are built one letter at a time!" All winter, Rocket practices his letters, spelling out words and even writing them in the snow as he waits for spring and his teacher to return. The illustrations, done in oils and colored pencil, are sweet and beguiling; the character of Rocket was based on Tad Hills's own dog, shown in a photo on the back flap.
GERM: The combination of singing and sounding out words and hearing stories read aloud is one fine way to become not just a reader, but also a lover of books and stories. Ask your children what other words they think Rocket should learn how to read and spell, as did Loreli Stochaj, librarian at Franklin School in Summit, NJ, with her first graders. (See page 86 in this handbook to see an example.) Gather up a menagerie of stuffed animals and have your children read aloud stories to them. (If you can bring in a real dog for the children to read to, all the better.) Meet a dog who opens his own bookstore in *Dog Loves Books* by Louise Yates.
RELATED TITLES: Berne, Jennifer. *Calvin Can't Fly: The Story of a Bookworm Birdie.* Sterling, 2010. / Bloom, Becky. *Wolf!* Orchard, 1999. / Harris, Robie H. *Maybe a Bear Ate It!* Orchard, 2008. / Hills, Tad. *Duck & Goose.* Schwartz & Wade, 2006. / Kirk, David. *Library Mouse.* Abrams, 2007. / Knudsen, Michelle. *Library Lion.* Candlewick, 2006. / Lies, Brian. *Bats at the Library.* Houghton Mifflin, 2008. / McPhail, David. *Fix-It.* Dutton, 1984. / Numeroff, Laura Joffe. *Beatrice Doesn't Want To.* Candlewick, 2004. / Sierra, Judy. *Wild About Books.* Knopf, 2004. / Stein, David Ezra. *Interrupting Chicken.* Candlewick, 2010. / Stevens, April. *Waking Up Wendell.* Illus. by Tad Hills. Schwartz & Wade, 2007. / Willems, Mo. *City Dog, Country Frog.* Hyperion, 2010. / Willems, Mo. *We Are in a Book!* Hyperion, 2010. / Yates, Louise. *Dog Loves Books.* Knopf, 2010.
SUBJECTS: BIRDS. BOOKS AND READING. DOGS. LANGUAGE ARTS. LITERACY. PERSEVERANCE.

[J] | | | | |
I Am Going! **(Elephant & Piggie series) Willems, Mo. Illus. by the author. Hyperion, 2010. {ISBN-13: 978-1-42311-990-6; 57p.} E (Gr. PreK-1)**
(SEE PAGE 11 FOR ANNOTATION)

[J*] |A| | | |
Interrupting Chicken. **Stein, David Ezra. Illus. by the author. Candlewick, 2010. {ISBN-13: 978-0-7636-4168-**
     9; 32p.} E (Gr. PreK-2) 2011 Caldecott Honor
Putting his little red chicken to bed, Papa opens a big book of fairy tales. "And of course you are not going to
interrupt the story tonight, are you?" he says. "Oh no, Papa, I'll be good," says the little chicken, nestled under the
covers of her bed. In the middle of "Hansel and Gretel," though, Chicken leaps into the book, shouting, "Out jumped
a little red chicken and she said, 'DON'T GO IN! SHE'S A WITCH!'" In the book within the book, Hansel and
Gretel head off the page, leaving the witch sitting on her front stoop, looking frustrated. Papa says, "You interrupted
the story. Try not to get so involved." He begins anew with "Little Red Riding Hood" and "Chicken Little," but each
time, Little Red Chicken pipes up, inserting herself directly into the fairy tales' illustrations, warning Little Red
Riding Hood not to talk to strangers, and informing Chicken Little not to panic. Way out illustrations done in
"watercolor, water-soluble crayon, china marker pen, opaque white ink, and tea" (tea?) portray Papa with pince-nez
on his yellow beak and a huge red comb like Elvis run amok. The little red chicken, with a similar comb, big round
white eyes, pointy clodhopper-ish red feet, and jaunty green tail feathers, sure knows how to get involved in a good
story, and even tells one of her own to put her tired Papa to sleep.
GERM: Have your listeners retell the three stories in Papa's book. Ask them how Chicken might interrupt other
fairy tales, like "The Three Little Pigs" or "The Three Bears." Talk about bedtime stories; survey how many of your
kids hear a bedtime story or book each night and what their before-bed rituals are. On page 87 in this handbook, see
the terrific four-part fairy tale lesson developed by Maren Vitali, librarian at Milltown School in Bridgewater, NJ.
RELATED TITLES: Berne, Jennifer. *Calvin Can't Fly: The Story of a Bookworm Birdie.* Sterling, 2010. / Bloom,
Becky. *Wolf!* Orchard, 1999. / Child, Lauren. *Beware of the Storybook Wolves.* Scholastic, 2001. / Child, Lauren.
Who's Afraid of the Big Bad Book? Hyperion, 2003. / Cousins, Lucy. *Yummy: Eight Favorite Fairy Tales.*
Candlewick, 2009. / Emberley, Michael. *Ruby.* Little, Brown, 1990. / Emberley, Rebecca, and Ed Emberley.
Chicken Little. Roaring Brook, 2009. / Hoberman, Mary Ann. *You Read to Me, I'll Read to You: Very Short Fairy
Tales to Read Together.* Little, Brown, 2004. / Marshall, James. *Red Riding Hood.* Dial, 1987. / O'Malley, Kevin.
Gimme Cracked Corn and I Will Share. Walker, 2007. / Pinkney, Jerry. *Little Red Riding Hood.* Little, Brown,
2007. / Stein, David Ezra. *Pouch.* Putnam, 2009. / Watt, Mélanie. *Chester's Masterpiece.* Kids Can, 2010.
SUBJECTS: BEDTIME. BEDTIME STORIES. BOOKS AND READING. CHICKENS. FAIRY TALES.
FATHERS. HUMOROUS FICTION. LANGUAGE ARTS. STORYTELLING.

[J*] | |B| | |
Knuffle Bunny Free: An Unexpected Diversion. **Willems, Mo. Illus. by the author. Balzer + Bray, 2010. {ISBN-**
     13: 978-0-06-192957-1; 48p.} E (Gr. PreK-2)
In the third and concluding installment of the award-winning Knuffle Bunny saga, Trixie and her parents are on their
way to Holland to visit Trixie's Oma and Opa. On the plane, Trixie plays with and reads to her stuffed friend and
then conks out in her seat. It's not until after her arrival, when she's drinking chocolate milk in the garden with her
grandmother, that she realizes something. There's her daddy, in the kitchen, talking with Opa, turning to look at the
thunderstruck face and big eyes of his traumatized daughter, and realizing exactly what has happened: Knuffle
Bunny is still on the plane. He calls the airline, but the plane is on its way to China. All that week, Trixie tries to be
brave and enjoy the sights and the fun things they do, but she misses her Knuffle Bunny. Oma and Opa get her a
brand new Funny-Bunny-Wunny-Doll Extreme that can walk, dance, and even speak Dutch, but that's no help. One
night, she has a cathartic dream about her rabbit and the places he is visiting around the world and the children he is
cheering up. The dream is depicted in a four-page gatefold panorama of Knuffle Bunny, floating through a series of
eight black and white photos, set against a deep blue background. The snapshots show children playing with the
bunny in an Indian courtyard, outside a Mongolian yurt, on a playground in London, and on a palm tree–filled beach
in the tropics. Trixie awakes, with new acceptance and insight, better able to enjoy the rest of her visit. Two
surprises await her on the return home that will get readers thinking.
GERM: Discussion point: Why didn't the new bunny doll help Trixie feel better? How does Trixie's dream help
her? On the plane home, Trixie aids the crying baby in the seat behind her with a selfless act. What selfless acts have
you performed or received? Find Judy Freeman's teachers guide for *Knuffle Bunny* and *Knuffle Bunny Too* at
www.pigeonpresents.com/grownup.aspx. At **www.pigeonpresents.com/pals-knuffle.aspx,** you'll find games,
activities, and reproducibles. On page 93 in this handbook, see the worksheet that librarian Loreli Stochaj did for her
first grades students at Franklin School in Summit, New Jersey. Then, on page 94, see the four-part research lesson,
"Postcards from Another Country," developed around the book by librarian Maren Vitali at Milltown School in
Bridgewater, NJ.

RELATED TITLES: Feiffer, Jules. *I Lost My Bear.* Morrow, 1998. / Grey, Mini. *Traction Man Is Here!* Knopf, 2005. / Grey, Mini. *Traction Man Meets Turbodog.* Knopf, 2008. / Willems, Mo. *Don't Let the Pigeon Drive the Bus!* Hyperion, 2003. (And others in the Pigeon series.) / Willems, Mo. *Knuffle Bunny: A Cautionary Tale.* Hyperion, 2004. / Willems, Mo. *Knuffle Bunny Too: A Case of Mistaken Identity.* Hyperion, 2007.
SUBJECTS: AIRPLANES. BABIES. FAMILY LIFE. GENEROSITY. GRANDPARENTS. LOST AND FOUND POSSESSIONS. NETHERLANDS. STUFFED ANIMALS. TOYS.

[J*] | | | | |
Let's Say Hi to Friends Who Fly! (Cat the Cat series) Willems, Mo. Illus. by the author. Balzer + Bray, 2010.
{ISBN-13: 978-0-06-172846-4; 24p.} E (Gr. PreK-1)
(SEE PAGE 7 FOR ANNOTATION)

[J] |A|B|H| |
Ling & Ting: Not Exactly the Same! Lin, Grace. Illus. by the author. Little, Brown, 2010. {ISBN-13: 978-0-316-02452-5; 43p.} E (Gr. PreK-2) 2011 Geisel Honor
Meet identical twins, Chinese American girls, Ling and Ting, who insist they are not *exactly* the same, even though they dress identically and have the same haircut. In the first of six short chapters, Ting sneezes just as the barber is cutting her bangs. Whoops! He lops off an unexpected hunk. Now the girls look different, and we, the readers, can tell who's who. In subsequent chapters, Ling attempts a magic card trick, the girls make a batch of Chinese dumplings, Ling has trouble eating with chopsticks, Ting goes to the library, and Ting tells Ling a story that incorporates details of all the other chapters. Fresh and fun, this beginning reader sports delectable, colorful black-outlined illustrations. Lin's is a voice we have not heard before in an easy reader, and it hits the spot.
GERM: Children can write and illustrate their own vignettes about their own siblings and family.
RELATED TITLES: Blumenthal, Deborah. *Don't Let the Peas Touch!: And Other Stories.* Scholastic, 2004. / DiCamillo, Kate. *Bink and Gollie.* Candlewick, 2010. / Frazee, Marla. *A Couple of Boys Have the Best Week Ever.* Harcourt, 2008. / Fucile, Tony. *Let's Do Nothing!* Candlewick, 2009. / Lin, Grace. *Dim Sum for Everyone.* Knopf, 2001. / Lin, Grace. *Fortune Cookie Fortunes.* Knopf, 2004. / Lin, Grace. *Where the Mountain Meets the Moon.* Little, Brown, 2009. / Wong, Janet. *Apple Pie 4th of July.* Harcourt, 2002.
SUBJECTS: CHINESE AMERICANS. EASY READERS. INDIVIDUALITY. MULTICULTURAL BOOKS. SISTERS. TWINS.

[J] |A| | | |
LMNO Peas. Baker, Keith. Illus. by the author. Simon & Schuster/Beach Lane, 2010. {ISBN-13: 978-1-4169-9141-0; 32p.} E (Gr. PreK-2)
"We are peas—alphabet peas! / We work and play in the ABCs." In a sprightly rhyming jaunt through the alphabet, an active array of personified little green peas list and demonstrate their varied jobs, from acrobats to zoologist. On each page, the jovial peas cluster around and are dwarfed by an oversized letter of the alphabet, starting with an orange A and, on the next page, a lavender B: "We're acrobats, artists, and astronauts in space / We're builders, bathers, and bikes in a race." Pastel-hued illustrations that look like watercolors but are actually done digitally portray, among others, a troupe of acrobat peas using hula-hoops; an artist pea in a black beret, painting a still life; and an astronaut pea in a purple rocket ship.
GERM: Whether you're getting ready for Career Day, studying nouns, or celebrating rhymes and the alphabet, this picture book celebration will make you hap-pea. Children can act out each of the pea professions and activities in narrative pantomime, where you read the text and they become the pea-ple. Don't miss the blurb about the author on the back flap, which states he is from Peattle, Washington and hopes that someday there will be "peas everywhere on Earth." Your pep-pea crew can come up with adjectives ending in "ppy" and then draw pea portraits of the little veggies looking sloppy or grumpy or drippy. Bring in fresh peas and have children shell them. Each child takes a pea and decides what occupation it should have that was not mentioned in the book. Children can draw pictures of the pea, the letter, and the job, or use fabrics and found materials to make a 3-D scene, dressing the pea, perhaps, and creating a background. If the pea is to be a basketball player, for instance, the artist could make a tiny basketball out of clay and a net with a pipe cleaner and some string.

EASY FICTION / PICTURE BOOKS, cont.

RELATED TITLES: Baker, Keith. *Big Fat Hen.* Harcourt, 1994. / Baker, Keith. *Just How Long Can a Long String Be?!* Scholastic/Arthur A. Levine, 2009. / Baker, Keith. *Quack and Count.* Harcourt, 2000. / MacDonald, Suse. *Alphabatics.* Simon & Schuster, 1986. / Markes, Julie. *Shhhhh! Everybody's Sleeping.* HarperCollins, 2005. / Rosenthal, Amy Krouse. *Little Pea.* Chronicle, 2005. / Slate, Joseph. *Miss Bindergarten Takes a Field Trip with Kindergarten.* Dutton, 2001. / Werner, Sharon. *Alphabeasties and Other Amazing Types.* Blue Apple, 2009.
SUBJECTS: ALPHABET BOOKS. CREATIVE DRAMA. LANGUAGE ARTS. OCCUPATIONS. PEAS. PERSONIFICATION. SOCIAL STUDIES. STORIES IN RHYME.

[J] | | |H|S|
Me and You. Browne, Anthony. Illus. by the author. Farrar, 2010. {ISBN-13: 978-0-374-34908-0; 25p.} E (Gr. PreK-2)
Here's an unusual retelling of "The Three Bears" that is oddly unsettling and thought provoking. On the right hand page is a recounting of the tale told from the point of view of the narrator, a young bear who lives in a spacious, sunny yellow house with his sweater-clad, middle class bear parents. On the wordless left-hand pages, in a series of sepia-toned panels, a golden-haired girl dressed in a brown sweatshirt sets out along grim, brick-walled streets with her mother. Chasing a loose balloon, the somber child loses her way. Meanwhile, the bears set off for a stroll in the park while their porridge is cooling. ("Daddy talked about *his* work and Mommy talked about *her* work. I just messed around," says the contented little bear, standing on his head on a park bench.) Passing broken windows and a gloomy iron fence, the girl comes upon the sunlit house, so out of place in her urban landscape. She eats the porridge, breaks the chair, ands heads up to the bedrooms, which is where the disapproving bears find her. Off she runs, through rain and snow, past a graffiti-filled wall. "I wonder what happened to her," the bear muses, staring out his window. The final pages offer a hopeful ending to the story as the girl finds her way back into the light, where her mother is waiting to envelop her in a hug.
GERM: Note Browne's dedication: "For all the underdogs." The two points of view—first person and omniscient observer—show two worlds, but you've probably never thought of Goldilocks as an underdog before. Children can narrate the wordless pictures, giving the girl her own voice as to what she thinks and feels as she finds her way to the Bears' alternate world. Do use this book with older children when talking about the many ways one can choose to tell a story.
RELATED TITLES: Aylesworth, Jim. *Goldilocks and the Three Bears.* Scholastic, 2003. / Brett, Jan. *Goldilocks and the Three Bears.* Putnam, 1987. / Brett, Jan. *The Three Snow Bears.* Putnam, 2007. / Browne, Anthony. *The Shape Game.* Farrar, 2003. / Browne, Anthony. *Willy the Dreamer.* Candlewick, 1998. / Buehner, Caralyn, and Mark Buehner. *Goldilocks and the Three Bears.* Dial, 2007. / Elya, Susan Middleton. *Rubia and the Three Osos.* Disney/Hyperion, 2010. / Ernst, Lisa Campbell. *Goldilocks Returns.* Simon & Schuster, 2000. / Ernst, Lisa Campbell. *Stella Louella's Runaway Book.* Simon & Schuster, 1998. / Lowell, Susan. *Dusty Locks and the Three Bears.* Henry Holt, 2001. / Marshall, James. *Goldilocks and the Three Bears.* Dial, 1988. / Stanley, Diane. *Goldie and the Three Bears.* HarperCollins, 2003.
SUBJECTS: BEARS. FOLKLORE. GOLDILOCKS STORIES. PARODIES. POINT OF VIEW.

[J*] | | | | |
Miss Brooks Loves Books! (And I Don't). Bottner, Barbara. Illus. by Michael Emberley. Knopf/Borzoi, 2010. {ISBN-13: 978-0-375-84682-3; 26p.} E (Gr. PreK-2)
A laconic and skeptical first grader, clad in overalls, a pink and green striped cap pulled down low over her spiky brown hair, and glasses, describes her wacky, over-the-top school librarian. Miss Brooks is an effervescent book cheerleader who dresses up in costumes to read books like *Where the Wild Things Are* and *The Very Hungry Caterpillar.* She tells the girl, "I want you to get as excited about books as I am." At Halloween, when each child has to find a poem to share, the child makes up her own. "Eek! A freak," she recites stoically. "Well, it's a start," Miss Brooks says. All year, Miss Brooks inundates her kids with books; but in May, she tells the class about something "truly terrifying: Book Week!" Each child is to pick a favorite book to present, make a costume, and show why he or she really loves that story. "I'll never love a book the way you do," the girl tells Miss Brooks, who responds, "Don't be so sure." She asks her mother if they can move. "My mother says there's a librarian in every town." She finds her classmates' reports too flowery, furry, clickety, and yippity. All the books Miss Brooks loads in her backpack to read with her mom, she dismisses as too kissy, pink, and silly. "You're as stubborn as a wart," her mother says. Then comes the epiphany, the one we Miss Brooks sympathizers strive to reach with every child. "I want to read a story about warts!" the girl shouts. Her mom reads her William Steig's *Shrek,* and she is hooked! "Read it again," she demands. Whew! At last! Another book-lover transformed by the power of a great book.

GERM: What a lead-in book to Book Week celebrations! Michael Emberley's pencil outlined ink and watercolor illustrations of the skinny-legged, boot-wearing, wild-haired, oft-costumed librarian will make you want to rummage through your closets for book outfits and to mix it up more with your kids. And, of course, read *Shrek* to see how a stubborn, snorty, warty ogre can make a kid's day. *Shrek* is the first book the narrator ever loved. What should she read next? Have kids recommend books explaining what she'd like about each one. Ask them what was the first book that they fell in love with? What was special about it?

RELATED TITLES: Bottner, Barbara. *Bootsie Barker Bites.* Putnam, 1992. / Ernst, Lisa Campbell. *Stella Louella's Runaway Book.* Simon & Schuster, 1998. / Finchler, Judy, and Kevin O'Malley. *Miss Malarkey Leaves No Reader Behind.* Walker, 2006. / Garland, Michael. *Miss Smith's Incredible Storybook.* Dutton, 2003. / Harris, Robie H. *Mail Harry to the Moon!* Illus. by Michael Emberley. Little, Brown, 2008. / Hoberman, Mary Ann. *You Read to Me, I'll Read to You: Very Short Stories to Read Together.* Illus. by Michael Emberley. Little, Brown, 2001. / Knudsen, Michelle. *Library Lion.* Candlewick, 2006. / Morris, Carla. *The Boy Who Was Raised by Librarians.* Peachtree, 2007. / Numeroff, Laura Joffe. *Beatrice Doesn't Want To.* Candlewick, 2004. / Polacco, Patricia. *Aunt Chip and the Great Triple Creek Dam Affair.* Philomel, 1996. / Polacco, Patricia. *Thank You, Mr. Falker.* Philomel, 1998. / Sierra, Judy. *Wild About Books.* Knopf, 2004. / Steig, William. *Shrek.* Farrar, 2010, c1990. / Thaler, Mike. *The Librarian from the Black Lagoon.* Scholastic, 1997. / Williams, Suzanne. *Library Lil.* Dial, 1997.

SUBJECTS: BOOKS AND READING. LANGUAGE ARTS. LIBRARIANS. MOTHERS. PERSONAL NARRATIVES. SCHOOLS.

[J] | | | | |

Mr. President Goes to School. Walton, Rick. Illus. by Brad Sneed. Peachtree, 2010. {ISBN-13: 978-1-56145-538-6; 32p.} E (Gr. K-5)

Life in the Oval Office isn't always easy for a commander-in-chief. "Mr. President was having a crummy day," begins a tale of politics and hokey-pokey. The National Gopher Society is demanding that gophers be allowed in the Rose Garden, the vice president just gave away the president's ping pong table, and Madam Secretary of State calls to say Bulrovia is threatening war with Snortburg. The dispirited lanky leader disguises himself in a floppy hat, fake nose with mustache and glasses, and a trench coat and walks seven and a half blocks to Mrs. Appletree's kindergarten class where the world is a little simpler. Upon learning his name is Louis, the tall grey-haired teacher says, "I had a student named Louis once. He's an important man now." After a satisfying day of finger painting, outdoor recess, building with blocks, a snack of milk and cookies, a nap, storytime, and a round of the hokey-pokey, Mr. President is ready to face the White House once again. He invites the glowering prime ministers from Bulrovia and Snortburg into the Oval Office and makes them work out their problems, kindergarten style, putting into practice everything he learned in kindergarten earlier in the day. Including the hokey-pokey, of course.

GERM: This "Everything-I-Need-to-Know-I-Learned-in-Kindergarten" themed story makes you wish that more world problems could be solved with such obvious common sense. Have your kids make a list of all the other things they learned in kindergarten. Then get up and do the hokey-pokey. Children can write up a list of advice for our current president on how to solve the world's problems.

RELATED TITLES: Cronin, Doreen. *Duck for President.* Simon & Schuster, 2004. / DiPucchio, Kelly. *Grace for President.* Hyperion, 2008. / Feiffer, Kate. *President Pennybaker.* Simon & Schuster, 2008. / Krosoczka, Jarrett. *Max for President.* Knopf, 2004. / Smith, Lane. *Madam President.* Hyperion, 2008. / St. George, Judith. *So You Want to Be President?* Philomel, 2000. / Stier, Catherine. *If I Were President.* Albert Whitman, 1999. / Winters, Kay. *My Teacher for President.* Dutton, 2004.

SUBJECTS: COOPERATION. KINDERGARTEN. PICTURE BOOKS FOR ALL AGES. PRESIDENTS. SOCIAL STUDIES. TEACHERS. WHITE HOUSE.

[J] | | | | |

My Garden. Henkes, Kevin. Illus. by the author. Greenwillow, 2010. {ISBN-13: 978-0-06-171517-4; 32p.} E (Gr. PreK-1)

A barefoot, brown-haired little girl in a wide-brimmed straw hat and a pink dress explains how she helps her mother in the garden, watering, weeding, and chasing away the lettuce-eating rabbits. She muses, "It's hard work, and my mother's garden is very nice, but if I had a garden . . ." The rest of the story contains her fantastical speculations on what would happen. "In my garden, the flowers could change color just by thinking about it—pink, blue, green, purple. Even patterns." The warm ink and watercolor illustrations on the facing page show her delight with a pair of sunflowers transformed, with pink petals and polka dots. In her garden, the rabbits would be chocolate; a jellybean bush would grow from jellybeans she planted, and the tomatoes would be as big as beach balls. A joyful mood piece, her monologue gets us fantasizing with "what ifs."

GERM: What a sweet and imaginative introduction to a science lesson on plants, and gardens, and how things grow. The logical conclusion would be to plant a garden outside with your children, or a window box with fast-growing seeds like string beans or morning glories. Best yet, depending on the time of year, would be sunflowers, since the transformation from seed to ten-foot plant is so miraculous. You could try planting seashells, as the little girl does, but don't expect them to root. Try this as a writing prompt: If I had a garden . . . .

RELATED TITLES: Brown, Peter. *The Curious Garden.* Little, Brown, 2009. / Coy, John. *Two Old Potatoes and Me.* Knopf, 2003. / Ehlert, Lois. *Leaf Man.* Harcourt, 2005. / Falwell, Cathryn. *Mystery Vine: A Pumpkin Surprise.* Greenwillow, 2009. / Henkes, Kevin. *Chrysanthemum.* Greenwillow, 1991. / Henkes, Kevin. *A Good Day.* Greenwillow, 2007. / Lobel, Anita. *Alison's Zinnia.* Greenwillow, 1990. / Schaefer, Lola M. *Pick, Pull, Snap!: Where Once a Flower Bloomed.* HarperCollins, 2003.

SUBJECTS: FLOWERS. GARDENING. GARDENS. IMAGINATION. PERSONAL NARRATIVES. PLANTS. SCIENCE.

[J] | | | | |

***Oh No!, or, How My Science Project Destroyed the World.* Barnett, Mac. Illus. by Dan Santat. Disney/Hyperion Books, 2010. {ISBN-13: 978-1-42312-312-5; 34p.} E (Gr. PreK-3)**

The cover is a medium shot of a bespectacled, brown-haired girl who is looking alarmed. An ornery frog is reflected in one lens of her big round glasses; in the other, a robot. In the background, choppers are flying and smoke is billowing ominously. You'll conclude, correctly, that things are not looking good. Diving right into the book, there's the same girl, wearing a brown jumper, walking down a rubble-strewn street past the pharmacy with a bus protruding from the shattered second floor window. "I knew it," she says. "I never should have built a robot for the science fair." Where the other kids entered the usual projects—homemade volcanoes, growing seeds, the "why is my cat so obese" cat diet chart—her first prize entry was for advanced robotics. The paneled, graphic novel-style Photoshop illustrations, filled with banners and store signs in Japanese, like *Godzilla* movies of old, burst with ominous shadows, explosions, and general mayhem as the monster runs amok through the city. "Looks like I'm going to have to fix this," she says, seeing the robot atop Union Station. "Hey, Robot! Knock it off already!" she hollers. "I should have given it ears," she chides herself, and holds up a sign saying, "Cut it out, Buster," but of course, she never taught it to read either. She's got just the solution, though: a giant attack toad.

GERM: "I knew it," is a sentence your kids will adopt for themselves by the open end of this zany sci fi romp. Ask kids to come up with ideas for how she is now going to control that toad? Have them continue the story in captions and drawings, employing science project ideas and technology. Judy Sierra's narrative poem, *The Secret Science Project That Almost Ate the School* is a picture book on the same wavelength.

RELATED TITLES: Benton, Jim. *The Fran That Time Forgot.* Simon & Schuster, 2005. (And others in the Franny K. Stein, Mad Scientist series.) / Bush, Timothy. *Benjamin McFadden and the Robot Babysitter.* Crown, 1998. / Clement, Rod. *Just Another Ordinary Day.* HarperCollins, 1997. / Clements, Andrew. *Double Trouble in Walla Walla.* Millbrook, 1998. / Cole, Joanna. *The Magic School Bus and the Science Fair Expedition.* Scholastic, 2006. / Cowan, Catherine. *My Life with the Wave.* Lothrop, 1997. / Feiffer, Jules. *Meanwhile . . . .* HarperCollins, 1997. / Long, Melinda. *How I Became a Pirate.* Harcourt, 2003. / Seuss, Dr. *Bartholomew and the Oobleck.* Random House, 1949. / Shannon, David. *A Bad Case of Stripes.* Scholastic, 1998. / Sierra, Judy. *The Secret Science Project That Almost Ate the School.* Simon & Schuster, 2006. / Smith, Lane. *Math Curse.* Viking, 1995. / Van Allsburg, Chris. *Jumanji.* Houghton Mifflin, 1981. / Van Allsburg, Chris. *Zathura: A Space Adventure.* Houghton Mifflin, 2002. / Varon, Sara. *Robot Dreams.* Roaring Brook/First Second, 2007.

SUBJECTS: FANTASY. HUMOROUS FICTION. PERSONAL NARRATIVES. PICTURE BOOKS FOR ALL AGES. ROBOTS. SCIENCE EXPERIMENTS. SCIENCE FAIRS. SCIENCE FICTION. SCIENCE PROJECTS. TOADS.

[J*] | | | | |

Pete the Cat: I Love My White Shoes. **Litwin, Eric. Illus. by James Dean. HarperCollins, 2010. {ISBN-13: 978-0-06-190622-0; 30p.} E (Gr. PreK-1)**

Pete the Cat, a lanky, skinny-tailed, indigo-hued kitty with big, almond-shaped yellow eyes, is sauntering down the street in his brand-new lace-up sneakers and singing this song: "I love my white shoes, I love my white shoes, I love my white shoes." Oh, no! Pete steps in a large pile—actually an entire hill—of strawberries. "What color did it turn his shoes?" it asks at the bottom of the page. Your listeners will yell out, "RED!" On the next page, against an all-red background, there is a full-page view of Pete's foot, clad in its now-red shoe. "Did Pete cry? Goodness, no!" In fact, there's Pete with a thought bubble above his head, reading "Everything is cool!" He just changes the lyrics a bit, singing, "I love my red shoes . . ." as he continues on his laid-back, mellow stroll. Pete steps next in a pile of blueberries, and then a large puddle of mud. Scratchy pen and inks outline the bold-colored watercolors of unflappable Pete, set against a background of primary colors. When he steps in a bucket of water that washes the colors away, he ambles along, his sneaks squeaking, singing, "I love my wet shoes . . ." The moral of his story? "No matter what you step in, keep walking along and singing your song . . . . . . because it's all good."

GERM: Go to **www.YouTube.com** to listen to or download the author telling the story and singing Pete the Cat's song, which you won't get out of your head for a long time. Your kids will learn this interactive story the first time you read it aloud, and will continue to act it out, sing it, and tell it to everyone. "Goodness, no!" will become part of your vocabulary. Ask what other colorful, squishy things Pete might step in, and sing about them. On the publisher's website, **www.harpercollinschildrens.com/petethecat**, there's a template of Pete's shoes you can print out and then cut out to play "Pin Your Shoe on Pete the Cat." Get your own Pete the Cat doll at **www.merrymakersinc.com**. And when life is getting you stressed, step back and consider Pete's go-with-the-flow way of looking at the world. It's all good.

RELATED TITLES: Cabrera, Jane. *Cat's Colors.* Dial, 1997. / Cabrera, Jane. *If You're Happy and You Know It.* Holiday House, 2005. / Ehlert, Lois. *Color Zoo.* HarperCollins, 1989. / Fox, Mem. *Where Is the Green Sheep?* Harcourt, 2004. / Harter, Debbie. *The Animal Boogie.* Barefoot, 2000. / Harter, Debbie. *Walking Through the Jungle.* Barefoot, 1997. / Martin, Bill, Jr. *Brown Bear, Brown Bear, What Do You See?* Henry Holt, 1983. / Numeroff, Laura. *If You Give a Cat a Cupcake.* HarperCollins, 2008. / Seeger, Laura Vaccaro. *Lemons Are Not Red.* Roaring Brook, 2004. / Underwood, Deborah. *The Quiet Book.* Houghton Mifflin, 2004. / Willems, Mo. *Cat the Cat, Who Is That?* Balzer + Bray, 2010.

SUBJECTS: CATS. CHANTABLE REFRAIN. COLOR. CREATIVE DRAMA. SHOES. SINGING. STORIES IN RHYME. STORIES TO TELL.

[j] | | | | |

The Pirate of Kindergarten. **Lyon, George Ella. Illus. by Lynne Avril. Atheneum, 2010. {ISBN-13: 978-1-41695-024-0; 40p.} E (Gr. PreK-1) 2011 Schneider Family Book Award for Young Children**

Ginny loves going to Reading Circle in her classroom, even when the children laugh at her when she knocks over chairs on the way. It's not easy for her to navigate, when she sees two of everything. To read a book, she puts her nose right on the page, but she still sees double. Scissors are tricky: on the rabbit picture Ms. Cleo hands out, Ginny cuts out three ears instead of two. On vision screening day, when she sees two of each letter, the nurse asks, "Do you know that most people see only one?" No, she didn't know that. Ginny cries. The eye doctor prescribes glasses and a black eye patch, which makes her look like a pirate, but now she can see everything, including her beloved books, just once. The chalk pastel, acrylic, and prismacolor pencil illustrations are friendly and easy to see by a group.

GERM: Double vision is a problem we haven't seen addressed in children's books before. Ginny's story is based on the author's own experiences as a child. The winner of this year's Schneider Family Book Award for Young Children, given to books that best exemplify a child's experience dealing with disabilities, this upbeat story will help your children empathize with others who are different.

RELATED TITLES: Buzzeo, Toni. *Adventure Annie Goes to Kindergarten.* Dial, 2010. / Cooper, Ilene. *Jake's Best Thumb.* Dutton, 2008. / Davis, Patricia A. *Brian's Bird.* Albert Whitman, 2000. / Headley, Justina Chen. *The Patch.* Charlesbridge, 2006. / Millman, Isaac. *Moses Goes to a Concert.* Farrar, 1998.

SUBJECTS: KINDERGARTEN. PEOPLE WITH DISABILITIES. SCHNEIDER FAMILY AWARD. SCHOOLS. VISION. VISION DISORDERS.

EASY FICTION / PICTURE BOOKS, cont.

[J] |A| | |S|

The Quiet Book. Underwood, Deborah. Illus. by Renata Liwska. Houghton Mifflin, 2010. {ISBN-13: 978-0-547-21567-9; 32p.} E (Gr. PreK-2)

"There are many kinds of quiet," begins this quietly unassuming but revelatory exploration of the concept. We follow a group of animal kids—a rabbit, some bears, a moose, a mouse, and a porcupine—through the daily aspects of their lives, from "First one awake quiet" to "Sound asleep quiet." In between are illustrated situations that will have you nodding your head in recognition: "Others telling secrets quiet," "Last one to get picked up from school quiet," and "Top of the roller coaster quiet." The softly colored pencil illustrations give the book a classic feel reminiscent of Ruth Kraus's *A Hole is to Dig* or Else Holme Minarik's "Little Bear" books. The sheer winsomeness of each page will make this a book to read aloud and discuss, but also to pore over, since each picture tucks in a little story. On one page, the caption reads "Trying not to hiccup quiet." In the foreground is a trio of birds playing flute, banjo, and triangle, in concert atop a tree stump. In the background, a bench of spectators looks on as an adult bear holds a distressed white rabbit kid upside down by the feet.

GERM: As you show each page to children, read the caption and have them examine the illustration and describe the situation. Afterwards, they can write and illustrate more "quiet" situations or do the opposite and take a closer look at the word "noisy." On page 90 in this handbook, see how Keri Peloso's second grade class at Milltown School in Bridgewater, New Jersey, wrote and illustrated their own sequel, *The Loud Book*.

RELATED TITLES: Edwards, Pamela Duncan. *Slop Goes the Soup: A Noisy Warthog Word Book.* Hyperion, 2001. / Elkin, Benjamin. *The Loudest Noise in the World.* Viking, 1954. / Gal, Susan. *Night Lights.* Knopf, 2009. / Johnson, David A. *Snow Sounds: An Onomatopoeic Story.* Houghton Mifflin, 2006. / MacDonald, Ross. *Achoo! Bang! Crash!: The Noisy Alphabet.* Hyperion, 2001. / Showers, Paul. *The Listening Walk.* HarperCollins, 1991. / Spier, Peter. *Crash! Bang! Boom!* Doubleday, 1990. / Underwood, Deborah. *The Noisy Book.* Houghton Mifflin, 2011.

SUBJECTS: ANIMALS. LANGUAGE ARTS. QUIETUDE.

[J] |A| | | |

Rubia and the Three Osos. Elya, Susan Middleton. Illus. by Melissa Sweet. Disney/Hyperion, 2010. (Gr. PreK-2) E {ISBN-13: 978-1-42311-252-5; 34p.}

In a charming Spanish language-laden, rhyming retelling of "The Three Bears," Mamá suggests a walk before dinner—"It's part of my South Woods Plan, so I'll be thinner." Off they go, and into their *casita* steps Little Miss Rubia, curls made of *oro*, clad in a pair of red cowboy boots. Blithely, she drinks up the *sopa*, breaks the smallest *silla*, and takes a snooze in one of *las tres camas*. Melissa Sweet's colorful watercolor, pencil, and mixed media illustrations are sunny and filled with good humor. Note the different ending to the traditional folktale: Rubia runs away from the bears, sure, but when she gets home, she cooks up a new pot of *sopa* to replace what she ate, says "*Lo siento*" [I'm sorry] to Bébé, and glues his *silla* back together. By the last page, she's sitting on the couch with them, singing along to Papá's guitar. As Papá says, "Our house *es tu casa*," and readers will feel at home there, too.

GERM: Listeners will have a joyous time, figuring out the meanings of each Spanish word in context, and there's a glossary and pronunciation guide to all 35 Spanish words and phrases, in case they get stumped or your Spanish pronunciation is less fluent than you thought. For more fun with folklore and Spanish, meet a cast of well-known characters in Elya's equally stellar *Fairy Trails: A Story Told in English and Spanish.*

RELATED TITLES: Aylesworth, Jim. *Goldilocks and the Three Bears.* Scholastic, 2003. / Brett, Jan. *Goldilocks and the Three Bears.* Putnam, 1987. / Brett, Jan. *The Three Snow Bears.* Putnam, 2007. / Browne, Anthony. *Me and You.* Farrar, 2010. / Buehner, Caralyn, and Mark Buehner. *Goldilocks and the Three Bears.* Dial, 2007. / Elya, Susan Middleton. *Eight Animals Bake a Cake.* Putnam, 2002. / Elya, Susan Middleton. *Fairy Trails: A Story Told in English and Spanish.* Bloomsbury, 2005. / Ernst, Lisa Campbell. *Goldilocks Returns.* Simon & Schuster, 2000. / Ernst, Lisa Campbell. *Stella Louella's Runaway Book.* Simon & Schuster, 1998. / Lowell, Susan. *Dusty Locks and the Three Bears.* Henry Holt, 2001. / Marshall, James. *Goldilocks and the Three Bears.* Dial, 1988. / Paul, Ann Whitford. *Mañana, Iguana.* Holiday House, 2004. / Paul, Ann Whitford. *Tortuga In Trouble.* Holiday House, 2009. / Stanley, Diane. *Goldie and the Three Bears.* HarperCollins, 2003.

SUBJECTS: BEARS. FOLKLORE. GOLDILOCKS STORIES. LANGUAGE ARTS. MULTICULTURAL BOOKS. SPANISH LANGUAGE. STORIES IN RHYME.

[J*] | | | |S|

Shark Vs. Train. **Barton, Chris. Illus. by Tom Lichtenheld. Little, Brown, 2010. {ISBN-13: 978-0-316-00762-7; 32p.} E (Gr. PreK-2)**

Facing each other on the cover, with teeth bared and menacing looks on their fierce profiles, are a big turquoise-colored shark and a smoke-emitting gray-blue train engine, obviously gearing up for an intense confrontation. In the middle of the endpapers sits a toy box. "GRRRRR," mutters the little toy shark inside. "CHUGRRR-CHUG," responds the toy train. On the next page, two boys, one blonde and one redhead, race over to dig through the toy box. Each grabs a toy of choice, one holding the growling shark in his fist and the other the train, with its five cars dangling. On the title page, the toys continue to threaten each other. In a delicate little dialogue balloon, the shark sneers, "I'M GOING TO CHOO-CHOO YOU UP AND SPIT YOU OUT," and the unintimidated train responds, "HA! I'M GOING TO FIN-ISH YOU, MACKEREL-BREATH." "Who will win?" it says in red letters. On the next page, the competition begins in earnest. Shark wins in the ocean; Train wins the race on the railroad tracks. Each page brings a new trial. Roasting marshmallows on a stick? Train has a clear advantage, holding the stick over his smokestack. Shark eats the pins at the bowling alley. "That counts as a strike, right?" he says, grinning fiendishly. "This is why you guys have a bad reputation," Train reproves. When Mom calls the boys for lunch, they toss shark and train into the toy box until next time. The watercolor and colored pencil illustrations are jammed with hilarious details that will make kids want to dig out their own favorite toys and start playing.

GERM: When you get to the title page, with its tantalizing "Who will win?" question, you may want to stop for a mini-discussion on what kids think the story will be about and which toy will be triumphant. Or not. Your listeners may insist on turning the page without any delay. Look at the insets on the back cover, listing the personified duo's favorite color, food, and game. Kids can draw and label portraits of their best toys. Download the very cute activity guide for the book, which you'll find at **http://tomlichtenheld.com/childrens_books/sharkvstrain.html**. This best buddy book of the year joins *Let's Do Nothing* by Tony Fucile and *A Couple of Boys Have the Best Week Ever* by Marla Frazee for a perfect testosterone-filled trio of books about imaginative play. In all three books, examine the all-important endpapers and the story-filled lead-up pages to the title page.

RELATED TITLES: Barton, Chris. *The Day-Glo Brothers: The True Story of Bob and Joe Switzer's Bright Ideas and Brand-New Colors.* Charlesbridge, 2009. / Bee, William. *And the Train Goes.* Candlewick, 2007. / Crews, Donald. *Freight Train.* Greenwillow, 1978. / Crews, Donald. *Inside Freight Train.* HarperCollins, 2001. / Crews, Nina. *Below.* Henry Holt, 2006. / Feiffer, Jules. *Meanwhile . . .* HarperCollins, 1997. / Fucile, Tony. *Let's Do Nothing!* Candlewick, 2009. / Grey, Mini. *Traction Man Is Here!* Knopf, 2005. / Grey, Mini. *Traction Man Meets Turbodog.* Knopf, 2008. / Hubble, Patricia. *Trains: Steaming! Pulling! Huffing!* Marshall Cavendish, 2005. / Lichtenheld, Tom. *Bridget's Beret.* Henry Holt/Christy Ottaviano, 2010. / MacDonald, Ross. *Another Perfect Day.* Roaring Brook, 2002. / Portis, Antointette. *Not a Box.* Chronicle, 2006. / Rosenthal, Amy Krouse. *Duck! Rabbit!* Illus. by Tom Lichtenheld. Chronicle, 2009. / Rosenthal, Amy Krouse. *Yes Day!* Illus. by Tom Lichtenheld. HarperCollins, 2009. / Shea, Bob. *Dinosaur vs. Bedtime.* Hyperion, 2008.

SUBJECTS: COMPETITION. FRIENDSHIP. HUMOROUS FICTION. IMAGINATION. PERSONIFICATION. PLAY. SHARKS. TOYS. TRAINS.

[j] |A| | | |

A Sick Day for Amos McGee. **Stead, Philip C. Illus. by Erin E. Stead. Roaring Brook, 2010. {ISBN-13: 978-1-59643-402-8; 32p.} E (Gr. PreK-1) 2011 Caldecott Medal; 2011 Charlotte Zolotow Honor Book**

Amos McGee rises early, dons his zookeeper's uniform, and takes the 6 a.m. bus to his job at the city zoo. Each day, he makes time for visiting with his friends, playing chess with the elephant, running races with the tortoise (who never loses), sitting quietly with the shy penguin, loaning his handkerchief to the runny-nosed rhinoceros, and reading stories to the owl, who is afraid of the dark. When Amos awakes with the sniffles and sneezes, the animals decide to take the bus to Amos's house and take care of him for a change. The pencil and woodblock printed illustrations of the gentle, elderly zookeeper and his animal friends are just plain sweet.

GERM: Do a zoo-themed story hour with another zoo-themed Caldecott book, *May I Bring a Friend* by Beatrice Schenk De Regniers. You may want to have your children make get-well cards for Amos, taking on the voice of one of the animals at the zoo.

EASY FICTION / PICTURE BOOKS, cont.

RELATED TITLES: Bateman, Teresa. *Farm Flu.* Albert Whitman, 2001. / Campbell, Rod. *Dear Zoo: A Lift-the-Flap Book.* Little Simon, 2007, c1982. / Cherry, Lynne. *Who's Sick Today?* Dutton, 1988. / De Regniers, Beatrice Schenk. *May I Bring a Friend.* Atheneum, 1964. / Garland, Michael. *Last Night at the Zoo.* Boyds Mills, 2001. / Gelman, Rita Golden. *I Went to the Zoo.* Scholastic, 1993. / Loomis, Christine. *One Cow Coughs: A Counting Book for the Sick and Miserable.* Ticknor & Fields, 1994. / Paxton, Tom. *Going to the Zoo.* Morrow, 1996. / Rathmann, Peggy. *Good Night, Gorilla.* Putnam, 1994. / Rex, Adam. *Pssst!* Harcourt, 2007. / Rose, Deborah Lee. *Birthday Zoo.* Albert Whitman, 2002. / Sierra, Judy. *Wild About Books.* Knopf, 2004. / Thomas, Shelley Moore. *Get Well, Good Knight.* Dutton, 2002. / Yolen, Jane. *How Do Dinosaurs Get Well Soon?* Blue Sky/Scholastic, 2003.
SUBJECTS: ANIMALS. CALDECOTT MEDAL. COMPASSION. FRIENDSHIP. KINDNESS. SICK. ZOO ANIMALS. ZOO KEEPERS.

[J] | |B| |S|
Snook Alone. **Nelson, Marilyn. Illus. by Timothy Basil Ering. Candlewick, 2010. {ISBN-13: 978-0-7636-2667-9; 48p.} E (Gr. 2-6)**
Abba Jacob, a monk who lives in a hermitage on a tropical island in the Indian Ocean, works and prays all day long, accompanied by his little black and white dog, Snook. Snook, rat terrier, catches the mice and rats in the kitchen and outside while Abba Jacob harvests fruit, works on the hermitage's wiring, or cleans up. When the monk is asked, along with two other men, to catalogue the plant and animal species of the uninhabited local islands, Snook comes, too, to catch the numerous mice and rats who have been eating the sea-birds' eggs. On the tiny island of Avocaire, a storm blows in, and Abba Jacob, unable to find his dog, must leave him behind. Ering's paintings are nothing short of spectacular. Seascapes filled with billowing clouds drifting across the azure skies, deep greens of the sea, and the ochre tones of the sand, are sweeping and dramatic. Add in the whimsical, cartoonish, rotund little monk, a fringe of hair encircling his round bald head, clad in white toga and sandals, running with his skinny arms and legs akimbo, a rapturous smile lighting up his kind face. Then there's Snook, racing through each page, wriggling with the joy of helping his master and then experiencing the shock of finding himself alone on the beach. Never have you seen a more soulful dog. Over the next many days, the resourceful Snook digs for fresh water, watches the huge clacking chungoma land crab take over his warren, catches fish to eat, walks among the egg-laying sea turtles, and waits "for his friend's soothing voice to emerge from its hiding place beneath the waves." It's Robinson Crusoe for dogs and, aside from the relief of the happy ending, your heart will ache with worry for the most loyal dog ever. The text is not an easy read. Newbery Honor author, Marilyn Nelson (*Carver, a Life in Poems*), has written a long, eloquent free verse–like story, rich with description, some of which will elude your listeners, though they should love the sound of it, unlike any other book you can name.
GERM: If you're looking for a way to talk about the use of imagery and characterization in stories, here you go. It's also a meditation on love, faith, and loyalty, so you may find yourself reaching for it at holiday time.
RELATED TITLES: Dennis, Brian. *Nubs: The True Story of a Mutt, a Marine & a Miracle.* Little, Brown, 2009. / Hest, Amy. *The Dog Who Belonged to No One.* Abrams, 2008. / Willems, Mo. *City Dog, Country Frog.* Hyperion, 2010.
SUBJECTS: DOGS. FRIENDSHIP. ISLANDS. LOST. LOYALTY. MONKS. PICTURE BOOKS FOR OLDER READERS. SEASHORE. SURVIVAL. TURTLES.

[J] | | | | |
Splinters. **Sylvester, Kevin. Illus. by the author. Tundra, 2010. {ISBN-13: 978-0-88776-944-3; 40p.} E (Gr. 1-4)**
Cindy Winters loves playing hockey on frozen ponds, but playing in a real league costs more than her parents can afford. Doing odd jobs, the enterprising girl earns enough money to join a team, but Coach Blister's daughters, the Blister sisters, are jealous and spiteful, and make her look bad on the ice. The scornful coach benches Cindy and makes her clean the uniforms and tape the hockey sticks. Cindy longs to get her chance to shine at the upcoming tryouts for the all-star hockey team. Then her fairy goaltender, an old woman only two feet tall, dressed in skates, mask, and old-fashioned leather goalie pads, appears and slashes Cindy across the leg with her magic hockey stick. "Ouch!" cries Cindy, but when she looks down, she's clad in a stunning white-and-gold uniform and a new pair of white leather skates. ("Not glass?" she asks, no doubt thinking of another girl. "Not very practical for hockey," says the fairy.) Awaiting her in the driveway is a shiny new Zamboni. At the tryouts, Head Coach Charmaine Prince despairs of finding a worthy star player until Cindy hits the ice. Knowing the spell will end when the final buzzer sounds, Cindy rushes off, leaving behind one skate, and, well, you know how the rest will work out. Pencil and watercolor illustrations capture the action and joy of the game and the humor and drama of the reworked fairy tale.

GERM: Phys Ed teachers are going to love this one. The Cinderella story has spawned so many innovative parodies. Explore the sports setting of this story and with Frances Minters's *Cinder Elly*, which incorporates basketball. Then have your kids pick a sport or hobby and figure out the elements they'd need (including equipment, characters, plots, and magic elements) to incorporate that activity into the Cinderella story. Teresa Bateman's *The Princesses Have a Ball* retells "The Twelve Dancing Princesses" with a basketball motif.

RELATED TITLES: Auch, Mary Jane. *The Princess and the Pizza.* Holiday House, 2002. / Bateman, Teresa. *The Princesses Have a Ball.* Albert Whitman, 2002. / Buehner, Caralyn. *Fanny's Dream.* Dial, 1996. / Craft, K. Y. *Cinderella.* SeaStar Books, 2000. / Ehrlich, Amy. *Cinderella.* Illus. by Susan Jeffers. Dutton, 2004. / Hughes, Shirley. *Ella's Big Chance: A Jazz-Age Cinderella.* Simon & Schuster, 2004. / Jackson, Ellen. *Cinder Edna.* Lothrop, 1994. / Ketteman, Helen. *Bubba the Cowboy Prince: A Fractured Texas Tale.* Scholastic, 1997. / Lowell, Susan. *Cindy Ellen: A Wild Western Cinderella.* Orchard, 1997. / McClintock, Barbara. *Cinderella.* Scholastic, 2005. / Minters, Frances. *Cinder Elly.* Viking, 1993. / Myers, Bernice. *Sidney Rella and the Glass Sneaker.* Macmillan, 1985. / Whipple, Laura. *If the Shoe Fits: Voices from Cinderella.* McElderry, 2002.

SUBJECTS: CINDERELLA STORIES. HOCKEY. LANGUAGE ARTS. PARODIES. PICTURE BOOKS FOR ALL AGES. SPORTS. STORIES TO TELL.

[J] | |B| | |

There's Going to Be a Baby. **Burningham, John. Illus. by Helen Oxenbury. Candlewick, 2010. {ISBN-13: 978-0-7636-4907-4; 48p.} E (Gr. PreK-1)**

In one of the most visually magnificent picture books this year, a dark-haired mother answers the many questions her little boy has after she tells him, "There's going to be a baby." As they walk through the falling snow (the boy balancing on a wall, his mother holding his hand and an umbrella, in a scene that looks like it's been inspired by a Japanese print, but done in ink and digitally colored), she tells him the baby will arrive in fall when it's ready. He'd like the baby to be a boy—Peter or Spider-Man. Above his head, you can see his thought balloon of a baby in a yellow and red Spiderbaby outfit. Stopping in a cafe for tea and ice cream, the mother says, "Maybe when the baby grows up, it will be a chef and work in a restaurant." Picturing the baby in chef's whites, the boy says, "I don't think I'd eat anything that was made by the baby." On the next double page are six panels, backed in gray cartoon-style tiny Benday Dots, of the baby making and flipping pancakes in the air. As the year passes and the mother's belly swells, the two go to a museum, a garden, the zoo, the beach, the bank, and the doctor's; at each new place, the boy imagines the baby in a related profession. Grandad comes to take the boy to the hospital. The boy says, with great wisdom, after having spent the year imagining what might be, "Grandad, the baby will be our baby. We're going to love the baby, aren't we?" And we, upon finishing this innovative and tender book, can only say, "Yes, we are."

GERM: First, let's look at the pedigrees of the two creators of this book. Oxenbury is the winner of three Kate Greenway Medals in England, while Burningham has won two. Burningham burst upon the American scene with *Come Away from the Water, Shirley* in 1971; each quirky new book has been a visually arresting cause for celebration, including last year's stunner, *It's a Secret.* As he said in an interview about writing and illustrating for children, "The 11th Commandment should have been 'Thou Shalt Not Bore.'" Oxenbury came out of retirement last year to do the glorious paintings for *Ten Little Fingers and Ten Little Toes,* by Mem Fox. Thankfully, she's back. Children's book illustrators can live forever, so here's hoping there are many more books coming from first-time collaborators, Burningham and Oxenbury. Here's the clincher: did you realize that the two have been married to each other for more than 45 years and raised three children? Just thought you'd like to know.

RELATED TITLES: Anholt, Catherine, and Laurence Anholt. *Catherine and Laurence Anholt's Big Book of Little Children.* Candlewick, 2003. / Ashman, Linda. *Babies on the Go.* Harcourt, 2003. / Burningham, John. *Come Away from the Water, Shirley.* Red Fox, 2000, c1977. / Burningham, John. *It's a Secret.* Candlewick, 2009. / Burningham, John. *Mr. Gumpy's Outing.* Henry Holt, 1971. / Fox, Mem. *Ten Little Fingers and Ten Little Toes.* Illus. by Helen Oxenbury. Harcourt, 2008. / Frazee, Marla. *The Boss Baby.* Beech Lane, 2010. / Frazee, Marla. *Walk On!: A Guide for Babies of All Ages.* Harcourt, 2006. / Harris, Robie H. *Hi, New Baby!* Candlewick Press, 2000. / Harris, Robie H. *Mail Harry to the Moon!* Little, Brown, 2008. / Keats, Ezra Jack. *Peter's Chair.* Viking, 1967. / Lloyd-Jones, Sally. *How to Be a Baby, by Me, the Big Sister.* Schwartz & Wade, 2007. / Ormerod, Jan. *101 Things to Do with a Baby.* Lothrop, 1984. / Root, Phyllis. *What Baby Wants.* Candlewick, 1998. / Rosen, Michael. *We're Going on a Bear Hunt.* Illus. by Helen Oxenbury. McElderry, 1989. / Schwartz, Amy. *A Teeny Tiny Baby.* Orchard, 1994. / Solheim, James. *Born Yesterday: The Diary of a Young Journalist.* Philomel, 2010. / Trivizas, Eugene. *The Three Little Wolves and the Big Bad Pig.* Illus. by Helen Oxenbury. McElderry, 1993. / Van Leeuwen, Jean. *Benny & Beautiful Baby Delilah.* Dial, 2006. / Waddell, Martin. *Farmer Duck.* Illus. by Helen Oxenbury. Candlewick, 1992.

SUBJECTS: BABIES. BROTHERS AND SISTERS. IMAGINATION. MOTHERS.

[J*] | | | | |
Time to Sleep, Sheep the Sheep. (Cat the Cat series) Willems, Mo. Illus. by the author. Balzer + Bray, 2010. {ISBN-13: 978-0-06-172847-1; 24p.} E (Gr. PreK-1)
(SEE PAGE 8 FOR ANNOTATION)

[J*] |A| | |S|
We Are in a Book! (Elephant & Piggie series) Willems, Mo. Illus. by the author. Hyperion, 2010. {ISBN-13: 978-1-42313-308-7; 64p.} E (Gr. PreK-1) 2011 Geisel Honor
(SEE PAGE 11 FOR ANNOTATION)

[J*] | | | | |
What's Your Sound, Hound the Hound? (Cat the Cat series) Willems, Mo. Illus. by the author. Balzer + Bray, 2010. {ISBN-13: 978-0-06-172844-0; 24p.} E (Gr. PreK-1)
(SEE PAGE 8 FOR ANNOTATION)

WINNERS!:
100+ Best Children's Books of 2010

FICTION BOOKS

[J*] | |B| | |

The Adventures of Nanny Piggins. **Spratt, R. A. Illus. by Dan Santat. Little, Brown, 2010. {ISBN-13: 978-0-316-06819-2; 239p.} FIC (Gr. 3-7) 2010 Booklist Editors' Choice, "Top of the List," Youth Fiction Book**

Desperate to find a nanny for his three children—eleven-year-old Derrick, nine-year-old Samantha, and seven-year-old Michael—Mr. Green, a parsimonious and dreadfully boring lawyer, is nevertheless too cheap to post an ad in the papers. Instead, he pounds a sign on his front lawn. After three weeks with no response, he is only too willing to hire the four-foot pig who knocks on the door, especially when she tells him her fee is a whole ten cents an hour. In a Mary Poppins story run amok, Nanny Piggins, whose only previous job experience is as a flying pig at the circus, supposes her new job can't be any harder than being blasted out of a cannon. The children immediately fall in love with their new nanny who announces, "I'm going to go to the kitchen and go through all the cupboards looking for things that contain sugar. Then eat as much as I can until I feel sick. You can join me if you like." She lets them eat chocolate before, after, and instead of breakfast, encourages them to read trashy literature at the dining table, and spends the $500 Mr. Green gives her to buy school uniforms for the children on a joyous day of terrifying rides at the amusement park. Horrified at the modern art on display at the local art gallery, she enters her own self-portrait, like the Mona Lisa, but with trotters and a snout, in their portrait competition, and accuses the gallery of pigism when they disqualify her painting. Each hilarious chapter is a self-contained, chocolate-smeared adventure, a feast of the absurd, just crying to be read aloud. Who wouldn't want a nanny like Nanny Piggins? Originally published in Australia, there will be two sequels coming, we hope, soon.

GERM: Nanny Alison, who tries to take over Nanny Piggins's job, consults a book called *How to Raise Children Properly*, with chapter headings including "When to Lock a Child in the Cellar." Have children come up with the chapter headings that Nanny Piggins would use if she wrote a book on the same subject. Make a list of 10 Life Lessons According to Nanny Piggins (which will undoubtedly contain references to chocolate, cake, and pie). Pair this with Mary Poppins, of course, and other absurdist chapter books like *School!: Adventures at the Harvey N. Trouble Elementary School* by Kate McMullan and *Sideways Stories from Wayside School* by Louis Sachar.

RELATED TITLES: Bond, Michael. *A Bear Called Paddington.* Houghton Mifflin, 1960. (And others in the Paddington Bear series.) / Broach, Elise. *Masterpiece.* Henry Holt, 2008. / Dahl, Roald. *Matilda.* Viking, 1988. / Evans, Douglas. *Apple Island or, The Truth About Teachers.* Front Street, 1998. / Fleming, Candace. *The Fabled Fourth Graders of Aesop Elementary School.* Schwartz & Wade, 2007. / King-Smith, Dick. *Clever Lollipop.* Candlewick, 2003. / Jonell, Lynne. *Emmy and the Incredible Shrinking Rat.* Henry Holt, 2007. / McMullan, Kate. *School!: Adventures at the Harvey N. Trouble Elementary School.* Feiwel and Friends, 2010. / Sachar, Louis. *Sideways Stories from Wayside School.* Morrow, 1985. (And others in the Wayside School series.) / Travers, P. L. *Mary Poppins.* Harcourt, 1934. (And others in the Mary Poppins series.)

SUBJECTS: BABYSITTERS. BEARS. BROTHERS AND SISTERS. FANTASY. FOOD HUMOROUS FICTION. NANNIES. PIGS.

FICTION BOOKS, cont.

[J*] | | |H| |

Big Nate: In a Class by Himself. Peirce, Lincoln. Illus. by the author. HarperCollins, 2010. {ISBN-13: 978-0-06-194434-5; 214p.} FIC (Gr. 3-6)

Nate Wright may look like an average sixth grader, and he admits he's not exactly Joe Honor Role; nevertheless, he just knows he is destined for greatness. This morning, when he looks through his binoculars into the bedroom of his best friend, Francis, next door, he gets a shock. Francis is reading his social studies textbook. This can only mean one thing. A TEST! His teacher, Mrs. Godfrey, AKA Venus de Silo (and you can find his list of 19 additional nicknames for her on page 82), has already threatened him with summer school if he does poorly on another test. Could he study now, before he goes to school? Afraid not. His book is in his locker, his class notes consist of doodles, and Nate knows he's dead. At school, Nate gets in trouble in science lab, dissecting a squid with his second best friend, Teddy, and Mr. Galvin goes Full Godfrey on them. ("GLOSSARY: When a teacher completely snaps and starts screaming, it's called a Full Godfrey. When Mrs. Godfrey does it, it's called Monday.") Racing to the flagpole, he whams full speed into Principal Nichols, knocking him down. Nate even forgets his lunch, though Teddy gives him a fortune cookie. The fortune is amazing: "Today you will surpass all others." Nate is elated. "It looked like today was going to stink out loud, and now everything's completely turned around!" Unfortunately, the only things in which he seems to be unsurpassed today are getting in trouble and racking up detentions in every single subject.

GERM: Nate's cocky ruminations are buttressed with cartoon panels, spot art, sidebars, and occasional full-page cartoons drawn on lined notebook paper. Based on the author's popular syndicated comic, this side-splitting "Wimpy Kid"–like graphic novel will be a huge hit with readers, who will be relieved to know the second book, *Big Nate Strikes Again*, is already out, with more to come! *I Smell a Pop Quiz!: A Big Nate Book* is a collection of comic strips. At the website, **www.bignatebooks.com**, you can read all of the Big Nate comic strips going back to 2000, watch a video interview conducted by Jeff Kinney, and even make your own Big Nate comic strip.

RELATED TITLES: Angleberger, Tom. *The Strange Case of Origami Yoda.* Amulet, 2010. / Byars, Betsy. *The 18th Emergency.* Viking, 1973. / Ferraiolo, Jack D. *The Big Splash.* Amulet, 2008. / Gauthier, Gail. *A Year with Butch and Spike.* Putnam, 1998. / George, Kristine O'Connell. *Swimming Upstream: Middle School Poems.* Clarion, 2002. / Getz, David. *Almost Famous.* Henry Holt, 1992. / Gorman, Carol. *Dork on the Run.* HarperCollins, 2002. / Holm, Jennifer L., and Matthew Holm. *Babymouse: Our Hero.* Random House, 2005. (And others in the Babymouse series.) / Kinney, Jeff. *Diary of a Wimpy Kid: Rodrick Rules.* Amulet, 2008. (And others in the Wimpy Kid series.) / Korman, Gordon. *This Can't Be Happening at Macdonald Hall.* Scholastic, 1978. / McMullan, Kate. *School!: Adventures at the Harvey N. Trouble Elementary School.* Feiwel and Friends, 2010. / Tashjian, Janet. *My Life As a Book.* Henry Holt, 2010. / Vail, Rachel. *Justin Case: School, Drool, and Other Daily Disasters.* Feiwel and Friends, 2010. / Vernon, Ursula. *Dragonbreath.* Dial, 2009. / Yee, Lisa. *Stanford Wong Flunks Big-Time.* Scholastic, 2005.

SUBJECTS: BEHAVIOR. CARTOONS AND COMICS. GRAPHIC NOVELS. HUMOROUS FICTION. MIDDLE SCHOOLS. PERSONAL NARRATIVES. SCHOOLS. TEACHERS.

[J*] | | | | |

Clementine, Friend of the Week. Pennypacker, Sara. Illus. by Marla Frazee. Hyperion, 2010. {ISBN-13: 978-1-42311-355-3; 161p.} FIC (Gr. 1-4)

As Clementine explains to her best friend, Margaret, on their bus ride home from school on Monday, today was the best day. She was picked to be Friend of the Week by her teacher, which means she will get to tell her autobiography to the class, be line leader, collect the milk money, and feed the fish. Best of all, on Friday she will get a special "Friend of the Week" booklet, where each of the kids in her third grade class will fill in a page describing what they think of her. Now a worldly wise fourth grader, Margaret still has her "Friend of the Week" booklet from last year, and reluctantly allows Clementine to come up to her apartment and see it. Ever the authority, Margaret advises Clementine to give everyone in her class compliments and maybe even presents so they'll write good things. Unfortunately, because of a misunderstanding, Margaret becomes furious with Clementine and now the two are on the outs, though Clementine doesn't even know why. Worse still, the unthinkable happens. Clementine's beloved kitten, Moisturizer, disappears from the apartment and no one can find him. Being Friend of the Week is turning into Clementine's most miserable week ever.

GERM: In this handbook on page 101, you'll find the complete text to Judy's guide for this fourth (and maybe even best) book in the series. Go to: **http://disney.go.com/** to download both the Clementine Friendship Party Kit, with reproducible pages, and Judy Freeman's Teacher's Guide to all four books in the series. Type "Clementine" in the Search Bar and click on the title when it comes up; then click on "Teaching Tools" for the guide and "Learn More" and the "Extras" for the Party Kit.

RELATED TITLES: Cabot, Meg. *Allie Finkle's Rules for Girls: The New Girl.* Scholastic, 2008. (And others in the Allie Finkle series.) / Cleary, Beverly. *Ramona Quimby, Age 8.* Morrow, 1981. (And others in the Ramona series.) / Creech, Sharon. *Granny Torrelli Makes Soup.* HarperCollins, 2003. / Danziger, Paula. *Amber Brown Is Not a Crayon.* Putnam, 1994. (And others in the Amber Brown series.) / Gifford, Peggy. *Moxy Maxwell Does Not Love Writing Thank You Notes.* Schwartz & Wade, 2008. (And others in the Moxy Maxwell series.) / Hannigan, Katherine. *Ida B: And Her Plans to Maximize Fun, Avoid Disaster, and (Possibly) Save the World.* Greenwillow, 2004. / Look, Lenore. *Ruby Lu, Brave and True.* Atheneum, 2004. / Pennypacker, Sara. *Clementine.* Hyperion, 2006. / Pennypacker, Sara. *Clementine's Letter.* Hyperion, 2008. / Pennypacker, Sara. *The Talented Clementine.* Hyperion, 2007. / Weeks, Sarah. *Oggie Cooder.* Scholastic, 2008.
SUBJECTS: ARGUMENTS. BEST FRIENDS. BOSTON (MASS.). CATS. CONFLICT RESOLUTION. FAMILY LIFE. FRIENDSHIP. HUMOROUS FICTION. LOST AND FOUND POSSESSIONS. PERSONAL NARRATIVES. SCHOOLS. SELFLESSNESS. TEACHERS.

[J] | | | | |
Cloud Tea Monkeys. Peet, Mal, and Elspeth Graham. Illus. by Juan Wijngaard. Candlewick, 2010. {ISBN-13: 978-0-7636-4453-6; 46p.} FIC (Gr. 1-4)
Tashi accompanies her mother and two other women on the long walk to the tea plantation, where they work for the bad-tempered Overseer gathering tea leaves and buds in heavy wicker baskets. When the long-tailed, black-faced, wild monkeys invade the plantation each day, Tashi sits under a tree and shares her fruit with them. In return, they groom her long dark hair. Tashi's mother has a cough and a fever; too sick to work, she stays home in bed for two days. With no money to pay the doctor, she will not get well. Frightened at this prospect, Tashi drags her mother's basket to the plantation, but the scornful overseer won't allow the little girl to pick tea. When the monkeys see her weeping, the leader, the one she calls Rajah, and other adult monkeys take her basket and disappear up the mountains and into the clouds. They return with the basket filled with extraordinary tea leaves they have gathered. His Excellency, the Royal Tea Taster, has just arrived for a surprise visit to examine the women's baskets to see if any of the teas they have gathered are good enough to be drunk by Her Majesty the Empress. Tashi's tea more than exceeds his expectations. Magnificent bordered full-page ink and gouache illustrations face each page of text, giving the story an elegant, timeless look. The solemn text reads like a classic literary folktale, and was, in fact, inspired by tea-picking tales of the Himalayan region of China.
GERM: Questions to ask: Why do the monkeys gather tea for Tashi? What do you think cloud tea tastes like? Brew some nice tea leaves and have a wee tea party.
RELATED TITLES: DiCamillo, Kate. *The Magician's Elephant.* Candlewick, 2009. / Fleischman, Sid. *The White Elephant.* Greenwillow, 2006. / Lin, Grace. *Where the Mountain Meets the Moon.* Little, Brown, 2009. / Reibstein, Mark. *Wabi Sabi.* Little, Brown, 2008. / Steig, William. *Brave Irene.* Farrar, 1986.
SUBJECTS: CONDUCT OF LIFE. HIMALAYAS. KINDNESS. MONKEYS. MOTHERS. MOUNTAINS. MULTICULTURAL BOOKS. SICK. TEA.

[J*] | | | |S|
Cosmic. Boyce, Frank Cottrell. HarperCollins/Walden Pond, 2010. ISBN-13: 978-0-06-183683-1; 313p.} FIC (Gr. 5-8)
Liam Digby begins his astonishing and hilarious narrative with this: "Mom, Dad—if you're listening—you know I said I was going to the South Lakeland Outdoor Activity Center with the school? To be completely honest, I'm not exactly in the Lake District. To be completely honest, I'm more sort of in space." This is Liam's explanation, narrated into his mobile phone, of how he got into this bit of a life-threatening dilemma. Along with four other children, he is now on board the *Infinite Possibility*, a rocket now spinning hopelessly out of control about 200,000 miles above Earth, lost in space. It all came about because Liam may only be twelve, but he's taller than anyone in his school, having grown seven inches over the summer, and already has a deep voice and stubble on his chin. This makes others believe he's far older than he is, leading the headmistress at his school, for example, to mistake him for a new teacher. When he and his friend, Florida Kirby, stop in at the Porsche dealer to look at the cars, the salesman assumes Liam is her father, and even offers to let him test drive a car. He spends hours playing World of Warcraft on his computer, where he's a Level Forty elf, but even though he's Gifted and Talented at school, kids still call him "freak" and "Wolverine." When he gets the call on his mobile from Drax Communications to visit Infinity Park in China, home of The Biggest Thrill Ride in the History of the World, called the Rocket, and to become the Greatest Dad Ever, he jumps at the chance, even though he's not exactly a dad. He feels he's mastered Level One of Being a Dad by observing his own father, though, and studying Dad's ridiculous book, *Talk to Your Teen.* Now all he needs is a daughter, and if he can talk Florida into playing along, they'll be on their way to China.

FICTION BOOKS, cont.

GERM: Liam makes a list of the five types of conversations his Dad has. See if your students can add examples of what their parents say. In impersonating a dad, Liam needs to figure out dadly skills, which include boring things like golf. Ask your students to write him a letter with the information he needs to beat out the four other dads and be named chaperone of the four children going into space. Note that Alan Bean, the fourth man to walk on the moon, shows up as a character in the story. To see his contributions to the space program and to see what he's doing these days, read *Mission Control, This Is* Apollo: *The Story of the First Voyages to the Moon* by Andrew Chaikin, with full color oil paintings by, well, Alan Bean.

RELATED TITLES: Boyce, Frank Cottrell. *Framed.* HarperCollins, 2005. / Boyce, Frank Cottrell. *Millions.* HarperCollins, 2004. / Burleigh, Robert. *One Giant Leap.* Philomel, 2009. / Chaikin, Andrew, with Victoria Kohl. *Mission Control, This Is* Apollo: *The Story of the First Voyages to the Moon.* Illus. by Alan Bean. Viking, 2009. / Connor, Leslie. *Crunch.* HarperCollins/Katherine Tegen, 2010. / Dahl, Roald. *Charlie and the Chocolate Factory.* Knopf, 1964. / Dowd, Siobhan. *The London Eye Mystery.* Random House/David Fickling, 2008. / Floca, Brian. *Moonshot: The Flight of* Apollo 11. Atheneum, 2009. / Klass, David. *Stuck on Earth.* Farrar/Frances Foster, 2010. / Mikaelsen, Ben. *Countdown.* Hyperion, 1996. / Reeve, Philip. *Larklight.* Bloomsbury, 2006. / Ride, Sally. *To Space and Back.* Lothrop, 1986.

SUBJECTS: ADVENTURE AND ADVENTURERS. ASTRONAUTS. FATHERS. HUMOROUS FICTION. INTERPLANETARY VOYAGES. OUTER SPACE—EXPLORATION. PERSONAL NARRATIVES. SCIENCE. SCIENCE FICTION. SIZE. SPACE FLIGHT TO THE MOON. VOYAGES AND TRAVELS.

[J] | | | | |

Dragonbreath: Curse of the Were-wiener. **Vernon, Ursula. Illus. by the author. Dial, 2010. {ISBN-13: 978-0-8037-3469-2; 200p.} FIC (Gr. 3-5)**

Third and maybe wackiest in the series so far, this hybrid novelette starts with Danny Dragonbreath, in the middle of a scary dream lit by a full moon, where he has a premonition that there is something wrong with his best friend, Wendall, an iguana. At lunchtime in the school cafeteria that day, Danny's overly large and bright red hot dog bites Wendall's finger, which is definitely not a normal occurrence. By the next day, Wendall's finger has turned candy-apple red, and his back is growing hair. Sneaking into the cafeteria's walk-in freezer to investigate, Danny finds an unusual package of hot dogs with the label "Were-Wieners, a product of Transylvania." At the school library, the two pals find a book in the mythology and folklore section called *A Child's Garden of Lycanthropy*, but there's nothing in it about were-wieners. Next, they call the 1-800 number on the hot dog package label, and speak to Reginald at Wurst-R-Us. (My favorite line: Reginald yells out, "Vlad! Another batch of the were-wieners went feral!") Reginald tells them they must find and kill the pack leader, the alpha wurst, with a silver skewer within three days or Wendall will become its minion. A late-night trip to the sewer to release a rogue potato salad, an "ancient enemy of the hot dog," might be their only hope. Witty one-liners and black and green toned illustrations on every page, often incorporating balloon dialogue, graphic novel style, will keep readers rolling.

GERM: Danny and Wendall do a search for werewolf books in the library's OPAC. You can tie this into your own computer catalog lessons, having students look up some of the subjects that have been covered in the books of the Dragonbreath series, including werewolves, samurai, volcanoes, ninja frogs, and giant squid. If your students don't know the folklore section of the library, introduce them to the pleasures of 398.2, which encompasses the same kinds of extreme adventures upon which Danny and Wendall thrive. Check out the animated webisode at **www.penguin.com/Dragonbreath**. For endless puns and classroom humor, also read Kate McMullan's *School!: Adventures at the Harvey N. Trouble Elementary School.*

RELATED TITLES: Benton, Jim. *The Fran That Time Forgot.* (And others in the Franny K. Stein, Mad Scientist series.) Simon & Schuster, 2005. / Bolger, Kevin. *Zombiekins.* Razorbill, 2010. / Holm, Jennifer L., and Matthew Holm. *Babymouse: Our Hero.* Random House, 2005. (And others in the Babymouse series.) / McMullan, Kate. *School!: Adventures at the Harvey N. Trouble Elementary School.* Feiwel and Friends, 2010. / Pilkey, Dav. *The Adventures of Captain Underpants: An Epic Novel.* Scholastic/Blue Sky, 1997. / Stadler, Alexander. *Julian Rodriguez: Episode One: Trash Crisis on Earth.* Scholastic, 2008. / Vernon, Ursula. *Dragonbreath.* Dial, 2009. / Vernon, Ursula. *Dragonbreath: Attack of the Ninja Frogs.* Dial, 2010. / Vernon, Ursula. *Dragonbreath: Lair of the Bat Monster.* Dial, 2011. / Wight, Eric. *Frankie Pickle and the Closet of Doom.* Simon & Schuster, 2009. (And others in the Frankie Pickle series.)

SUBJECTS: DRAGONS. FANTASY. GRAPHIC NOVELS. HUMOROUS FICTION. IGUANAS. SCHOOL LUNCHROOMS, CAFETERIAS, ETC. SCHOOLS. WEREWOLVES.

FICTION BOOKS, cont.

[J] |A|B|H| |

The Dreamer. **Ryan, Pam Munoz. Illus. by Peter Sis. Scholastic, 2010. {ISBN-13: 978-0-439-26970-4; 372p.}**
> **FIC (Gr. 4-8) 2011 Belpré Author Medal and 2010 Boston Globe-Horn Book Honor for Fiction and Poetry**

Recuperating from an illness, Neftalí Reyes is supposed to stay in bed and do his math homework, but he is so easily distracted by everything around him. Instead, he listens to the music of the rain and looks out the window at the Andes Mountains and imagines he's the captain of a ship on the ocean, far from his country, Chile. His father, a large looming man, thunders, "Stop that incessant daydreaming! . . . Do you want to be a skinny weakling forever and amount to nothing? . . . Your mother was the same, scribbling on bits of paper, her mind always in another world." Neftalí's mother died of a fever two months after his birth. While his demanding, domineering father is a constant terror in his life, Mamadre, his stepmother, is his support. Neftalí is a daydreamer, seeing the poetry of the world around him. He stutters when he speaks and is painfully shy. Ryan has created a lyrical and wondrous novel based on the early years of Chile's most famous son, the poet Pablo Neruda. The bookmaking is luscious, with a metallic blue and green dust jacket, green print, and ethereal green pen and ink illustrations.

GERM: Neftali collects words, loving the rhythm of locomotive, chocolate, oregano, and iguana. Ask your students to make a list of the words that they love the sound of. Read aloud the Neruda poems at the back of the book. Neftalí's toy sheep that was passed to him through a hole in the fence near his house by an unknown child became a constant companion. According to the author's note, Neruda kept that sheep for many years, and looked for a replacement after it was destroyed in a house fire. Why do you think it was so important to him that he never forgot it? Do you have a possession that you hope to keep always? What is it and why is it important to you? Students will be fascinated to see photographs of Neruda at **www.Fundacionneruda.org**. There you'll also find a dry timeline of his life—read aloud the entries for July 12, 1904 (his birth) through 1920. Discuss what the timeline left out that you learned from *The Dreamer*. If you are able to read Spanish with any degree of fluency (or know someone who does), it would be so effective to read aloud one of his poems first in English and then in Spanish. You can find all of his poetry online in both languages. For instance, at the back of the book, read aloud "Ode to the Lizard." You'll find the poem in its original Spanish as "Oda a La Lagartija." Have children see which words they can recognize and compare the two texts side by side. Pair this with Deborah Kogan Ray's picture book bio of Neruda, *To Go Singing Through the World*. Look up a discussion guide to the book at **www.bookwizard.scholastic.com**.

RELATED TITLES: Bryant, Jen. *A River of Words: The Story of William Carlos Williams*. Eerdmans, 2008. / Kerley, Barbara. *Walt Whitman: Words for America*. Scholastic, 2004. / Lasky, Kathryn. *A Voice of Her Own: The Story of Phillis Wheatley, Slave Poet*. Candlewick, 2002. / Ray, Deborah Kogan. *To Go Singing Through the World*. Farrar, 2006. / Ryan, Pam Muñoz. *Becoming Naomi Leon*. Scholastic, 2004. / Ryan, Pam Muñoz. *Esperanza Rising*. Scholastic, 2000. / Ryan, Pam Muñoz. *Riding Freedom*. Scholastic, 1998.

SUBJECTS: AUTHORS. BIOGRAPHICAL FICTION. CHILE—HISTORY—20TH CENTURY. HISTORICAL FICTION. LANGUAGE ARTS. MULTICULTURAL BOOKS. NERUDA, PABLO, 1904-1973. POETS.

[j] | | | |S|

The Familiars. **Epstein, Adam Jay, and Andrew Jacobson. Illus. by Bobby Chiu. HarperCollins, 2010. {ISBN-13: 978-0-06-196108-3; 360p.} FIC (Gr. 4-7)**

Stealing a fish at the fishmongers, mangy black-and-white alley cat, Aldwyn, is pursued through the streets of Bridgetower by the ruthless, crossbow-wielding bounty hunter, Grimslade. Diving into an open window, the wily, wise-cracking cat finds himself in a room filled with hundreds of animal cages containing familiars, animals with extraordinary magical powers, waiting to be chosen as companions to spellcasting witches or wizards. Jack, a wizard apprentice celebrating his eleventh birthday, spots Aldwyn, who has slipped into an empty cage, and, of course, chooses him. The shopkeeper thinks Aldwyn must be a telekinetic bicolor, but truly, the cat boasts no magic powers, except for his extraordinary street smarts and a talent for getting into trouble. Brought into the countryside, Aldwyn and Jack join two other children and their familiars—a sharp-tongued blue jay named Skylar, and a fly-loving red-eyed tree frog named Gilbert. Trouble is brewing in the kingdom, and when the three children are captured by the rogue Queen Loranella, it will be up to the three familiars to find and rescue them.

GERM: An appealing read-aloud or read-alone, this fast-paced and entertaining quest fantasy focuses on the talking animals instead of the kids, which animal-lovers will adore. Since Sony Pictures Animation has already optioned the story, it would be fun to have students each take a chapter and make an illustrated storyboard of it. The paperback is due out soon, so buying a class set would make sense for this project.

RELATED TITLES: Bearn, Emily. *Tumtum & Nutmeg: Adventures Beyond Nutmouse Hall.* Little, Brown, 2009. / Black, Holly, and Tony DiTerlizzi. *The Spiderwick Chronicles, Book 1: The Field Guide.* Simon & Schuster, 2003. (And others in the Spiderwick series.) / Edwards, Julie. *The Last of the Really Great Whangdoodles.* HarperCollins, 1974. / Hunter, Erin. *The Hunter.* (Warriors series, Book 1.) HarperCollins, 2003. / Ibbotson, Eva. *The Secret of Platform 13.* Dutton, 1998. / Rowling, J. K. *Harry Potter and the Sorcerer's Stone.* (And all the others in the Harry Potter series.) Scholastic, 1998. / Selden, George. *The Cricket in Times Square.* Farrar, 1960. / White, E. B. *Charlotte's Web.* HarperCollins, 1952.
SUBJECTS: ADVENTURE AND ADVENTURERS. BIRDS. CATS. FANTASY. FROGS. MAGIC. WIZARDS.

[J*] |A|B| | |
Heart of a Samurai: Based on the True Story of Nakahama Manjiro. Preus, Margi. Illus. by Nakahama Manjiro and others. Abrams/Amulet, 2010. (Gr. 5-8) FIC {ISBN-13: 978-0-810-98981-8; 301p.} **2011 Newbery Honor**

In January of 1841, the Year of the Ox, after a storm led to eight days of drifting at sea in their small fishing boat, five Japanese fishermen, including fourteen-year-old Nakahama Manjiro, encountered an island inhabited by thousands of birds. They spent the next five months on Bird Island, as they named it, subsisting on raw bird meat. They knew the law in Japan: "Any person who leaves the country and later returns will be put to death," because Japanese officials feared their minds might be poisoned by foreign devils. In June, the five were rescued by an American whaling ship, the John Howland. Captain Whitfield took a liking to Manjiro and the boy, renamed John Mung by the other sailors, began to learn English and earn his keep aboard the ship. Two years later, he went home with the captain to New Bedford, Massachusetts, where he attended school and apprenticed as a cooper. All of these are well-documented facts about Manjiro, known as the first Japanese person ever to set foot on American soil. It's what the author has done with these facts—turning them into an elegant, believable, enthralling, and altogether stellar novel impossible to put down—that makes it so worthy of its Newbery Honor. How Manjiro deals with prejudice, homesickness, and unfamiliar customs in his eleven years away from home will intrigue and engross readers.
GERM: Discuss the customs that Manjiro found puzzling and unfamiliar. Students can research nineteenth century Japan, closed to all foreigners for 250 years, to compare and contrast it with America in terms of its customs, dress, food, and society. Compare Preus's novelization with the nonfiction account, *Shipwrecked! The True Adventures of a Japanese Boy* by Rhoda Blumberg and with Emily Arnold McCully's nonfiction picture book biography, *Manjiro: The Boy Who Risked His Life for Two Countries.* By the way, if you go to **www.teachingbooks.net** and find the Author Name Pronunciations link, you can hear the author explain how her name is pronounced.
RELATED TITLES: Avi. *The True Confessions of Charlotte Doyle.* Orchard, 1990. / Blumberg, Rhoda. *Commodore Perry in the Land of the Shogun.* Lothrop, 1985. / Blumberg, Rhoda. *Shipwrecked! The True Adventures of a Japanese Boy.* HarperCollins, 2001. / Bradford, Chris. *Young Samurai: The Way of the Warrior.* Disney/Hyperion, 2008. / Hoobler, Dorothy, and Thomas Hoobler. *The Ghost in the Tokaido Inn.* Philomel, 1999. (And others in the Samurai Mystery series.) / Kadohata, Cynthia. *Weedflower.* Atheneum, 2006. / McCully, Emily Arnold. *Manjiro: The Boy Who Risked His Life for Two Countries.* Farrar, 2008. / Murphy, Jim. *Gone a-Whaling: The Lure of the Sea and the Hunt for the Great Whale.* Clarion, 1998. / Paterson, Katherine. *The Master Puppeteer.* HarperCollins, 1975. / Paterson, Katherine. *The Sign of the Chrysanthemum.* HarperCollins, 1973.
SUBJECTS: ADVENTURE AND ADVENTURERS. BIOGRAPHICAL FICTION. HISTORICAL FICTION. JAPAN. NAKAHAMA, MANJIRO, 1827-1898—FICTION. MULTICULTURAL BOOKS. SHIPS. SHIPWRECKS. SOCIAL STUDIES. SURVIVAL. VOYAGES AND TRAVELS.

FICTION BOOKS, cont.

[J*] | | | | |

How Tía Lola Learned to Teach. **Alvarez, Julia. Knopf, 2010. {ISBN-13: 978-0-375-86460-5; 144p.} FIC (Gr. 3-6)**

In this delicious stand-alone sequel to *How Tía Lola Came to Stay*, Miguel and Juanita Guzman's adored aunt from the Dominican Republic is now living with them in snowy Vermont, helping their newly divorced Mami to take care of them. When the principal of the children's school calls to ask Tía Lola if she will volunteer and teach Spanish to the students, Tía Lola is apprehensive. She doesn't speak English very well, she never went past fourth grade, and she worries that she's not educated enough to teach the students at Bridgeport Elementary. Miguel isn't so sure he wants his larger-than-life aunt coming to his fifth grade classroom, but she is an instant hit. She teaches the children Spanish songs, encourages them to use their imaginations, and, in Juanita's third grade classroom, organizes a Spanish treasure hunt. Told in present tense by an omniscient narrator, the story introduces some serious issues, but always infused with gentle humor and affection. The children's father, Papi, comes to visit with his girlfriend, Carmen, and they may be getting married. On a visit to New York City, Miguel disobeys his father and tries to take the subway alone. And Tía Lola's visa expires, which means she may be deported to the Dominican Republic. Through it all, Tía Lola is a warm breeze that will make readers yearn for such a loving and lovable relative.

GERM: Each chapter is headed with one of Tía Lola's Spanish sayings, which figures in the lessons the children learn about themselves, with the help of their understanding aunt. Make a chart of her aphorisms. Give children a list of the English translations and see how many they can match, using recall and looking for recognizable words. (See the Table of Contents for the complete list in Spanish, with English translations.) Ask them to pick one of the sayings and explain how it relates to their own lives. Then have them tell or write an anecdote about a relative who has had an impact on them. Compile a list of pithy sayings that your students have heard from their family elders.

RELATED TITLES: Alvarez, Julia. *Before We Were Free*. Knopf, 2002. / Alvarez, Julia. *Return to Sender*. Knopf, 2009. / Applegate, Katherine. *Home of the Brave*. Feiwel & Friends, 2007. / Fleming, Candace. *Lowji Discovers America*. Atheneum, 2005. / Marsden, Carolyn. *The Gold-Threaded Dress*. Candlewick, 2002. / Medina, Jane. *The Dream on Blanca's Wall: Poems in English and Spanish*. Wordsong/Boyds Mills, 2004. / Ryan, Pam Muñoz. *Esperanza Rising*. Scholastic, 2000. / Singh, Vandana. *Younguncle Comes to Town*. Viking, 2006.

SUBJECTS: AUNTS. DIVORCE. DOMINICAN AMERICANS. FAMILY LIFE. HISPANIC AMERICANS. IMMIGRATION AND EMIGRATION. LANGUAGE ARTS. MULTICULTURAL BOOKS. SCHOOLS. SPANISH LANGUAGE. VERMONT.

[J] | | | | |

Ivy's Ever After. **Lairamore, Dawn. Holiday House, 2010. {ISBN-13: 978-0-8234-2261-6; 311p.} FIC (Gr. 4-7)**

Princess Ivory Isadora Imperia Irene, who insists on being called Ivy, is not your typical compliant, well-behaved, proper princess. Perhaps it is because Ivy's mother died after giving birth to her, her fairy godmother disappeared soon after, and her father, the king, has become increasingly simple minded since his wife's death. Instead of playing the harp and doing embroidery, the impetuous girl has the run of Ardendale's rundown old castle, with the approval of her indulgent father, though not of her stern nursemaid, Tildy. At age ten, Ivy learns something shocking from an old book, *An Annotated History of Ardendale*. Hundreds of years ago, a treaty was negotiated with the dragons that had been terrorizing the kingdom. On her fourteenth birthday, the first-born daughter of the king is to be locked in a white stone tower, guarded by a dragon. The first prince to slay the dragon will win the princess's hand and gain the dragon's treasure as well. A month before her fourteenth birthday, Prince Romil of Glacia arrives to compete for Ivy's hand. Though she thinks him dashing at first, she soon realizes that he is cold, calculating, and willing to do anything to take over the throne. She decides to do everything she can to scare him off, but he is undeterred, and now her very life could be in danger. What she really needs is the help of her fairy godmother, Drusilla. As a tale of a spunky princess who enlists the help of her tower guard, a small, fire-impaired dragon named Eldridge, and sets out to find Drusilla, this is a spirited and enjoyable fairy tale–like read aloud.

GERM: Do a princess/dragon booktalk with some of the titles listed below.

RELATED TITLES: Bath, K. P. *The Secret of Castle Cant*. Little, Brown, 2004. / Coombs, Kate. *The Runaway Princess*. Farrar, 2006. / Fletcher, Susan. *Shadow Spinner*. Atheneum, 1998. / Hale, Shannon. *Princess Academy*. Bloomsbury, 2005. / Kindl, Patrice. *Goose Chase*. Houghton Mifflin, 2001. / Knudsen, Michelle. *The Dragon of Trelian*. Candlewick, 2009. / Levine, Gail Carson. *Ella Enchanted*. HarperCollins, 1997. / Lin, Grace. *Where the Mountain Meets the Moon*. Little, Brown, 2009. / Stanley, Diane. *Bella at Midnight*. HarperCollins, 2006. / Wrede, Patricia. *Dealing with Dragons*. Harcourt, 1990.

SUBJECTS: CONFORMITY. DRAGONS. FAIRY GODMOTHERS. FANTASY. GOATS. KINGS AND RULERS. PRINCES AND PRINCESSES.

FICTION BOOKS, cont.

[J] | | | | |

The Junkyard Wonders. **Polacco, Patricia. Illus. by the author. Philomel, 2010. {ISBN-13: 978-0-399-25078-1; 48p.} FIC (Gr. 2-6)**

Spending a year with her father and Gramma in Michigan, Trisha is excited about going to a new school where no one will tease her for being in a special class, as she was in her old school in California. She even has a new friend, Kay. Her new teacher, stout, grey-haired Mrs. Peterson in Room 206, says, "Welcome to the junkyard," and gives them a definition of the word "genius" to memorize starting with, "Genius is neither learned nor acquired . . ." and tells them, "The definition describes every one of you." Trisha likes these kids, all different and odd, like super-tall Jody, who has a disease that makes him grow too fast; Gibbie, with Tourette's; Stuart, with diabetes; Ravanne, who never speaks; and her new soul mate, Thom, who others call Sissy Boy because ballet is his life. But she's already been rejected by Kay who doesn't want a junkyard kid at her lunch table, and she's devastated at being in a special class once again. Luckily, Mrs. Peterson is that unforgettable teacher who brings out the genius in each of her students, and makes them embrace their differences, in spite of the harassment of a nasty bully and his pals.

GERM: Polacco, a national treasure in the children's book world, makes readers understand and accept how kids tick, and incorporates here issues not customarily covered in a picture book, including a gay character, Thom, and the death of a child. (Don't worry—both situations are handled beautifully.) You've probably already met Trisha in *Thank You, Mr. Falker*, about the teacher who taught her to read. What will make kids snap to attention is the last page, where a note from the author updates the lives of Thom and Gibbie, which is when they will realize that Trisha is actually Patricia Polacco and this story is true. Mrs. Peterson takes her class to the junkyard and has each group collect materials that can be made into something new. She reads aloud Dickens and poetry. Look how she has the class form groups—using the scents of lemon, cinnamon, and almonds. All are ideas we can synthesize with our own kids. At a time when teachers are being reviled nationwide, how heartening it is to be reminded of why we went into teaching in the first place. We can only hope we make the same kind of differences in the lives of the kids we teach.

RELATED TITLES: Borden, Louise. *Good Luck, Mrs. K.* McElderry, 1999. / Haddix, Margaret Peterson. *Because of Anya.* Simon & Schuster, 2002. / Hill, Kirkpatrick. *The Year of Miss Agnes.* McElderry, 2000. / Houston, Gloria. *My Great Aunt Arizona.* HarperCollins, 1992. / Klise, Kate. *Stand Straight, Ella Kate: The True Story of a Real Giant.* Dial, 2010. / Levy, Elizabeth. *Keep Ms. Sugarman in the Fourth Grade.* HarperCollins, 1991. / Polacco, Patricia. *Chicken Sunday.* Philomel, 1992. / Polacco, Patricia. *The Lemonade Club.* Philomel, 2007. / Polacco, Patricia. *Mrs. Mack.* Philomel, 1998. / Polacco, Patricia. *An Orange for Frankie.* Philomel, 2004. / Polacco, Patricia. *My Rotten, Redheaded Older Brother.* Simon & Schuster, 1994. / Polacco, Patricia. *Thank You, Mr. Falker.* Philomel, 1998.

SUBJECTS: AUTOBIOGRAPHICAL FICTION. BIOGRAPHICAL FICTION. BULLIES. DEATH. FRIENDSHIP. INTERPERSONAL RELATIONS. INVENTIONS AND INVENTORS. LEARNING DISABILITIES. PEOPLE WITH DISABILITIES. SCHOOLS. SELF-ESTEEM. TEACHERS.

[J] |A| | | |

Mockingbird: (Mok'ing-bûrd). **Erskine, Kathryn. Philomel, 2010. {ISBN-13: 978-0-399-25264-8; 235p.} FIC (Gr. 4-7) 2011 National Book Award**

Caitlin and her dad are reeling from the school shooting death of her fourteen-year-old brother, Devon. As a ten-year-old with Asperger's, Caitlin has difficulty reading people's faces, understanding emotion, and comprehending her brother leaving her. She's not allowed in Devon's room to go to her hidey-hole anymore. "Not since The Day Our Life Fell Apart and Dad slammed Devon's door shut and put his head against it and cried and said, *No no no no no.*" Back at school, she has a session with Mrs. Brooks, her counselor, who encourages her talk about the funeral. Though Caitlin can spout dictionary definitions of words, in conversation, she takes them literally. When Mrs. Brooks asks if she can still feel Devon's presence, Caitlin wonders what he would feel like. Caitlin doesn't want him around in a "different way," like Mrs. Brooks describes; she wants him around in the same old way, making her popcorn, and teaching her not to be weird so kids won't laugh at her. She has a TRM—a Tantrum Rage Meltdown—from missing him. At school she confronts Josh, who she thinks of as loud and evil, and whose cousin was one of the shooters at Devon's school, for pushing William, an autistic boy. Josh says, cruelly, "It's not my fault her brother is dead." Researching the heart for a report, she finds this irrefutable statement: "A gunshot to the Heart is almost always fatal." It's not until her counselor has her spend recess time on the playground that she makes her first friend ever, a sad-eyed little kindergarten boy named Michael, who misses his mother. What she doesn't realize is that his mother, a teacher, was one of the other victims of the shooting. Hearing the word Closure used in the context of the shooting, she seeks a way to find Closure for herself and her father. Her matter-of-fact narration, using italics instead of quotes for dialogue, allows us to empathize with how an Asperger's child sees the world, and root for her as she finds a way to get connected to her new world.

GERM: Okay, you are not going to be reading this compelling and devastating novel aloud, unless you have a constitution of iron or don't mind weeping copiously in front of and/or with your students, but it is a must read. Themes from Harper Lee's *To Kill a Mockingbird*, a movie and book Devon loved, give the book its title and its moral core; even Devon's nickname for Caitlin was Scout. An Author's Note explains that the story was inspired by the senseless killings at Virginia Tech in 2007.

RELATED TITLES: Baskin, Nora Raleigh. *Anything but Typical.* Simon & Schuster, 2009. / Choldenko, Gennifer. *Al Capone Does My Shirts.* Putnam, 2004. / Couloumbis, Audrey. *Getting Near to Baby.* Putnam, 1999. / Creech, Sharon. *The Wanderer.* HarperCollins, 2000. / Dowd, Siobhan. *The London Eye Mystery.* Random House/David Fickling, 2008. / Fry, Virginia Lynn. *Part of Me Died, Too: Stories of Creative Survival Among Bereaved Children and Teenagers.* Dutton, 1995. / Hest, Amy. *Remembering Mrs. Rossi.* Candlewick, 2007. / Lee, Harper. *To Kill a Mockingbird.* HarperCollins, 1999. / Lord, Cynthia. *Rules.* Scholastic, 2006. / Martin, Ann M. *A Corner of the Universe.* Scholastic, 2002. / Martin, Ann M. *Everything for a Dog.* Feiwel & Friends, 2009. / Park, Barbara. *Mick Harte Was Here.* Knopf, 1995. / Potter, Ellen. *Slob.* Philomel, 2009. / Recorvits, Helen. *Goodbye, Walter Malinski.* Farrar, 1999. / Spinelli, Jerry. *Loser.* HarperCollins, 2002. / Tarshis, Lauren. *Emma-Jean Lazarus Fell Out of a Tree.* Dial, 2007. / Urban, Linda. *A Crooked Kind of Perfect.* Harcourt, 2007.

SUBJECTS: ASPERGER'S SYNDROME. BROTHERS AND SISTERS. DEATH. EMOTIONS. EMPATHY. FATHERS. GRIEF. PERSONAL NARRATIVES. SCHOOL SHOOTINGS. SCHOOLS. TEACHERS.

[j] |A| | | |
Moon Over Manifest. Vanderpool, Clare. Delacorte, 2010. {ISBN-13: 978-0-385-73883-5; 351p.} FIC (Gr. 5-8)
     2011 Newbery Medal
In the spring of 1936, with the Depression still in full swing, eleven-year-old rough-and-tumble Abilene Tucker, wearing overalls and carrying a satchel containing her most special possession, her daddy's broken compass, arrives by train in the small mining town of Manifest, Kansas. Her daddy, Gideon, has just gotten a railroad job in Iowa, and since Abilene has only just recovered from a dangerously infected cut on her knee, he has decided to send her back to the place where he grew up, in the care of an old friend, Pastor Howard, AKA Shady. Shady's ramshackle place seems to be one part saloon, one part carpenter shop, and one part church, but he's kind to Abilene, who hopes to find out more about her daddy's early life. Instead, she finds, under a loose floorboard in her room, a cigar box filled with mementoes and old letters dated 1918, written from a young soldier named Ned Gillen to someone named Jinx. With her new friends, cousins Lettie and Ruthanne, Abilene sets out to unravel the town's long-held secrets. Tightly constructed, the novels segues from Abilene's snappy and observant narrative to World War I homefront tales of two decades past, told through local newspaper stories, Ned's letters, and the you-are-there stories about Ned and young con artist, Jinx, told to Abilene by an old Hungarian woman, Miss Sadie, a local fortune teller or diviner. Many issues figure into this complex tale, including the nefarious doings of the local Ku Klux Klan, unfair labor practices the immigrant community must accept from the corrupt mine owner, moonshine-making in a time of Prohibition, a murder, and the identity of a mysterious someone known as The Rattler. Will readers have the chops and the staying power to follow the convoluted story to its ultimately satisfying conclusion? There's the rub.

GERM: You can compare and contrast this with another Depression era story of a kid on the road, *Bud, Not Buddy*, by Christopher Paul Curtis. Kids can do some research into World War I, including the influenza pandemic of 1918 that took so many lives. Go to **www.teachingbooks.net/show.cgi?f=awards2011** to hear the author introduce and read an excerpt from the book.

RELATED TITLES: Curtis, Christopher Paul. *Bud, Not Buddy.* Delacorte, 1999. / Freedman, Russell. *Children of the Great Depression.* Clarion, 2005. / Hesse, Karen. *Out of the Dust.* Scholastic, 1997. / Holm, Jennifer L. *Turtle in Paradise.* Random House, 2010. / McCutcheon, John. *Christmas in the Trenches.* Peachtree, 2006. / Morpurgo, Michael. *War Horse.* Scholastic, 2007, c1982. / Peck, Richard. *A Long Way from Chicago.* Dial, 1998. / Phelan, Matt. *The Storm in the Barn.* Candlewick, 2009.

SUBJECTS: DEPRESSIONS—1929—U.S. FATHERS. HISTORICAL FICTION. KANSAS. NEWBERY MEDAL. PERSONAL NARRATIVES. SECRETS. SOCIAL STUDIES. WORLD WAR, 1914-1918.

FICTION BOOKS, cont.

[J] | | | | |

My Life As a Book. Tashjian, Janet. Illus. by Jake Tashjian. Henry Holt, 2010. {ISBN-13: 978-0-8050-8903-5; 211p.} FIC (Gr. 4-7)

"I DON'T WANT TO READ THIS BOOK," cries twelve-year-old Derek in the first line of his present tense narrative. Ever since his teacher has pegged him as a "reluctant reader," he's been working overtime to thwart his mother who bribes him with one chocolate chip for every page he reads. As he tells it, he actually does like to read, as long as it's comics like *Calvin and Hobbes* or *Garfield*. Because he loves to draw, he takes the list of vocabulary words his teacher, reading tutor, and mom insist that he keep, and he draws tiny little stick figures (there are almost 200 of them scattered through the margins of the book) that define each word in context. As he notes, "Anything to get out of reading." This summer, though, he needs to read three books on his teacher's summer reading list and write a report on one of them. Derek insists this is not doable on his schedule, and is doing everything he can to avoid it. When he finds a ten-year-old newspaper from Martha's Vineyard in the attic, with the headline "Local Girl Found Dead on Beach," he gets curious, especially when his mother won't answer his questions about it. Learning that he was somehow involved in the girl's death, back when he was a toddler, he wants more than anything to go to Massachusetts to find out more. Instead, his mother signs him up for six weeks of Learning Camp.

GERM: Derek is a crackerjack cartoonist; his fine line doodles are on target and more often than not, ingenious. The word "investigate" has a stick figure wearing a Sherlock Holmes–style deerstalker cap, leaning over to peer at the ground with his magnifying glass; "punishment" shows a disgruntled kid, perched on a chair in a corner. Your kids are going to be delighted poring over these, especially when they learn that the author's fourteen-year-old son, Jake, drew them all. Now you have a whole new way for children to do their vocabulary word assignments that will definitely appeal to the right-brained artists in your group who hate to read but live to draw.

RELATED TITLES: Angleberger, Tom. *The Strange Case of Origami Yoda.* Amulet, 2010. / Gantos, Jack. *Joey Pigza Swallowed the Key.* Farrar, 1998. / Kinney, Jeff. *Diary of a Wimpy Kid: Rodrick Rules.* Amulet, 2008. (And others in the Wimpy Kid series.) / Peirce, Lincoln. *Big Nate: In a Class by Himself.* HarperCollins, 2010. / Tarshis, Lauren. *Emma-Jean Lazarus Fell Out of a Tree.* Dial, 2007. / Vail, Rachel. *Justin Case: School, Drool, and Other Daily Disasters.* Feiwel and Friends, 2010. / Yee, Lisa. *Stanford Wong Flunks Big-Time.* Scholastic, 2005.

SUBJECTS: BOOKS AND READING. DEATH. DOGS. FAMILY LIFE. LANGUAGE ARTS. PERSONAL NARRATIVES. SECRETS. SUMMER.

[J] | | | | |

A Nest for Celeste: A Story About Art, Inspiration, and the Meaning of Home. Cole, Henry. Illus. by the author. HarperCollins/Katherine Tegen, 2010. {ISBN-13: 978-0-06-170410-9; 342p.} FIC (Gr. 3-6)

In her nook beneath the dusty floorboards of Oakley Plantation's dining room, Celeste, an industrious mouse, spends her days weaving baskets from the blades of dried grasses. When two domineering rats bully her into entering the dining room to forage for food, Celeste gets her first glimpse of the house's two human visitors: Mr. Audubon, an artist, and his fourteen-year-old assistant, Joseph. They have come to New Orleans to paint portraits of all the birds in Louisiana as part of Audubon's quest to capture lifelike and life-sized images of every species of bird in North America. That night, the gray house cat stalks Celeste, who escapes to a second floor bedroom and finds safety in Joseph's leather boot. Little One, as Joseph calls her affectionately, soon learns to sit in his shirt pocket, her head poking out, or to perch contentedly on his shoulders as he works on his drawings for Mr. Audubon. When Joseph brings a wild wood thrush into his room, Celeste tries but is unable to free the bird, whose name is Cornelius, from his cage. Venturing outside to find some dogwood berries for Cornelius, she is caught in a thunderstorm and flood that carries her far from home. Like Brian Selznick did in his Caldecott winner, *The Invention of Hugo Cabret*, Henry Cole has interspersed his narrative with captivating full-page pencil drawings on nearly every page.

GERM: Audubon himself would surely approve of and appreciate the many detailed close-ups of the good mouse, Celeste, and the different birds she encounters on her journey. While this is a lyrical fantasy of a talking mouse, note that she does not speak with any of the humans, though she understands everything Joseph says. It is, as well, a historical account of Audubon's visit to the plantation in 1821 with his assistant, Joseph, as the Afterword makes clear. The two made their way across America, where Audubon painted life-sized portraits of more than 400 bird species. In the novel, readers learn the uncomfortable truth about the way Audubon captured his birds on canvas: he first killed each bird and pinned it to a wooden board. Joseph questions the ethics of killing the birds in order to make them look alive, something readers will be interested to discuss. Check out Audubon's original paintings and text descriptions from his 1840 "First Octavo Edition," on the Audubon Society's website at **www.audubon.org/bird/BoA/BOA_index.html**.

FICTION BOOKS, cont.

RELATED TITLES: Bearn, Emily. *Tumtum & Nutmeg: Adventures Beyond Nutmouse Hall.* Little, Brown, 2009. / Brenner, Barbara. *On the Frontier with Mr. Audubon.* Boyds Mills, 1997. / Burleigh, Robert. *Into the Woods: John James Audubon Lives His Dream.* Atheneum, 2003. / Davies, Jacqueline. *The Boy Who Drew Birds: A Story of John James Audubon.* Houghton Mifflin. 2003. / DiCamillo, Kate. *The Miraculous Journey of Edward Tulane.* Candlewick, 2006. / Hoose, Phillip. *The Race to Save the Lord God Bird.* Farrar, 2004. / King-Smith, Dick. *Babe, the Gallant Pig.* Crown, 1985. / King-Smith, Dick. *Clever Lollipop.* Candlewick, 2003. / King-Smith, Dick. *Martin's Mice.* Crown, 1989. / King-Smith, Dick. *The School Mouse.* Hyperion, 1995. / Lawson, Robert. *Ben and Me: An Astonishing Life of Benjamin Franklin by His Good Mouse, Amos.* Little, Brown, 1939. / Selden, George. *The Cricket in Times Square.* Farrar, 1960. / Selznick, Brian. *The Invention of Hugo Cabret: A Novel in Words and Pictures.* Scholastic, 2007. / White, E. B. *Charlotte's Web.* HarperCollins, 1952.
SUBJECTS: ARTISTS. AUDUBON, JOHN JAMES, 1785-1851. BIRDS. FANTASY. HISTORICAL FICTION. HUMAN-ANIMAL RELATIONSHIPS. LOUISIANA. MASON, JOSEPH, 1807-1883. MICE. NEW ORLEANS (LA.). SCIENCE.

[J*] |A|B|H|S|
One Crazy Summer. Williams-Garcia, Rita. HarperCollins/Amistad, 2010. {ISBN-13: 978-0-06-076088-5; 218p.} FIC (Gr. 5-8) 2011 Newbery Honor; 2011 Coretta Scott King Author Medal; 2010 National Book Award Finalist; Scott O'Dell Award for Historical Fiction
If you're old enough to remember the summer of 1968, right after the assassinations of Martin Luther King, Jr. and Robert Kennedy, it seems like yesterday, but for children, it's distant history. There are many poignant and inspirational middle grade novels about the civil rights era—*The Watsons Go to Birmingham, 1963* is one outstanding example—but until now, virtually none about its more radical aftermath. That summer, the Black Panthers in Oakland, California were posing with rifles to show their resistance to the authorities, but also running free breakfast programs and childcare centers for the community. Into this scenario steps our narrator, eleven-year-old Delphine Gaither, who is shepherding her two quarrelsome younger sisters, nine-year-old Vonetta and seven-year-old Fern, on a plane from New York to spend a month with their mother, Cecile, in Oakland. Their Pa has decided they need to know her, though she abandoned the family when Fern was a baby, leaving them to be raised by their grandmother, Big Ma. Delphine has memories of her mother writing on walls and arguing with Papa, but she is still stunned to reconnect with her tall, no-nonsense, angry mother who may look like "a colored movie star," but makes it clear that she considers her daughters' visit a huge intrusion. "Cecile was no kind of mother. Cecile didn't want us. Cecile was crazy." A real mother would cook them dinner; Cecile sends them to get take-out at Ming's, tells them they are not allowed in her kitchen, and sends them to The People's Center, run by the Black Panthers, for breakfast every day. Cecile is a poet, known as Sister Nzila to the Panthers, and she might win your designation as Worst Mother in a children's book, but she is a nuanced and surprising character. Delphine's story overflows with her unvarnished observations about the Panthers, the differences between black Oakland and white San Francisco, and how the girls cope when their mother is arrested.
GERM: This will be a fascinating Book Club selection to read and discuss. Students will want to do some research about the Panthers and their controversial ideas, actions, and the consequences. Expect to see some major awards for this vivid portrayal of a girl who considers herself plain and steady, who has taken over mothering her two sisters, who wants to know why her mother left, and who chronicles her world with such clarity.
RELATED TITLES: Birdsall, Jeanne. *The Penderwicks: A Summer Tale of Four Sisters, Two Rabbits, and a Very Interesting Boy.* Knopf, 2005. / Bridges, Ruby. *Through My Eyes.* Scholastic, 1999. / Choldenko, Gennifer. *Al Capone Does My Shirts.* Putnam, 2004. / Creech, Sharon. *The Wanderer.* HarperCollins, 2000. / Curtis, Christopher Paul. *The Watsons Go to Birmingham, 1963.* Delacorte, 1995. / Grimes, Nikki. *The Road to Paris.* Putnam, 2006. / Holm, Jennifer L. *Turtle in Paradise.* Random House, 2010. / Hoose, Phillip. *Claudette Colvin: Twice toward Justice.* Farrar/Kroupa, 2009. / Magoon, Kekla. *The Rock and the River.* Aladdin, 2009. / McWhorter, Diane. *A Dream of Freedom: The Civil Rights Movement from 1954 to 1968.* Scholastic, 2004. / O'Connor, Barbara. *How to Steal a Dog.* Frances Foster/Farrar, 2007. / Thor, Annika. *A Faraway Island.* Delacorte, 2009. / Wolfson, Jill. *What I Call Life.* Henry Holt, 2005. / Woodson, Jacqueline. *Locomotion.* Putnam, 2003.
SUBJECTS: AFRICAN AMERICANS. BLACK PANTHER PARTY. CALIFORNIA. CIVIL RIGHTS MOVEMENT. FAMILY PROBLEMS. HISTORICAL FICTION. MOTHERS. MULTICULTURAL BOOKS. OAKLAND (CALIF.)—HISTORY—20TH CENTURY. PERSONAL NARRATIVES. POETS. SAN FRANCISCO. SISTERS. SOCIAL STUDIES. SUMMER. VACATIONS.

FICTION BOOKS, cont.

[J*] | | | | |
Out of My Mind. Draper, Sharon M. Atheneum, 2010. {ISBN-13: 978-1-4169-7170-2; 295p.} FIC (Gr. 4-8)
     2011 Josette Frank Award for Fiction (Bank Street College of Education)
"I have never spoken one single word. I am almost eleven years old." The narrator is Melody, who has cerebral palsy. Though she can't speak, she has a prodigious memory, recalling word-for-word everything she sees and hears. When Melody gets frustrated, she screeches and flails her body in what she calls "tornado explosions," and not even her own mother knows what's wrong. Despite one doctor's pronouncement that Melody is severely brain-damaged, her mother believes she is intelligent, and enrolls her in a special needs class in a local elementary school where she is strapped in a wheelchair all day, using a primitive communication board to point to phrases like "yes," "no," and "maybe" with her thumb. As Melody explains in her remarkable narrative, "It's like I live in a cage with no door and no key, and I have no way to tell someone how to get me out." A whole new world opens up when she gets an electric wheelchair and a new high-tech computer and speech device called a Medi-Talker which allows her to say "I love you" to her parents for the first time. Mainstreamed into a fifth grade inclusion class for her major subjects, Melody tries out for the Whiz Kids competition, coached by her history teacher, Mr. Demming. No one, including her teacher, believes she can succeed. "They think my brain is messed up like the rest of me," she types to Catherine, her special assistant, though she perseveres and aces the quiz team tests.
GERM: Don't assume that this is a heartwarming tale of a girl who overcomes her illness to triumph over the odds. Cerebral palsy is not curable. Melody faces disappointments and setbacks that would be daunting or devastating for anyone. She's a fighter, though, and her honest narrative will get kids thinking about and appreciating all the things they do without thinking, like walking and talking. This will be one electric classroom read-aloud and is bursting with discussion possibilities.
RELATED TITLES: Baskin, Nora Raleigh. *Anything but Typical.* Simon & Schuster, 2009. / Choldenko, Gennifer. *Al Capone Does My Shirts.* Putnam, 2004. / Codell, Esmé Raji. *Sahara Special.* Hyperion, 2003. / Dowd, Siobhan. *The London Eye Mystery.* Random House/David Fickling, 2008. / Gantos, Jack. *Joey Pigza Swallowed the Key.* Farrar, 1998. / Konigsburg, E. L. *The View from Saturday.* Atheneum, 1996. / Lord, Cynthia. *Rules.* Scholastic, 2006. / Miller, Sarah Elizabeth. *Miss Spitfire: Reaching Helen Keller.* Atheneum, 2007. / Sonnenblick, Jordan. *After Ever After.* Scholastic, 2010. / Spinelli, Jerry. *Loser.* HarperCollins, 2002. / Tarshis, Lauren. *Emma-Jean Lazarus Fell Out of a Tree.* Dial, 2007. / Trueman, Terry. *Stuck in Neutral.* HarperCollins, 2000. / Urban, Linda. *A Crooked Kind of Perfect.* Harcourt, 2007. / Wolff, Virginia Euwer. *Probably Still Nick Swanson.* Henry Holt, 1988.
SUBJECTS: CEREBRAL PALSY. COMMUNICATION. FAMILY PROBLEMS. INTERPERSONAL RELATIONS. PEOPLE WITH DISABILITIES. PERSONAL NARRATIVES. SCHOOLS.

[J*] | | | |S|
The Red Pyramid. Riordan, Rick. Disney/Hyperion, 2010. {ISBN-13: 978-1-42311-338-6; 516p.} FIC (Gr. 5-9)
Here's fourteen-year-old Carter Kane, speaking directly to us, as transcribed from a digital recording: "We only have a few hours, so listen carefully. If you're hearing this story, you're already in danger . . . I guess it started in London, the night our dad blew up the British Museum." Since his mother died in a mysterious accident when he was eight, Carter and his archaeologist dad, the famed Egyptologist, Dr. Julius Kane, have traveled the world, going to digs, visiting museums, and living out of suitcases. Sadie has been living with her maternal grandparents in London. Due to a contentious custody battle, Carter and his dad are only allowed visitation rights with Sadie two days a year. The two kids couldn't be less alike. Carter favors his African American dad, with dark brown skin and brown eyes, while Sadie, with her British accent, fair skin, light brown hair, and blue eyes, takes after her mother. Sadie's the rebellious one, dying her hair in streaks of bright colors and resenting her separation from her father. On Christmas Eve, on the way to the British Museum, the three stop at Cleopatra's Needle, the ancient Egyptian obelisk, where Dad reveals that their mom died at that very spot. Dad promises to tell them more when they get to the museum, where, as he says, "I'm going to make everything right again." Instead, he inadvertently summons five deadly gods who have been trapped in the Rosetta Stone. The resulting explosion leaves the gallery in ruins and the stone in shards. Carter watches in horror as a fiery man appears and conjures a glowing sarcophagus around Dr. Kane, which then sinks into the floor and disappears. As the children quickly discover, the blood of the pharaohs runs through their veins; they are the most powerful royal children to be born in centuries. Can they summon enough magic to rescue their father and reconcile the gods with the Per Ankh, the House of Life, before Set—the Red Lord and evil god of chaos—destroys North America and more? Their ensuing race takes them to their Uncle Amos's invisible mansion in Brooklyn, New York; to the top of the Washington Monument; to Graceland, Elvis's estate in Memphis; and to Camelback Mountain in Phoenix, Arizona, where Set is building a massive red pyramid. The Demon Days are here and Carter and Sadie have only five days to fend off or befriend a host of gods, demons, and other magical creatures that can't wait to kill them, and bring back order to the universe.

FICTION BOOKS, cont.

GERM: Welcome to Book 1 of The Kane Chronicles. Tremendously inventive, exhilarating, and just plain fun, this is nonetheless a challenging read, integrating a weighty dose of Egyptian mythology into the Kane kids' sassy narratives. Go to **http://disney.go.com/disneybooks/kanechronicles/** and look for the Egyptian Event Kit. There you can print out a helpful chart describing each of the many gods and magicians you meet in *The Red Pyramid*, which is, well, a godsend if you're having trouble keeping them all straight. (Guaranteed, Riordan's tenacious fans will read the book more than once, which will help them decipher the arc of the Kane kids' complicated quest.) On the Web site, you can also play the Red Pyramid Puzzle, and download and listen to chapter one of the audio book. Book Two of the trilogy is due out in 2011.

RELATED TITLES: Alexander, Lloyd. *The Book of Three.* Henry Holt, 1964. / Billingsley, Franny. *The Folk Keeper.* Simon & Schuster, 1999. / Collins, Suzanne. *Gregor the Overlander.* Scholastic, 2003. / Divakaruni, Chitra Banerjee. *The Conch Bearer.* Roaring Brook, 2003. / LaFevers, R. L. *Theodosia and the Serpents of Chaos.* Houghton Mifflin, 2007. (And others in the Theodosia series.) / Langrish, Katherine. *Troll Fell.* HarperCollins, 2004. / L'Engle, Madeleine. *A Wrinkle in Time.* Farrar, 1962. / Pratchett, Terry. *The Wee Free Men.* HarperCollins, 2003. / Pullman, Philip. *The Golden Compass.* Knopf, 1996. (And others in the His Dark Materials series.) / Riordan, Rick. *The Lightning Thief.* Miramax/Hyperion, 2005. (And others in the Percy Jackson & the Olympians series.) / Rollins, James. *Jake Ransom and the Skull King's Shadow.* HarperCollins, 2009. / Rowling, J. K. *Harry Potter and the Sorcerer's Stone.* Scholastic, 1998. (And others in the Harry Potter series.) / Scott, Michael. *The Alchemyst: The Secrets of the Immortal Nicholas Flamel.* Delacorte, 2007. / Stroud, Jonathan. *The Amulet of Samarkand.* Hyperion, 2003.

SUBJECTS: ADVENTURE AND ADVENTURERS. BROTHERS AND SISTERS. GODS AND GODDESSES. EGYPT. FANTASY. MAGIC. MUSEUMS. MYTHOLOGY, EGYPTIAN. PERSONAL NARRATIVES. SECRETS. VOYAGES AND TRAVELS.

[J*] | | | | |

School!: Adventures at the Harvey N. Trouble Elementary School. McMullan, Kate. Illus. by George Booth. Feiwel and Friends, 2010. {ISBN-13: 978-0-312-37592-8; 149p.} FIC (Gr. 2-5)

On Hotsy-Totsy Monday, Ron Faster, a very fast runner, runs to the bus stop and boards the school bus driven by Mr. Stuckinaditch. "Good morning, Mr. Stuckinaditch," he says. "Are you going to get stuck in a ditch today?" "Why would I do that?" asks Mr. Stuckinaditch, who stops to pick up other students, including Viola Fuss and little Izzy Normal. All of a sudden, CLONK! The bus gets stuck in a ditch. Ron runs to fetch Mr. Justin Case, who always carries a chain in his tow truck—just in case. At school, there's the principal, Miss Ingashoe, having a bit of trouble walking; if you look at her foot in the tiny pen and ink spot illustration, you'll see it's because she is, indeed, missing a shoe. Then there are the two custodians, Janitor Iquit and Assistant Janitor Quitoo, who quit when Oopsie Spiller spills his cup of orange juice in the hall. "This is not normal," says little Izzy Normal every time something not normal happens, which is often at the Harvey N. Trouble Elementary School. There's a substitute in Ron's class today, Mr. Norman Don't-know, and he seems to be clueless about things like fractions, vowels, or the Roman Empire. He does seem to have a briefcase full of cupcakes, cookies, and party hats, so the whole class gets to celebrate the birthday of classmate, Abby Birthday, of course. Four more chapters celebrate the other tippy-toppy, super-duper, hunky-dory, and yowie-ka-zowie days of the week with Ron and the other nutty kids and teachers, from Anita Dawg to Mrs. Doremi Fasollatido, bald as a billiard ball without her wig. Get ready for a wholelotta crazy puns and frantic little illustrations scattered on every page.

GERM: Read a chapter a day over the course of a zany week. Your kids can answer the same question Ron's father, a retired race car driver, asks him every afternoon: "What did you learn at school today, son?" They can also come up with new punnish names for themselves, and untangle the many puns in the book, some of which they'll get right away, and some that even you will need to puzzle over. Speaking of Justin Case, another very cute school novel with similarly tiny sketches is *Justin Case: School, Drool, and Other Daily Disasters* by Rachel Vail.

RELATED TITLES: Angleberger, Tom. *The Strange Case of Origami Yoda.* Amulet, 2010. / Birney, Betty G. *The World According to Humphrey.* Putnam, 2004. / Dahl, Roald. *Matilda.* Viking, 1988. / Evans, Douglas. *Apple Island or, The Truth About Teachers.* Front Street, 1998. / Fleischman, Paul. *The Dunderheads.* Candlewick, 2009. / Fleming, Candace. *The Fabled Fourth Graders of Aesop Elementary School.* Schwartz & Wade, 2007. / Peirce, Lincoln. *Big Nate: In a Class by Himself.* HarperCollins, 2010. / Sachar, Louis. *Sideways Stories from Wayside School.* Morrow, 1985. (And others in the Wayside School series.) / Scieszka, Jon, and Francesco Sedita. *Spaceheadz.* (SPHDZ, Book #1!) Simon & Schuster, 2010. / Spratt, R. A. *The Adventures of Nanny Piggins.* Little, Brown, 2010. / Vail, Rachel. *Justin Case: School, Drool, and Other Daily Disasters.* Feiwel and Friends, 2010. / Vernon, Ursula. *Dragonbreath: Curse of the Were-wiener.* Dial, 2010.

SUBJECTS: BUSES. HUMOROUS FICTION. LANGUAGE ARTS. PLAYS ON WORDS. PUNS AND PUNNING. SCHOOLS. TEACHERS. WORDPLAY.

FICTION BOOKS, cont.

[J] |A| | | |

Smile! **Telgemeier, Raina. Illus. by the author. Graphix, 2010. {ISBN-13: 978-0-545-13205-3; 213p.} FIC (Gr. 5-8) 2010 Boston Globe-Horn Book Honor for Nonfiction**

Racing her two girlfriends to the front porch after her scout meeting, eleven-year-old Raina trips and falls, knocking out one front tooth and driving the other up into her gum. If you're terrified of dentists and Novocain, you might stop reading this colorful graphic novel, based on the author's own experiences, right here, but you'll be missing Raina's compelling journey of tooth agony that stretches from sixth grade through high school. It's hard enough to be an adolescent, dealing with the teasing, crushes, and trials of daily life, but Raina must juggle friendship, boys, and school with her ever-present dental ordeals, including surgery, extractions, implants, endless braces, and headgear. In spite of it, or, really, because of it, Raina emerges more self aware and confident, disentangling herself from unkind friends and honing her talent for art. The paneled illustrations are comic book bright and accessible, and the book reads itself, taking us back to San Francisco in the 1980s, including the 1989 World Series earthquake.

GERM: Students could parse the text as a time capsule of the simpler pre-texting years of the 1980s and 90s, and do a bit of research to find out how life was different and/or the same way back then. They will also be inspired to create their own graphic autobiographies, concentrating on retelling a simple anecdote about something they'd like to remember (or wish they could forget) from their own lives. They'll love looking at the author's smile in her photo on the back page, and want to dig into Telgemeier's graphic novel versions of Ann M. Martin's Baby-sitter's Club series.

RELATED TITLES: Angleberger, Tom. *The Strange Case of Origami Yoda.* Amulet, 2010. / Draper, Sharon M. *Out of My Mind.* Atheneum, 2010. / Ignatow, Amy. *The Popularity Papers: Research for the Social Improvement and General Betterment of Lydia Goldblatt & Julie Graham-Chang.* Abrams/Amulet Books, 2010. / Kinney, Jeff. *Diary of a Wimpy Kid: Greg Heffley's Journal.* Amulet, 2007. (And others in the Wimpy Kid series.) / Peirce, Lincoln. *Big Nate: In a Class by Himself.* HarperCollins, 2010. (And others in the Big Nate series.) / Sonnenblick, Jordan. *After Ever After.* Scholastic, 2010. / Telgemeier, Raina. *The Baby-sitter's Club #1: Kristy's Great Idea: A Graphic Novel.* Graphix, p2006. (And others in the Baby-sitter's Club Graphic Novel series.) / Young, Karen Romano. *Doodlebug: A Novel in Doodles.* Feiwel & Friends, 2010.

SUBJECTS: AUTOBIOGRAPHY. BRACES. CARTOONS AND COMICS. DENTISTS. EARTHQUAKES. FRIENDSHIP. GRAPHIC NOVELS. ORTHODONTICS. PERSONAL NARRATIVES. SAN FRANCISCO. SELF-ESTEEM. TEETH.

[J] | | | | |

Spaceheadz. **(SPHDZ, Book #1!) Scieszka, Jon, and Francesco Sedita. Illus. by Shane Prigmore. Simon & Schuster, 2010. {ISBN-13: 978-1-41697-951-7; 163p.} FIC (Gr. 3-5)**

It's Michael K.'s first day in a new school, P.S. 868, in a new city, Brooklyn, New York, and though he's only been there for twenty minutes, it's already seriously weird. His new teacher, Mrs. Halley, has put him in the slow group with two strange new kids. How strange? The new girl just ate half of his pencil, and the new boy has just told him that they are Spaceheadz from another planet. They talk in TV jingles like "JUST DO IT" and "I'M LOVING IT!" and try to recruit him to Mission SPHDZ. Aliens don't invade fifth grade classrooms in Brooklyn, New York and expect you to help them save the world, do they? Meanwhile, in a noisy, tiny, one-room apartment overlooking the Brooklyn-Queens Expressway, Agent Umber receives an urgent call on his AAA Picklephone® from his Chief at the Anti Alien Agency, informing him they are on Alert Level Red. As Agent Umber says, "I promise, as always, to Protect and to Serve and to Always Look Up." What are the coordinates of the dangerous alien activity? Look on Umber's computer screen and there it is: P.S. 858. This is sci-fi "Get Smart" for kids, but with a spy that's even more discombobulated than Maxwell Smart. In alternating chapters, Michael K. can't quite believe that Major Fluffy, the class hamster, is the Mission Leader, and Agent Umber keeps getting knocked out. Graphically, the layout is a standout, interspersing all-black pages and white print with regular pages, though the print tends to veer at odd angles and there are loads of comical comic-like black and white illustrations. There are also many pages of odd and far out facts about things like different types of waves and electromagnetic fields. Over-the-top slapstick humor seals the deal—kids will love the look of this and wait impatiently for the next installment. Fortunately, the mission—to recruit 3.14 million earthlings to be Spaceheadz so the Earth will not be turned off—continues in *Spaceheadz, Book #2!*.

GERM: For the interactive component, kids can become SPHDZ at **www.sphdz.com**, check out the AAA at **antialienagency.com**, and visit Mrs. Halley's class website at **mrshalleyscomets.com**. For Judy Freeman's Reader's Theater script of chapters one and three of *Spaceheadz*, go to page 180 in this handbook.

FICTION BOOKS, cont.

RELATED TITLES: Anderson, M. T. *Whales on Stilts.* Harcourt, 2005. / Benton, Jim. *The Fran That Time Forgot.* Simon & Schuster, 2005. (And others in the Franny K. Stein, Mad Scientist series.) / Gauthier, Gail. *My Life Among the Aliens.* Putnam, 1996. / Pilkey, Dav. *The Adventures of Captain Underpants: An Epic Novel.* Scholastic/Blue Sky, 1997. / Scieszka, Jon. *Knights of the Kitchen Table.* Viking, 1991. (And others in the Time Warp Trio series.) / Scieszka, Jon. *Knucklehead: Tall Tales & Mostly True Stories About Growing Up Scieszka.* Viking, 2008. / Scieszka, Jon. *The Stinky Cheese Man and Other Fairly Stupid Tales.* Viking, 1992. / Stadler, Alexander. *Julian Rodriguez: Episode One: Trash Crisis on Earth.* Scholastic, 2008. / Vernon, Ursula. *Dragonbreath.* Dial, 2009. (And others in the Dragonbreath series.) / Wight, Eric. *Frankie Pickle and the Closet of Doom.* Simon & Schuster, 2009.

SUBJECTS: BROOKLYN (NEW YORK, N.Y.) EXTRATERRESTRIALS. FAMILY LIFE. HUMOROUS FICTION. MOVING, HOUSEHOLD. NEW YORK CITY. READER'S THEATER. SCHOOLS. SCIENCE FICTION. SPY STORIES. TEACHERS.

[J*] |A| | | |
The Strange Case of Origami Yoda. **Angleberger, Tom.** Illus. by the author. Amulet, 2010. {ISBN-13: 978-0-8109-8425-7; 141p.} FIC (Gr. 3-6) Judy Freeman's 2011 Best of the Best for Fiction

Tommy begins the first entry in his case file with this: "The big question: Is Origami Yoda real? . . . Does he really know things? Can he see the future? . . . Or is he just a hoax that fooled a whole bunch of us at McQuarrie Middle School?" To get solid answers and scientific evidence, Tommy has asked each person who was helped by Origami Yoda, classmate Dwight's little paper-folded finger puppet, to write down his or her account, which he has compiled here, along with his own analysis. He has even allowed his skeptical friend Harvey, who is sure Origami Yoda is just a "green paperwad," to add his commentary at the end of each testimonial, and another friend, Kellen, to supply the many adorable cartoon doodles that decorate the margins of the crumpled notebook paper-like pages. The first encounter with Origami Yoda happens on PTA Fun Night, when Tommy has finally decided to get up and ask Hannah to dance. Dwight wiggles the finger puppet and says, in a squeaky voice that doesn't even sound very Yoda-like, "Rush in fools do." Tommy decides the statement means "Fools are in a rush," and stays where he is, which turns out to be good advice, saving his butt, as he quickly recognizes. After that, everyone wants help from Origami Yoda, including Kellen, who gets an embarrassing water stain on his pants, and Cassie, who accidentally breaks her teacher's bust of Shakespeare and hides it in her backpack. The only kid who doesn't actually tell his story for Tommy's case file is Dwight, himself. Dwight is that weird, seemingly clueless kid who barfed in class when he ate thirteen helpings of canned peaches, who picks his nose, and the one who always ruins it for everyone, as his teachers put it. He's also the origami master who walks around with the puppet perched on the tip of his index finger, dispensing Jedi-wise advice to his eager classmates.

GERM: What's truly interesting is watching Dwight, whom we only see from others' points of view, and figuring out how he ticks. Have your kids compile a list of adjectives that define Dwight's character and see how their opinions of him change. This quirky, comical book has proved a huge hit with middle grade kids who wish they had an Origami Yoda they could ask for guidance in their dealings with friends, teachers, and the opposite sex. In the meantime, they can make their own Origami Yodas using Tommy's paperfolding instructions and diagrams at the back of the book. You'll also find the instructions on page 114 in this handbook, and learn some tricks on page 116. You can print them out at **www.origamiyoda.com**, which also includes the author's blog and kids' responses to the book. As Yoda might say, "Paperfolding you must try."

RELATED TITLES: Amato, Mary. *The Word Eater.* Holiday House, 2000. / Fletcher, Ralph. *Flying Solo.* Clarion, 1998. / Gauthier, Gail. *A Year with Butch and Spike.* Putnam, 1998. / Kinney, Jeff. *Diary of a Wimpy Kid: Greg Heffley's Journal.* Amulet, 2007. (And others in the Wimpy Kid series.) / McMullan, Kate. *School!: Adventures at the Harvey N. Trouble Elementary School.* Feiwel and Friends, 2010. / Peirce, Lincoln. *Big Nate: In a Class by Himself.* HarperCollins, 2010. / Rocklin, Joanne. *For Your Eyes Only!* Scholastic, 1997. / Shreve, Susan. *Jonah the Whale.* Scholastic, 1998. / Tarshis, Lauren. *Emma-Jean Lazarus Fell Out of a Tree.* Dial, 2007. / Tashjian, Janet. *My Life As a Book.* Henry Holt, 2010. / Vail, Rachel. *Justin Case: School, Drool, and Other Daily Disasters.* Feiwel and Friends, 2010. / Yee, Lisa. *Stanford Wong Flunks Big-Time.* Scholastic, 2005.

SUBJECTS: BEHAVIOR. ECCENTRICS AND ECCENTRICITIES. FINGER PUPPETS. HUMOROUS FICTION. INTERPERSONAL RELATIONS. MIDDLE SCHOOLS. ORIGAMI. PERSONAL NARRATIVES. SCHOOLS. SCIENCE. WRITING. YODA (FICTITIOUS CHARACTER).

[J*] |A| | |S|

A Tale Dark & Grimm. **Gidwitz, Adam. Dutton, 2010. {ISBN-13: 978-0-525-42334-8; 250p.} FIC (Gr. 5-7)**
Using the characters of Hansel and Gretel to represent the Everychild in the realm of fairy tales, Gidwitz serves up eight sizzling fairy tales, some familiar, some not, loosely based on stories by the Brothers Grimm. His compelling and conversational retellings contain warnings for the fainter of heart, such as: "Are there any small children in the room right now? If so, it would be best if we just let them think this is really the end of the story and hurried them off to bed." If you've read your Grimm, you know they are often bloody, violent, and scary as all get-out, but ultimately, evil is punished, and the upstanding triumph. Over the course of their journey, Hansel and Gretel get their heads cut off by their parents, the king and queen of the kingdom of Grimm, and are almost cooked and eaten by an old baker woman. Gretel cuts off her own finger to save her seven step-brothers, who have been turned into birds, and thwarts a handsome but murderous young man (in a variant of the English fairy tale, "Mr. Fox," by Joseph Jacobs). Hansel becomes a hairy, meat-eating beast in the Lebenwald, the Wood of Life; is killed by a huntsman and then revived; is gambled away to the Devil; and travels to Hell where he must pluck three golden hairs from the Devil's head. Whew. This is heavy stuff, but it reads like a dream. Okay, a nightmare, but one that children will relish as they root for the siblings to triumph, find better parents, and ultimately save their kingdom.
GERM: Introduce the life and works of Jacob and Wilhelm Grimm. At **www.pitt.edu/~dash/grimm.html**, you'll find a chronology and links to the tales, though certainly not all of the 200 stories in their influential 1815 collection, *Kinder- und Hausmärchen* (Children's and Household Tales) are appropriate for children. You will also find links to versions from other countries, which makes for some interesting reading. You'll want students to compare some of the chapters with the tales on which they're based, such as "Faithful Johannes" (also known as "Faithful John"), "Hansel and Gretel," "The Seven Ravens," "The Robber Bridegroom" (though that one's particularly gory), and "The Devil with the Three Golden Hairs." You'll find translations of all of the tales at **www.surlalunefairytales.com/authors/grimms.html#CONTENTS**. As for sparking some open-ended discussion, try some of these questions: Why do these stories still speak to us? What do they mean? What do we know about life from reading them? How did the author weave all of these stories together? How are you like or unlike Hansel and/or Gretel?
RELATED TITLES: Andersen, Hans Christian. *The Wild Swans.* Retold by Deborah Hautzig. Knopf, 1992. / Babbitt, Natalie. *Ouch: A Tale from Grimm.* HarperCollins, 1998. / Fletcher, Susan. *Shadow Spinner.* Atheneum, 1998. / Garcia, Laura Gallego. *The Legend of the Wandering King.* Scholastic, 2005. / Kindl, Patrice. *Goose Chase.* Houghton Mifflin, 2001. / Langrish, Katherine. *Troll Fell.* HarperCollins, 2004. / Levine, Gail Carson. *Ella Enchanted.* HarperCollins, 1997. / Levine, Gail Carson. *The Fairy's Return and Other Princess Tales.* HarperCollins, 2006. / Lin, Grace. *Where the Mountain Meets the Moon.* Little, Brown, 2009. / Marcantonio, Patricia Santos. *Red Ridin' in the Hood: And Other Cuentos.* Farrar, 2005. / McKinley, Robin. *Beauty.* HarperCollins, 1978. / Napoli, Donna Jo. *The Prince of the Pond.* Dutton, 1992. / Pullman, Philip. *I Was a Rat!* Knopf, 2000. / Shulman, Polly. *The Grimm Legacy.* Putnam, 2010. / Stanley, Diane. *Bella at Midnight.* HarperCollins, 2006. / Vande Velde, Vivian. *Tales from the Brothers Grimm and the Sisters Weird.* Harcourt, 1995.
SUBJECTS: ADVENTURE AND ADVENTURERS. BROTHERS AND SISTERS. CHARACTERS IN LITERATURE. FAIRY TALES. FANTASY. FOLKLORE. KINGS AND RULERS. LANGUAGE ARTS.

[J] |A|B| | |

Turtle in Paradise. **Holm, Jennifer L. Random House, 2010. {ISBN-13: 978-0-375-83688-6; 191p.} FIC (Gr. 3-6) 2011 Newbery Honor**
A peppery first sentence introduces us to the tell-it-like-it-is narrator, ten-year-old Turtle. "Everyone thinks children are as sweet as Necco Wafers, but I've lived long enough to know the truth; kids are rotten." It's June, 1935, and Turtle is on her way to Key West, Florida with her cat Smokey. Mama, back in New Jersey, has a new job as a housekeeper for a mean rich lady who hates kids, and she has a new boyfriend, Archie, a traveling salesman. That's why Turtle is moving in with her Aunt Minerva, Mama's sister, whom she has never even met. Key West is where Mama grew up, a place where the natives call themselves Conchs (pronounced "conks") after the shelled mollusks, and where Turtle's slew of cousins still live. As Turtle notes, "Too bad she didn't tell me that they were all snotty boys," referring to her three rambunctious cousins—eleven-year-old Beans, nine-year-old Kermit, and four-year-old Buddy. Beans is the leader of the Diaper Gang, a group of boys who baby-sit crying babies for their grateful mothers. The boys are pros at changing diapers and applying their secret formula, a white powder that cures diaper rash just like that. Their first rule? No girls allowed. Turtle gets a job diving for sponges with a kind fisherman, Slow Poke, who used to know her mother; deals with her grandmother, Nana Philly, who has had a stroke but is still meaner than a scorpion; and is caught up in a hurricane while searching for buried treasure. Based on family stories she heard from her great-great grandmother, once again Holm delivers a punchy and entertaining historical narrative that creates a memorable sense of place.

GERM: Make a cut-up, which is what Conch kids love to do. Each kid brings whatever fruit or vegetable (even raw onions) they find laying around or hanging on a tree—banana, mango, pineapple, and even potatoes. Cut everything up, and season with old sour, as described in the text (or just use fresh lime and salt; you might want to leave out the hot peppers). At the very least, bring in an avocado pear to slice and give everyone a taste. (You mainlanders probably call it an avocado).

RELATED TITLES: Birdsall, Jeanne. *The Penderwicks: A Summer Tale of Four Sisters, Two Rabbits, and a Very Interesting Boy.* Knopf, 2005. / Choldenko, Gennifer. *Al Capone Does My Shirts.* Putnam, 2004. / Curtis, Christopher Paul. *Bud, Not Buddy.* Delacorte, 1999. / DiCamillo, Kate. *Because of Winn-Dixie.* Candlewick, 2000. / Holm, Jennifer L. *Our Only May Amelia.* HarperCollins, 1999. / Holm, Jennifer L. *Penny from Heaven.* Random House, 2006. / Ibbotson, Eva. *Journey to the River Sea.* Dutton, 2002. / Levine, Gail Carson. *Dave at Night.* HarperCollins, 1999. / Peck, Richard. *A Long Way from Chicago.* Dial, 1998. / Peck, Richard. *A Season of Gifts.* Dial, 2009. / Peck, Richard. *A Year Down Yonder.* Dial, 2000. / Recorvits, Helen. *Goodbye, Walter Malinski.* Farrar, 1999. / Williams-Garcia, Rita. *One Crazy Summer.* HarperCollins/Amistad, 2010.

SUBJECTS: ADVENTURE AND ADVENTURERS. COUSINS. DEPRESSIONS—1929—U.S. FAMILY LIFE. FLORIDA. HISTORICAL FICTION. HUMOROUS FICTION. HURRICANES. KEY WEST (FLA.). MOTHERS. PERSONAL NARRATIVES. SOCIAL STUDIES.

WINNERS!:
100+ Best Children's Books of 2010

NONFICTION & BIOGRAPHY BOOKS

[J*] |A|B|H|S|
Ballet for Martha: Making Appalachian Spring. **Greenberg, Jan, and Sandra Jordan. Illus. by Brian Floca.**
Roaring Brook/Flash Point, 2010. {ISBN-13: 978-1-59643-338-0; 48p.} 780 (Gr. 2-6) 2011 Sibert
Honor; 2011 Orbis Pictus Award for Outstanding Nonfiction for Children
First there was the story, told in dance, about a pioneer family on the American frontier in western Pennsylvania,
written and choreographed by dancer, Martha Graham. Then there was the music, composed by Aaron Copland,
inspired by and incorporating the Shaker hymn, "Simple Gifts." And finally, there was the set, spare and simple,
designed by sculptor Isamu Noguchi. How the classic ballet, "Appalachian Spring," came together in a collaboration
between dancer, musician, and artist is chronicled in a stately, elegant nonfiction picture book, with magnificent pen
and ink and watercolors by the versatile Brian Floca. His portraits capture the new ballet style of Graham's dancers,
as described in the graceful, pared down, but quote-filled present tense text. Graham said, "I wanted something more
from dance . . ." and "My dancers never fall to simply fall. They fall to rise." In the dance studio, Martha and the
dancers work on the dance steps, not always an easy process. Martha has a screaming tantrum, throwing a shoe
before she figures out the movement she wants. "The dancers wait. Martha always figures it out." Isamu Noguchi's
set starts as miniature models that would fit into a matchbook, with angular beams and a narrow rocking chair. At
the top of the score he is composing at his piano, Copland writes the words, "Ballet for Martha." After months of
rehearsal, they are ready. The second half of the book moves to opening night, October 30, 1944, in Washington,
D.C., with a sequence of sweeping full-page and spot illustrations. They offer a glimpse of the majesty and
excitement of that first performance, with the then 50-year-old Martha dancing the lead role as the Pioneer Woman.
It'll give you goose bumps. The final pages provide information about the three principals, a bibliography, source
notes, and black and white photos.
GERM: It's tricky to figure out the audience for this spectacular book, but it's well worth reading aloud, playing
Copland's score as you go, because you and your kids have never really seen a book like this before. As a
demonstration of the collaborative power of art, music, and dance, and how they came together to create a new kind
of American ballet, it will enrich any humanities curriculum or inspire you to develop one. Amazingly, you can
watch the entire ballet, filmed in 1944 in black and white, with the original cast, and with the haunting Copland
score, separated into four 10-minute clips, at **www.YouTube.com**.
RELATED TITLES: Floca, Brian. *Lightship.* Atheneum, 2007. / Floca, Brian. *Moonshot: The Flight of* Apollo 11.
Atheneum, 2009. / Freedman, Russell. *Martha Graham: A Dancer's Life.* Clarion, 1998. / Greenberg, Jan. *Romare
Bearden: Collage of Memories.* Abrams, 2003. / Greenberg, Jan, and Sandra Jordan. *Action Jackson.* Roaring
Brook, 2002. / Greenberg, Jan, and Sandra Jordan. *Christo and Jeanne-Claude: Through the Gates and Beyond.*
Roaring Brook, 2008. / Greenberg, Jan, and Sandra Jordan. *Chuck Close Up Close.* Roaring Brook, 2002. / Hale,
Christy. *The East-West House: Noguchi's Childhood in Japan.* Lee & Low, 2009. / Li, Cunxin. *Dancing to
Freedom: The True Story of Mao's Last Dancer.* Walker, 2008. / Reich, Susanna. *José!: Born to Dance.* Simon &
Schuster, 2005. / Siegel, Siena Cherson. *To Dance: A Memoir.* Atheneum, 2006.
**SUBJECTS: APPALACHIAN SPRING. ARTISTS. BALLET. COLLABORATION. COMPOSERS—
BIOGRAPHY. COPLAND, AARON, 1900-1990. DANCE. DANCERS. GRAHAM, MARTHA, 1894-1991.
MUSIC. NOGUCHI, ISAMU, 1904-1988. WOMEN—BIOGRAPHY.**

[J] | | | | |
Biblioburro: A True Story from Columbia. **Winter, Jeanette. Illus. by the author. {ISBN-13: 978-1-41699-778-8; 32p.} 020 (Gr. K-6)**

"People around here love stories. I'm trying to keep that spirit alive in my own way." That quote is from Luis Soriano, a teacher, who in 2000, found a way to bring books to children and adults who live in remote villages in the hills of Columbia. Jeanette Winter looks for true stories of people who have done something to make the world more beautiful (an allusion to the selfless retired librarian in Barbara Cooney's classic picture book, *Miss Rumphius*), and then writes and illustrates small, spare accounts of these people—like librarian Alia Muhammad Baker, who rescued the books from her library when Basra was being bombed during the Iraq War; and Wangari Maathai, the Nobel Peace Prize winner, who started the Green Belt Movement in Kenya by planting trees. She pares down her texts so even the youngest children get the gentle message. With colorful folk-art acrylics filled with the lush foliage and indigenous animals of Columbia, set against a white background, her latest account reads like a folktale: "Deep in the jungles of Columbia, there lives a man who loves books. His name is Luis." His house overflowing and his wife grumbling about all the books, Luis gets an idea. He buys two burros, Alfa and Beto, builds crates to hang on their backs, loads them with books, and sets out for the faraway village of El Tormento. When a bandit threatens him, Luis says, "Please let us pass. The children are waiting." The bandit takes a book, growling, "Next time I want silver!" When Luis arrives, he hands out little piglet masks to the awaiting children and reads "The Three Little Pigs." His mission will have an impact on our jaded children who take books and libraries for granted.

GERM: The questions to ask include: Why does Luis take it upon himself to go out on his burros every weekend to bring books to people he doesn't even know? Why is it important for those people to have books? The actual account of his encounter with the robber is startling. According to the article about the Biblioburro on Wikipedia, "A copy of Paulo Coelho's 1990 novel *Brida* was stolen by bandits, who tied-up Soriano after attempting to rob him and discovered he had no money." To see photos of Luis and his burros, go to his website, **www.fundacionbiblioburro.com**. It is in Spanish, but you'll find links to English news stories about his life.

RELATED TITLES: Appelt, Kathi. *Down Cut Shin Creek: The Pack Horse Librarians of Kentucky.* HarperCollins, 2001. / Cooney, Barbara. *Miss Rumphius.* Viking, 1982. / Gonzalez, Lucia. *The Storyteller's Candle/La Velita de los Cuentos.* Children's Book Press, 2008. / Mora, Pat. *Tomás and the Library Lady.* Knopf, 1997. / Polacco, Patricia. *Aunt Chip and the Great Triple Creek Dam Affair.* Philomel, 1996. / Polacco, Patricia. *Thank You, Mr. Falker.* Philomel, 1998. / Ruurs, Margaret. *My Librarian Is a Camel: How Books Are Brought to Children Around the World.* Boyds Mills, 2005. / Sierra, Judy. *Wild About Books.* Knopf, 2004. / Williams, Suzanne. *Library Lil.* Dial, 1997. / Winter, Jeannette. *Follow the Drinking Gourd.* Knopf, 1989. / Winter, Jeanette. *The Librarian of Basra: A True Story from Iraq.* Harcourt, 2005. / Winter, Jeanette. *Mama: A True Story in Which a Baby Hippo Loses His Mama During the Tsunami, but Finds a New Home, and a New Mama.* Harcourt, 2006. / Winter, Jeanette. *September Roses.* Farrar, 2004. / Winter, Jeanette. *The Tale of Pale Male: A True Story.* Harcourt, 2007. / Winter, Jeanette. *Wangari's Trees of Peace: A True Story from Africa.* Harcourt, 2008.

SUBJECTS: BIOGRAPHY. BOOKS AND READING. COLUMBIA. COMPASSION. GENEROSITY. LANGUAGE ARTS. LIBRARIANS. LIBRARIES. MULTICULTURAL BOOKS. PICTURE BOOKS FOR ALL AGES. SELFLESSNESS. SORIANO, LUIS. TRAVELING LIBRARIES.

[j] | |B| |S|
Black Jack: The Ballad of Jack Johnson. **Smith, Charles R. Illus. by Shane W. Evans. Roaring Brook/Neal Porter, 2010. {ISBN-13: 978-1-59643-473-8; 40p.} B (Gr. 2-5)**

Bold, full bleed illustrations in deep blues and browns and a large print, rhyming, rap-like text make this picture book biography of the African American fighter, Jack Johnson, a standout. Looking at Jack Johnson on the book's cover with his shaved head, clenched fists, and bulging muscles, you'll think you're about to read a tall tale, and indeed, his indomitable, larger-than-life persona and tenacious drive to fight seems Herculean. Born to former slaves in Texas in 1878, Jack was bullied by other boys until his mother said, "Jack, fight back!" He did, and found fighting came easy to him. As a young man earning money with his fists, Jack was a sharp dresser, a driver of classy cars, and "a mighty, fightin' man" who wanted to be the best fighter, black or white, in spite of heavyweight, Jim Jeffries' pronouncement: "I will never fight a Negro." In 1910 in Reno, Nevada, Jack at last fought and defeated Jim Jeffries, making history as the world's first black heavyweight champion.

GERM: Even if you're not a boxing fan, you'll find this an inspirational read-aloud that will startle kids who think the battle for racial equality started with Martin Luther King. An afterword—"And Then What Happened?"—discusses the obstacles he faced as a brave, outspoken black man when others wanted to "keep him in his place." As he said, quoted on the very first page, "Because my ancestors came here before anyone had dreamed of a United States, I consider myself a pure-blooded American." Go to **ww.google.com/images** and look up Jack Johnson to see scores of photographs of him fighting, posing, and behind the wheel.

RELATED TITLES: Burleigh, Robert. *Stealing Home: Jackie Robinson Against the Odds.* Simon & Schuster, 2007. / Cline-Ransome, Lesa. *Major Taylor, Champion Cyclist.* Atheneum, 2004. / Cline-Ransome, Lesa. *Satchel Paige.* Simon & Schuster, 2000. / Myers, Walter Dean. *Harlem.* Scholastic, 1997. / Myers, Walter Dean. *Muhammad Ali: The People's Champion.* HarperCollins/Amistad, 2010. / Nelson, Kadir. *We Are the Ship: The Story of Negro League Baseball.* Hyperion/Jump at the Sun, 2008. / Robinson, Sharon. *Testing the Ice: A True Story About Jackie Robinson.* Illus. by Kadir Nelson. Scholastic, 2009. / Winter, Jonah. *Muhammad Ali: Champion of the World.* Schwartz & Wade, 2007. / Winter, Jonah. *Roberto Clemente: Pride of the Pittsburgh Pirates.* Atheneum, 2005. / Wise, Bill. *Louis Sockalexis: Native American Baseball Pioneer.* Lee & Low. 2007.
SUBJECTS: AFRICAN AMERICANS—BIOGRAPHY. ATHLETES—BIOGRAPHY. BIOGRAPHY. BOXERS (SPORTS). JOHNSON, JACK, 1878-1946. MULTICULTURAL BOOKS. PREJUDICE. RACE RELATIONS. SOCIAL STUDIES. SPORTS—BIOGRAPHY.

[J*] |A| | | |
Bones: Skeletons and How They Work. **Jenkins, Steve. Illus. by the author. Scholastic, 2010. {ISBN-13: 978-0-5450-4651-0 48p.} 573.7 (Gr. K-5) Judy Freeman's 2011 Best of the Best for Nonfiction**
Jenkins captivates nonfiction readers regularly with his mini-forays into the animal kingdom. He has examined tails (*What Do You Do with a Tail Like This?*), color (*Living Color*), and animal locomotion (*Move!*). Perhaps his most striking book is the big, red *Actual Size*, which depicts animals in whole and part, with cut paper collage that seems so real, kids want to touch the pages to feel the texture. This time he takes on the subject of skeletons, comparing human bones with those of dozens of animals (including the elephant, two-toed sloth, frog, and leopard), in another oversized showstopper. The blood-red cover with the title in curvy white letters and the mottled gray illustration of a toothy, grinning, life-sized human skull will make this book a hot ticket item. It begins, "Bones are alive . . . The bones in an animal's body form its skeleton . . . Remove an animal's skeleton, and it would become a helpless, squishy sack of skin." (Can't you just hear your kids saying, "Oooohhh" when they hear that?) Each double page contains a brief text (in white print against a monochrome dark-colored background) and bone-colored collage illustrations of one part of a human skeleton, comparing and contrasting it with an assortment of animals. Starting with the hand and arm, the pages move sequentially through the foot and leg, ribs, backbone, and skull. Compare the human rib cage, with its 12 pairs of ribs, with the 24 pairs on a two-toed sloth and the fused ribs on a box turtle. Then open up the double gatefold page to a starting four-page panorama of the skeleton of a six foot python, actual size, and count the almost 200 pairs of ribs. After learning about each set of bones we come upon another big wow of a page, labeled "Some Assembly Required." On an indigo background are all 206 bones in an adult human body, shown one-fourth actual size. Open up the gate-folds, turn the book sideways, and view the completed skeleton, grinning and waving at us. Back matter is equally compelling, with more facts and smaller drawings of bones.
GERM: As a first look at anatomy or a tie-in to all those Halloween skeletons, the book will get readers thinking about the bones under their own skin. Have them feel different parts of their bodies—hips, knees, ankles, toes, spine, etc.—to find the bones within, and hold a flashlight up to their palms to see the bones in their hands. From the information in the book, I assembled a list of terms and definitions that I turned into two worksheets: a word search and a crossword puzzle for children to do after you've shared the book with them. There are many make-your-own puzzle sites on the web where you can create free worksheets, but the one I liked the best was **www.armoredpenguin.com.** See the results on pages 120-122 of this handbook.
RELATED TITLES: Balestrino, Philip. *The Skeleton Inside You.* HarperCollins, 1989. / Beccia, Carlyn. *I Feel Better with a Frog in My Throat: History's Strangest Cures.* Houghton Mifflin, 2010. / Cole, Joanna. *The Magic School Bus Inside the Human Body.* Scholastic, 1989. / Cuyler, Marjorie. *Skeleton Hiccups.* Simon & Schuster, 2002. / Jenkins, Steve. *Actual Size.* Houghton Mifflin, 2004. / Jenkins, Steve. *Living Color.* Houghton Mifflin, 2004. / Jenkins, Steve, and Robin Page. *What Do You Do With a Tail Like This?* Houghton Mifflin, 2003. / Parker, Steve. *Skeleton.* DK, 2004. / Seuling, Barbara. *You Blink Twelve Times a Minute: And Other Freaky Facts About the Human Body.* Picture Window, 2009. / Seuling, Barbara. *You Can't Sneeze with Your Eyes Open and Other Freaky Facts About the Human Body.* Dutton, 1986. / Seuling, Barbara. *Your Skin Weighs More than Your Brain and Other Freaky Facts About Your Skin, Skeleton, and Other Body Parts.* Picture Window, 2008.
SUBJECTS: ANATOMY. BODY, HUMAN. SCIENCE. SKELETON.

[J] |A| | | |

Dave the Potter: Artist, Poet, Slave. **Hill, Laban Carrick. Illus. by Bryan Collier. Little, Brown, 2010. {ISBN-13: 978-0-316-10731-0; 42p.} 738 (Gr. 2-8) 2011 Caldecott Honor Book and Coretta Scott King Illustrator Medal**

Here's a haunting picture book, written in free verse, illustrated with magnificent full-bleed watercolor and collage art, and based on the work of a real person, known as Dave the Potter and Dave the Slave. Dave was a slave in South Carolina, one of only two potters who could throw huge pots as large as forty gallons, which meant he could manage a sixty pound lump of clay on his wheel. Many of his pots, now collector's items, still exist. Remarkably, Dave often composed and wrote poems in the still-damp clay, on the sides of his pots, starting in 1836, when he was seventeen. Not much is known about his life, and this is not a biography, though there is biographical information at the back. It is, instead, a celebration of his art, a painted and poetic explanation of how he must have worked, mixing and wedging the clay, centering the clay on the wheel, and then boring down into the rounded cylinder of clay. "Dave kicked / his potter's wheel / until it spun / as fast as / a carnival's wheel of fortune. / Like a / magician / pulling / a rabbit / out of / a hat, / Dave's hands, buried / in the mounded mud, / pulled out the shape of a jar." Open up the gate-folded page, and there's an extraordinary four-panel illustration of Dave's hands, opening up the base of the clay, and pulling up the sides. (As someone who made pots in high school and college, I can tell you it does feel magical, centering the clay and then throwing a pot, and Collier's extraordinary brown-toned paintings capture the look and sensation of pulling a pot from a centered disk of spinning clay.) We see him adding a coil to the rim of the pot, grinding the glaze, and then writing a poem with a stick under the pot's rim. Because no one knows what Dave looked like, Collier used a bearded model he felt "reflected the spirit of Dave." As a tribute to an artist who made his mark, almost unheard of for a slave, this book will give you goose bumps.

GERM: Appended is an essay about Dave's life and poetry, with the text of seven of his rhyming couplets. For more information on Dave's life and information on his pots and his poems, go to **http://leonardtodd.com**. Bring out clay so children can make small pinch pots and perhaps even write poems on their walls.

RELATED TITLES: Giovanni, Nikki. *Rosa.* Henry Holt, 2005. / Hill, Laban Carrick. *Harlem Stomp!: A Cultural History of the Harlem Renaissance.* Little, Brown, 2010. / Lasky, Kathryn. *A Voice of Her Own: The Story of Phillis Wheatley, Slave Poet.* Candlewick, 2002. / Levine, Ellen. *Henry's Freedom Box: A True Story.* Scholastic, 2007. / McCully, Emily Arnold. *Wonder Horse: The True Story of the World's Smartest Horse.* Henry Holt, 2010. / Nelson, Vaunda Micheaux. *Bad News for Outlaws: The Remarkable Life of Bass Reeves, Deputy U.S. Marshal.* Carolrhoda, 2009. / Park, Linda Sue. *A Single Shard.* Clarion, 2002. / Polacco, Patricia. *January's Sparrow.* Philomel, 2009. / Rappaport, Doreen. *Martin's Big Words: The Life of Dr. Martin Luther King, Jr.* Illus. by Bryan Collier. Hyperion, 2001.

SUBJECTS: AFRICAN AMERICANS—BIOGRAPHY. ARTISTS. BIOGRAPHY. DAVE THE POTTER, 1801?-1870?. MULTICULTURAL BOOKS. PICTURE BOOKS FOR OLDER READERS. POETS. POTTERS. SLAVES. SOCIAL STUDIES.

[J*] | | | |S|

The Extraordinary Mark Twain (According to Susy). **Kerley, Barbara. Illus. by Edwin Fotheringham. Scholastic, 2010. {ISBN-13: 978-0-545-12508-6; 44p.} FIC (Gr. 3-6)**

At age 13, Susy Clemens, adored oldest daughter of Samuel Clemens (better known to the world as Mark Twain), wrote her own secret biography of her famous father, keeping it hidden under her pillow. She observed, "It troubles me to have so few people know Papa, I mean really know him. They think of Mark Twain as a humorist, joking at everything." In this robust, oversized picture book, Susy sets the record straight. Kerley's narrative notes how Susy studied her father, then age 50, noting his habits and his fine and not-so-fine qualities. Attached to the center of every other double-page spread is a 5" X 4" insert, labeled "Journal." Open it up to find an excerpt from Susy's actual (and uncorrected) writings that take him far from the realm of exalted writer. One page reads, "He <u>has</u> got a temper but we all of us have in this family. . . . He is . . . oh <u>so</u> absent minded! . . . He smokes a great deal almost incessantly. . . . Papa uses very strong language." Susy's notebook, kept over the course of a year, from 1885-1886, ran 130 pages; it's a rare pleasure to read these brief but illuminating observations, filled with anecdotes and quotes.

NONFICTION AND BIOGRAPHY BOOKS, cont.

GERM: Not only is this a window into the life and personality of Twain, it serves as a splendid instructional manual on how to write a biography. At the back of the book, along with the detailed Author's Note, timeline of Twain's life, and list of sources for every quote, is Kerley's own detailed outline, "Writing an Extraordinary Biography," which lays out the steps Susy took to write hers. You'll find a printable version to use with your students on the author's website at: **www.barbarakerley.com/WritingABio.html.** Show and tell Twain's books, and compare photographs of him with Fotheringham's splendid paintings. If you can't make it to Hartford (and it's most definitely a trip worth taking), you can go on a virtual tour of the ornate Tiffany-designed house at **www.marktwainhouse.org.** Then have students pick admired members of their own family and write notebook biographies about them.

RELATED TITLES: Corey, Shana. *Annette Kellerman, Who Swam Her Way to Fame, Fortune, & Swimsuit History!* Illus. by Edwin Fotheringham. Scholastic, 2009. / Fleischman, Sid. *The Trouble Begins at 8: A Life of Mark Twain in the Wild, Wild West.* Greenwillow Books, 2008. / Kerley, Barbara. *The Dinosaurs of Waterhouse Hawkins.* Illus. by Brian Selznick. Scholastic, 2001. / Kerley, Barbara. *Walt Whitman: Words for America.* Scholastic, 2004. / Kerley, Barbara. *What to Do About Alice?: How Alice Roosevelt Broke the Rules, Charmed the World, and Drove Her Father Teddy Crazy!* Illus. by Edwin Fotheringham. Scholastic, 2008. / Krull, Kathleen. *Lives of the Writers: Comedies, Tragedies (and What the Neighbors Thought).* Harcourt, 1994. / Krull, Kathleen. *The Road to Oz: Twists, Turns, Bumps, and Triumphs in the Life of L. Frank Baum.* Knopf, 2008. / Stanley, Diane, and Peter Vennema. *Charles Dickens: The Man Who Had Great Expectations.* Morrow, 1993. / Yolen, Jane. *The Perfect Wizard: Hans Christian Andersen.* Dutton, 2004.
SUBJECTS: AUTHORS—BIOGRAPHY. AUTHORSHIP. BIOGRAPHY. CLEMENS, SUSY, 1872-1896. DIARIES. LANGUAGE ARTS. TWAIN, MARK, 1835-1910. WRITING.

[J] | | | | |
The Hallelujah Flight. **Bildner, Phil. Illus. by John Holyfield. Putnam, 2010. {ISBN-13: 978-0-399-24789-7; 32p.} E (Gr. 1-6)**
Told from the point of view of airplane mechanic, Thomas Allen, this is a fictionalized but fact-based account of his partnership with stunt pilot, James Banning, the first African American aviator to obtain a license in the U.S. Mocked as "The Flying Hoboes" by the crew at the local airport, the two nevertheless planned to fly their two-person, open cockpit OXX6 Eagle Rock plane from Los Angeles to New York City, and by gum, they did just that. They left LA on September 19, 1932 and didn't even make it out of California before they needed to stop for repairs. At each stop they made, people gave them food, fuel, and supplies in exchange for getting to sign their names on the plane's wing. "Hallelujah," Thomas would say. "Hallelujah right back at you," Banning would reply. Though they encountered prejudice at some of their stops, including being denied access to one airport and food at a restaurant, the two flyers persevered and arrived in New York on October 9, 1932, getting a heroes' welcome in Harlem. Exuberant full bleed acrylic paintings add energy and ebullience to this inspirational story about two daredevils you probably haven't encountered before.

GERM: Pair with books about other flying firsts, like Bessie Coleman, African American pilot, in *Fly High!: The Story of Bessie Coleman* by Louise Borden and Mary Kay Kroeger, *Ruth Law Thrills a Nation* by Don Brown, and *Flight: The Journey of Charles Lindbergh* by Robert Burleigh. Discussion Point: What obstacles did Banning and Allen face and why was their flight so remarkable? With older children, share this website: **earlyaviators.com/ebanning.htm,** for a photograph and a newspaper account of Banning's tragic death in a plane crash at age 33, due, in part, to racism.

RELATED TITLES: Borden, Louise, and Mary Kay Kroeger. *Fly High!: The Story of Bessie Coleman.* McElderry, 2001. / Brown, Don. *Ruth Law Thrills a Nation.* Ticknor & Fields, 1993. / Brown, Tami Lewis. *Soar, Elinor!* Farrar, 2010. / Burleigh, Robert. *Flight: The Journey of Charles Lindbergh.* Philomel, 1991. / Grimes, Nikki. *Talkin' about Bessie: The Story of Aviator Elizabeth Coleman.* Orchard, 2002. / Joseph, Lynn. *Fly, Bessie, Fly.* Simon & Schuster, 1998. / Lindbergh, Reeve. *Nobody Owns the Sky: The Story of "Brave Bessie" Coleman.* Candlewick, 1996. / Moss, Marissa. *Brave Harriet.* Harcourt, 2001. / Ryan, Pam Muñoz. *Amelia and Eleanor Go for a Ride.* Scholastic, 1999. / Smith, Sherri L. *Flygirl.* Putnam, 2009.
SUBJECTS: AFRICAN AMERICANS. AIR PILOTS. AIRPLANES. BANNING, JAMES HERMAN, 1900-1933. BIOGRAPHICAL FICTION. FLIGHT. HISTORICAL FICTION. MULTICULTURAL BOOKS. PICTURE BOOKS FOR OLDER READERS. SCIENCE. SOCIAL STUDIES. TRANSCONTINENTAL FLIGHTS.

[J] | | | | |

Henry Aaron's Dream. Tavares, Matt. Illus. by the author. Candlewick, 2010. {ISBN-13: 978-0-7636-3224-3; 40p.} 796.357 (Gr. 2-6)

Like many young boys who love baseball, Henry Aaron imagined himself in the big leagues when he played in his yard. His father said, "Ain't no colored ball players," but that didn't stop Henry from swinging at bottle caps and tin cans with a broom handle. At the time, in the 1940s in Mobile, Alabama, there were baseball fields all over the city, all with the sign "Whites Only"; it was actually against the law for black kids to play ball with white kids. It wasn't until Henry was 12 that Mobile opened Carver Park, its first "Colored Only" ballpark, where he played with his friends, holding his bat right-handed, with his left hand on top. On April 15, 1947, listening on the radio as Jackie Robinson played his first game with the Brooklyn Dodgers, Henry knew his own dream could now come true, in spite of all the adversity that Robinson faced. When the Dodgers played an exhibition game in Mobile, Henry went with his father, sitting in the colored section, telling him that he'd be playing ball with Jackie someday. In 1951, when he was still in high school, Henry joined the semi-pro Mobile Black Bears, playing on Sundays for $10 a game. Next, he joined the Indianapolis Clowns, a Negro League team, where he was spotted by a scout for the Braves who asked him to try batting the correct way, with his right hand on top. Henry did, and hit a home run. This inspirational picture book biography, with large, bravura, action-jammed illustrations done in watercolor, ink, and pencil, describes his seasons in the minors, playing for a Braves Class A team in southern towns "where black people and white people weren't even allowed to play checkers together." Where the text describes the white players' celebration of their pennant win in Savannah, there's an illustration of Henry, who had been named Most Valuable Player, playing cards with other black players in a restaurant's kitchen. And, for a satisfying climax, there's a marvelous double page depiction of Henry, in his first game in the majors in 1954, sliding safely into second base, as Jackie Robinson tries to tag him out. What an amazing story!

GERM: Backmatter includes an Author's Note about Aaron's subsequent career, and a full page of his stats, from 1952 to 1976. Look up "Hank Aaron" at **www.YouTube.com**, and you can see scores of videos, including the April 8, 1974 game where he hit his 715th home run, breaking Babe Ruth's record.

RELATED TITLES: Burleigh, Robert. *Stealing Home: Jackie Robinson Against the Odds.* Simon & Schuster, 2007. / Cline-Ransome, Lesa. *Satchel Paige.* Simon & Schuster, 2000. / Curtis, Gavin. *The Bat Boy & His Violin.* Simon & Schuster, 1998. / Golenbock, Peter. *Teammates.* Harcourt, 1990. / Nelson, Kadir. *We Are the Ship: The Story of Negro League Baseball.* Hyperion/Jump at the Sun, 2008. / Robinson, Sharon. *Testing the Ice: A True Story About Jackie Robinson.* Illus. by Kadir Nelson. Scholastic, 2009. / Uhlberg, Myron. *Dad, Jackie, and Me.* Peachtree, 2005. / Winter, Jonah. *Roberto Clemente: Pride of the Pittsburgh Pirates.* Atheneum, 2005. / Wise, Bill. *Louis Sockalexis: Native American Baseball Pioneer.* Lee & Low. 2007.

SUBJECTS: AARON, HANK, 1934-. AFRICAN AMERICANS—BIOGRAPHY. ATHLETES— BIOGRAPHY. BASEBALL PLAYERS. BIOGRAPHY. MULTICULTURAL BOOKS. NEGRO LEAGUES. PREJUDICE. RACE RELATIONS. SPORTS—BIOGRAPHY.

[J] | | | | |

Henry Knox: Bookseller, Soldier, Patriot. Silvey, Anita. Illus. by Wendell Minor. Clarion, 2010. {ISBN-13: 978-0-618-27485-7; 40p.} B (Gr. 3-6)

We tend to be familiar with all the big names from the American Revolution, like Paul Revere and George Washington. Now, in this handsome and fascinating picture book biography, meet a man whose contribution to the war was incalculable, even though you may never have heard of him. The seventh of ten sons, Henry Knox was born in Boston in 1750. At the age of nine, Henry quit his studies and got a job as a bookseller's assistant to help support his family after his father deserted them. As a six-foot, 250-pound teenager, his three passions were books, cannons, and food. In 1771, at age twenty-one, Henry opened the London Book Store in Boston, which soon became a fashionable gathering place for British officers stationed in the city, but also for supporters of the American rebels' cause. After the battle of Lexington and Concord in 1775, Henry devised a plan to transport cannons and other weapons captured from the British at Fort Ticonderoga, New York to Boston, three hundred miles away. On December 5, 1775, Henry oversaw the conveyance of fifty-nine cannons—120,000 pounds of them—across Lake Champlain by boat and then dragged on sleds pulled by oxen down to Saratoga and then Albany, across the frozen Hudson River, through the heavy snows in the Berkshires, and on to Framingham. On March 4, 1776, the Continental army moved the cannons into the hills overlooking Boston Harbor. Sir Howe, the British general said, "The rebels have done more in one night than my whole army would have done in a month." Outmaneuvered, Howe called for the British army to evacuate the city. What had been dubbed Knox's Folly proved a brilliant mission by the man who became the head of artillery for the Continental Army. This compellingly told event in history is made even more concrete by the bold and imposing acrylic double-page paintings done on wood panels, which give the book an authentic folk-art, you-are-there look.

GERM: The interesting question to pose is this: What if Henry Knox had failed in his mission to bring artillery to Boston? How might things have been different? How might your own life be different? Another excellent picture book to share is *Let It Begin Here!: Lexington and Concord: First Battles of the American Revolution* by Dennis Brindell Fradin.

RELATED TITLES: Adler, David A. *Heroes of the Revolution.* Holiday House, 2003. / Chandra, Deborah, and Madeline Comora. *George Washington's Teeth.* Farrar, 2003. / Fleming, Candace. *The Hatmaker's Sign: A Story by Benjamin Franklin.* Orchard, 1998. / Fradin, Dennis Brindell. *Let It Begin Here!: Lexington and Concord: First Battles of the American Revolution.* Walker, 2005. / Freedman, Russell. *Lafayette and the American Revolution.* Holiday House, 2008. / Freedman, Russell. *Washington at Valley Forge.* Holiday House, 2008. / Fritz, Jean. *And Then What Happened, Paul Revere?* Putnam, 1996. / Fritz, Jean. *What's the Big Idea, Ben Franklin?* Putnam, 1976. / Fritz, Jean. *Will You Sign Here, John Hancock?* Putnam, 1997. / Harness, Cheryl. *Thomas Jefferson.* National Geographic, 2004. / Lasky, Kathryn. *A Voice of Her Own: The Story of Phillis Wheatley, Slave Poet.* Candlewick, 2002. / Longfellow, Henry Wadsworth. *The Midnight Ride of Paul Revere.* Illus. by Christopher Bing. Handprint, 2001. / Minor, Wendall. *Yankee Doodle America: The Spirit of 1776 from A to Z.* Putnam, 2006. / Woodruff, Elvira. *George Washington's Socks.* Scholastic, 1991. /
SUBJECTS: BIOGRAPHY. GENERALS—UNITED STATES—BIOGRAPHY. KNOX, HENRY, 1750-1806. SOCIAL STUDIES. U.S.—HISTORY—REVOLUTION, 1775-1783.

[J*] | | | | |
***I Feel Better with a Frog in My Throat: History's Strangest Cures.* Beccia, Carlyn. Illus. by the author. Houghton Mifflin, 2010. {ISBN-13: 978-0-547-22570-8; 48p.} 610 (Gr. 3-6)**
If you have a cough, a cold, a sore throat, a wound, a stomachache, a fever, or a headache, perhaps you have a home remedy you swear by, whether it is tea, chicken soup, lozenges, or a good doctor. In this collection of cures that were considered effective way back when, from prehistoric times to the nineteenth century, see which ones actually worked. Arranged by ailment, each is introduced by a cover page with a set of labeled inset illustrations of three or more cures and their origins. The first page, titled "History's Strangest Cures for Coughs," asks, "Did any of these cures help?" Picture A, showing five yellow caterpillars in a glass vase, is labeled "Caterpillar Fungus (Origin: Ancient China)"; B, with a frog resting on his back in a bowl, says "Frog Soup (Origin: Sixteenth-century England)"; while C shows a beaver munching on a log, labeled "Cherry Bark (Origin: Native American)". Before turning the page, ask your group to predict which one (or ones) worked. A handsome and comic full-page illustration, done in digital mixed-media, accompanies each answer, with a paragraph explaining the use and effectiveness of each cure. For instance, caterpillar fungus, still used in traditional Chinese medicine, may boost the immune system; frog soup, made from nine frogs, didn't work; but cherry bark boiled into tea contains hydrocyanic acid, used in modern cough and cold remedies. Some of the cures are pretty icky, which will make some readers very happy.
GERM: For each section, children will be making educated guesses, relating ways their own families treat each malady, and learning some surprising facts about health and history. Students can do some research into ways we treat each malady these days. Before and/or after reading the book aloud, try the "I Feel Better with a Frog in My Throat" worksheet on page 118 in this handbook.
RELATED TITLES: Beccia, Carlyn. *Raucous Royals: Test your Royal Wits: Crack Codes, Solve Mysteries, and Deduce Which Royal Rumors are True.* Houghton Mifflin, 2008. / Cherry, Lynne, and Mark J. Plotkin. *The Shaman's Apprentice: A Tale of the Amazon Rain Forest.* Harcourt, 1998. / Jenkins, Steve. *Bones: Skeletons and How They Work.* Scholastic, 2010. / Seuling, Barbara. *You Blink Twelve Times a Minute: And Other Freaky Facts About the Human Body.* Picture Window, 2009. / Seuling, Barbara. *You Can't Sneeze with Your Eyes Open and Other Freaky Facts About the Human Body.* Dutton, 1986.
SUBJECTS: MEDICINE. SCIENCE. SICK.

[J] |A|B|H| |

Kakapo Rescue: Saving the World's Strangest Parrot. (Scientists in the Field series) Montgomery, Sy. Photos by Nic Bishop. Houghton Mifflin, 2010. {ISBN-13: 978-0-618-49417-0; 74p.} 639.9 (Gr. 4-8) 2011 Sibert Medal

In another on-the-spot adventure by the writer/photographer team of Montgomery and Bishop, the duo fly to tiny Codfish Island, a windswept speck off of New Zealand's southern coast, to research the work being done to save the endangered kakapo (pronounced KAR-ka-poe) parrot. These unusual flightless, nocturnal birds, the world's rarest and heaviest parrots at nine pounds, have whiskers like a cat's, can growl like a dog, and can live up to a century. And there are only eighty-seven left. Montgomery's text covers the history and almost extinction of the birds. When the Maori came to New Zealand seven centuries ago, they hunted and ate the parrots, and the Europeans that came after 1769 proved even more disastrous. She chronicles "the roller-coaster story of just one part of one hatching season, a story of heartbreak and thrills, of hard work and luck, of science and guesswork." Bishop's color photographs capture the parrots and the people who work to save them. It's quite a compelling package.

GERM: Go to **www.YouTube.com** and enter "kakapo" in the search bar to see a video of the parrot in action.
RELATED TITLES: Hiaasen, Carl. *Hoot.* Knopf, 2002. / Montgomery, Sy. *Quest for the Tree Kangaroo: An Expedition to the Cloud Forest of New Guinea.* Houghton Mifflin, 2006. / Montgomery, Sy. *The Snake Scientist.* Houghton Mifflin, 1999. / Montgomery, Sy. *The Tarantula Scientist.* Houghton Mifflin, 2004. (And others in the Scientists in the Field series.) / Schulman, Janet. *Pale Male: Citizen Hawk of New York City.* Knopf, 2008. / Turner, Pamela S. *The Frog Scientist.* Houghton Mifflin, 2009. / Turner, Pamela S. *Gorilla Doctors: Saving Endangered Great Apes.* Houghton Mifflin, 2005. (And others in the Scientists in the Field series.) / Wolf, Sallie. *The Robin Makes a Laughing Sound: A Birder's Journal.* Charlesbridge, 2010.
SUBJECTS: ANIMALS. BIRDS. ENDANGERED SPECIES. KAKAPO. PARROTS. SCIENCE. SCIENTISTS.

[J] | | | |S|

Kubla Khan: The Emperor of Everything. Krull, Kathleen. Illus. by Robert Byrd. Viking, 2010. {ISBN-13: 978-0-670-01114-8; 42p.} B (Gr. 3-6)

Continuing her string of engrossing biographies about extraordinary people most children have never encountered, Krull now takes on "the least known, most mysterious of history's great leaders" who extended the Mongol Empire of his grandfather, Genghis Khan. Born in Mongolia in 1215, Kubla Khan started riding horses at age three. At that time, boys were trained to be warriors, ready to fight from age fourteen to seventy. Spectacular, full-bleed Asian-style illustrations in black fine lines and vibrant inks show Mongolian men on horseback, hunting, raiding and burning a town, and setting up their movable round tents. The text contains many startling facts. About Mongolian nomads and their ponies: "In the worst of times, when there was absolutely no food, a pony even provided nourishment. A rider would cut into the skin of his mount and drink a bit of blood, then continue on the journey." Kubla Khan had four wives, countless concubines (good luck explaining that one), and one hundred children. At age forty-five, when Kubla was elected Khan of all Khans, he still wanted to conquer China, which he did in 1271, setting up a four hundred room palace in what is now Beijing. His birthday parties numbered forty thousand guests, and at his New Year's festival, five thousand elephants carried in his gifts from all over the realm. Nothing like a wee bit of excess, though the narrative also chronicles the good things he did in the thirty years of his reign, considered a golden age for theater, literature, science, agriculture, and education.

GERM: As a read-aloud biography, this is full of lively anecdotes. Students can discuss or write a comparison of Kubla Khan's governing style with that of U.S. presidents or other modern day rulers. One interesting question to consider is this: Was Kubla Khan a good leader? Why or why not? Look at the whimsical but informative map that spreads across the endpapers, and marks, in olive green, the extent of Kubla Khan's Mongol Empire across most of Asia. Have students make their own maps of their known worlds, adding tiny drawings of local landmarks. Pair the book with Russell Freedman's picture book biography, *The Adventures of Marco Polo*, since he claimed to have spent many years in the court of the great Kubla Khan. The marvel that most impressed Marco Polo was the use of paper money, "a way of creating money out of nothing." Pull out a dollar bill and ask why it is considered valuable.
RELATED TITLES: Cole, Joanna. *Ms. Frizzle's Adventures: Imperial China.* Scholastic, 2005. / Freedman, Russell. *The Adventures of Marco Polo.* Scholastic, 2006. / Freedman, Russell. *Confucius: The Golden Rule.* Scholastic, 2002. / Lewin, Ted, and Betsy Lewin. *Horse Song: The Naadam of Mongolia.* Lee & Low, 2008. / Montgomery, Sy. *Saving the Ghost of the Mountain: An Expedition Among Snow Leopards in Mongolia.* Houghton Mifflin, 2009. (And others in the Scientists in the Field series.) / O'Connor, Jane. *The Emperor's Silent Army: Terracotta Warriors of Ancient China.* Viking, 2002.
SUBJECTS: BIOGRAPHY. CHINA. KINGS AND RULERS. KUBLAI KHAN, 1216-1294. MONGOLS—BIOGRAPHY. MULTICULTURAL BOOKS. SOCIAL STUDIES.

[J] |A|B| | |

Lafayette and the American Revolution. Freedman, Russell. Illus. with paintings and reprods. Holiday House, 2010. {ISBN-13: 978-0-82342-182-4; 88p.} B (Gr. 6-9) 2011 Sibert Honor

Americans recall Lafayette as the Frenchman who came to fight alongside George Washington during the Revolutionary War. Freedman's impeccably researched and written biography, liberally illustrated with color paintings, reproductions, engravings, and portraits, will surprise you with the facts. Gilbert de Lafayette was a wealthy nineteen-year-old nobleman who defied the king's order forbidding French subjects to go to the aid of the American colonists, and surreptitiously sailed from France to join the revolutionaries. While he had attended the most exclusive military school in France, he had no experience on any actual battlefield. Married at sixteen to fourteen-year-old Adrienne, he reluctantly joined the royal court of Louis XVI and Marie Antoinette at Versailles where he spoke little and danced badly. While the French government was helping the American rebels in secret, Lafayette was determined to volunteer his services in person, with prospects of glory instead of pay. When he and several other French officers arrived in Philadelphia after an 800-mile, thirty-two day hike from South Carolina over rutted roads, they were turned away at the statehouse door by a Congressman who told them, "It seems that French officers have a great fancy to enter our service without being invited." Realizing it could be advantageous to take on the wealthy young man whose family connections might help them, Congress soon accepted Lafayette into the army as a major general, serving directly under Washington. This back story is eye-opening. How he and forty-five-year-old Washington bonded like father and son, and how Lafayette grew into his command is one of the great stories of the Revolutionary War.

GERM: Have students research the lasting effects of Lafayette on American society today, looking up places (like parks, streets, cities, and schools) named after him. Pair the book with Freedman's *Washington at Valley Forge.* On the publisher's website, **www.holidayhouse.com**, you can download an Educator's Guide to both titles.

RELATED TITLES: Adler, David A. *Heroes of the Revolution.* Holiday House, 2003. / Fradin, Dennis Brindell. *Let It Begin Here!: Lexington and Concord: First Battles of the American Revolution.* Walker, 2005. / Freedman, Russell. *Washington at Valley Forge.* Holiday House, 2008. / Fritz, Jean. *And Then What Happened, Paul Revere?* Putnam, 1996. / Fritz, Jean. *What's the Big Idea, Ben Franklin?* Putnam, 1976. / Fritz, Jean. *Why Not, Lafayette?* Putnam, 1999. / Fritz, Jean. *Will You Sign Here, John Hancock?* Putnam, 1997. / Harness, Cheryl. *Thomas Jefferson.* National Geographic, 2004. / Murphy, Jim. *The Crossing: How George Washington Saved the American Revolution.* Scholastic, 2010. / Silvey, Anita. *Henry Knox: Bookseller, Soldier, Patriot.* Clarion, 2010. / Woodruff, Elvira. *George Washington's Socks.* Scholastic, 1991.

SUBJECTS: BIOGRAPHY. GENERALS—BIOGRAPHY. LAFAYETTE, GILBERT, MARQUIS DE, 1757-1834. SOCIAL STUDIES. U.S.—HISTORY—REVOLUTION, 1775-1783. WASHINGTON, GEORGE, 1732-1799.

[J*] |A|B| | |

Nic Bishop Lizards. Bishop, Nic. Photos by the author. Scholastic, 2010. {ISBN-13: 978-0-545-20634-1; 48p.} 596 (Gr. PreK-4)

By now, we expect each new animal book by Nic Bishop to burst with astonishing full-page color photographs and expertly crafted descriptions, and this one sure doesn't disappoint. Each page contains one topic sentence that you can read to the youngest listeners, and then a brief essay of fascinating facts that will make even the most jaded readers stop and say, "No kidding!" Did you know there are about 5,000 types of lizards, including iguanas, chameleons, geckos, skinks, and monitors? The largest lizard, the Komodo dragon from Indonesia, "is big enough to kill a water buffalo." The smallest, a dwarf gecko from the Caribbean, "is small enough to curl up on your thumbnail." Sharing the page with those meaty facts is a double-page color photo of a glass lizard, which looks just like a snake. Read the caption, and you'll learn, "Glass lizards can blink and they have ear holes. Snakes do not have eyelids, or ears that you can see." Look closely, and you'll find its ear hole. Other remarkable photos show a bearded dragon hatching from its egg, a shingleback skink whose tail looks just like its head, and four contented looking marine iguanas basking in the sun. But wait! There's more! This is a Nic Bishop book, after all. That means there will be gate-folded photos, and though there is only one, it's a four-page doozey of a basilisk lizard hopping across the surface of water, racing " . . . up to twenty steps a second, so its feet barely have time to sink." (OK, he tells us, according to scientists, we could do that too, if we could just run 65 miles an hour . . .) One more treat awaits, and that's Nic's Author's Note at the back, explaining how he flew to Perth, Australia and drove for days just to find the thorny devil he photographed in the book, and how he built a pool inside his own house so he could photograph that water-skimming basilisk in action.

GERM: After you read this book aloud, have your listeners complete the "Do You Know Lizards" worksheet on page 123 of this handbook. Show all of Bishop's books and talk about his photographs, captions, and the information and style of his texts. Initiate a photography project where children put together their own booklets in the same manner, first taking photos of a wild or domestic animal, then researching and writing up an interesting factual narrative to accompany the pictures.

RELATED TITLES: Arnosky, Jim. *All About Alligators.* Scholastic, 1994. / Arnosky, Jim. *All About Frogs.* Scholastic, 2002. / Bishop, Nic. *Nic Bishop Butterflies and Moths.* Scholastic, 2009. / Bishop, Nic. *Nic Bishop Frogs.* Scholastic, 2008. / Bishop, Nic. *Nic Bishop Marsupials.* Scholastic, 2009. / Bishop, Nic. *Nic Bishop Spiders.* Scholastic, 2007. / Cowley, Joy. *Chameleon, Chameleon.* Photos by Nic Bishop. Scholastic, 2005. / Cowley, Joy. *Red-Eyed Tree Frog.* Photos by Nic Bishop. Scholastic, 1999. / Cowley, Joy. *Snake and Lizard.* Kane Miller, 2008. / Florian, Douglas. *Lizards, Frogs, and Polliwogs: Poems and Paintings.* Harcourt, 2001. / Jenkins, Martin. *Chameleons Are Cool.* Candlewick, 1997. / Kessler, Cristina. *Konte Chameleon Fine, Fine, Fine!: A West African Folk Tale.* Boyds Mills, 1997. / Martin, James. *Chameleons: Dragons in the Trees.* Crown, 1991. / Mwenye Haditi. *Crafty Chameleon.* Little, Brown, 1987. / Wiesner, David. *Art & Max.* Clarion, 2010.
SUBJECTS: ANIMALS. LIZARDS. REPTILES AND AMPHIBIANS. SCIENCE.

[J] | | | | |
1+1=5: And Other Unlikely Additions. LaRochelle, David. Illus. by Brenda Sexton. Sterling, 2010. {ISBN-13: 978-1-40275-995-6; 32p.} 513.2 (Gr. PreK-2)

On the first page of this intriguing head trip of an arithmetic book is the first problem, boxed, in big black letters: 1 + 1 = 3. In the bordered, colorful, full-page, digitally rendered illustration are two animals—they look like a horse and a goat—reading books titled *Mythical Beasts* and *Barnyard Buddies.* Turn the page for the goofily logical answer to the math question: 1 unicorn + 1 goat = 3 horns! (OK, this one is too tricky to figure out from the first picture, since the horns are not visible until you turn the page. For several of the problems, you really need to show both illustrations if your kids can have a fair chance at deducing the answer. Not a problem; just use a piece of oak tag to cover the answer on the second page.) But kids will say, "Ohhh. I get it!" and be eager to tackle the other 14 problems. One page reads: "1 + 1 = 11?" In the illustration, you see a basketball resting next to a leg and foot clad in a sneaker; facing them are a leg and foot in a black ice skate, standing beside a hockey puck. Sports nuts will call out the answer: 1 basketball team + 1 hockey team = 11 players! For each problem, astute arithmeticians must use clues in the illustrations to puzzle out the two addends and then add them up to see if they fit.

GERM: So that your kids can see and consider all the details in the illustrations, it would be great to use a document camera. Have them pair up and discuss their possible answers together, and see what kinds of solutions they propose. Then have them make up a new addition problem and illustrate it like a greeting card, with the problem and a picture containing a clue on the outside, and the solution and illustration showing all the components on the inside. Children can present their problems and illustrations for the rest of the class to solve.

RELATED TITLES: Adler, David A. *Easy Math Puzzles.* Holiday House, 1997. / Day, Nancy Raines. *Double Those Wheels.* Dutton, 2003. / Dodds, Dayle Ann. *Minnie's Diner.* Candlewick, 2004. / Franco, Betsy. *Counting Our Way to the 100th Day!* McElderry, 2004. / Franco, Betsy. *Mathematickles!* McElderry, 2003. / Leedy, Loreen. *Mission: Addition.* Holiday House, 1997. / Leedy, Loreen. *2 X 2 = BOO!: A Set of Spooky Multiplication Stories.* Holiday House, 1995. / Michelson, Richard. *Ten Times Better.* Marshall Cavendish, 2000. / Pinczes, Elinor J. *One Hundred Hungry Ants.* Houghton Mifflin, 1993. / Sayre, April Pulley, and Jeff Sayre. *One Is a Snail, Ten Is A Crab; A Counting by Feet Book.* Candlewick, 2003. / Schwartz, David M. *How Much Is a Million?* Lothrop, 1985. / Tang, Greg. *The Grapes of Math.* Scholastic, 2001. / Tang, Greg. *Math-terpieces: The Art of Problem Solving.* Scholastic, 2003. / Ziefert, Harriet. *Math Riddles.* Viking, 1997.
SUBJECTS: ADDITION. COUNTING BOOKS. GUESSING GAMES. MATHEMATICS.

NONFICTION AND BIOGRAPHY BOOKS, cont.

[J] | | | |S|

Pop!: The Invention of Bubble Gum. McCarthy, Meghan. Illus. by the author. Simon & Schuster/Paula Wiseman, 2010. {ISBN-13: 978-1-41697-970-8; 32p.} 664 (Gr. K-4)

In the "Wow! I never knew that!" department, find out how Walter Diemer, an accountant at the Fleer family's candy factory in Philadelphia, came up with a whole new kind of gum in 1928. (Did you know that chewing gum has been around for centuries, and before that, people chewed sap or resin from trees?) After his boss gave up hope of inventing a gum with which chewers could blow bubbles, Walter spent months experimenting with different mixtures and flavors. When he finally concocted a substance that bubbled and popped, he poured in pink coloring, the only one he had at hand, and voilà! Bubble gum! They called it Double Bubble, and it was an instant hit. Walter said, "I've done something with my life. I've made kids happy around the world." As with all of McCarthy's delightful nonfiction picture books, her dapper, full bleed acrylic illustrations are peopled with smiling, googly-eyed folks, and her pared down text is just right to read aloud to any age.

GERM: At the back, there's a double page containing a bibliography, interesting nuggets about Diemer's later life, and delectable facts about gum. For instance, did you know chewing sugarless gum can prevent tooth decay? And studies have shown that chewing gum helps you concentrate. Mind you, when you share this book with your kids, they're going to be demanding gum. How can you say no? Matthew Cordell's outrageously funny picture book, *Trouble Gum,* about two piglet brothers who wreak havoc with gum, may be the natural deterrent you need. From Jon Agee's book of tongue twister poems, *Orangutan Tongs: Poems to Tangle Your Tongue,* read the poem "Bubble," which starts, "The world's biggest bubblegum bubble / was blown in the town of O'Toole." Celebrate gum in song with "Choo'n Gum," a fabulous novelty song you might recognize, made famous in the 1950s by Teresa Brewer. You can hear her sing it at **www.youtube.com/watch?v=a18sZGr8lIE**, and find the lyrics in this handbook on page 180.

RELATED TITLES: Agee, Jon. *Orangutan Tongs: Poems to Tangle Your Tongue.* Disney/Hyperion, 2009. / Barton, Chris. *The Day-Glo Brothers: The True Story of Bob and Joe Switzer's Bright Ideas and Brand-New Colors.* Charlesbridge, 2009. / Cordell, Matthew. *Trouble Gum.* Feiwel & Friends, 2009. / Jones, Charlotte Foltz. *Accidents May Happen: Fifty Inventions Discovered by Mistake.* Delacorte, 1996. / Jones, Charlotte Foltz. *Mistakes That Worked.* Doubleday, 1991. / McCarthy, Meghan. *Aliens Are Coming!: The True Account of the 1938 War of The Worlds Radio Broadcast.* Knopf, 2006. / McCarthy, Meghan. *Astronaut Handbook.* Knopf, 2008. / McCarthy, Meghan. *City Hawk: The Story of Pale Male.* Simon & Schuster, 2007. / McCarthy, Meghan. *Seabiscuit the Wonder Horse.* Simon & Schuster/Paula Wiseman, 2008. / McCarthy, Meghan. *Strong Man: The Story of Charles Atlas.* Knopf, 2007. / McCully, Emily Arnold. *Marvelous Mattie: How Margaret E. Knight Became an Inventor.* Farrar, 2006. / St. George, Judith. *So You Want to Be an Inventor?* Philomel, 2002. / Wheeler, Lisa. *Bubble Gum, Bubble Gum.* Little, Brown, 2004. / Wulffson, Don. *The Kid Who Invented the Popsicle: And Other Surprising Stories About Inventions.* Dutton, 1997.

SUBJECTS: BIOGRAPHY. BUBBLE GUM. CHEWING GUM. INVENTIONS AND INVENTORS. SCIENCE. SOCIAL STUDIES.

[J] | | | | |

The Secret Cave: Discovering Lascaux. McCully, Emily Arnold. Illus. by the author. Farrar, 2010. {ISBN-13: 978-0-374-36694-0; 36p.} 944 (Gr. 2-6)

In what the Author's Note calls "a fictional recreation based on anecdotal accounts," in 1940, three boys in the French village of Montignac accompany Marcel, an older boy, to see what he has discovered: the opening of what he thinks might be a tunnel dug by a nobleman long ago. Using a knife, they enlarge the hole until they can squeeze through. They crawl through the wet tunnel, with only Marcel's homemade lamp to dispel the dark. Instead of finding gold treasure, stashed by a long-ago count, they enter a huge cave and see a large reddish-brown cow painted on the wall. In each chamber, they find more animal paintings. Though they look brand-new, Jacques Marcal recognizes them as paintings made by prehistoric people, which he learned about from his teacher, Monsieur Laval. McCully's dark atmospheric ink and watercolor illustrations of the cave paintings capture the eerie grandeur of this underground wonderland. Marcel is disappointed not to have found the count's gold but Jacques recognizes the paintings as a different sort of treasure. When they finally tell Monsieur Laval about their cave, he is doubtful until he, along with most of the children of the village, follows the boys into the first great hall. "This treasure comes straight from our ancestors to all people everywhere," he declares. Determined that no one will deface their cave, they sleep in front of the entrance for months. Though World War II is raging, their discovery is reported in newspapers worldwide. After the war, Marcel and Jacques stayed on as official guardians and guides at the caves, now known as Lascaux.

GERM: The endpapers display a map that gives you an idea of how extensive these caves are. The Author's Note contains a black and white photo of Jacques and Marcel and archaeologists in the Hall of the Bulls and some astonishing facts. The caves had remained sealed for about 17,000 years, which had kept the colors from fading on the 600 paintings and 1,500 engravings. Take a virtual tour of Lascaux that feels like you are wending your way through the tunnels with a flashlight, stopping to look at the amazing brown-hued paintings, at **www.lascaux.culture.fr/#/fr/00.xml**.

RELATED TITLES: Gibbons, Gail. *Caves and Caverns.* Harcourt, 1993. / McCully, Emily Arnold. *The Ballot Box Battle.* Knopf, 1996. / McCully, Emily Arnold. *Manjiro: The Boy Who Risked His Life for Two Countries.* Farrar, 2008. / McCully, Emily Arnold. *Marvelous Mattie: How Margaret E. Knight Became an Inventor.* Farrar, 2006. / McCully, Emily Arnold. *Mirette on the High Wire.* Putnam, 1992. / McCully, Emily Arnold. *My Heart Glow: Alice Cogswell, Thomas Gallaudet and the Birth of American Sign Language.* Hyperion, 2008. / McCully, Emily Arnold. *Wonder Horse: The True Story of the World's Smartest Horse.* Henry Holt, 2010. / Millman, Isaac. *Hidden Child.* Farrar, 2005. / Sayre, Henry M. *Cave Paintings to Picasso: The Inside Scoop on 50 Art Masterpieces.* Chronicle Books, 2003.

SUBJECTS: ART, PREHISTORIC. CAVE PAINTINGS. FRANCE. HISTORICAL FICTION. LASCAUX CAVE (FRANCE). SCIENCE. SOCIAL STUDIES. WORLD WAR, 1939-1945.

[J*] |A| | | |

Shake, Rattle & Turn that Noise Down!: How Elvis Changed Music, Me, and Mom. Stamaty, Mark Alan. Illus. by the author. Knopf, 2010. {ISBN-13: 978-0-375-84685-4; 32p.} 782.4 (Gr. 2-6)

Elvis Presley lovers, unite and meet a guy whose whole life has been defined by the King. When author and cartoonist Mark Stamaty turned eight in 1955, his parents gave him his own radio. As he states in his comic book-style autobiography about two pivotal years of his childhood, "Back then, lots of things we now take for granted did not even exist. Things like personal computers, cell phones, video games, video cameras, iPods, and CDs." (Your kids will be thinking, Wow, this dude is seriously old!") At first, he listened to gentle popular songs and to classical music, which made his mother happy. One day, he was in his room, listening to the radio, when the announcer said, "Here's the newest record from that singer everyone is talking about, Elvis Presley." Up till here, the illustrations are cartoon panels captioned with narration and balloon dialogue, done in an attractive mélange of graphite, ink, gouache, watercolor, polymer paint, and colored pencils. Turn the page, though, and pouring out of the radio in huge yellow letters on an indigo background, are the lyrics that knock the kid into the air: **YOUAINNUTHINBUTTAHOUNDDOGCRYINALLATIME!** His mother rushes into the room, pulling out her hair, shrieking, **"STOP IT! STOP IT! STOP IT! TURN THAT DOWN! I CAN'T STAND IT! WHAT IS THAT?! WHAT IS WRONG WITH YOU?! ARE YOU CRAZY?! I'M LOSING MY MIND!"** (Poor mom. It's always hard on the parents when a new style of music captures the heart and minds of our youth. Think back to your childhood. Who were the singers that drove your parents insane?) She forbids him to bring any Elvis records into the house, except "Love Me Tender," forgetting there's a flip side to every 45. (OK, you're going to need to show kids what a 45 was.) He sings along with Elvis, using a tennis racket for his guitar, and wiggling his hips. He combs his hair into a pompadour, and all of the boys ask him to fix their hair, too. At the annual Blue-and-Gold Cub Scout Dinner, where everyone is expected to perform a skit, his den forms a group, the Jordanaires, with Mark as Elvis. He's a smash hit and Mom is so proud!

GERM: A delightful and hilarious personal narrative, the book jumps off the charts with its backmatter: photos of Mark in Elvis gear that night, and then, on the next page, a color photo of Mark in 1993, then a political cartoonist for the Washington Post, doing his Elvis imitation in the oval office for another Elvis fan, President Bill Clinton. The final page is a nine-paneled black and white photomontage of grown-up Mark morphing into Elvis. Too funny! What a great excuse to put on "Hound Dog" and other Elvis tunes. For older kids, pair this with Shelley Pearsall's *All Shook Up*, about a boy whose divorced dad becomes an Elvis impersonator, and Richard Peck's *A Season of Gifts*, where a boy's older sister is a rabid Elvis fan. There's also a great scene in Rick Riordan's *The Red Pyramid* where Graceland gets destroyed. Play some Elvis Presley music and wiggle those hips! Ask your kids to describe or write about something they've done that they'll remember for the rest of their lives.

RELATED TITLES: Denenberg, Barry. *All Shook Up: The Life and Death of Elvis Presley.* Scholastic, 2001. / Pearsall, Shelley. *All Shook Up.* Knopf, 2008. / Peck, Richard. *A Season of Gifts.* Dial, 2009. / Riordan, Rick. *The Red Pyramid.* Disney/Hyperion, 2010. / Scieszka, Jon. *Knucklehead: Tall Tales & Mostly True Stories About Growing Up Scieszka.* Viking, 2008. / Siegel, Siena Cherson. *To Dance: A Memoir.* Atheneum, 2006. / Sís, Peter. *The Wall: Growing Up Behind the Iron Curtain.* Farrar/Frances Foster, 2007. / Stamaty, Mark Alan. *Alia's Mission: Saving the Books of Iraq.* Knopf, 2004. / Stamaty, Mark Alan. *Who Needs Donuts?* Knopf, 2001, c1973.

SUBJECTS: AUTOBIOGRAPHY. BIOGRAPHY. CARTOONS AND COMICS. MOTHERS. MUSIC. PERSONAL NARRATIVES. PRESLEY, ELVIS, 1935-1977. ROCK MUSIC.

[J] | | | | |

Sit-In: How Four Friends Stood Up by Sitting Down. Pinkney, Andrea Davis. Illus. by Brian Pinkney. Little, Brown, 2010. {ISBN-13: 978-0-316-07016-4; 40p.} 323.1196 (Gr. 2-6) 2011 Flora Stieglitz Straus Award for Nonfiction (Bank Street College of Education)

"We must . . . meet hate with love." Those are the words, in huge teal letters, that greet you when you open up this remarkable and visually arresting picture book, the words that inspired four African American college freshmen to begin their sit-in at the Woolworth's lunch counter in Greensboro, North Carolina on February 1, 1960. Their order? "A doughnut and coffee, with cream on the side." David, Joseph, Franklin, and Ezell watched quietly as the waitress served all of the white customers, and stayed there until the man in charge of the store closed it down. The next day, more students showed up, and soon there were lunch counter protests all over the South. Even when angry whites flung food and insults at them—"We don't serve your kind."—they stayed. "We must meet violence with nonviolence," Dr. King said, and even when they were arrested and jailed, young people continued to protest segregated restaurants, libraries, buses, parks, and pools, until those wrongs were corrected. "A doughnut and coffee, with cream on the side, is not about food—it's about pride." Brian Pinkney's sweeping brush strokes on full-page watercolors. highlighted with India ink, are real standouts in portraying the hope and patience of those brave students who refused to back down, and Andrea Davis Pinkney's poetic and inspirational prose will get you all fired up.

GERM: The backmatter contains an annotated, illustrated timeline of other dates in the movement, a photo of the four students sitting at the Woolworth's lunch counter, a longer essay about the sit-in, and a bibliography, including websites. You'll find much to explore at **www.sitins.com** and **www.sitinmovement.org**, including: photographs; original newspaper articles; and information about the International Civil Rights Center & Museum, housed in the former Woolworth's building, where you can still see the actual lunch counter. Carole Boston Weatherford's *Freedom on the Menu* is a fictional account of the sit-in, told from the eyes of a young African American girl. Other moving and inspirational picture books about segregation and the Civil Rights Movement include Matt Faulkner's *A Taste of Colored Water*, about segregated drinking fountains; Marybeth Lorbiecki's *Sister Anne's Hand*s, about a black teacher who encounters racism from her white students; *Child of the Civil Rights Movement*, an autobiographical account by Paula Young Shelton, daughter of Andrew Young; *Freedom Summer*, about segregation at a swimming pool; and the one that sums up the humanity of the issue, Jacqueline Woodson's *The Other Side*.

RELATED TITLES: Evans, Freddi Williams. *A Bus of Our Own*. Albert Whitman, 2001. / Golenbock, Peter. *Teammates*. Harcourt, 1990. / Lorbiecki, Marybeth. *Sister Anne's Hands*. Dial, 1998. / McKissack, Patricia C. *Goin' Someplace Special*. Atheneum, 2001. / McWhorter, Diane. *A Dream of Freedom: The Civil Rights Movement from 1954 to 1968*. Scholastic, 2004. / Mitchell, Margaree King. *Uncle Jed's Barber Shop*. Simon & Schuster, 1993. / Rappaport, Doreen. *Martin's Big Words*. Hyperion, 2001. / Shelton, Paula Young. *Child of the Civil Rights Movement*. Schwartz & Wade, 2010. / Shore, Diane Z., and Jessica Alexander. *This Is the Dream*. Amistad, 2006. / Weatherford, Carole Boston. *Freedom on the Menu: The Greensboro Sit-ins*. Dial, 2005. / Wiles, Deborah. *Freedom Summer*. Atheneum, 2001. / Woodson, Jacqueline. *The Other Side*. Putnam, 2001.

SUBJECTS: AFRICAN AMERICANS. BIOGRAPHY. CIVIL RIGHTS MOVEMENT. MULTICULTURAL BOOKS. PREJUDICE. RACE RELATIONS. SOCIAL STUDIES. U.S.—HISTORY—TWENTIETH CENTURY.

[J] | | | | |

Soar, Elinor! Brown, Tami Lewis. Illus. by Francois Roca. Farrar, 2010. {ISBN-13: 978-0-374-37115-9; 40p.} B (Gr. 2-6)

From her first airplane ride at age six in a three-seater Farman pusher biplane that gave $5 rides above the Long Island potato fields in 1917, Elinor Smith loved being in the air. She began flying lessons at age ten, and made her first solo flight at fifteen. At sixteen, in 1928, Elinor became the youngest flyer in the U.S. Newspapers derided her as the "Flying Flapper" and one male stunt pilot bet her she couldn't fly under one of the bridges that spanned the East River in New York City. She decided she'd fly under all four: the Brooklyn, Manhattan, Williamsburg, and Queensboro. In a picture book account of that remarkable stunt and how she pulled it off, the detailed full-bleed paintings in handsome shades of brown and blue are glorious and awe-inspiring. On Sunday, October 21, 1928, dressed in her lucky sneakers and red leather jacket, seventeen-year-old Elinor was in the cockpit, ready to take off from Roosevelt Field in Long Island, when Charles Lindbergh (who had already made his record-breaking solo flight across the Atlantic the year before) came up to her and said, "Good luck, kid. Keep your nose down on the turns." The text recounts her challenges in dipping under each bridge, culminating with her vertical bank between two ships as she flew her Waco 10 sideways under the Brooklyn Bridge. "She'd shown the world what a girl could do—soar!"

GERM: The Author's Note includes several sepia-toned photographs of this remarkable girl, and information about her subsequent flights, including setting an endurance record for a 26-hour flight that is still unbroken. The fact that the author was able to interview Elinor, who died in 2010 at age 98, makes this account even more immediate and inspirational for readers. "Children must be allowed to dream and have a horizon to work toward," said Elinor. Write that quote on the board and ask your children what their dream horizons include. Introduce picture books about other brave and groundbreaking early pilots including James Banning, the first U.S.-licensed African American aviator, in *The Hallelujah Flight* by Phil Bildner; Ruth Law, who broke a distance record in 1916, in *Ruth Law Thrills a Nation* by Don Brown; and Bessie Coleman, the first African-American woman pilot, in *Fly High!: The Story of Bessie Coleman* by Louise Borden and Mary Kay Kroeger. Read about Lucky Lindy's flight from Roosevelt Field to Paris in *Flight: The Journey of Charles Lindbergh* by Robert Burleigh.
RELATED TITLES: Bildner, Phil. *The Hallelujah Flight.* Putnam, 2010. / Borden, Louise, and Mary Kay Kroeger. *Fly High!: The Story of Bessie Coleman.* McElderry, 2001. / Brown, Don. *Alice Ramsey's Grand Adventure.* Houghton Mifflin, 1997. / Brown, Don. *Ruth Law Thrills a Nation.* Ticknor & Fields, 1993. / Burleigh, Robert. *Flight: The Journey of Charles Lindbergh.* Philomel, 1991. / Grimes, Nikki. *Talkin' about Bessie: The Story of Aviator Elizabeth Coleman.* Orchard, 2002. / Joseph, Lynn. *Fly, Bessie, Fly.* Simon & Schuster, 1998. / Lindbergh, Reeve. *Nobody Owns the Sky: The Story of "Brave Bessie" Coleman.* Candlewick, 1996. / Moss, Marissa. *Brave Harriet.* Harcourt, 2001. / Ryan, Pam Muñoz. *Amelia and Eleanor Go for a Ride.* Scholastic, 1999. / Szabo, Corinne. *Sky Pioneer: A Photobiography of Amelia Earhart.* National Geographic, 1997.
SUBJECTS: AIR PILOTS. AIRPLANES. BIOGRAPHY. FLIGHT. SCIENCE. SMITH, ELINOR, 1911-2010. SOCIAL STUDIES. WOMEN—BIOGRAPHY.

[J] | | | | |
Summer Birds: The Butterflies of Maria Merian. **Engle, Margarita. Illus. by Julie Paschkis. Henry Holt, 2010. {ISBN-13: 978-0-8050-8937-0; 32p.} 595.78 (Gr. 1-4)**
Thirteen-year-old Maria Merian explains how she captures insects to study them, especially caterpillars and summer birds, the medieval term for butterflies and moths. "Neighbors would accuse me of witchcraft if they knew." Maria observes caterpillars, which she keeps in jars, and discovers they are born from eggs laid by summer birds. She notes how they spin cocoons, and then emerge as winged creatures, changing from one form to another. In her notebook, she paints detailed pictures of caterpillars, frogs, and flowers, and anticipates the time when she will be a grown-up, free to travel to faraway lands to paint nature. Maria's spare but impassioned personal narrative and description of what we now call metamorphosis is accompanied by fanciful, colorful paintings outlined in fine brown lines, that have the look of medieval folk art, old prints, and batiks.
GERM: Every child who has seen Eric Carle's *The Very Hungry Caterpillar* knows how a caterpillar becomes a butterfly. The historical note at the back describes how, in seventeenth century Germany, Europeans believed in spontaneous generation—that beetles, worms, caterpillars and frogs were evil "beasts of the devil," formed from mud. Children will be astounded and inspired to learn that a teenager could, through careful observation and perseverance, make such an important and far-reaching discovery about metamorphosis that disproved the prevailing wisdom. We adults will marvel that a young woman of that time would be recognized and remembered as a scientist and painter. To see some of Merian's original paintings and read fascinating information about her later life and her paintings, look her up at **www.Wikipedia.com**, which gives a nicely detailed account. Find out more about "summer birds" and other creatures that change forms in Nic Bishop's *Butterflies and Moths* and Nic Bishop's *Frogs.* Meet Mary Anning, another self-taught nineteenth century scientist whose fossil discoveries in Cornwall, England changed thinking about those creatures we call dinosaurs, in Don Brown's *Rare Treasure: Mary Anning and Her Remarkable Discoveries.* If you're feeling a bit silly after all of this serious information, recite "Cecil Was a Caterpillar" with your students, on page 183 of this handbook.
RELATED TITLES: Bishop, Nic. *Nic Bishop Butterflies and Moths.* Scholastic, 2009. / Brown, Don. *Rare Treasure: Mary Anning and Her Remarkable Discoveries.* Houghton Mifflin, 1999. / Carle, Eric. *The Very Hungry Caterpillar.* Philomel, 1987, c1969. / Heiligman, Deborah. *From Caterpillar to Butterfly.* HarperCollins, 1996. / Lasky, Kathryn. *One Beetle Too Many: The Extraordinary Adventures of Charles Darwin.* Candlewick Press, 2009. / McCully, Emily Arnold. *Marvelous Mattie: How Margaret E. Knight Became an Inventor.* Farrar, 2006.
SUBJECTS: BIOGRAPHY. BUTTERFLIES. CATERPILLARS. INSECTS. MERIAN, MARIA SIBYLLA, 1647-1717. METAMORPHOSIS. NATURALISTS. SCIENCE. SCIENTISTS. WOMEN—BIOGRAPHY.

[J] | | | | |

***A Wizard from the Start: The Incredible Boyhood & Amazing Inventions of Thomas Edison.* Brown, Don. Illus. by the author. Houghton Mifflin, 2010. {ISBN-13: 978-0-547-19487-5; 32p.} B (Gr. 1-4)**

This brief picture book biography, filled with interesting anecdotes and quotes, hits the highlights of Edison's life, experimenting, tinkering, and reading. Growing up in Port Huron, Michigan, Tom was home-schooled by his mother after his teacher called the daydreaming boy "addled." The full-page watercolors pull us right in to each dramatic moment. There's Tom and a pal fooling around with acids and chemicals in the basement, his anxious mother hovering at the top of the stairs. Anticipate the pain as he is about to get his ear boxed by an angry railroad worker after his chemistry experiment in the baggage car caused a fire. Then watch him save a three-year-old boy, snatching him from the path of an oncoming freight train. The inspirational text is easy to read aloud, just enough to make listeners of all ages curious about the prolific inventor.

GERM: Go back to the page where Tom, at the public library, started at the first book on the bottom shelf and read every book. Ask your children what effect these books had on Edison's life. Challenge them to read a whole shelf of books at the library and report back on what they've learned. As a fourteen-year-old boy, working as a railroad "news butch," selling newspapers, candy, and cigars to the commuters in Detroit, he wrote and printed his own newspaper on the train. "The more to do, the more to be done," he wrote. Discuss how he lived that sentiment. Have them look up a list of his many inventions and consider his own words about his 1,093 patents: "I never did a day's work in my life. It was all fun." Have your students learn the Morse code as Edison did to earn a coveted job as a tramp telegraph operator. If Edison was alive today, what recent inventions would he most admire? What still needs to be invented?

RELATED TITLES: Brown, Don. *Odd Boy Out: Young Albert Einstein.* Houghton Mifflin, 2004. / Brown, Don. *One Giant Leap: The Story of Neil Armstrong.* Houghton Mifflin, 1998. / Brown, Don. *Ruth Law Thrills a Nation.* Houghton Mifflin, 1993. / Delano, Marfé Ferguson. *Inventing the Future: A Photobiography of Thomas Alva Edison.* National Geographic, 2002. / Dooling, Michael. *Young Thomas Edison.* Holiday House, 2005. / Gutman, Dan. *Qwerty Stevens Back in Time: The Edison Mystery.* Simon & Schuster, 2001. / Moore, Floyd C. *I Gave Thomas Edison My Sandwich.* Albert Whitman, 1995. / Old, Wendie. *To Fly: The Story of the Wright Brothers.* Clarion, 2002. / St. George, Judith. *So You Want to Be an Inventor?* Philomel, 2002.

SUBJECTS: BIOGRAPHY. EDISON, THOMAS ALVA. ENGINEERS. INVENTIONS AND INVENTORS. SCIENCE. SCIENTISTS.

WINNERS!:
100+ Best Children's Books of 2010

POETRY AND FOLKLORE BOOKS

[J] |A|B|H| |
Dark Emperor & Other Poems of the Night. Sidman, Joyce. Illus. by Rick Allen. Houghton Mifflin, 2010.
    {ISBN-13: 978-0-547-15228-8; 32p.} 811 (Gr. 3-6) 2011 Newbery Honor
"To all of you who crawl and creep, / who buzz and chirp and hoot and peep, / who wake at dusk and throw off sleep; / Welcome to the night." Sidman welcomes us all with another dozen insightful, playful, thoughtful poems, this time about nocturnal animals and other nighttime inhabitants of the woods. Facing each poem, on the right-hand page, is a moonlit linoleum print, hand-colored with gouache, portraying the creature in its nighttime habitat, and a descriptive, factual paragraph about it. The package is irresistible, a robust combustion of all types of poems—a ballad, a lament, a concrete poem, and even a love poem from a primrose moth to its only true love, the primrose— and facts that startle, inform, and surprise. Meet a snail at moonrise climbing its "slick trail of silver," a baby porcupette, a singing cricket with its "searing, unstoppable sound," and, of course, the title creature with "mesmerizing eyes," as described by a mouse that fears its "hooked face and hungry eye."
GERM: One magical thing about these poems is the riddle-ness of them. Most do not identify the subject except in the title. When you read these aloud, leave off the title and ask your children to listen for clues to identify the subject of the poem. Go to **www.joycesidman.com/darkemperorTG.html** for a teacher's guide to the book, and a link to the Merle Travis' song "Dark As a Dungeon," the tune Sidman used to go with "Ballad of the Wandering Eft." Sing it, of course.
RELATED TITLES: Esbensen, Barbara Juster. *Echoes for the Eye: Poems to Celebrate Patterns in Nature.* HarperCollins, 1996. / Franco, Betsy. *Bees, Snails, & Peacock Tails: Patterns and Shapes . . . Naturally.* McElderry, 2008. / Ruddell, Deborah. *A Whiff of Pine, a Hint of Skunk: A Forest of Poems.* McElderry, 2009. / Sidman, Joyce. *Butterfly Eyes and Other Secrets of the Meadow.* Houghton Mifflin, 2006. / Sidman, Joyce. *Red Sings from Treetops: A Year in Colors.* Houghton Mifflin, 2009. / Sidman, Joyce. *Song of the Water Boatman & Other Pond Poems.* Houghton Mifflin, 2005. / Sidman, Joyce. *This Is Just to Say: Poems of Apology and Forgiveness.* Houghton Mifflin, 2007. / Sidman, Joyce. *Ubiquitous: Celebrating Nature's Survivors.* Harcourt, 2010.
SUBJECTS: ANIMALS—POETRY. NATURE—POETRY. NIGHT—POETRY. POETRY—SINGLE AUTHOR. SCIENCE—POETRY.

[J] |A| | | |

Guyku: A Year of Haiku for Boys. Raczka, Bob. Illus. by Peter H. Reynolds. Houghton Mifflin, 2010. {ISBN-13: 978-0-547-24003-9; 48p.} 811 (Gr. PreK-4) 2011 Claudia Lewis Award for Poetry (Bank Street College of Education)

In a series of guy-centric haiku, six per season starting with spring, a multicultural cast of young boys laugh and play their way outside through an activity-packed year. "With baseball cards and / clothes pins we make our bikes sound / like motorcycles." Exuberant brown-toned watercolors tinged with green and yellow accompany the hand-printed haiku, one per page. Kite-flying, dam-building, rock-skipping, leaf-raking, snowball-pitching boys, playing alone or in pairs, observe and comment on the natural world as they revel in the freedom of unsupervised, unregimented play. "The best part about / kicking this stone home from school / is there are no rules."

GERM: In his "Why I Illustrated *Guyku*" note, Peter H. Reynolds states, "The invitation for boys to swim in the 'poem pond' needs to be issued more often and more loudly." Raczka's Author's Note at the back of the book, titled "Why I Wrote *Guyku*," states that haiku is "a wonderful form of poetry for guys like us. Why? Because haiku is an observation of nature and nature is a place where guys love to be." He says that the 24 haiku poems are about things he did as a boy or that his sons have done. Naturally, you'll want to give equal time, having your kids write and illustrate "Girlku," or maybe "Petku." At Van Holten School in Bridgewater, NJ, the second grade students of Becky Gara, Helen Kyritsis, and Lisa D'Ascensio wrote and illustrated a dazzling book of wild animal haiku they called *Zooku.* See page 91 in this handbook for excerpts. Also read the story told in haiku, of a stray dog that finds a family in *Dogku* by Andrew Clements.

RELATED TITLES: Barton, Chris. *Shark Vs. Train.* Little, Brown, 2010. / Clements, Andrew. *Dogku.* Simon & Schuster, 2007. / Frazee, Marla. *A Couple of Boys Have the Best Week Ever.* Harcourt, 2008. / Fucile, Tony. *Let's Do Nothing!* Candlewick, 2009. / Hopkins, Lee Bennett, comp. *Sharing the Seasons: A Book of Poems.* McElderry, 2010. / Lin, Grace, and Ranida T. McKneally. *Our Seasons.* Charlesbridge, 2006. / Prelutsky, Jack. *If Not for the Cat.* Greenwillow, 2004. / Reibstein, Mark. *Wabi Sabi.* Little, Brown, 2008. / Sidman, Joyce. *Red Sings from Treetops: A Year in Colors.* Houghton Mifflin, 2009.

SUBJECTS: BOYS—POETRY. HAIKU. LANGUAGE ARTS. POETRY—SINGLE AUTHOR. SEASONS—POETRY.

[J] |A| | | |

In the Wild. Elliott, David. Illus. by Holly Meade. Candlewick, 2010. {ISBN-13: 978-0-7636-4497-0; 32p.} 811 (Gr. PreK-1)

While his first similarly designed poetry book, *On the Farm,* was all about domestic animals, now Elliott takes on the mostly larger and often dangerous wild animals of the world in 14 poems just right for the youngest listeners. Each oversized two-page spread is a masterful rendering, in watercolor and woodblock print, of an animal in its natural habitat. The rhyming wordplay is always arresting. Of the giraffe, standing tall on the African plain, he writes: "Stilt-walker! / Tree-topper! / Long-necked / showstopper!" Familiar beasts include the elephant, zebra, rhinoceros, panda, kangaroo, and wolf. "Dear Orangutan," starts one, styled as a letter, and ends with, "How nice to have someone like you / sitting in our family tree. / Sincerely from your cousin, / Me." A real class act, poetry-wise.

GERM: Listeners can identify the biomes from which the animals hail. There's one terrific fact on the endpapers. The author states, "Writing the poems for this book, I learned that there are just four great cats." Stop and see if your group can name them: tiger, lion, jaguar, and leopard. What makes them great cats? They are the only cats that can roar! Older children can use these poems and pictures as inspiration to research, write, and illustrate new ones.

RELATED TITLES: Elliott, David. *Finn Throws a Fit.* Candlewick, 2009. / Elliott, David. *On the Farm.* Candlewick, 2008. / Florian, Doug. *Beast Feast.* Harcourt, 1994. / Florian, Douglas. *Omnibeasts: Animal Poems and Paintings.* Harcourt, 2004. / Ghigna, Charles. *Animal Tracks: Wild Poems to Read Aloud.* Abrams, 2004. / Lewis, J. Patrick. *A Hippopotamustn't and Other Animal Verses.* Dial, 1990. / Prelutsky, Jack, comp. *The Beauty of the Beast: Poems from the Animal Kingdom.* Knopf, 1997. / Prelutsky, Jack. *If Not for the Cat.* Greenwillow, 2004. / Ruddell, Deborah. *A Whiff of Pine, a Hint of Skunk: A Forest of Poems.* McElderry, 2009. / Sidman, Joyce. *Butterfly Eyes and Other Secrets of the Meadow.* Houghton Mifflin, 2006. / Sidman, Joyce. *Song of the Water Boatman & Other Pond Poems.* Houghton Mifflin, 2005. / Whipple, Laura. *Eric Carle's Animals, Animals.* Philomel, 1989.

SUBJECTS: ANIMALS—POETRY. POETRY—SINGLE AUTHOR. SCIENCE—POETRY.

[J*] |A|B|H| |
Mirror, Mirror: A Book of Reversible Verse. **Singer, Marilyn. Illus. by Josée Masse. Dutton, 2010. {ISBN-13: 978-0-525-47901-7; 32p.} 811 (Gr. 3-6) Judy Freeman's 2011 Best of the Best for Poetry**
Fourteen reverso poems—read first from top to bottom, and then rearranged so the bottom line becomes the top—take on the double-sided nature of fairy tales. In "Cinderella's Double Life" she muses, "I'll be shining / these shoes / till the clock strikes midnight." Next to that poem is the same poem, reprinted so the last line is first and the first line is last. Those same lines now begin the second poem, but with new punctuation and line breaks that change the entire mood and meaning: Now Cinderella crows, "Till the clock strikes midnight, / these shoes! / I'll be shining / at the ball." On the facing page is a bifurcated illustration of Cinderella polishing shoes on the left, and dancing with the prince under the moon on the right. Same words, whole new story. "In the Hood," presents Little Red Riding Hood, first from her viewpoint, and then from the wolf's. It's all insidiously clever and delightful.
GERM: For each pair of poems, listeners will need to discern the narrator or point of view. These would be wonderful for pairs of children to read aloud and show a book of the corresponding fairy tale. What a clever way to review (or introduce) tales every literate person should know. Your poets can try their hands at writing new reversos. In her Author's Note, Singer says, "It is a form that is both challenging and fun—rather like creating and solving a puzzle." Dig deeper into the Cinderella story with the point of view poems in Laura Whipple's *If the Shoe Fits*.
RELATED TITLES: Gaiman, Neil. *Instructions.* HarperCollins, 2010. / Gidwitz, Adam. *A Tale Dark & Grimm.* Dutton, 2010. / Hoberman, Mary Ann. *You Read to Me, I'll Read to You: Very Short Fairy Tales to Read Together.* Little, Brown, 2004. / Stein, David Ezra. *Interrupting Chicken.* Candlewick, 2010. / Whipple, Laura. *If the Shoe Fits: Voices from Cinderella.* McElderry, 2002.
SUBJECTS: CHARACTERS IN LITERATURE. FAIRY TALES. LANGUAGE ARTS. POETRY—SINGLE AUTHOR.

[J] | | | | |
Ol' Bloo's Boogie-Woogie Band and Blues Ensemble. **Huling, Jan. Illus. by Henri Sorensen. Peachtree, 2010. {ISBN-13: 978-1-56145-436-5; 32p.} 398.2 (Gr. 1-5)**
When Ol' Bloo Donkey overhears the farmer planning to "put the poor beast outta his misery," he decides to set out for New Orleans where folks might appreciate his "beee-yoooo-ti-ful singin' voice," though according to the folksy narrator, his voice reminds one of "the sound an accordion makes fallin' down a flight of stairs." On his way, Ol' Bloo Donkey meets up with three other "silver-throated varmints": a flea-bit old hound named Gnarly Dog; One-Eyed Lemony Cat, with a black patch over one eye; and grizzled old Rusty Red Rooster. Together they plan to sing in a honky-tonk, figuring "them big city folk won't know what hit 'em." Seeing a cabin, they decide to sing for their supper, especially when they spy the banquet of gumbo, po-boys, pralines, and bread puddin' on the table inside, attended by three rough-looking thieves. The four break into song (or an awful shriek, from the robbers' perspective) and crash through the window, scaring the three men into the woods. This laconic retelling of the Brothers Grimm folktale, "The Bremen-Town Musicians," has been reset in the woods outside of New Orleans, illustrated with a combination of expressive full-page oil paintings and black silhouettes.
GERM: Compare this revamped version with Kevin O'Malley's joke-riddled *Animal Crackers Fly the Coop*, and be sure to read the original story, "The Bremen Town Musicians," which you'll find on page 184 in this handbook, to see from whence these stories sprang. This would make a lively Reader's Theater script.
RELATED TITLES: Doucet, Sharon Arms. *Lapin Plays Possum: Trickster Tales from the Louisiana Bayou.* Farrar, 2002. / Grimm, Jacob, and Grimm, Wilhelm. *The Bremen Town Musicians.* North-South, 1992. / Kesey, Ken. *Little Tricker the Squirrel Meets Big Double the Bear.* Viking, 1990. / Krosoczka, Jarrett J. *Punk Farm.* Knopf, 2005. / O'Malley, Kevin. *Animal Crackers Fly the Coop.* Walker, 2010. / Plume, Ilse. *The Bremen-Town Musicians.* Bantam, 1980. / Salley, Coleen. *Epossumondas Plays Possum.* Harcourt, 2009. (And others in the Epossumondas series.) / Thomassie, Tynia. *Feliciana Feydra LeRoux: A Cajun Tall Tale.* Little, Brown, 1995.
SUBJECTS: ANIMALS—FOLKLORE. CATS—FOLKLORE. DOGS—FOLKLORE. DONKEYS—FOLKLORE. FOLKLORE—GERMANY. LOUISIANA. MUSICIANS—FOLKLORE. ROBBERS AND OUTLAWS—FOLKLORE. ROOSTERS—FOLKLORE. SINGERS—FOLKLORE. STORIES TO TELL.

[J] |A| |H| |

Pocketful of Posies: A Treasury of Nursery Rhymes. Mavor, Sally. Illus. by the author. Houghton Mifflin, 2010.
 {ISBN-13: 978-0-618-73740-6; 72p.} 398.8 (Gr. PreK-1)

You'll recognize most of the 64 nursery rhymes selected for this handsome collection, but will be awestruck at the illustrations. What Sally Mavor calls "playing with a needle and thread" is a tactile, warm, and adorable panorama of hand-stitched scenes, described as "hand-sewn fabric relief collages." The backgrounds of each page are made from a soft, felt blanket-like material that makes you feel warm and cozy just looking at it. Then she adds embroidered trees and flowers, houses crafted from bark, buttons and other miniature found materials, and a multicultural cast of children fashioned from yarn and lace, wearing tiny, colorful hand-knitted and sewn outfits. Children will want to feel the pages, as they look three-dimensional, and are oh, so charming. There's much to recite here, as well, like: "I'm dusty Bill / from Vinegar Hill. / Never had a bath / and never will."

GERM: Keep a scraps basket of old cut up knits, placemats, towels, and other bits you'd otherwise toss, so your little ones can make pictures out of fabrics, yarns, and textiles. This will be a much-appreciated holiday present or a gift for a newborn, as well as a classroom book for all early childhood classrooms.

RELATED TITLES: Crews, Nina. *The Neighborhood Mother Goose.* Greenwillow, 2004. / Denton, Kady MacDonald, comp. *A Child's Treasury of Nursery Rhymes.* Kingfisher, 1998. / DePaola, Tomie. *Tomie dePaola's Mother Goose.* Putnam, 1985. / Fabian, Bobbi, comp. *Twinkle, Twinkle: An Animal Lover's Mother Goose.* Dutton, 1997. / Foreman, Michael, comp. *Michael Foreman's Playtime Rhymes.* Candlewick, 2002. / Hoberman, Mary Ann. *You Read to Me, I'll Read to You: Very Short Mother Goose Tales to Read Together.* Little, Brown, 2005. / Lamont, Priscilla, comp. *Ring-a-Round-a-Rosy: Nursery Rhymes, Action Rhymes and Lullabyes.* Little, Brown, 1990. / Lobel, Arnold. *The Random House Book of Mother Goose.* Random House, 1986. / Long, Sylvia, comp. *Sylvia Long's Mother Goose.* Chronicle, 1999. / Moses, Will, comp. *Will Moses Mother Goose.* Philomel, 2003.

SUBJECTS: LANGUAGE ARTS. MOTHER GOOSE. NURSERY RHYMES. POETRY—ANTHOLOGIES.

[J] | | | | |

The Red Hen. Emberley, Rebecca, and Ed Emberley. Illus. by Rebecca Emberley and Ed Emberley. Roaring
 Brook, 2010. {ISBN-13: 978-1-59643-492-9; 32p.} 398.2 (Gr. PreK-1)

The Emberley father and daughter team are back with an equally wacky companion to last year's chicken story, *Chicken Little.* In a new telling of the familiar tale, Red Hen finds a wonderful recipe for a "Simply Splendid Cake." When she asks, "Who will help me gather the ingredients?", the cat and the rat say, "Not I." "Bribbit," says the frog, which is obviously frog for "Not I," and will be your kids' favorite new word. "All right then, I shall do it myself," says Red Hen. Overlaid geometric cutouts of the recalcitrant animals in wildly bright colors against a white background would make Matisse proud, and will make children laugh.

GERM: In one of the best new additions to storytime of the year, the repetition is delightful for joining in, and everyone will want to act it out. Putting together a colorful set of flannelboard characters shouldn't be too complex for a retelling with audience participation. The recipe for the cake is appended, too, if you're feeling peckish.

RELATED TITLES: Emberley, Ed. *Go Away, Big Green Monster!* Little, Brown, 1993. / Emberley, Rebecca. *Three Cool Kids.* Little, Brown, 1995. / Emberley, Rebecca, and Ed Emberley. *Chicken Little.* Roaring Brook, 2009. / Galdone, Paul. *The Little Red Hen.* Clarion, 1979. / Ketteman, Helen. *Armadilly Chili.* Albert Whitman, 2004. / Kimmelman, Leslie. *The Little Red Hen and the Passover Matzah.* Holiday House, 2010. / Paul, Ann Whitford. *Mañana, Iguana.* Holiday House, 2004. / Pinkney, Jerry. *The Little Red Hen.* Dial, 2006. / Stevens, Janet, and Susan Stevens Crummel. *Cook-a-Doodle-Doo!* Harcourt, 1999. / Sturges, Philemon. *The Little Red Hen (Makes a Pizza).* Dutton, 1999.

SUBJECTS: ANIMALS—FOLKLORE. BIRDS—FOLKLORE. CATS—FOLKLORE. CHANTABLE REFRAIN—FOLKLORE. CHICKENS—FOLKLORE. CREATIVE DRAMA—FOLKLORE. FOLKLORE. FROGS—FOLKLORE. HUMOROUS FOLKLORE. RATS—FOLKLORE. READER'S THEATER. STORIES TO TELL.

[J] | | | | |

Sharing the Seasons: A Book of Poems. Hopkins, Lee Bennett, comp. Illus. by David Diaz. McElderry, 2010. {ISBN-13: 978-1-4169-0210-2; 83p.} 811 (Gr. 2-6)

A sunstorm of colors pours from every page of this magnificent poetry collection, with twelve well-chosen poems for each of the seasons, starting with Spring. Diaz's full-bleed mixed media illustrations of children and animals reveling in each season look like they're stenciled onto the page and illuminated. Every figure shimmers with rays of radiant seasonal colors that make you feel exhilarated. Read the acknowledgments page and you'll see that Hopkins commissioned many of the poems directly from the 27 authors, instead of harvesting already-published poems, which is why few will seem familiar or old hat; most will feel fresh, substantial, and surprising, summing up all the things you never realized you felt about the seasons.

GERM: You'll be eager to share these aloud. Have children each pick a favorite season and write and illustrate a poem about it.

RELATED TITLES: Andrews, Julie, and Emma Walton Hamilton. *Julie Andrews' Collection of Poems, Songs, and Lullabies.* Little, Brown, 2009. / Hopkins, Lee Bennett, comp. *Amazing Faces: Poems.* Lee & Low, 2010. / Hopkins, Lee Bennett, comp. *Oh, No! Where Are My Pants? And Other Disasters: Poems.* HarperCollins, 2005. / Hopkins, Lee Bennett, comp. *Sky Magic: Poems.* Dutton, 2009. / Kennedy, Caroline. *A Family of Poems: My Favorite Poetry for Children.* Hyperion, 2005. / Kennedy, Dorothy M., and X. J. Kennedy, comps. *Talking Like the Rain: A First Book of Poems.* Little, Brown, 1992. / Martin, Bill, Jr., and Michael Sampson. *The Bill Martin Jr Big Book of Poetry.* Simon & Schuster, 2008. / Raczka, Bob. *Guyku: A Year of Haiku for Boys.* Houghton Mifflin, 2010. / Sidman, Joyce. *Red Sings from Treetops: A Year in Colors.* Houghton Mifflin, 2009. / Yolen, Jane, ed. *Switching on the Moon: A Very First Book of Bedtime Poems.* Candlewick, 2010.

SUBJECTS: POETRY—ANTHOLOGIES. SCIENCE—POETRY. SEASONS—POETRY.

[J] | | | | |

Switching on the Moon: A Very First Book of Bedtime Poems. Yolen, Jane, ed. Illus. by G. Brian Karas. Candlewick, 2010. {ISBN-13: 978-0-7636-4249-5; 95p.} 398.8 (Gr. PreK-1)

Sixty sweet, simple, image-rich bedtime poems are paired with gorgeous, evocative, full-page gouache, acrylic, and pencil paintings. Divided into three categories—Going to Bed, Sweet Dreams, and In the Night—each poem and page is a revelation. Some are beyond well known, like "The Star" by Jane Taylor. (You remember that one, starting with "Twinkle, twinkle, little star.") Others are jaunty and fun, like "Naughty Soap Song" by Dorothy Addis, which begins, "Just when I'm ready to / Start on my ears, / This is the time that my / Soap disappears." Some of the illustrations are childlike and funny; others are just plain ravishing, sweeping across the page in a pageant of night. There's "Rock-a-bye, Baby," of course, but on the facing page is the West Indian version of the lullaby, "Rack-a-bye baby," which begins, "Rack-a-bye, baby, / Pon tap a tree tap." The usual suspects in children's poetry are here—Douglas Florian, Jane Yolen, Marilyn Singer, Mary Ann Hoberman, and Lee Bennett Hopkins are just a few we know and love—but there are many surprises in Yolen's expert selections.

GERM: With its multicultural cast of sleepy and not-so-sleepy children before, during, and after bedtime, this is a gift book that will keep on giving every night when you share a poem or three. Read it at bedtime storyhours and during the day, too, when you can ask your charges what bedtime poems their parents recite at night.

RELATED TITLES: Andrews, Julie, and Emma Walton Hamilton. *Julie Andrews' Collection of Poems, Songs, and Lullabies.* Little, Brown, 2009. / Gal, Susan. *Night Lights.* Knopf, 2009. / Hopkins, Lee Bennett, comp. *Climb into My Lap: First Poems to Read Together.* Simon & Schuster, 1998. / Hopkins, Lee Bennett, comp. *Sharing the Seasons: A Book of Poems.* McElderry, 2010. / Kennedy, Caroline. *A Family of Poems: My Favorite Poetry for Children.* Hyperion, 2005. / Kennedy, Dorothy M., and X. J. Kennedy, comps. *Talking Like the Rain: A First Book of Poems.* Little, Brown, 1992. / Martin, Bill, Jr., and Michael Sampson. *The Bill Martin Jr Big Book of Poetry.* Simon & Schuster, 2008. / Yolen, Jane, and Andrew Fusek Peters, eds. *Here's a Little Poem: A Very First Book of Poetry.* Candlewick, 2007.

SUBJECTS: BEDTIME—POETRY. NIGHT—POETRY. NURSERY RHYMES. POETRY—ANTHOLOGIES. SCIENCE—POETRY. SLEEP—POETRY.

[J*] | | | | |

The 3 Little Dassies. **Brett, Jan. Illus. by the author. Putnam, 2010. {ISBN-13: 978-0-399-25499-4; 32p.} E (Gr. PreK-2)**

Three little dassies—soft-furred, little, brown, big-eyed, black-nosed rodents also called rock hyraxes—wave goodbye to their family, and set out across the Namib Desert on their own. Mimbi, Pimbi, and Timbi, clad in colorful long-sleeved cotton gowns and flat-topped turbans, seek a cooler, less crowded place where they will be safe from big eagles. When the sisters arrive at the foot of a mountain, they are welcomed by handsome, smiling Agama Man, a dapper redheaded agama lizard, dressed in a green jacket and fedora. Mimbi builds her house of long grasses, Pimbi uses drift wood to make a wooden house, and Timbi works all day to build one of stone. Overhead flies a big old eagle, looking for food for his hungry chicks. "I see you, dassie," he screeches, "I'll flap and I'll clap and I'll blow your house in." He picks up each of the first two dassies in his talons and deposits them atop the mountain in his nest with his two white chicks. As with all Jan Brett books, the side illustrations tell part of the story; in the framed side panels, Agama Man scrambles up the rocks to reach and rescue the sisters. In the meantime, the eagle is unable to blow in Timbi's stone house, and is soon scared off by the dassies, whereupon there's a nice pourquoi tale–like explanation of why eagles' feathers are now as black as soot.

GERM: Brett's story was inspired by a camping trip in Namibia in southern Africa where she first spotted little rock dassies, a red-headed agama lizard, and eagles, who eat dassies. The clothing of the three sisters is based on the dresses and hats worn by the Herero women. Borders incorporate African fabrics, and delicately colored watercolor and gouache paintings are majestic and downright magnificent. Compare this re-set version of "Three Little Pigs" story with the original of course, but also with the two versions set in the American desert: *The Three Little Javelinas* by Susan Lowell and *The Three Little Tamales* by Eric A. Kimmel. See Judy Freeman's Reader's Theater script of *The 3 Little Dassies* on page 146 of this handbook.

RELATED TITLES: Brett, Jan. *The Easter Egg.* Putnam, 2010. / Brett, Jan. *Goldilocks and the Three Bears.* Putnam, 1987. / Brett, Jan. *The Hat.* Putnam, 1997. / Brett, Jan. *Honey . . . Honey . . . Lion!: A Story from Africa.* Putnam, 2005. / Brett, Jan. *The Mitten: A Ukrainian Folktale.* Penguin, 1989. / Brett, Jan. *The Three Snow Bears.* Putnam, 2007. / Brett, Jan. *Trouble with Trolls.* Putnam, 1992. / Kimmel, Eric A. *The Three Little Tamales.* Marshall Cavendish, 2009. / Lowell, Susan. *The Three Little Javelinas.* Rising Moon, 1992. / Marshall, James. *The Three Little Pigs.* Dial, 1989. / Moser, Barry. *The Three Little Pigs.* Little, Brown, 2001. / Paul, Ann Whitford. *Tortuga In Trouble.* Holiday House, 2009. / Scieszka, Jon. *The True Story of the 3 Little Pigs.* Viking, 1989. / Zemach, Margot. *The Three Little Pigs: An Old Story.* Farrar, 1988.

SUBJECTS: AFRICA. DASSIES. FOLKLORE. LANGUAGE ARTS. LIZARDS. NAMIB DESERT (NAMIBIA). PARODIES. REPTILES AND AMPHIBIANS. ROCK HYRAXES. THREE LITTLE PIGS.

[J] |A| | |S|

Ubiquitous: Celebrating Nature's Survivors. **Sidman, Joyce. Illus. by Beckie Prange. Harcourt, 2010. {ISBN-13: 978-0-618-71719-4; 36p.} 811 (Gr. 3-6)**

Starting with and celebrating the earliest form of life on earth, bacteria, poet Sidman offers a seven-line diamante, "First Life." On the facing page is a detailed paragraph of facts about how life began four billion years ago in the form of bacteria. (Did you know bacteria can clone themselves every twenty minutes and that there are "more bacteria than any other living thing on earth.") Then there is the gorgeous illustration covering the page, a linocut hand-colored with glowing watercolors. The 13 equally striking poems that follow move sequentially, from a mollusk (500 million years old) to lichen (400 million years old), sharks (375 million years old), scarab, diatoms, a gecko, and ending with a human baby (100,000 years old). As always, Sidman's poetry—some free verse, some rhyming—abounds with startling and soulful imagery that is a fest to share with others.

GERM: The Author's Note recommends two fascinating resources: The Tree of Life Project at **www.tolweb.org/tree/**, hosted by the University of Arizona, and the Encyclopedia of Life at **www.eol.org**. For more information, go to the author's own website at **www.joycesidman.com**. The endpapers will generate sheer astonishment, once you examine it closely to realize it is a compressed timeline of earth's history, with the subject of each poem marked off. The Illustrator's Note explains how she compressed each geologic period with colored string 46 meters long, with one centimeter equaling one million years. Have your kids stretch out a string down the hallway to mark off the different periods and eras. What this book does is generate a thrilling sense of wonder about our place in the history and future of the planet. No mean feat.

RELATED TITLES: Esbensen, Barbara Juster. *Echoes for the Eye: Poems to Celebrate Patterns in Nature.* HarperCollins, 1996. / Franco, Betsy. *Bees, Snails, & Peacock Tails: Patterns and Shapes . . . Naturally.* McElderry, 2008. / Jenkins, Steve. *Life on Earth: The Story of Evolution.* Houghton Mifflin, 2002. / Sidman, Joyce. *Butterfly Eyes and Other Secrets of the Meadow.* Houghton Mifflin, 2006. / Sidman, Joyce. *Dark Emperor & Other Poems of the Night.* Houghton Mifflin, 2010. / Sidman, Joyce. *Red Sings from Treetops: A Year in Colors.* Houghton Mifflin, 2009. / Sidman, Joyce. *Song of the Water Boatman & Other Pond Poems.* Houghton Mifflin, 2005. / Sidman, Joyce. *This Is Just to Say: Poems of Apology and Forgiveness.* Houghton Mifflin, 2007.
SUBJECTS: BIOLOGY—POETRY. NATURE—POETRY. POETRY—SINGLE AUTHOR. SCIENCE—POETRY.

[J] | | | | |
You Read to Me, I'll Read to You Very Short Fables to Read Together. **Hoberman, Mary Ann. Illus. by Michael Emberley. Little, Brown, 2010. {ISBN-13: 978-0-316-04117-1; 32p.} 811 (Gr. PreK-3)**
Hoberman's spirited "You Read to Me, I'll Read to You" series of retold stories-in-rhyme for two voices has been a godsend for getting pairs of kids reading with expression, fluency, proficiency, and joy. In this irresistible new collection, thirteen fables are retold from the contrasting points of view of animal duos. The first poem is an introduction, explaining how to perform the fables with a partner. Included are the iconic ("The Boy Who Cried Wolf," "The Lion and the Mouse") and the less known ("The Ant and the Dove," "The Fox and the Stork"). The first fable is instantly familiar. "I'm a tortoise" it says in orange print on the left side of the page. "I'm a hare. You're a slowpoke," it says in green on the right. "I don't care" is the next left-hand line, completing the rhyme. In the accompanying series of adorable pencil and watercolor illustrations, the sensible green tortoise and the jazzy brown rabbit, clad in bike shorts and shades, dare each other to a race. Just look at that cocky, hyperactive hare, stretched out atop his bike, shoulders on the handlebars, rear on the seat, legs sticking straight out, having a snooze as the tortoise wheels past him. You know who's going to win this race. The moral is meant to be read in unison by both players: "Moral: Just keep up an even pace. / Slow and steady wins the race."
GERM: These are marvelous to read in pairs, sure, but if you have a document camera, try them as a choral reading, splitting your group in half. Afterwards, pairs can pick and practice a poem to perform. Compare the selections with their corresponding prose counterparts. With "The Lion and the Mouse," you can also pull in Jerry Pinkney's wordless Caldecott winner, *The Lion & the Mouse.* With "The Fox and the Grapes," and its dialogue between the dapper-suited fox and a bunch of personified purple grapes, read Margie Palatini's *Lousy, Rotten, Stinkin' Grapes.*
RELATED TITLES: Hoberman, Mary Ann. *It's Simple, Said Simon.* Knopf, 2001. / Hoberman, Mary Ann. *The Llama Who Had No Pajama: 100 Favorite Poems.* Harcourt, 1998. / Hoberman, Mary Ann. *The Seven Silly Eaters.* Harcourt, 1997. / Hoberman, Mary Ann. *You Read to Me, I'll Read to You: Very Short Fairy Tales to Read Together.* Little, Brown, 2004. / Hoberman, Mary Ann. *You Read to Me, I'll Read to You: Very Short Mother Goose Tales to Read Together.* Little, Brown, 2005. / Hoberman, Mary Ann. *You Read to Me, I'll Read to You: Very Short Stories to Read Together.* Little, Brown, 2001. / Morpurgo, Michael. *The McElderry Book of Aesop's Fables.* McElderry, 2005. / Palatini, Margie. *Lousy Rotten Stinkin' Grapes.* Simon & Schuster, 2009. / Pinkney, Jerry. *Aesop's Fables.* SeaStar, 2000. / Pinkney, Jerry. *The Lion & the Mouse.* Little, Brown, 2009.
SUBJECTS: AESOP. ANIMALS—POETRY. FABLES. FOLKLORE—POETRY. LANGUAGE ARTS. POETRY—SINGLE AUTHOR. READER'S THEATER. STORIES IN RHYME.

BOOKS JUDY CHOSE NOT TO REVIEW
FOR THIS PROGRAM

NOTE: There's no sane way to review 200+ children's books in a one-day workshop, so I had to omit those titles I felt we could live without. Although many of these titles are worth buying for a library collection, none were on my personal "Best of the Year" list. Since the **WINNERS!** Conference is geared to books for grades K-6, I also omitted most of the Young Adult titles for grades 7 and up. (See that list on page 67.)

[j] | | | |S| ***Alchemy and Meggy Swann.*** Cushman, Karen. Clarion, 2010. {ISBN-13: 978-0-547-23184-6; 167p.} FIC (Gr. 5-8)

[j] |A| | | | ***Back of the Bus.*** Reynolds, Aaron. Illus. by Floyd Cooper. Philomel, 2010. {ISBN-13: 978-0-399-25091-0; 32p.} E (Gr. 1-4)

[j] |A| | | | ***The Bat Scientists.*** Carson, Mary Kay. Illus. by Tom Uhlman. Houghton Mifflin, 2010. {ISBN-13: 978-0-547-19956-6; 79p.} 599.4 (Gr. 6-8)

[j] | | | |S| ***Benno and the Night of Broken Glass.*** Wiviott, Meg. Illus. by Josée Bisaillon. Kar-Ben, 2010. {ISBN-13: 978-0-8225-9929-6; 32p.} E (Gr. 2-5)

[j] |A| | | | ***Black Elk's Vision: A Lakota Story.*** Nelson, S. D. Illus. by the author. Abrams, 2010. {ISBN-13: 978-0-8109-8399-1; 47p.} 978.004 (Gr. 4-8)

[j] | | | |S| ***The Chicken Thief.*** Rodriguez, Béatrice. Illus. by the author. Enchanted Lion, 2010. {ISBN-13: 978-1-59270-092-9; 26p.} E (Gr. PreK-1)

[j] |A|B| | | *Countdown.* Wiles, Deborah. Scholastic, 2010. {ISBN-13: 978-0-545-10605-4; 377p.} FIC (Gr. 5-7)

[j] |A| | | | ***Dear Primo: A Letter to My Cousin.*** Tonatiuh, Duncan. Illus. by the author. Abrams, 2010. {ISBN-13: 978-0-8109-3872-4; 32p.} E (Gr. 1-3) 2011 Belpré Illustrator Honor

[j] |A| | | | ***Departure Time.*** Matti, Truus. Trans. by Nancy Forest-Flier. Namelos, 2010. {ISBN-13: 978-1-60898-087-1; 214p.} FIC (Gr. 5-8) 2011 Batchelder Award

[j] | | | |S| ***Don't Want to Go!*** Hughes, Shirley. Illus. by the author. Candlewick, 2010. {ISBN-13: 978-0-7636-5091-9; 32p.} E (Gr. PreK-K)

[j] | | | |S| ***Emily's Fortune.*** Naylor, Phyllis Reynolds. Illus. by Ross Collins. Delacorte, 2010. {ISBN-13: 978-0-385-73616-9; 147p.} FIC (Gr. 3-6)

[j] |A| | |S| ***The Fantastic Secret of Owen Jester.*** O'Connor, Barbara. Farrar/Frances Foster, 2010. {ISBN-13: 978-0-374-36850-0; 168p.} FIC (Gr. 4-7)

[j] |A| | | | ***Farm.*** Cooper, Elisha. Illus. by the author. Orchard, 2010. {ISBN-13: 978-0-545-07075-1; 40p.} E (Gr. PreK-3)

[_] |A| | | | ***Fiesta Babies.*** Tafolla, Carmen. Illus. by Amy Córdova. Tricycle, 2010. {ISBN-13: 978-1-58246-372-8; 20p.} E (Gr. PreK) 2011 Belpré Illustrator Honor

[j] | |B| | | ***Fort Mosé and the Story of the Man Who Built the First Free Black Settlement in Colonial America.*** Turner, Glennette Tilley. Abrams, 2010. {ISBN-13: 978-0-81094-056-7; 42p.} 975.9 (Gr. 4-8)

[j] |A| | | | ***Grandma's Gift.*** Velasquez, Eric. Illus. by the author. Walker, 2010. {ISBN-13: 978-0-8027-2083-2; 32p.} E (Gr. 1-3) 2011 Belpré Illustrator Medal

[j] |A| | | | ***Growing Patterns: Fibonacci Numbers in Nature.*** Campbell, Sarah. Photos by Sarah Campbell and Richard Campbell. Boyds Mills, 2010. {ISBN-13: 978-1-59078-752-6; 32p.} 512.7 (Gr. 2-5)

[j] | | |H| | ***Happy Birthday, Sophie Hartley.*** Greene, Stephanie. Clarion, 2010. {ISBN-13: 978-0-547-25128-8; 127p.} FIC (Gr. 3-5)

[j] | | | |S| ***Here Comes the Garbage Barge!*** Winter, Jonah. Illus. by Red Nose Studio. Schwartz & Wade, 2010. {ISBN-13: 978-0-375-85218-3; 34p.} E (Gr. 1-4)

[j] | | | | | ***Hereville: How Mirka Got Her Sword.*** Deutsch, Barry. Illus. by Jake Richmond. Abrams/Amulet, 2010. {ISBN-13: 978-0-8109-8422-6; 137p.} 741.5 (Gr. 4-8) 2011 Sydney Taylor Book Award for Older Readers

[j] |A| | | | ***Hip-Pocket Papa.*** Markle, Sandra. Illus. by Alan Marks. Charlesbridge, 2010. {ISBN-13: 978-1-57091-708-0; 32p.} 597.8 (Gr. K-3) 2011 Charlotte Zolotow Honor Book

[j] |A|B| | | *The Hive Detectives: Chronicle of a Honey Bee Catastrophe.* Burns, Loree Griffin. Houghton Mifflin, 2010. {ISBN-13: 978-0-547-15231-8; 66p.} 638 (Gr. 5-8)

[j] |A| | | | *How to Clean a Hippopotamus: A Look at Unusual Animal Partnerships.* Jenkins, Steve, and Robin Page. Houghton Mifflin, 2010. {ISBN-13: 978-0-547-24515-7; 32p.} 591.7 (Gr. 1-3)

[j] | | |H| | *I Know Here.* Croza, Laurel. Illus. by Matt James. Groundwood, 2010. {ISBN-13: 978-0-88899-923-8; 32p.} E (Gr. 1-4) 2010 Boston Globe-Horn Book Award for Picture Book

[j] | | | |S| *Insect Detective.* Voake, Steve. Illus. by Charlotte Voake. Candlewick, 2010. {ISBN-13: 978-0-7636-4447-5; 32p.} 595.7 (Gr. PreK-2)

[j] | | | | | *Jimi Sounds Like a Rainbow: A Story of the Young Jimi Hendrix* by Gary Golio, Gary. Illus. by Javaka Steptoe. Clarion, 2010. {ISBN-13: 978-0-618-85279-6; 32p.} B (Gr. 3-6) 2011 Coretta Scott King Illustrator Honor

[j] | | | |S| *Keeper.* Appelt, Kathi. Illus. by August Hall. Atheneum, 2010. {ISBN-13: 978-1-4169-5060-8; 399p.} FIC (Gr. 4-7)

[j] | |B| | | *The Last Best Days of Summer.* Hobbs, Valerie. Farrar/Frances Foster, 2010. {ISBN-13: 978-0-374-34670-6; 197p.} FIC (Gr. 5-8)

[j] |A| | | | *Me, Frida.* Novesky, Amy. Illus. by David Diaz. Abrams, 2010. {ISBN-13: 978-0-8109-8969-6; 32p.} B (Gr. 3-6) 2011 Belpré Illustrator Honor

[j] |A|B| | | *Meanwhile: Pick Any Path: 3,856 Story Possibilities.* Shiga, Jason. Illus. by the author. Abrams/Amulet, 2010. {ISBN-13: 978-0-8109-8423-3; unp.} FIC (Gr. 4-6)

[j] | | |H| | *Mirror.* Baker, Jeanne. Illus. by the author. Candlewick, 2010. {ISBN-13: 978-0-7636-4848-0; 40p.} E (Gr. K-4)

[j] | |B| | | *Miss Lina's Ballerinas.* Maccarone, Grace. Illus. by Christine Davenier. Feiwel and Friends, 2010. {ISBN-13: 978-0-312-38243-8; 40p.} E (Gr. PreK-3)

[j] | | | |S| *Monsters Eat Whiny Children.* Kaplan, Bruce Eric. Illus. by the author. Simon & Schuster, 2010. {ISBN-13: 978-1-4169-8689-8; 34p.} E (Gr. K-2)

[j] |A| | | | *The Night Fairy.* Schlitz, Laura Amy. Illus. by Angela Barrett. Candlewick, 2010. {ISBN-13: 978-0-7636-3674-6; 117p.} FIC (Gr. 2-5)

[j] |A| | | | *90 Miles to Havana.* Flores-Galbis, Enrique. Roaring Brook, 2010. {ISBN-13: 978-1-59643-168-3; 292p.} FIC (Gr. 4-7) 2011 Belpré Author Honor

[j] | |B|H| | *Nini Lost and Found.* Lobel, Anita. Illus. by the author. Knopf, 2010. {ISBN-13: 978-0-375-85880-2; 34p.} E (Gr. PreK-1) 2010 Booklist Editors' Choice "Top of the List," Youth Picture Book

[j] |A| | |S| *Ninth Ward.* Rhodes, Jewell Parker. Little, Brown, 2010. {ISBN-13: 978-0-316-04307-6; 217p.} FIC (Gr. 5-8) 2011 Coretta Scott King Author Honor

[j] |A| | | | *¡Ole! Flamenco.* Ancona, George. Photos by the author. Lee & Low, 2010. {ISBN-13: 978-1-60060-361-7; 46p.} 793.3 (Gr. 3-6) 2011 Belpré Author Honor

[j] | | | |S| *Olympians 2: Athena, Grey-eyed Goddess.* O'Connor, George. First Second, 2010. {ISBN-13: 978-1-59643-649-7; 76p.} 741.5 (Gr. 5-9)

[j] |A| | | | *Pecan Pie Baby.* Woodson, Jacqueline. Illus. by Sophie Blackall. Putnam, 2010. {ISBN-13: 978-0-399-23987-8; 32p.} E (Gr. K-2)

[j] | |B| | | *A Pig Parade Is a Terrible Idea.* Black, Michael Ian. Illus. by Kevin Hawkes. Simon & Schuster, 2010. {ISBN-13: 978-1-416-97922-7; 32p.} E (Gr. PreK-2)

[j] | |B| | | *Pingpong Perry Experiences How a Book Is Made.* Donovan, Sandra. Picture Window, 2010. {ISBN-13: 978-1-40485-759-9; 24p.} 002 (Gr. 1-4)

[j] | |B| | | *Rain School.* Rumford, James. Illus. by the author. Houghton Mifflin, 2010. {ISBN-13: 978-0-547-24307-8; 32p.} E (Gr. PreK-2)

[j] |A| | | | *Ruth and the Green Book.* Ramsey, Calvin Alexander. Illus. by Floyd Cooper. Carolrhoda, 2010. {ISBN-13: 978-0-7613-5255-6; 32p.} E (Gr. 2-5)

[j] |A| | | | *Saltypie: A Choctaw Journey from Darkness into Light.* Tingle, Tim. Illus. by Karen Clarkson. Cinco Puntos, 2010. {ISBN-13: 978-1-933693-67-5; 40p.} 973.04 (Gr. 3-6)

[j] | | | |S| *Seasons.* Blexbolex. Trans. from French by Claudia Bedrick. illus. by the author. Enchanted Lion, 2010. {ISBN-13: 978-1-59270-095-0; 180p.} E (Gr. PreK-1)

[j] | | | | | *Seeds of Change.* Johnson, Jen Cullerton. Illus. by Sonia Lynn Sadler. Lee & Low, 2010. {ISBN-13: 978-1-60060-367-9; 40p.} B (Gr. 1-5) 2011 Coretta Scott King/John Steptoe New Talent (Illustrator) Award

BOOKS JUDY CHOSE NOT TO REVIEW FOR THIS PROGRAM, cont.

[j] |A| | | | *Shadow.* Lee, Suzy. Illus. by the author. Chronicle, 2010. {ISBN-13: 978-0-8118-7280-5; 36p.} E (Gr. PreK-1)

[j] | |B| | | *Sleepover at Gramma's House.* Joosse, Barbara. Illus. by Jan Jutte. Philomel, 2010. {ISBN-13: 978-0-399-25261-7; 38p.} E (Gr. PreK-1)

[j] | |B| | | *Take Me with You.* Marsden, Carolyn. Candlewick, 2010. {ISBN-13: 978-0-7636-3739-2; 160p.} FIC (Gr. 4-7)

[j] | | | |S| *13 Treasures.* Harrison, Michelle. Little, Brown, 2010. {ISBN-13: 978-0-316-04148-5; 355p.} FIC (Gr. 5-8)

[j] |A| | | | *Trickster: Native American Tales: A Graphic Collection.* Dembicki, Matt, ed. Fulcrum, 2010. {ISBN-13: 978-1-55591-724-1; 231p.} 398.2 (Gr. 6-12)

[j] |A| | | | *Tuck Me In.* Hacohen, Dean. Illus. by Sherry Scharschmidt. Candlewick, 2010. {ISBN-13: 978-0-7636-4728-5; 40p.} E (Gr. PreK-1)

[j] | |B| | | *Tumbleweed Skies.* Sherrard, Valerie. Fitzhenry & Whiteside, 2010. {ISBN-13: 978-1-554-55113-2; 153p.} FIC (Gr. 3-6)

[j] | |B| | | *The Unsinkable Walker Bean.* Renier, Aaron. Illus. by the author. First Second, 2010. {ISBN-13: 978-1-59643-453-0; 191p.} 741.5 (Gr. 4-7)

[j] | | |H| | *The Village Garage.* Karas, G. Brian. Illus. by the author. Henry Holt/Christy Ottaviano, 2010. {ISBN-13: 978-0-8050-8716-1; 32p.} E (Gr. PreK-2)

[j] |A| | | | *We Shall Overcome: A Song That Changed the World.* Stotts, Stuart. Illus. by Terrance Cummings. Clarion, 2010. {ISBN-13: 978-0-547-18210-0; 72p.} 782.42162 (Gr. 4-8)

[j] | | | |S| *What If?* Seeger, Laura Vaccaro. Illus. by the author. Roaring Brook/Neal Porter, 2010. {ISBN-13: 978-1-59643-398-4; 32p.} E (Gr. PreK-1)

[j] |A| | | | *Yucky Worms.* French, Vivian. Illus. by Jessica Ahlberg. Candlewick, 2010. {ISBN-13: 978-0-7636-4446-8; 28p.} E (Gr. PreK-2)

[j] | |B| | | *Zora and Me.* Bond, Victoria Bond, and T. R. Simon. Candlewick, 2010. {ISBN-13: 978-0-763-64300-3; 170p.} FIC (Gr. 5-8) 2011 Coretta Scott King/John Steptoe New Talent (Author) Award

YOUNG ADULT BOOKS FOR GRADES 7 AND UP
THAT WERE ON THIS YEAR'S LISTS

(With a couple of exceptions, WINNERS! only covers books
for Grades PreK through 6)

| |B| | | *After Ever After.* Sonnenblick, Jordan. Scholastic, 2010. {ISBN-13: 978-0-439-83706-4; 260p.} FIC (Gr. 6-8) 2011 Schneider Family Book Award for Middle School

| | | |S| *Annexed.* Dogar, Sharon. Houghton Mifflin, 2010. {ISBN-13: 978-0-547-50195-6; 341p.} FIC (Gr. 8-12)

| |B|H| | *As Easy as Falling off the Face of the Earth.* Perkins, Lynne Rae. Illus. by the author. Greenwillow, 2010. {ISBN-13: 978-0-06-187091-0; 352p.} FIC (Gr. 7-12)

| | | |S| *Black Hole Sun.* Gill, David Macinnis. Greenwillow, 2010. {ISBN-13: 978-0-06-167304-7; 340p.} FIC (Gr. 8-12)

| |B| | | *Borrowed Names: Poems About Laura Ingalls Wilder, Madam C. J. Walker, and Their Daughters.* Atkins, Jeannine. Henry Holt, 2010. {ISBN-13: 978-0-8050-8934-9; 209p.} 811 (Gr. 7-9)

| | | |S| *Confessions of the Sullivan Sisters.* Standiford, Natalie. Scholastic, 2010. {ISBN-13: 978-0-545-10710-5; 313p.} FIC (Gr. 8-12)

| | |H|S| *A Conspiracy of Kings.* Turner, Megan Whalen. Greenwillow, 2010. {ISBN-13: 978-0-06-187093-4; 316p.} FIC (Gr. 7-10) 2010 Boston Globe-Horn Book Honor for Fiction and Poetry

| |B| | | *The Curse of the Wendigo.* Yancey, Rick. Simon & Schuster, 2010. {ISBN-13: 978-1-416-98450-4; 424p.} FIC (Gr. 9-12)

|A|B| |S| *Fever Crumb.* Reeve, Philip. Scholastic, 2010. {ISBN-13: 978-0-545-20719-5; 325p.} FIC (Gr. 6-9)

| | | |S| *Finnikin of the Rock.* Marchetta, Melina. Candlewick, 2010. {ISBN-13: 978-0-7636-4361-4; 399p.} FIC (Gr. 7-12)

|A| | | | *The Firefly Letters: A Suffragette's Journey to Cuba.* Engle, Margarita. Henry Holt, 2010. {ISBN-13: 978-0-8050-9082-6; 151p.} 811 (Gr. 7-12) 2011 Belpré Author Honor

| |B| | | *For the Win.* Doctorow, Cory. Tor, 2010. {ISBN-13: 978-0-765-32216-6; 475p.} FIC (Gr. 10-12)

| | |H| | *Forge.* Anderson, Laurie Halse. Atheneum, 2010. {ISBN-13: 978-1-41696-144-4; 297p.} FIC (Gr. 6-8)

| | | |S| *Frederick Douglass: A Noble Life.* Adler, David A. Holiday House, 2010. {ISBN-13: 978-0-8234-2056-8; 138p.} B (Gr. 7-12)

| | | |S| *The Good, the Bad, and the Barbie: A Doll's History and Her Impact on Us.* Stone, Tanya Lee. Viking, 2010. {ISBN-13: 978-0-670-01187-2; 130p.} 688.7 (Gr. 7-12)

| | | |S| *The Grimm Legacy.* Shulman, Polly. Putnam, 2010. {ISBN-13: 978-0-399-25096-5; 325p.} FIC (Gr. 6-9)

| | |H|S| *Incarceron.* Fisher, Catherine. Dial, 2010. {ISBN-13: 978-0-8037-3396-1; 442p.} FIC (Gr. 7-10)

| | | |S| *King of Ithaka.* Barrett, Tracy. Henry Holt, 2010. {ISBN-13: 978-0-8050-8969-1; 261p.} FIC (Gr. 8-12)

| | | | | *Lockdown.* Myers, Walter Dean. HarperTeen, 2010. {ISBN-13: 978-0-06-121480-6; 247p.} FIC (Gr. 7-12) 2011 Coretta Scott King Author Honor; 2010 National Book Award Finalist

| |B| | | *The Marbury Lens.* Smith, Andrew. Feiwel and Friends, 2010. {ISBN-13: 978-0-312-61342-6; 358p.} FIC (Gr. 10-12)

| |B| | | *Mockingjay.* Collins, Suzanne. Scholastic, 2010. {ISBN-13: 978-0-439-02351-1; 390p.} FIC (Gr. 7-12)

| |B| | | *Monsters of Men.* (Chaos Walking series, Book Three) Ness, Patrick. Candlewick, 2010. {ISBN-13: 978-0-763-64751-3; 608p.} FIC (Gr. 9-12)

|A|B| | | *Nothing.* Teller, Janne. Trans. from the Danish by Martin Aitken. Atheneum, 2010. {ISBN-13: 978-1-4169-8579-2; 227p.} FIC (Gr. 7-12) 2011 Batchelder Honor and 2011 Printz Honor

| | |H|S| *The Notorious Benedict Arnold: A True Story of Adventure, Heroism, & Treachery.* Sheinkin, Steve. Roaring Brook/Flash Point, 2010. {ISBN-13: 978-1-59643-486-8; 337p.} B (Gr. 7-12)

| | | |S| *Num8ers.* Ward, Rachel. Scholastic/Chicken House, 2010. {ISBN-13: 978-0-545-14299-1; 325p.} FIC (Gr. 8-12)

| | |S| *Ostrich Boys.* Gray, Keith. Random, 2010. {ISBN-13: 978-0-375-85843-7; 297p.} FIC (Gr. 8-12)

| |B| | | *Pathfinder.* Card, Orson Scott. Simon & Schuster/Simon Pulse, 2010. {ISBN-13: 978-1-416-99176-2; 662p.} FIC (Gr. 8-12)

| | | |S| *Revolution.* Donnelly, Jennifer. Delacorte, 2010. {ISBN-13: 978-0-385-73763-0; 496p.} FIC (Gr. 8-12)

| | |H| | *Revolver.* Sedgwick, Marcus. Roaring Brook, 2010. {ISBN-13: 978-1-59643-592-6; 204p.} FIC (Gr. 8-12) 2011 Printz Honor

| |B| |S| *The Ring of Solomon: A Bartimaeus Novel.* Stroud, Jonathan. Hyperion/Disney, 2010. {ISBN-13: 978-1-4231-2372-9; 416p.} FIC (Gr. 9-12)

| |B| | | *Set to Sea.* Weing, Drew. Illus. by the author. Fantagraphics, 2010. {ISBN-13: 978-1-606-99368-2; 144p.} FIC (Gr. 8-12)

|A| | | | *Ship Breaker.* Bacigalupi, Paolo. Little, Brown, 2010. {ISBN-13: 978-0-316-05621-2; 326p.} FIC (Gr. 7-12) 2011 Printz Medal; 2010 National Book Award Finalist

| |B| | | *Sir Charlie: Chaplin, the Funniest Man in the World.* Fleischman, Sid. Greenwillow, 2010. {ISBN-13: 978-0-0618-9640-8; 268p.} B (Gr. 6-10)

| | |H| | *The Sky Is Everywhere.* Nelson, Jandy. Dial, 2010. {ISBN-13: 978-0-8037-3495-1; 275p.} FIC (Gr. 8-12)

| | | |S| *Sugar Changed the World: A Story of Magic, Spice, Slavery, Freedom, and Science.* Aronson, Marc, and Marina Budhos. Clarion, 2010. {ISBN-13: 978-0-618-57492-6; 166p.} 664.109 (Gr. 8-12)

|A|B|H|S| *They Called Themselves the K.K.K.: The Birth of an American Terrorist Group.* Bartoletti, Susan Campbell. Houghton Mifflin, 2010. {ISBN-13: 978-0-618-44033-7; 172p.} 322.420973 (Gr. 7-12) 2011 YALSA Award for Excellence in Nonfiction for Young Adults; 2010 Booklist Editors' Choice "Top of the List," Youth Nonfiction Book

| |B| |S| *The Things a Brother Knows.* Reinhardt, Dana. Random House/Wendy Lamb, 2010. {ISBN-13: 978-0-375-84455-3; 245p.} FIC (Gr. 8-12) 2011 Sydney Taylor Book Award for Teen Readers

| | | |S| *Three Rivers Rising: A Novel of the Johnstown Flood.* Richards, James. Knopf, 2010. {ISBN-13: 978-0-375-85885-7; 293p.} FIC (Gr. 7-12)

|A| | | | *A Time of Miracles.* Bondoux, Anne-Laure. Trans. from the French by Y. Maudet. Delacorte, 2010. {ISBN-13: 978-0-385-73922-1; 180p.} FIC (Gr. 7-12) 2011 Batchelder Medal

| | | |S| *Time You Let Me In: 25 Poets Under 25.* Nye, Naomi Shihab. Greenwillow, 2010. {ISBN-13: 978-0-06-189637-8; 236p.} 811.608 (Gr. 8-12)

| | | |S| *Toads and Diamonds.* Tomlinson, Heather. Henry Holt, 2010. {ISBN-13: 978-0-8050-8968-4; 278p.} FIC (Gr. 7-12)

| | | |S| *Trash.* Mulligan, Andy. Random/David Fickling, 2010. {ISBN-13: 978-0-385-75214-5; 232p.} FIC (Gr. 7-10)

| |B| | | *Unraveling Freedom: The Battle for Democracy on the Homefront during World War I.* Bausum, Ann. National Geographic, 2010. {ISBN-13: 978-1-42630-702-7; 88p.} 940.373 (Gr. 8-11)

| | |H|S| *The War to End All Wars: World War I.* Freedman, Russell. Clarion, 2010. {ISBN-13: 978-0-547-02686-2; 176p.} 940.3 (Gr. 7-12)

| |B| | | *Warriors in the Crossfire.* Flood, Bo. Front Street, 2010. {ISBN-13: 978-1-59078-661-1; 142p.} FIC (Gr. 6-9)

| | |H| | *The White Horse Trick.* Thompson, Kate. Greenwillow, 2010. {ISBN-13: 978-0-06-200416-1; 405p.} FIC (Gr. 7-10)

| | | |S| *Wicked Girls: A Novel of the Salem Witch Trials.* Hemphill, Stephanie. HarperCollins/Balzer & Bray, 2010. {ISBN-13: 978-0-06-185328-9; 408p.} FIC (Gr. 9-12)

|A|B| | | *Yummy: The Last Days of a Southside Shorty.* Neri, G. Illus. by Randy DuBurke. Lee & Low, 2010. {ISBN-13: 978-1-584-30267-4; 94p.} FIC (Gr. 8-12) 2011 Coretta Scott King Author Honor

| | | |S| *Zombies vs. Unicorns.* Black, Holly, and Justine Larbalestier, eds. McElderry, 2010. {ISBN-13: 978-1-4169-8953-0; 415p.} FIC (Gr. 9-12)

CELEBRATING

CHILDREN'S BOOKS

THINGS TO CONSIDER WHEN READING AND DISCUSSING BOOKS

Adapted from *Books Kids Will Sit Still For 3*
(Libraries Unlimited, 2006) by Judy Freeman

Here is my personal list of evaluative guideposts that I use when pondering the strengths and weaknesses of a new book.

PLOT — Plan of action; holds story together; how the story is arranged. Encompasses exposition, problem, rising action, conflict, climax, falling action (dénouement), resolution.

SETTING — Past, present, or future. Specific place, generic or universal setting; vital to the story (integral setting), or an unimportant backdrop.

CHARACTERIZATION — What types of protagonists and antagonists? (Flat, stereotyped, fully developed, round, etc.) How presented? (Through narration, character's conversations with self or others, character's thoughts, character's actions, physical description.) Major and minor; static (unchanging) or dynamic (changing).

POINT OF VIEW — How the reader learns of the events, character motivation, and climax. Told in first person, second person (rare), third person; omniscient, limited omniscient, objective.

THEME — Author's purpose in writing the story, going beyond the general plot; the underlying truths or lessons to be learned about life, stated explicitly or implicitly.

STYLE — What makes writing memorable. Smooth, fast-paced, full of vivid description of action; or stilted, moralistic, sentimental, didactic, and patronizing to the child reader. How is the story arranged: chronological, with flashbacks, episodic.

FORMAT — Shape, size, design of book; special features (pop-up, gatefold or die-cut pages, unusual cover or dust jacket design)

ILLUSTRATIONS — How do they complement / extend text? What style / medium is used?

COMPARISONS — With other books of same topic, theme, genre, style, author, etc.

20 BASIC QUESTIONS TO ASK YOURSELF
WHEN EVALUATING A NEW BOOK

Adapted from *Books Kids Will Sit Still For 3*
(Libraries Unlimited, 2006) by Judy Freeman

1.   Is the plot original or groundbreaking or surprising? Or is it predictable or preachy or overdone?

2.   How is the plot presented? (Flashback, chronological, episodic, etc.) Could you follow the thread of the story throughout?

3.   Do all of the events and supporting details make sense and work, within the context of the story? Are the facts accurate, even in a fantasy?

4.   Does the author have a recognizable narrative style? What is distinctive about it? Does it flow naturally with interesting language, varied sentence structure, and appeal to the reader, or does it feel clunky or choppy or soporific? What tone does the author use?

5.   Point of view: Who narrates the book? Is the narration believable? Were you able to lose yourself in the story and experience a willing suspension of disbelief?

6.   Are the main characters worth getting to know? Can you visualize them? Do you feel you got to know them well?

7.   Does the setting play an important part? If so, is it visually vivid, as in sci fi and fantasy, which may take place in an unfamiliar world?

8.   Are there any parts that you feel are very well or very poorly written? Did you want to keep reading without stopping, or did you keep putting the book down? As author James Patterson would say, does this book have Narrative Power that propels the book and makes you keep turning the pages?

9.   Is the ending satisfying, or does the story fall apart midway? Is it an open or closed ending?

10. What is the theme? Is it intuitive to the reader or thought-provoking, or didactic or moralistic? Will children grasp what the author wanted to say?

11. Do the illustrations fit the story? Do they extend the story or just restate it?

12. Is there anything remarkable about the format?

20 BASIC QUESTIONS TO ASK YOURSELF WHEN EVALUATING A NEW BOOK, cont.

13.   Does the cover work? Will it turn kids on, off, or leave them cold?

14.   When you think of the book, which scene or character first comes to mind? Will you think about this book in a week? A month? A year? Forever?

15.   What did you enjoy most/least about the book?

16.   What grades/age levels does this book best fit?

17.   What types of children will want to read this book and why?

18.   Do you agree with the published reviews (***Booklist***, ***Hornbook***, ***School Library Journal***, ***Publishers Weekly***, ***Kirkus***, ***The New York Times***, etc.)? Do the published reviews agree with each other?

19.   How can you use/present this book with children?

20.   What other books do you have on this topic or theme, or in this style, to which you can link this title for readers? How will this book strengthen your collection?

WINNERS & LOSERS

The "Experts" liked this book a lot. They are grown-ups. You are a kid. Kids are the ones who are going to read this book. The "Experts" are not always right. Sometimes they forget or misjudge what kids will like. When you read this book, give an honest opinion of what you think of it.

*AUTHOR*_____

TITLE _____

After completing your book, write a paragraph or more explaining exactly what you thought of it. You do not need to give a summary of the plot. Instead, consider these points:

THE ILLUSTRATIONS

THE STORY

TO WHOM WOULD YOU RECOMMEND THIS? WHY?

DOES THIS BOOK DESERVE TO BE CONSIDERED A "WINNER" OR A "LOSER"? EXPLAIN WHY.

BE VERY HONEST.

_____
_____
_____
_____
_____
_____
_____
_____
_____
_____
_____
_____
_____
_____
_____
_____
_____

Judy Freeman's LIST OF MEMORABLE
AUTHORS & ILLUSTRATORS
Updated Spring, 2011

In *Books Kids Will Sit Still For*, I drew up a list of authors and illustrators who had made a lasting contribution to children's literature and had accumulated a significant body of work. I broke the lists into suggested grade levels to assist teachers and librarians looking to institute monthly or weekly author/illustrator studies, either for reading aloud or having students familiarize themselves with an author's books. I update this list every year, and while it is in no way comprehensive, I hope you can use it as a way to familiarize yourself with some of the best in the children's literature field and to introduce new and worthy writers and artists to your media-dazed students. For additional suggestions, be sure to look at the lists that are one grade level above and below your students' grade, depending on their reading and maturity levels.

(Key: Author = A, Illustrator = I, Author/Illustrator = A/I)

PRESCHOOL, KINDERGARTEN, AND GRADE 1:

Kathi Appelt (A), Jim Arnosky (A/I), Jose Aruego (A/I), Frank Asch (A/I), Mary Jane Auch (A/I), Jim Aylesworth (A), Keith Baker (A/I), Molly Bang (A/I), Byron Barton (A/I), Bonny Becker (A), Robert J. Blake (A/I), Harry Bliss (I), Barbara Bottner (A), Jan Brett (A/I), Norman Bridwell (A/I), Marc Brown (A/I), Anthony Browne (A/I), Nick Bruel (A/I), Denise Brunkus (I), John Burningham (A/I), Toni Buzzeo, (A), Janell Cannon (A/I), Nancy Carlson (A/I), Eric Carle (A/I), Denys Cazet (A/I), Lauren Child (A/I), Eileen Christelow (A/I), Henry Cole (I), Ying Chang Compestine (A), Joy Cowley (A), Donald Crews (A/I), Doreen Cronin (A), Susan Stevens Crummel (A/I), Katie Davis (A/I), Anna Dewdney (A/I), Ariane Dewey (A/I), Arthur Dorros (A/I), Olivier Dunrea (A/I), Pamela Duncan Edwards (A), Tim Egan (A/I), Richard Egielski (A/I), Lois Ehlert (A/I), Michael Emberley (A/I), Lisa Campbell Ernst (A/I), Ian Falconer (A/I), Cathryn Falwell (A/I), Jules Feiffer (A/I), Candace Fleming (A), Denise Fleming (A/I), Brian Floca (A/I), Mem Fox (A), Saxton Freymann (A/I), Marla Frazee (A/I), Don Freeman (A/I), Bob Graham (A/I), Emily Gravett (A/I), Kevin Henkes (A/I), Amy Hest (A), Tad Hills (A/I), Mary Ann Hoberman (A), Holly Hobbie (A/I), Arthur Howard (A/I), Shirley Hughes (A/I), Pat Hutchins (A/I), Satomi Ichikawa (A/I), Simon James (A/I), Steve Jenkins (A/I), Dolores Johnson (A), Steve Johnson and Lou Fancher (I) / Ann Jonas (A/I), William Joyce (A/I), G. Brian Karas (A/I), Keiko Kasza (A/I), Ezra Jack Keats (A/I), Holly Keller (A/I), Eric A. Kimmel (A), Elisa Kleven (A/I), Daniel Kirk (A/I), David Kirk (A/I), Jarrett J. Krosoczka (A/I), Loreen Leedy (A/I), Helen Lester (A), Betsy Lewin (A/I), Tom Lichtenheld (A/I), Grace Lin (A/I), Leo Lionni (A/I), Arnold Lobel (A/I), Anita Lobel (A/I), Jonathan London (A), Loren Long (I), Suse MacDonald (A/I), James Marshall (A/I), Bill Martin, Jr. (A), Petra Mathers (A/I), Mercer Mayer (A/I), Barbara McClintock (A/I), Gerald McDermott (A/I), Patricia C. McKissack (A), Kate McMullan (A) and James McMullan (I), David McPhail (A/I), Holly Meade (I/I), Pierr Morgan (I), Barry Moser (A/I), Mother Goose (A), Roxie Munro (I) / Robert Munsch (A), Lynn Munsinger (I), Jon J Muth (A,/I), Kadir Nelson (I), Robert Neubecker (A), Vincent Nguyen (I), Laura Numeroff (A), Jane O'Connor (A), Helen Oxenbury (A/I), Margie Palatini (A/I), Leslie Patricelli (A/I), Lynne Rae Perkins (A/I), Wendy Pfeffer, Dav Pilkey (A/I), Daniel Pinkwater (A/I), Beatrix Potter (A/I), Giselle Potter (I), Robin Pulver (A), Chris Raschka (A/I), Peggy Rathmann (A/I), Eric Rohmann (A/I), Barry Root (I), Amy Krouse Rosenthal (A), Karen Rostoker-Gruber (A), Marisabina Russo (A/I), Carole Lexa Schaefer (A), Amy Schwartz (A/I), Laura Vaccaro Seeger (A/I), Maurice Sendak (A/I), David Shannon (A/I), Marc Simont (A/I), Marilyn Singer (A), Peter Sís (A/I), Joseph Slate (A), Brad Sneed (I), Gary Soto (A), Alexander Stadler (A/I), David Ezra Stein (S/I), Janet Stevens (A/I), Philemon Sturges (A), Simms Taback (A/I), Mark Teague (A/I), Jan Thomas (A/I), Bill Thomson (A/I), Martin Waddell (A/I), Eileen Stoll Walsh (A/I), Mélanie Watt (A/I), Rosemary Wells (A/I), Nadine Bernard Westcott (A/I), Bruce Whatley (I), David Wiesner (A/I), Mo Willems (A/I), Vera B. Williams (A/I), Kay Winters (A), Audrey Wood (A/I), Don Wood (A/I), Ed Young (A/I), Harriet Ziefert (A)

LIST OF MEMORABLE AUTHORS & ILLUSTRATORS, cont.

GRADE 2, 3, AND 4 (all authors, unless noted):

David A. Adler, Jon Agee, Hans Christian Andersen, Lynne Barasch, Barbara Bash (A/I), Nic Bishop (A/I), Michael Bond, Don Brown (A/I), Joseph Bruchac, Caralyn Buehner (A) and Mark Buehner (I), Eve Bunting, Stephanie Calmenson, Ann Cameron, Peter Catalanotto (I), Lynne Cherry (A/I), R. Gregory Christie (I), Beverly Cleary, Brock Cole (A/I), Joanna Cole, Raul Colón (I), Ellen Conford, Barbara Cooney (A/I), Pat Cummings (A/I), Roald Dahl, Paula Danziger, Bruce Degen (I), Demi (A/I), Tomie dePaola (A/I), David Diaz (I), Leo & Diane Dillon (A/I), Henrik Drescher (A/I), Tim Egan (A/I), Susan Middleton Elya, Candace Fleming, Douglas Florian (A/I), Edwin Fotheringham (I), Debra Frasier (A/I), Jean Fritz, Tony Fucile (A/I), Stephen Gammell (I), Kristine O'Connell George, Mordicai Gerstein (A/I), Gail Gibbons (A/I), Patricia Reilly Giff, Paul Goble (A/I), Nikki Grimes, Jacob and William Grimm, Brenda Guiberson (A/I), Kevin Hawkes (I), Jennifer L. Holm (A) and Matthew Holm (I), Lee Bennett Hopkins, Deborah Hopkinson, James Howe, Johanna Hurwitz, Trina Schart Hyman (I), Eva Ibbotson, Anne Isaacs, Tony Johnston, Maira Kalman (A/I), Steven Kellogg (A/I), X. J. Kennedy, Barbara Kerley, Rukhsana Khan, Eric A. Kimmel, Dick King-Smith, Rudyard Kipling, Suzy Kline, Kathryn Lasky, Patricia Lauber, Loreen Leedy (A/I), Julius Lester, Elizabeth Levy, Ted Lewin (I), J. Patrick Lewis, Myra Cohn Livingston, Lenore Look, David Macaulay (A/I), Ann M. Martin, Jacqueline Briggs Martin, Rafe Martin, Meghan McCarthy (A/I), Emily Arnold McCully (A/I), Megan McDonald, Susan Meddaugh (A/I), Eve Merriam, A. A. Milne, Claudia Mills, Wendell Minor (I), Tololwa M. Mollel, Pat Mora, Christopher Myers (I), Kadir Nelson (I), Kevin O'Malley (A/I), Mary Pope Osborne, Peggy Parish, Barbara Park, Bill Peet (A/I), Sara Pennypacker, Andrea Davis Pinkney, Brian Pinkney (I), Jerry Pinkney (I), Daniel Pinkwater (A/I), Hanoch Piven (A/I), Patricia Polacco (A/I), Jack Prelutsky, Gloria Rand (A) and Ted Rand (I), James Ransome (I), Deborah Kogan Ray (A/I), Peter H. Reynolds (A/I). James Rumford, Pam Muñoz Ryan, Joanne Ryder, Robert Sabuda (A/I), Louis Sachar, Robert D. San Souci, Allen Say (A/I), S. D. Schindler (I), Jon Scieszka, Brian Selznick (I), Dr. Seuss (A/I), Marjorie Weinman Sharmat, Joyce Sidman, Judy Sierra, Shel Silverstein, Seymour Simon, Peter Sís (A/I), David Small (I), Lane Smith (A/I), Chris K. Soenpiet (I), Gennady Spirin (I), Judith St. George, Diane Stanley (A/I), William Steig (A/I), Sarah Stewart, James Stevenson (A/I), Mark Teague (A/I), Chris Van Allsburg (A/I), Ursula Vernon, Judith Viorst, Bernard Waber (A/I), James Warhola (A/I), E. B. White, Laura Ingalls Wilder, Jeannette Winter (A/I), Jane Yolen, Paul O. Zelinsky (A/I)

GRADE 5 AND 6 (all authors, unless noted):

Arnold Adoff, Lloyd Alexander, Julia Alvarez, Jennifer Armstrong, Avi, Joan Bauer, Marion Dane Bauer, Rhoda Blumberg, Joseph Bruchac, Eve Bunting, Betsy Byars, Andrew Clements, Jane Leslie Conley, Bruce Coville, Sharon Creech, Lynn Curlee (A/I), Christopher Paul Curtis, Karen Cushman, Kate DiCamillo, Frances O'Roark Dowell, Nancy Farmer, Paul Fleischman, Sid Fleischman, Candace Fleming, Russell Freedman, Jack Gantos, Jean Craighead George, Patricia Reilly Giff, Dan Gutman, Mary Downing Hahn, Virginia Hamilton, Kevin Henkes, Karen Hesse, Jennifer L. Holm, Diana Wynne Jones, E. L. Konigsburg, Jeff Kinney, Gordon Korman, Kathleen Krull, Janet Taylor Lisle, Lois Lowry, Ann M. Martin, Sy Montgomery, Jim Murphy, Donna Jo Napoli, Phyllis Reynolds Naylor, Kenneth Oppel, Linda Sue Park, Katherine Paterson, James Patterson, Gary Paulsen, Richard Peck, Philip Pullman, Adam Rex, Rick Riordan, J. K. Rowling, Pam Muñoz Ryan, Louis Sachar, Laura Amy Schlitz, Brian Selznick (A/I), Jeff Smith (A/I), Lemony Snicket, Jordan Sonnenblick, Jerry Spinelli, Mildred Taylor, Vivian Vande Velde, Wendelin Van Draanen, Cynthia Voigt, Jacqueline Woodson, Valerie Worth, Laurence Yep, Jane Yolen

YOUTH MEDIA AWARDS, 2011

AMERICAN LIBRARY ASSOCIATION
ANNOUNCED JANUARY 10, 2011

NEWBERY MEDAL (**John Newbery Medal** for the author of most outstanding contribution to American literature for children)
- ❖ *Moon Over Manifest* by Clare Vanderpool. Delacorte, 2010.

NEWBERY HONOR BOOKS:
- *Turtle in Paradise* by Jennifer L. Holm. Random House, 2010.
- *Heart of a Samurai* by Margi Preus. Abrams/Amulet, 2010.
- *Dark Emperor and Other Poems of the Night* by Joyce Sidman, illus. by Rick Allen. Houghton Mifflin, 2010.
- *One Crazy Summer* by Rita Williams-Garcia. HarperCollins/Amistad, 2010.

CALDECOTT MEDAL (**Randolph Caldecott Medal** for illustrator of the most distinguished American picture book for children)
- ❖ *A Sick Day for Amos McGee* by Philip C. Stead, illustrated by Erin E. Stead. Roaring Brook Press/Neal Porter 2010.

CALDECOTT HONOR BOOKS:
- *Dave the Potter: Artist, Poet, Slave* by Laban Carrick Hill, illustrated by Bryan Collier. Little, Brown, 2010.
- *Interrupting Chicken* written and illustrated by David Ezra Stein. Candlewick, 2010.

PRINTZ MEDAL (**Michael L. Printz Award** for excellence in literature written for young adults)
- ❖ *Ship Breaker* by Paolo Bacigalupi. Little, Brown, 2010.

PRINTZ HONOR BOOKS:
- *Stolen* by Lucy Christopher. Scholastic/Chicken House, 2010.
- *Please Ignore Vera Dietz* by A. S. King. Knopf, 2010.
- *Revolver* by Marcus Sedgwick. Roaring Book, 2010.
- *Nothing* by Janne Teller. Atheneum, 2010.

GEISEL MEDAL (Theodor Seuss Geisel Award for most distinguished beginning reader book)
❖ *Bink and Gollie* by Kate DiCamillo and Alison McGhee, illustrated by Tony Fucile. Candlewick, 2010.

GEISEL HONOR BOOKS
- *Ling & Ting: Not Exactly the Same!* written and illustrated by Grace Lin. Little, Brown, 2010.
- *We Are in a Book!* written and illustrated by Mo Willems. Hyperion, 2010.

SIBERT MEDAL (Robert F. Sibert Medal for most distinguished informational book for children)
❖ *Kakapo Rescue: Saving the World's Strangest Parrot* by Sy Montgomery, photographs by Nic Bishop. Houghton Mifflin, 2010.

SIBERT HONOR BOOKS
- *Ballet for Martha: Making Appalachian Spring* by Jan Greenberg and Sandra Jordan, illustrated by Brian Floca. Roaring Brook/Neal Porter, 2010.
- *Lafayette and the American Revolution* by Russell Freedman. Holiday House, 2010.

CORETTA SCOTT KING (AUTHOR) BOOK AWARD (Recognizing an African American author of outstanding books for children and young adults)
❖ *One Crazy Summer* by Rita Williams-Garcia. HarperCollins/Amistad, 2010.

KING HONOR BOOK (AUTHOR)
- *Lockdown* by Walter Dean Myers. HarperCollins/Amistad, 2010.
- *Ninth Ward* by Jewell Parker Rhodes. Little, Brown, 2010.
- *Yummy: The Last Days of a Southside Shorty* by G. Neri, illustrated by Randy DuBurke. Lee & Low, 2010.

CORETTA SCOTT KING (ILLUSTRATOR) BOOK AWARD (Recognizing an African American illustrator of outstanding books for children and young adults)
❖ *Dave the Potter: Artist, Poet, Slave* by Laban Carrick Hill, illustrated by Bryan Collier. Little, Brown, 2010.

KING HONOR BOOK (ILLUSTRATOR)
- *Jimi Sounds Like a Rainbow: A Story of the Young Jimi Hendrix* by Gary Golio, illustrated by Javaka Steptoe. Clarion, 2010.

CORETTA SCOTT KING/JOHN STEPTOE NEW TALENT (AUTHOR) AWARD
❖ *Zora and Me* by Victoria Bond and T. R. Simon. Candlewick, 2010.

CORETTA SCOTT KING/JOHN STEPTOE NEW TALENT (ILLUSTRATOR) AWARD
❖ *Seeds of Change* by Jen Cullerton Johnson, illustrated by Sonia Lynn Sadler. Lee & Low, 2010.

PURA BELPRÉ (AUTHOR) AWARD (Honoring a Latino writer whose children's books best portray, affirm, and celebrate the Latino cultural experience)

❖ *The Dreamer* **by Pam Munoz Ryan, illustrated by Peter Sis. Scholastic, 2010.**

BELPRÉ HONOR BOOKS (AUTHOR)
- *Ole! Flamenco* by George Ancona, photographs by George Ancona. Lee & Low, 2010.
- *The Firefly Letters: A Suffragette's Journey to Cuba* by Margarita Engle. Henry Holt, 2010.
- *90 Miles to Havana* by Enrique Flores-Galbis. Roaring Brook, 2010.

PURA BELPRÉ (ILLUSTRATOR) AWARD (Honoring a Latino illustrator whose children's books best portray, affirm and celebrate the Latino cultural experience)

❖ *Grandma's Gift* **written and illustrated by Eric Velasquez. Walker, 2010.**

BELPRÉ HONOR BOOKS (ILLUSTRATOR)
- *Fiesta Babies* by Carmen Tafolla, illustrated by Amy Córdova. Tricycle, 2010.
- *Me, Frida* by Amy Novesky, illustrated by David Diaz. Abrams, 2010.
- *Dear Primo: A Letter to My Cousin* written and illustrated by Duncan Tonatiuh. Abrams, 2010.

SCHNEIDER FAMILY BOOK AWARD (For books that embody an artistic expression of the disability experience)

Schneider Award for Children, Ages 0 to 10:

❖ *The Pirate of Kindergarten* **by George Ella Lyon, illustrated by Lynne Avril. Atheneum, 2010.**

Schneider Award for Middle School, Ages 11-13:

❖ *After Ever After* **by Jordan Sonnenblick. Scholastic, 2010.**

Schneider Award for Teens, Ages 13-18:

❖ *Five Flavors of Dumb* **by Antony John. Dial, 2010.**

MILDRED L. BATCHELDER AWARD (For an outstanding children's book translated from a foreign language and subsequently published in the United States)

❖ *A Time of Miracles* **by Anne-Laure Bondoux, translated by Y. Maudet. Delacorte, 2010.**

BATCHELDER HONOR BOOKS
- *Departure Time* by Truus Matti, translated by Nancy Forest-Flier. Namelos, 2010.
- *Nothing* by Janne Teller, translated by Martin Aitken. Atheneum, 2010.

FREEMAN'S FAVORITES, 2001-2010

I read a lot of children's books, some great, some good, and some not so wonderful. Here's my average: for every 20 books I read, one will rise to the top like cream. When I find a book I love, I want to crow about it and share it with everyone. Nevertheless, I urge you not to take my word for it when I say a book is special. Compared to the under 12 set, I'm really, really old. How do I know what children will find unputdownable? I give it my best shot, though, reading as if I were 6 or 10 or 14, and am always elated when children agree with some of my choices.

Each year, I pull together all the new books I've fallen for, and head off to several local public schools to test them out on the people for whom these books are intended—real kids— to see if they like them, too. Sometimes I get it right, sometimes not. By the end of each year, I put together a list of my 100+ best books of the year in this, *The WINNERS! Handbook*, of which I publish a new edition each year, with annotated lists of my choices.

This year, as I finished compiling my list of best books, I applied my own 50-item selection criteria (see the "50 Ways To Recognize a Read-Aloud" chapter in *More Books Kids Will Sit Still For*, page 7), and selected my very favorite picture book, fiction, young adult, poetry, and nonfiction read-aloud for each year over the past decade. Singling out the books that I found most successful, provocative, fresh, child friendly, beloved, and pleasurable to read aloud is an instructive and intriguing exercise. Coming up with just one book per category can be agonizing.

You can tell a lot about a person by the books he or she loves. Your own list would most likely be vastly different from this one, so feel free to agree or disagree with me on any of my choices. I urge you to try compiling a list for yourself, and then ask your kids to come up with lists of their past favorite books. (Check my books, *More Books Kids Will Sit Still For* on page 23 for the "Freeman's Favorites" from 1984-1994 and *Books Kids Will Sit Still For 3* on page 67 for my choices from 1995-2005.) Teachers and librarians: post these lists around the room for children to find new choices of books to read. Parents, read the books on your children's lists, too. Talk about why you picked each book. Favorite books are best when shared.

My choices from the past decade, are as follows:

2001

PICTURE BOOK:	***And the Dish Ran Away with the Spoon* by Janet Stevens, illus. by the author. Harcourt, 2001. (Gr. PreK-2)** When Dish and Spoon disappear, Cat, Dog, and Cow set off to find them.
FICTION:	***Love That Dog* by Sharon Creech. HarperCollins, 2001. (Gr. 4-7)** Through poetry, a boy named Jack reflects on the life and death of his beloved dog, Sky.
YA:	***Flipped* by Wendelin Van Draanen. Knopf, 2001. (Gr. 6-8)** Juli is crazy about Bryce, Bryce thinks she's crazy.
POETRY:	***A Poke in the I: A Collection of Concrete Poems* selected by Paul Janeczko, illus. by Chris Raschka. Candlewick, 2001. (Gr. 3-8)** A very cool set of thirty concrete or shape poems, with wild and jazzy collage illustrations.
NONFICTION:	***The Dinosaurs of Waterhouse Hawkins* by Barbara Kerley, illus. by Brian Selznick. Scholastic, 2001. (Gr. 2-6)** No one knew what dinosaurs looked like until 1853, when Benjamin Waterhouse Hawkins built the first life-sized models in England.

2002

PICTURE BOOK: *I Stink* by Kate McMullan, illus. by Jim McMullan. HarperCollins, 2002. (Gr. PreK-2)
Narrated by a tough guy NYC garbage truck with real attitude.

FICTION: *Time Stops for No Mouse* by Michael Hoeye. Putnam, 2002. (Gr. 4-8)
Mild-mannered watchmaker mouse, Hermux Tantamoq, becomes embroiled in a dangerous mystery.

YA: *Big Mouth & Ugly Girl* by Joyce Carol Oates. HarperCollins, 2002. (Gr. 8-12)
Loner, Ursula Riggs, comes to the defense of class clown, Matt Donoghy, when he's accused of making threats against their high school.

POETRY: *FEG: Stupid (Ridiculous) Poems for Intelligent Children* by Robin Hirsch, illus. by Ha. (Little, Brown, 2002. (Gr. 4-8)
Two dozen nimble wordplay poems employ palindromes, spoonerisms, and other clever games and puzzles for tenacious readers to figure out.

NONFICTION: *Fireboat: The Heroic Adventures of the John J. Harvey* by Maira Kalman, illus. by the author. Putnam, 2002. (Gr. 1-6)
Astonishing and moving true picture book about the crewmembers of the John J. Harvey fireboat who helped fight the fires in lower Manhattan on 9/11.

2003

PICTURE BOOK: *Don't Let the Pigeon Drive the Bus* by Mo Willems, illus. by the author. Hyperion, 2003. (Gr. PreK-3)
"Can I drive the bus?" wheedles the Pigeon. Your kids, no matter what age, will talk back to him sternly and say, "No!"

FICTION: *The Tale of Despereaux: Being the Story of a Mouse, a Princess, Some Soup, and a Spool of Thread* by Kate DiCamillo, illus. by Timothy Basil Ering. Candlewick, 2003. (Gr. 3-8)
Oh, the drama, when big-eared mouse, Despereaux, is sentenced to death for talking to the human princess he reveres.

YA: *The First Part Last* by Angela Johnson. Simon & Schuster, 2003. (Gr. 8-12)
Sixteen-year-old Bobby is trying to raise his baby daughter, Feather, on his own.

POETRY: *Dogs Rule!* by Daniel Kirk, illus. by the author. Hyperion, 2003. (Gr. PreK-)
Twenty-two spirited poems, about and narrated by dogs, can even be sung with the accompanying CD, which you can download at **www.danielkirk.com**.

NONFICTION: *The Man Who Walked between the Towers* by Mordicai Gerstein, illus. by the author. Roaring Brook, 2003. (Gr. Adult)
French aerialist, Philippe Petit, walked on a cable stretched between the just-completed Twin Towers in New York City on August 7, 1974.

2004

PICTURE BOOK: *Knuffle Bunny* by Mo Willems, illus. by the author. Hyperion, 2004. (Gr. PreK-2)
Toddler, Trixie, says her first word when her beloved stuffed bunny goes missing.

FICTION: *Al Capone Does My Shirts* by Gennifer Choldenko. Putnam, 2004. (Gr. 5-8)
In 1935, when Moose Flanagan's father gets a job at Alcatraz prison, the family moves to the twelve-acre rock island in the middle of San Francisco Bay.

YA: *Airborn* by Kenneth Oppel. HarperCollins, 2004. (Gr. 5-9)
Aboard the airship, Aurora, riding high above the Pacificus, fifteen-year-old cabin boy, Matt Cruse, helps to rescue an unconscious man in a hot air balloon.

POETRY: *Technically, It's Not My Fault: Concrete Poems* by John Grandits, illus. by the author. Clarion, 2004. (Gr. 4-7)
Get to know sixth grader, Robert, through his concrete or shape poems about school, his sister, skateboards, talking backwards, and bloodcurdling screams.

NONFICTION: *Actual Size* by Steve Jenkins, illus. by the author. Houghton Mifflin, 2004. (Gr. PreK-5)
Eighteen animals, or parts of animals, from the tiny goby fish to the man-eating saltwater crocodile, are shown actual size in this spectacular science picture book.

2005

PICTURE BOOK: *Bad Kitty* by Nick Bruel, illus. by the author. Roaring Brook, 2005. (Gr. PreK-2)
In an alphabet book of bad food and even worse behavior, a black cat takes revenge when her people run out of kitty food.

FICTION: *The Lightning Thief* by Rick Riordan. Miramax/Hyperion, 2005. (Gr. 4-8)
Percy Jackson, troubled, dyslexic, ADHD kid has a bit of a problem on his sixth grade class field trip to the Metropolitan Museum of Art in New York City.

YA: *Harry Potter and the Half-Blood Prince* by J. K. Rowling, illus. by Mary Grandpré. Scholastic, 2005. (Gr. 5-Adult)
I've adored every Harry Potter book, but book six, which I read on the beach on vacation in sunny Puerto Rico, had me shivering in spite of the beautiful weather.

POETRY: *Runny Babbit: A Billy Sook* by Shel Silverstein, illus. by the author. HarperCollins, 2005. (Gr. 7-12)
There are twenty-foo feally runny pyming rhoems about Runny Babbit and pots of his lals in this bazy crook.

NONFICTION: *Encyclopedia Prehistorica: Dinosaurs* by Robert Sabuda and Matthew Reinhart, illus. by Robert Sabuda. Candlewick, 2005. (Gr. K-7)
While the intricate and inventive watercolored pop-ups will make dinosaur lovers gasp, there are meaty chunks of information on each page as well.

2006

PICTURE BOOK: *John, Paul, George & Ben* by Lane Smith, illus. by the author. Hyperion, 2006. (Gr. 1-4)
Follow the fictional childhoods of bold John Hancock, noisy Paul Revere, honest George Washington, clever Ben Franklin, and independent Tom Jefferson.

FICTION: *The Miraculous Journey of Edward Tulane* by Kate DiCamillo, illus. by Bagram Ibatoulline. Candlewick, 2006. (Gr. 4-7)
A china rabbit learns the hard way about the importance of love.

YA: *The Book Thief* by Marcus Zusak. Knopf, 2006. (Gr. 8-Adult)
Death himself chronicles the life of Liesel Meminger, a 9-year-old foster child in a small town outside Munich during World War II.

POETRY: *Frankenstein Makes a Sandwich: And Other Stories You're Sure to Like, Because They're All About Monsters, and Some of Them Are Also About Food. You Like Food, Don't You? Well, All Right Then* by Adam Rex, illus. by the author. Harcourt, 2006. (Gr. 2-8)
Get to know all those fabulous movie monsters in a collection of 20 poems and pictures that will have you screaming with laughter.

NONFICTION: *The American Story* by Jennifer Armstrong, illus. by Roger Roth. Knopf, 2006. (Gr. 3-8)
In a handsome and hefty volume that children and adults will pore over and reread is a dazzling chronology of 100 stories from American history.

2007

PICTURE BOOK: *Knuffle Bunny Too: A Case of Mistaken Identity* by Mo Willems, illus. by the author. Hyperion, 2007. (Gr. PreK-3)
Trixie and Sonja's almost identical stuffed Knuffle Bunnies get switched.

FICTION: *The Invention of Hugo Cabret* by Brian Selznick, illus. by the author. Scholastic, 2007. (Gr. 3-8)
This 500+ page Caldecott winner, about an orphan trying to survive alone in a Paris train station, is a magical combination of words and pictures.

YA: *The Absolutely True Diary of a Part-Time Indian* by Sherman Alexie, illus. by Ellen Forney. Little, Brown, 2007. (Gr. 8-Adult)
Adult author Sherman Alexie's first YA book, loosely autobiographical, is hard-hitting, heart-breaking, wildly funny, raunchy, profane, and unforgettable.

POETRY: *Good Masters! Sweet Ladies!: Voices from a Medieval Village* by Laura Amy Schlitz, illus. by Robert Byrd. Candlewick, 2007. (Gr. 5-8)
This Newbery Medal winner, a collection of 22 children's narratives in poetry, transports readers to an English manor house and village in 1255.

NONFICTION: *Nic Bishop Spiders* by Nic Bishop, photos. by the author. Scholastic, 2007. (Gr. PreK-4)
Even kids who think they hate spiders will be entranced by Bishop's color photos and fascinating fact-filled, easy-to-absorb text.

2008

PICTURE BOOK: *A Visitor for Bear* by Bonny Becker, illus. by Kady MacDonald Denton. Candlewick, 2008. (Gr. PreK-2)
Bear thinks he doesn't like visitors, and then Mouse pops up, small and bright-eyed.

FICTION: *The Underneath* by Kathi Appelt, illus. by David Small. Atheneum, 2008. (Gr. 4-8)
In an East Texas swamp converge an abandoned cat, an abused dog named Ranger, a trapper called Gar-Face, two kittens, Grandmother Moccasin, and a 100-foot alligator.

YA: *The Disreputable History of Frankie Landau-Banks* by E. Lockhar. Hyperion, 2008. (Gr. 7-12)
High school sophomore, Frankie, infiltrates the all-boys secret society at her boarding school.

POETRY: *The Bill Martin Jr Big Book of Poetry* by Bill Martin, Jr, and Michael Sampson, illus. by Steven Kellogg and others. Simon & Schuster, 2008. (Gr. PreK-3)
This big, brash, and beautiful volume is stuffed with almost 200 poems from 50+ poets, and illustrated by 13 well-known children's book illustrators.

NONFICTION: *We Are the Ship: The Story of Negro League Baseball* by Kadir Nelso. Hyperion/Jump at the Sun, 2008. (Gr. 3-Adult)
For all the sports lovers in your family, this Sibert Medal winner is a breathtaking tribute to baseball's Negro League players.

2009

PICTURE BOOK: *Let's Do Nothing!* by Tony Fucile, illus. by the author. Candlewick, 2009. (Gr. K-3)
Two boys prove doing nothing isn't as easy as it seems.

FICTION: *Where the Mountain Meets the Moon* by Grace Lin, illus. by the author. Little, Brown, 2009. (Gr. 2-5)
In a riveting quest novel, laced with Chinese folktales, Minli sets out to change her family's fortune.

YA: (tie) *How to Say Goodbye in Robot* by Natalie Standiford. Scholastic, 2009. (Gr. 8-12)
Beatrice, a late night insomniac, finds a fellow radio geek in loner Jonah Tate, whom the other seniors at her new school call Ghost Boy.

Leviathan by Scott Westerfeld, illus. by Keith Thompson. Simon & Schuster/Pulse, 2009. (Gr. 7-10)
In a steampunk version of the events leading up to WWI, it's Austrian Clanker machinery versus the English Darwinist biotech airbeast, Leviathan.

POETRY: *Julie Andrews' Collection of Poems, Songs, and Lullabies* by Julie Andrews and Emma Walton Hamilton, illus. by James McMullan. Little, Brown, 2009. (Gr. K-6)
A stunning collection of 136 poems for children of all ages.

NONFICTION: *Redwoods* by Jason Chin, illus. by the author. Roaring Brook/Flash Point, 2009. (Gr. K-4)
An innovative picture book-within-a-book about redwood trees.

2010

After looking over every title that received a starred review from any of the major journals, reading the hundreds of books on this year's Best Books lists, and polling all of my library friends and reviewers for their favorite picks (Thank you Kathleen Baxter, Elizabeth Bird, Jenny Brown, Susan Faust, Beth Gerall, Carol Levin, and Lisa Von Drasek for sharing . . .), I then have to get tough and pick my own favorites, which often end up being titles that are a bit under the radar.

In picking my very favorite books for this year, I realized that none of the titles on my following list won a big award, much to my great disappointment. I thought *City Dog, Country Frog* should have won at least a Caldecott Honor; would have been thrilled to see *The Strange Case of Origami Yoda*, a book that has been all the rage with middle grade readers, and for good reason, get a Newbery, though it's not the kind of book that typically wins; and would have fought for a Sibert had I been on that committee this year, for *Bones: Skeletons and How They Work*. Ah, well. Just because a book doesn't get a medal doesn't mean it can't be memorable, kid-friendly, and have staying power, which I think describes all of these books.

PICTURE BOOK:
City Dog, Country Frog by Mo Willems, illus. by Jon J Muth. Disney Hyperion, 2010. (Gr. PreK-2)
Through the seasons, City Dog and his new friend, Country Frog, play games and revel in their time together. A picture book for all ages. (see full review on page 9)

FICTION:
The Strange Case of Origami Yoda by Tom Angleberger, illus. by the author. Amulet, 2010. (Gr. 4-7)
The Yoda finger puppet worn by Dwight, the weirdest kid at McQuarrie Middle School, offers life-changing advice to any student who asks. (see full review on page 39)

YA:
Incarceron by Catherine Fisher. Dial, 2010. (Gr. 6-12)
In alternate chapters, Finn, an inmate in the vast prison system of Incarceron, plans to break out, something no prisoner but one has ever done, while Claudia, daughter of the Warden, breaks in. (see full review on page 67)

POETRY:
Mirror, Mirror: A Book of Reversible Verse by Marilyn Singer, illus. by Josée Masse. Dutton, 2010. (Gr. 3-6)
Fourteen reverso poems—read first from top to bottom, and then rearranged so the bottom line becomes the top—take on the double-sided nature of fairy tales. (see full review on page 59)

NONFICTION:
Bones: Skeletons and How They Work by Steve Jenkins, illus. by the author. Scholastic, 2010. (Gr. K-5)
Compare the bones in the human body with those of different animals and see what you look like from the inside out. (see full review on page 44)

JUDY FREEMAN'S BEST OF THE BEST OF THE DECADE

If I had to pick my one favorite picture book of the past decade, it would have to be Mo Willems's insouciant Caldecott Honor winner, ***Don't Let the Pigeon Drive the Bus***, in which children young and old engage in conversation with that persistent Pigeon. When I read it to three- and four-year-old preschoolers, they were unrelenting and vociferous, not cutting Pigeon a bit of slack in refusing his ever-hopeful attempts to drive that bus. Note that there are four Mo Willems books in my "Best of the Decade" lists. I am ever astonished by the power of Mo to captivate children with his words and pictures.

For fiction, my top pick for the past many years was ***Harry Potter and the Sorcerer's Stone***, the first in a series which has changed children's reading and adults' reactions to children's books forever, we hope. After 11 years, it is time for a new fave: ***The Invention of Hugo Cabret*** by the amazing Brian Selznick. What a groundbreaking book this is, with its masterful silent movie-like pencil illustrations that tell half of the story. One librarian dubbed it "cinematic fiction." I was at the award announcements at ALA when this book won the Caldecott. A 500-page novel winning the medal for most distinguished contribution to American illustration for children? There was screaming and shouting and cheering and clapping and foot stomping (and a lot of that was coming from me). I also was fortunate to hear Brian Selznick deliver his Newbery Speech six months later at the Newbery-Caldecott dinner, and it was spectacular. You can read the speech and watch the ebullient hand-created video he showed along with it here at **www.theinventionofhugocabret.com/slideshow_flash.htm**.

Young adult books had me stumped. Should I pick ***The Book Thief***, which is such a hard-hitting, emotionally wrenching book about the Holocaust and World War II? It has such an interesting narrator—Death—who says, "I can be amiable. Agreeable. Affable. And that's only the As. Just don't ask me to be nice. Nice has nothing to do with me." I also haven't stopped thinking about E. Lockhart's ***The Disreputable History of Frankie Landau-Banks*** since I first read it. Frankie wants to transcend her family's image of her as Bunny Rabbit and to prove herself a force. Was she heroic or just obsessed in her venture to be recognized as the equal of the privileged boys in her school? I'm still pondering this. The book that made me laugh and howl and gasp was ***The Absolutely True Diary of a Part-Time Indian*** by Sherman Alexie, which, with its mixture of cartoons and text looked like nothing else I had ever read. Knowing that Junior's story was loosely autobiographical made it all the more wrenching and outrageous and real. I'll go with this one, though I could be persuaded to change my mind.

Poetry proved difficult as well. There's the general hilarity and gorgeous movie monster-themed illustrations of Adam Rex's ***Frankenstein Makes a Sandwich*** with its running gag about the Phantom of the Opera who can't get certain pop songs out of his head, and dizzyingly funny poem titles like "Dracula Doesn't Know He's Been Walking Around All Night with Spinach in His Teeth." On the other hand, there's the elegant and dramatic ***Good Masters, Sweet Ladies*** by Laura Amy Schlitz, a book kids might not pick up on their own, but one that gives me goosebumps every time I read one of the narrative poems aloud. It looks like an illuminated manuscript. Do I go for the laughs or the goosebumps? Depends on my mood, I guess. You decide. I fiercely love both titles.

For nonfiction, ***Actual Size*** is a book I love to use with children when I do school visits and assemblies; it never fails to wow 'em. I love to give it as a present for all the cousins and nieces and nephews when they turn six or so. To see all those animals actual size, from the 12" eye of the giant squid to the gate-folded page of the saltwater crocodile that opens to reveal its toothy snout, is thrilling and just a bit scary for kids, which they find titillating. Me, too.

How Rocket Learned to Read Lesson, Grades K-1

by librarian Loreli Stochaj and her first grades students at Franklin School, Summit, New Jersey

After reading *How Rocket Learned to Read* by Tad Hills (Schwartz & Wade, 2010) to her first grade classes, Loreli Stochaj, crackerjack librarian at Franklin School in Summit, New Jersey, asked her students what other essential words they would teach to Rocket, the dog. They came up with wonderful seasonal words, including l-e-a-v-e-s, l-a-d-y-b-u-g, w-a-t-e-r, and s-n-o-w. Each child then filled in a Rocket page, drawing a seasonal picture and spelling out a new word for Rocket to learn. When the children shared their pictures, they spelled out their words for the others to identify.

Interrupting Fairy Tales: A Lesson Plan for Grades 2-4

by Maren Vitali, Librarian, Milltown School, Bridgewater, NJ (and bits by Judy Freeman)

Inspired by *Interrupting Chicken* by David Ezra Stein (Candlewick, 2010)

OBJECTIVES:
Children will recognize and articulate the difference between fairy tales and fictional stories.
Children will summarize the text of a fairy tale.
Children will "interrupt a fairy tale" in a style similar to *Interrupting Chicken.*

MATERIALS:
Interrupting Chicken by David Ezra Stein (Candlewick, 2010)
Assortment of well-known fairy tales, including Hansel and Gretel," "Little Red Riding Hood," and "Chicken Little" (all featured in the story, *Interrupting Chicken*); at least 12 others like "Sleeping Beauty," "Snow White," "Rumpelstiltskin;" plus 6-8 good but lesser known fairy tale picture books
Chart and writing paper for class summaries of fairy tales
Publishing paper for interrupting fairy tales
Paper, pencils, drawing materials

SESSION 1

PROCEDURE:
1. Ask the children to show you where the fairy tales (398.2) are in the library. Discuss: What is a folk or fairy tale? Where are they in the library? Why are they in a separate section from fiction or easy fiction/picture books? What are the titles of some of the folk and fairy tales you have heard or read? Record these titles on a chart or SMART board (or other interactive white board) as children name them, and hold up corresponding books to go along (i.e., "Cinderella," Snow White," etc.).
2. Ask children to tell you: What are the components of a folk or fairy tale? What sorts of things happen in them? Who are the main characters? Where do they take place? How do the stories begin ("Once upon a time") and end ("Happily ever after")?
3. Review (or introduce) Judy Freeman's chant, "Look for 398.2," with all joining in on the refrain and snapping their fingers in time to the rap as follows:

LOOK FOR 398.2

If you want a good story, let me tell you what to do—
LOOK FOR 398.2, LOOK FOR 398.2!

Prince or princess in hot water, trouble with a witch's brew—
LOOK FOR 398.2, LOOK FOR 398.2!

Fierce and fire-breathing dragons, shiny scales of green and blue—
LOOK FOR 398.2, LOOK FOR 398.2!

Ogres, leprechauns, and goblins all are waiting just for you—
LOOK FOR 398.2, LOOK FOR 398.2!

Find a tale from every country, from Australia to Peru—
LOOK FOR 398.2, LOOK FOR 398.2!
That's all you've got to do!

4. Hold up a variety of well-known tales. Handpick one to show that is not as well known and does not contain the traditional beginning and ending. Read aloud the first and last lines to demonstrate that not all stories begin and end with the words we expect. Do a picture walk of the story and have children tell you who the main characters are, describe the setting, and point out any magical elements they notice.

5. Have on hand a variety of lesser-known fairy tale picture books you've selected from the 398.2 shelves of your library. Hand out one book per trio of children. Each group will then spend five minutes looking over its story to locate and identify the following information (which you can list on the board so they'll remember):

- *Beginnings* that differ from "Once upon a time"
- *Endings* that differ from " . . . and they all lived happily ever after"
- *Settings*, including the country of origin
- *Main characters*, both heroes and villains
- *Hero's quest and/or magical elements* he or she encounters on the way

6. Starting with the first category, "Beginnings," ask each group to quickly identify aloud the title and author of its book, show the cover, and read aloud the beginning sentence. Then move on to "Endings," "Settings," "Characters," and "Quests."

FOLLOW UP:
Encourage students to check out folk and fairy tale books from the 398.2 section of the library.

SESSION 2

PROCEDURE:
1. Read aloud Caldecott Honor picture book, *Interrupting Chicken* by David Ezra Stein (Candlewick, 2010). Laugh like crazy.
2. Discuss how Little Chicken interrupts each story to change its outcome. Ask: What if Papa's bedtime book of fairy tales had contained more stories? Which other stories do you think should be in Papa's book and why?
3. Next, re-read and re-examine the summaries of each story Papa reads to Little Chicken. Show picture book versions of each of the stories (Hansel and Gretel," "Little Red Riding Hood," and "Chicken Little") that Chicken interrupts.
4. Explain that today, children will be choosing a fairy tale of their own to "summarize." Select a common fairy tale to model and have children collaboratively come up with a one-paragraph summary of it.
5. Allow the group to look for and select a well-known fairy tale (titles not already covered in *Interrupting Chicken*) on the shelves or lay out a dozen books on the tables for them to choose. Or hold up each tale you have selected and have each group each claim one. (Children can work alone or in pairs or trios for this activity.) You can have multiples of each title as needed.
6. Have children read their story and then write a brief summary. Remind them that a good summary will have all the key phrases or characteristic of the original story, but cannot contain every detail.

FOLLOW UP:
To find out if their summary is recognizable, have them share it with the class. If the other children can figure out the fairy tale from the summary, they have done a good job.

SESSION 3

PROCEDURE:

1. Review the plot points of *Interrupting Chicken*. Look specifically (and reread aloud) the summaries Papa reads to Little Chicken and have listeners note the climactic moment when Little Chicken chooses to interrupt, such as in "Hansel and Gretel." ("Out jumped a little red chicken, and SHE said, "DON'T GO IN! SHE'S A WITCH!") Then discuss how her actions change the whole story. ("So Hansel and Gretel didn't. THE END!")
2. Explain that today children will be interrupting their fairytales, Chicken-style.
3. Have the kids re-read their summaries and find a dramatic spot to interrupt them. They can then draw illustrations to go with their work—complete with pictures of Chicken interrupting the fairytale, written in a dialogue balloon, and her final sentence, which changes the outcome of the story.

FOLLOW UP:

Have children share their work.

THE LOUD BOOK

by the second graders in Keri Peloso's class
Milltown School, Bridgewater, New Jersey

Inspired by _The Quiet Book_ by Deborah Underwood,
illustrated by Renata Liwska (Houghton Mifflin, 2010)

laundrey tumbling loud

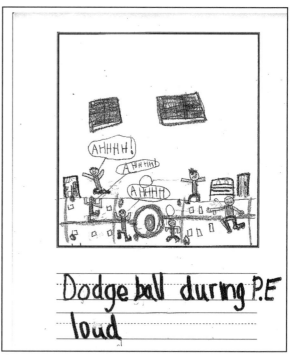

Dodge ball during P.E loud

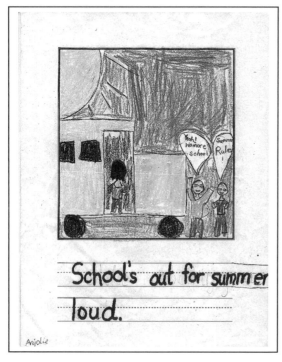

School's out for summer loud.

After reading about all the types of quiet there are in _The Quiet Book_ by Deborah Underwood, the second graders in Keri Peloso's class came up with many examples of quiet's opposite. They then put together their own book, _The Loud Book_, filled with their astute examples and colorful crayon and pencil illustrations.

Mind you, Underwood herself has already written her own companion book, and she used the same exact title: _The Loud Book_ (Houghton Mifflin, 2011), but the second graders scooped her! Theirs came out first, and though it may not be for sale on Amazon, it's still pretty darn adorable, as you can see from the three examples here.

ZOOKU: WRITING ANIMAL HAIKU

by the second graders of Becky Gara, Helen Kyritsis, and Lisa D'Ascensio, Van Holten School, Bridgewater, New Jersey

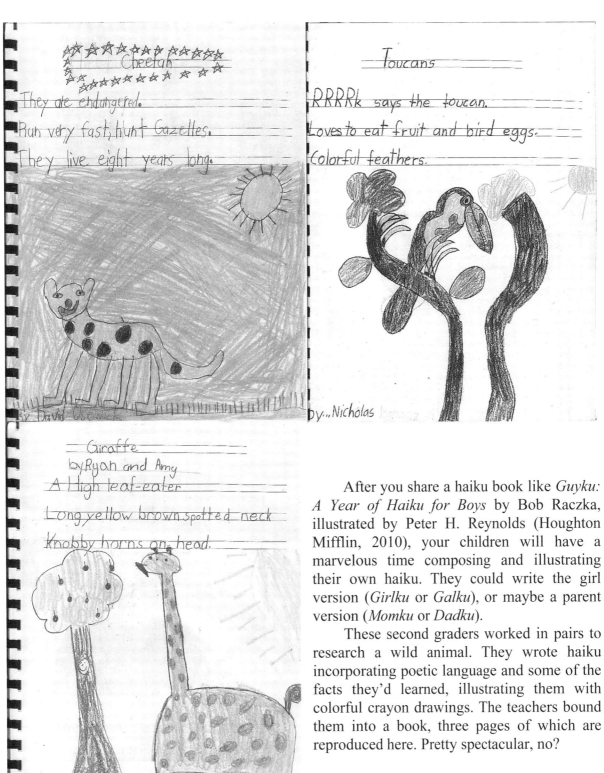

Cheetah
They are endangered.
Run very fast, hunt Gazelles.
They live eight years long.
by David Oc...

Toucans
RRRRk says the toucan.
Loves to eat fruit and bird eggs.
Colorful feathers.
by...Nicholas...

Giraffe
by Ryan and Amy
A High leaf-eater
Long yellow brown spotted neck
Knobby horns on head.

After you share a haiku book like *Guyku: A Year of Haiku for Boys* by Bob Raczka, illustrated by Peter H. Reynolds (Houghton Mifflin, 2010), your children will have a marvelous time composing and illustrating their own haiku. They could write the girl version (*Girlku* or *Galku*), or maybe a parent version (*Momku* or *Dadku*).

These second graders worked in pairs to research a wild animal. They wrote haiku incorporating poetic language and some of the facts they'd learned, illustrating them with colorful crayon drawings. The teachers bound them into a book, three pages of which are reproduced here. Pretty spectacular, no?

TIME TO EAT, HIPPO THE HIPPO!

by the first graders in Esther Loor's class, Milltown School, Bridgewater, New Jersey

Inspired by *Time to Sleep, Sheep the Sheep* in the Cat the Cat series written and illustrated by Mo Willems (Balzer + Bray, 2010)

In his winning new Cat the Cat series, Mo Willems manages to present witty, cohesive, and ridiculously easy to read stories using a mere 20 words per book, complete with repeated refrains, adorable illustrations, and a hefty dose of the absurd. It's rewarding for children to write new versions of these stories using the same formats and patterns. Mo often says he never draws anything in his books that a three- or four-year-old can't copy. Cat the Cat is the latest of his characters that children will delight in drawing, along with Pigeon, Knuffle Bunny, and Elephant and Piggie.

To create a delightful animal-filled book patterned after *Time to Sleep, Sheep the Sheep!*, Esther Loor's first graders worked in pairs. One child was responsible for creating the left-hand page, with Cat the Cat calling to an animal friend. The other partner created the facing page, with a drawing of that animal and its terse but cheerful response. It's a book children can read independently with great satisfaction and success.

Knuffle Bunny Free: A Writing and Illustrating Prompt

by librarian Loreli Stochaj and her first grades students at Franklin School, Summit, New Jersey

Inspired by the book, *Knuffle Bunny Free: An Unexpected Diversion* written and illustrated by Mo Willems (Balzer + Bray, 2010)

Name BrYanna   Class 1W

Today you heard <u>Knuffle Bunny Free</u> by Mo Willems. If you were going to take Knuffle Bunny on an adventure where would you take him? What would you do together?

I would take Ms.
Knuffle Bunny to
Costa Rica. I would
Cary her everywher I
go.

Knuffle Bunny Free: A Lesson Plan

Researching Foreign Countries: A Lesson Plan for Grades 2-4
by Maren Vitali, Librarian, Milltown School, Bridgewater, NJ

SESSION 1

OBJECTIVES:
Students will recognize the names and books of outstanding authors like Mo Willems and continue to develop an appreciation for a range of outstanding children's literature.
Students will brainstorm a list of interesting places in the world.

MATERIALS:
Knuffle Bunny Free: An Unexpected Diversion by Mo Willems (Balzer & Bray, 2010)
Other "Knuffle Bunny" books: *Knuffle Bunny* and *Knuffle Bunny Too*; other books by Mo Willems

PROCEDURE:
1. Discuss Mo Willems and ask students which titles they know. Show and describe his many titles, including *Don't Let the Pigeon Drive the Bus* and *City Dog, Country Frog*.
2. Do a picture walk through the first two "Knuffle Bunny" books.
3. Show the newest book, *Knuffle Bunny Free*, to class. Have children make predictions of what they think is going to happen to Trixie's stuffed rabbit this time.
4. Read aloud and revel in the story.
5. On the pages showing Trixie's dream of Knuffle Bunny traveling the world, ask children to try to identify the cities or countries shown in each photograph.
6. Explain that we are going to be doing some research on places Knuffle Bunny might have visited as he traveled around the world.
7. Have kid brainstorm "far away" places on Earth, and locate them on a globe or classroom map. Ask if any of them have been to the places they brainstormed and if so, what they saw there.

SESSION 2

OBJECTIVE:
Students will use netbooks to gather information about a landmark, city, and/or country that Knuffle Bunny could visit on his journey around the world.

MATERIALS:
Netbooks
"Postcards from Another Country" research sheet

PROCEDURE:
1. Review the places Trixie dreamed her stuffed bunny *Knuffle Bunny Free* visited.
2. Have students pick places they'd like to research.
3. Model how the kids will access the websites to gather the information they need to fill out their "Postcards from Another Country" worksheets.
4. Using these websites (or, if you have a subscription, the online version of *World Book* at **www.worldbook.com**), children locate information about their special places and fill it in on their worksheets. (NOTE: You can easily have children use print encyclopedias along with or instead of the websites. Truth be told, the information in *World Book* will be more detailed and accessible, and may contain better photographs of national landmarks.

FOLLOW UP:
Have students share one interesting fact they found.

Postcards from Another Country

Explore the websites listed below. Look at the various countries and choose one that sounds interesting to you.

http://www.factmonster.com/countries.html

http://kids.nationalgeographic.com/kids/places/find/

Once you have chosen a country, find and record the following information below:

COUNTRY: _____

CAPITAL: _____

SIZE: _____

POPULATION: _____

FORM OF GOVERNMENT/PRESIDENT: _____

POPULATION: _____

LANGUAGE: _____

MONEY: _____

GEOGRAPHY: _____

ANIMALS: _____

INTERESTING FACTS/INFORMATION
(IN YOUR OWN WORDS, PLEASE!):

1. _____
   _____
   _____

2. _____
   _____
   _____

3. _____
   _____
   _____

4. _____
   _____
   _____

5. _____
   _____
   _____

SESSION 3

OBJECTIVES:
Children will practice letter-writing skills.
Children will use their research to create a postcard from Knuffle Bunny that demonstrates and displays the information they learned about their country.

MATERIALS:
Knuffle Bunny Free: An Unexpected Diversion by Mo Willems
Sample postcards
Completed research sheets
Rough draft postcard template

PROCEDURE:
1. Discuss how writing a letter is different from other types of writing.
2. Talk about postcards how they are more concise and briefer than letters.
3. Today the kids are going to use their research to crate a postcard to Trixie from Knuffle Bunny. They need to make sure they include their facts about their country in a fun way. Show my sample.
4. Children compose a postcard message incorporating one or more facts about their country, as seen through the eyes of Knuffle Bunny.

FOLLOW UP:
Have kids share what they wrote.

SESSION 4

OBJECTIVES:
Children will search for and print out photographs using Google images.
Children will use their research to create a postcard, ostensibly from the point of view of Knuffle Bunny to his little girl, Trixie that demonstrates and displays the information they learned about their country.

MATERIALS:
Netbooks
Final postcard paper, crayons, colored pencils
Small drawings of Knuffle Bunny

PROCEDURE:
1. Have children use the netbooks to find a photograph of their country or a place that Knuffle Bunny could visit while there. Demonstrate how to do a Google image search.
2. Print the photos in black and white to replicate the style of the book. These pictures will be used as the front of the postcard. Students will need to include a heading that they draw on the picture like: "Greetings From . . ." or "It's a Beautiful Day in . . ."
3. While waiting for the pictures to print, they can write their final copy on the postcard itself.
4. Have children glue the photograph to one side of the postcard paper, and glue a little drawing of Knuffle Bunny on the photograph.

FOLLOW UP:
Have children read and share their postcards. (See next page for a postcard researched, written, and created by one of Maren Vitali's second graders.)

A SECOND GRADER'S POSTCARD
FROM KNUFFLE BUNNY TO TRIXIE

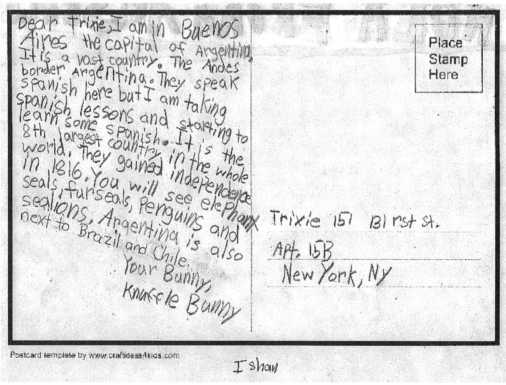

Dear Trixie, I am in Buenos Aires the capital of Argentina. It is a vast country. The Andes border Argentina. They speak Spanish here but I am taking Spanish lessons and starting to learn some Spanish. It is the 8th largest country in the whole world. They gained independence in 1816. You will see elephant seals, fur seals, Penguins and sealions. Argentina is also next to Brazil and Chile.
Your Bunny,
Knuffle Bunny

Place
Stamp
Here

Trixie 151 131 rst St.

Apt. 15B
New York, NY

Postcard template by www.craftideas4kids.com

Ishan

98

LOLLIPOP VIGNETTES: A Lesson Plan for Grades 2-4

by Maren Vitali, Librarian, Milltown School, Bridgewater, NJ (Mvitali@brrsd.k12.nj.us), with a few tweaks by Judy Freeman

Inspired by *Big Red Lollipop* by Rukhsana Khan (Viking, 2010)

OBJECTIVES:

Students will learn about vignettes and autobiography.

Students will write a vignette about their childhood—an autobiographical memory that involves something specific and unforgettable that happened to them when they were little.

MATERIALS:

Big Red Lollipop by Rukhsana Khan, illus. by Sophie Blackall (Viking, 2010)

Everything But the Horse by Holly Hobbie (Little, Brown, 2010

I Lost My Tooth in Africa by Penda Diakité (Scholastic, 2006)

Thank You Mr. Falker by Patricia Polacco (Philomel, 1998)

The Relatives Came by Cynthia Rylant (Atheneum, 2001, c1985)

When I Was Young in the Mountains by Cynthia Rylant (Dutton, 1982)

Uncle Andy's by James Warhola (Putnam, 2003)

Paper for rough and drafts.

Lollipop-shaped papers, 6-8" in diameter, with spiral drawn on them (or kids can draw their own spirals with red crayon, or, better yet, glitter glue sticks)

SESSION 1

PROCEDURE:

1. Talk about memories. What kind of things happened to you that you think you'll remember even when you turn 80? Ask kids to share some stories from when they were little.
2. Share several personal memories from when I was little and about my own children. Explain that I write them down so I will remember them forever.
3. Read *Big Red Lollipop*, which is based on something that happened to the author when she was young. Explain that this is called a personal narrative, and is also a vignette—a brief but indelible memory from a short period in time. Discuss: Why does the author still remember this event from her childhood?
4. Tell the children that today they will be writing down a brief but important memory that they recall like it was yesterday. It can be from last week, or last year, or when they were younger.

FOLLOW UP:

Have students begin work on their rough drafts and, if there is time, share their paragraphs.

SESSIONS 2 and 3

PROCEDURE:

1. Review *Big Red Lollipop*. Discuss how this is a short personal narrative, a brief memory from a short period in time.
2. Read/booktalk/display other picture book vignette stories from the list above.
3. Have kids finish working on their rough drafts and make a good copy. Then have them each select a key sentence or two from their stories, and copy it around the spiral on the lollipop-shaped paper.

FOLLOW UP:

Have kids share their lollipop vignettes. Attach a paint stick to the back of each lollipop paper. Make a bulletin board display of lollipops and their accompanying finished stories.

SAMPLE OF A LOLLIPOP VIGNETTE
Grade 3, Milltown School, Bridgewater, NJ

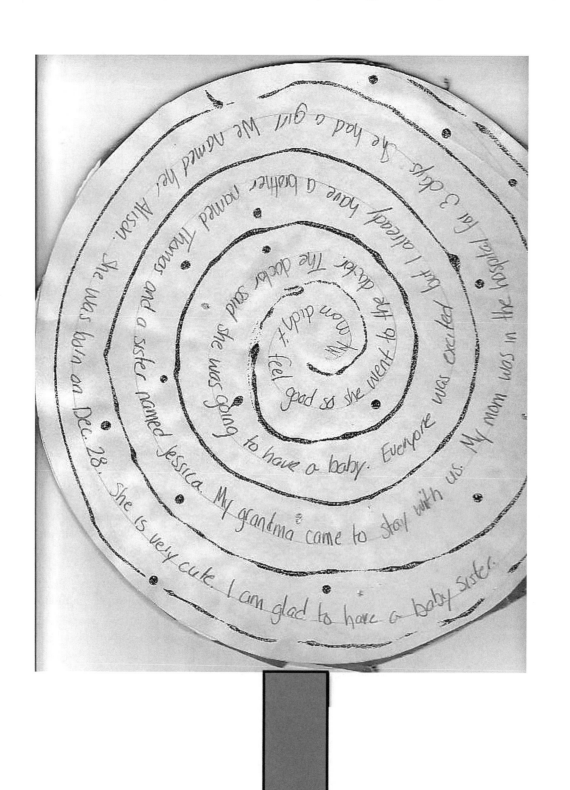

CLEMENTINE, FRIEND OF THE WEEK
A TEACHER'S GUIDE by Judy Freeman (www.JudyReadsBooks.com)

for *Clementine, Friend of the Week* by Sara Pennypacker, illustrated by Marla Frazee (Disney Hyperion, 2010). Printed with permission of the publisher, Disney Hyperion.

ABOUT THE GUIDE

In this guide, you will find an array of ideas, activities, writing and drawing prompts, discussion points, connections, and suggested projects you can use to delve deeper into the characters, plot, and themes introduced in *Clementine, Friend of the Week*. While you can't and shouldn't use all of these ideas, pick and choose the ones that best speak to your students, whether you're using the book as a read-aloud or a book for Guided Reading, Literature Circles, or Book Club discussion groups.

SUMMARY

As Clementine explains to her best friend, Margaret, on their bus ride home from school on Monday, today was the best day. She was picked to be Friend of the Week by her teacher, which means she will get to tell her autobiography to the class, be line leader, collect the milk money, and feed the fish. Best of all, on Friday she will get a special "Friend of the Week" booklet, where each of the kids in her third grade class will fill in a page describing what they think of her. Fourth grader Margaret still has her Friend of the Week booklet from last year, and reluctantly allows Clementine to come up to her apartment and see it. (It seems to be full of interesting comments, like, "Margaret is an extra-clean girl.") Ever the authority, Margaret advises Clementine to give everyone in her class compliments and maybe even presents so they'll write good things in her book, too.

Unfortunately, Margaret's older brother, Mitchell has put a piece of white tape over the "R" on the cover of her book, so it now says "Fiend of the Week." When Margaret notices it, she is furious, "like a cartoon person about to explode." Trying to be helpful, Clementine carefully peels off the offending tape and then shows Margaret what she's done. For some reason, that makes Margaret even madder. She bellows, " . . . AND YOU'RE NOT EVEN MY FRIEND AND I ONLY PLAY WITH YOU BECAUSE YOU LIVE IN MY BUILDING AND NOW YOU HAVE TO GO HOME!"

Now Clementine and Margaret are on the outs, and Clementine doesn't even know why. Worse still, the unthinkable happens. Clementine's beloved kitten, Moisturizer, disappears from the apartment and no one can find him. Being Friend of the Week is turning into Clementine's most miserable week ever.

For more about the Clementine books, including Judy Freeman's Teacher's Guide to the first three books in the series, go to **www.clementinebooks.com**.

BEST AT THIS, BLUE RIBBON FOR THAT

Riding the bus after school on Monday, Clementine is excited to tell Margaret about getting picked for Friend of the Week, where she'll get to tell her autobiography to the class, be line leader, collect the milk money, and feed the fish. Margaret is unimpressed, saying, "We did that when I was in third grade."

Clementine comes up to Margaret's apartment to see her booklet from last year. In Margaret's living room, next to the fireplace, is a whole bookcase filled with the many awards and trophies she has won. She and Clementine stand in front of the shelves, admiring them. Clementine says, "So I clasped my hands and we stood there having a moment of silence, staring at all the proof of how great Margaret was at everything. There sure was a lot of it. Three whole shelves of 'Best at This' and 'Blue Ribbon for That' lined up all neat and tight like groceries in the supermarket." *(page 3)*

DISCUSSION POINTS:

- Most people, including Clementine, never win trophies for what they do best, which in her case includes drawing and math. How does Clementine feel about Margaret's trophies?

- What if you could get a prize for the things you do best? What are your own special talents?

ACTIVITY:

- Students can design and make their own blue medals and awards plaques, making them freehand or on the computer. As an interesting art project, they could even construct handcrafted trophies. Each prize should be labeled with their names and the reason for the prize. (Encourage your kids to think of small but significant achievements, such as Tallest Snowman or Best Ear Wiggler.)

MORON – VILLAIN – PEST: ABBREVIATIONS AND ACRONYMS

Margaret's older brother Mitchell has 6 baseball trophies, each labeled M.V.P. Margaret tells Clementine the letters stand for "Moron – Villain – Pest." *(page 6)* Ask your kids if they know what the letters really stand for (Most Valuable Player).

ACTIVITY:

- Ask your group what other acronyms they know and what they stand for. Brainstorm a list, with examples like PTA, PB&J, and SPCA. Children can make up new acronyms and have others in the group try to figure out what the letters represent. (See the worksheet in this handbook on page 103.)

MARGARET'S COMPLIMENTS

Margaret shows Clementine her Friend of the Week booklet and reads aloud some of the compliments her classmates wrote. They include comments like, "I like having Margaret in class because she is neat," and "Margaret is helpfull. Every day she tells me what I do wrong." *(page 8)*

DISCUSSION POINTS:

- What is a compliment?
- How do the compliments fit Margaret's personality?

FIEND OF THE WEEK

Margaret is furious with Mitchell for covering the "R" in her Friend of the Week booklet so it now reads "Fiend of the Week." But when Clementine takes the booklet without Margaret seeing and peels of the tape, Margaret turns her fury on her friend. *"Who said you could read that?!"* she shrieks. Then she yells, "NOBODY'S GOING TO WRITE ANYTHING GREAT IN YOUR BOOKLET NO MATTER HOW MANY PRESENTS YOU GIVE THEM AND YOU'RE NOT EVEN MY FRIEND AND I ONLY PLAY WITH YOU BECAUSE YOU LIVE IN MY BUILDING AND NOW YOU HAVE TO GO HOME!" *(page 10)*

DISCUSSION POINTS:

- Why is Margaret so upset when Clementine touches her booklet of compliments?
- Why does Margaret blow up at Clementine and tell her she's not her friend?
- What does Clementine do in response?
- Have you ever had a fight with a good friend? What happened? How did you feel and what did you do?

CLEMENTINE'S BROTHER, CORN KERNEL

In this fourth book in the series, we still don't know Clementine's little brother's name, though she calls him any number of vegetable names, which your listeners may wish to track, like Corn Kernel, Yam, and Chili Pepper. When Clementine goes into the kitchen, she watches as he drags the big spaghetti pot out of the cupboard, turns it upside down over his head, and starts to whack on it with a big spoon, all the while laughing like crazy. She asks her mother, "Do you ever wonder if Corn Kernel is normal?" *(page 20)* Her mom doesn't think there's anything wrong with him.

WRITING PROMPTS:

- Write a character study about someone in your family, preferably a toddler, who does wacky things.
- Ask your parents to tell you what strange things you used to do when you were little.

MORON – VILLAIN – PEST:
ABBREVIATIONS AND ACRONYMS

Margaret's older brother Mitchell has 6 baseball trophies, each labeled M.V.P. She tells Clementine the letters stand for "Moron – Villain – Pest." As Clementine finds out later, that's not true. Do you know what the letters really stand for? An abbreviation is a shortened form of a word or phrase that makes it faster and easier to say or write (like U.S.A. for The United States of America or MVP for Most Valuable Player). An acronym, a type of abbreviation, is a made-up word, usually written in capitals, that is created by using the initial letter of a group of words (like AWOL, for Absent Without Leave).

DO YOU KNOW WHAT THESE LETTERS STAND FOR?

DIRECTIONS: Fill in each abbreviation or acronym below with its full phrase.

1.   PB&J = _ _ _ _ _ _   _ _ _ _ _ _   _ _ _   _ _ _ _ _

2.   TV = _ _ _ _ _ _ _ _ _

3.   PC = _ _ _ _ _ _ _ _   _ _ _ _ _ _ _

4.   PTA = _ _ _ _ _ _ - _ _ _ _ _ _   _ _ _ _ _ _ _ _ _ _

5.   NFL = _ _ _ _ _ _ _ _   _ _ _ _ _ _ _   _ _ _ _ _

6.   SPCA = _ _ _ _ _ _ _   _ _ _   _ _ _   _ _ _ _ _ _ _ _ _   _ _   _ _ _ _ _ _ _   _ _

             _ _ _ _ _ _

7.   YMCA = _ _ _ _ _   _ _ _ _ '   _ _ _ _ _ _ _ _   _ _ _ _ _ _ _ _ _ _

8.   ESP = _ _ _ _ _ _ _ _ _ - _ _ _ _ _ _   _ _ _ _ _ _ _ _ _

9.   IQ = _ _ _ _ _ _ _ _ _ _ _ _   _ _ _ _ _ _ _ _

10.   TTYL = _ _ _ _   _ _   _ _ _   _ _ _ _ _

11.   ROTFL = _ _ _ _ _ _ _   _ _   _ _ _   _ _ _ _ _ _ _ _ _ _ _

12.   MPH = _ _ _ _ _   _ _ _   _ _ _ _

13.   NASA = _ _ _ _ _ _ _ _   _ _ _ _ _ _ _ _ _ _   _ _ _   _ _ _ _ _   _ _ _ _ _ _ _ _ _ _ _ _ _

14.   SCUBA = _ _ _ _ - _ _ _ _ _ _ _ _ _   _ _ _ _ _ _ _ _ _   _ _ _ _ _ _ _ _ _   _ _ _ _ _ _ _ _

15.   POTUS = _ _ _ _ _ _ _ _ _   _ _   _ _ _   _ _ _ _ _ _   _ _ _ _ _ _

MAKE UP YOUR OWN ACRONYM: Write the acronym and the words it stands for below. Try it out on others to see if they can figure out what it means.

_____   =   _____

DO YOU KNOW WHAT THESE LETTERS STAND FOR? ANSWER KEY

1. PB&J = Peanut butter and jelly
2. TV = Television
3. PC = Personal computer
4. PTA = Parent-Teacher Association
5. NFL = National Football League
6. SPCA = Society for the Prevention of Cruelty to Animals
7. YMCA = Young Men's Christian Association
8. ESP = Extrasensory perception
9. IQ = Intelligence Quotient
10. TTYL = Talk to You Later
11. ROTFL = Rolling on the Floor Laughing
12. MPH = Miles per hour
13. NASA = National Aeronautics and Space Administration
14. SCUBA = Self-Contained Underwater Breathing Apparatus
15. POTUS = President of the United States

THE LITTLE RED HEN

When Clementine goes into the kitchen, her mother gives her a head of lettuce and a salad spinner to make salad for dinner. Clementine's mother is a big fan of the Little Red Hen Story. Her philosophy is, "Anyone who expects to eat something in our house should expect to help make it." Clementine tells us, "I always make a face about doing dinner chores, but the truth is, I *like* being in the steaming, clattery jumble of dinner-making with everybody else." *(page 24)*

DISCUSSION POINTS:

● What is the connection between the Little Red Hen Story and Clementine's mother's mealtime chores?

● What chores do you do in your family?

RELATED RESOURCES

● Don't assume your students know the story of the Little Red Hen. Have the ones who do retell it for the rest of the group. (If you don't remember the story, look for one of these splendid versions:
  Barton, Byron. *The Little Red Hen.* HarperCollins, 1993.
  Galdone, Paul. *The Little Red Hen.* Clarion, 1973. (There's a nice video of this story from Weston Woods, also available on YouTube at:
    http://www.youtube.com/watch?v=zr-yQGD9eAA).
  Pinkney, Jerry. *The Little Red Hen.* Dial, 2006.
  Zemach, Margot. *The Little Red Hen.* Farrar, 1983.

● You can also download, for free, a charmingly illustrated 1918 version of the story from Project Gutenberg at: **http://www.gutenberg.org/files/18735/18735-h/18735-h.htm**.

FIGHTING AND MAKING UP

Clementine doesn't exactly know why Margaret is so mad at her, and doesn't know what to do about not being friends anymore. Clementine's mother thinks they'll work it out, because the two girls have been friends since the day Margaret moved in, and that's what friends do. *(page 29)*

DISCUSSION POINTS:

● Describe how you made a friend.

● Have you ever had a fight with a friend? What started it?

● How did you make up or apologize or become friends again?

WRITING PROMPT:

- Maybe Clementine needs some feedback from someone who's had experience with making up from a fight—someone like you. Write Clementine a letter with your best advice on what she should do about Margaret.

GIVING COMPLIMENTS

Margaret tells Clementine she should give everybody in her class compliments all week so they'll give her some back when they write in her Friend of the Week booklet on Friday. On Tuesday, Clementine observes, "Giving people compliments turned out to be a lot harder than Margaret had made it sound." *(page 33)*

She compliments her classmate, Willy: "That's a huge bruise on your arm! Great colors!" To Joe, the shortest kid in her class, she says, "You look a little taller today. Maybe it's starting." She even tells the lunchroom lady that her hairnet makes her head look like a hornet's nest from the back.

DISCUSSION POINTS:

- Why is Clementine handing out compliments? What is unusual about them?

- Why and when should you give someone a compliment?

- When have you gotten or given a compliment and why? How did it make you feel?

ACTIVITY:

- Write a heartfelt compliment to someone you know. Sign it or don't sign it, but leave it where that person will find it.

EVERY DAY'S A HOLIDAY

On Saturday, all of the third and fourth graders will be meeting in Boston Common to hold a bike rally, which will raise money for their spring trip. All of the students are to decorate their bikes. Clementine knows she will have the "best-decorated bike in the history of life" because she plans to use some of her dad's decorations. *(page 36)*

Clementine's dad is the manager of the apartment building where the family lives. Dad says every day is some kind of holiday, and he decorates the lobby accordingly. For not just the normal holidays, but also wacky ones like Fruitcake-Toss Day, Punch-the-Clock Day, and Measure-Your-Feet Day, all actual observances, Dad has a comprehensive collection of plastic ornaments and decorations that he keeps in the basement. "Every week, he posts what special days are coming up on the lobby bulletin board, along with suggestions for how to celebrate." *(page 37)*

HOLIDAY RESOURCE:

- If you want a real list of actual holidays, including monthly, weekly, and daily, don't miss **http://www.brownielocks.com**, which is jam-packed with scores of both traditional and "bizarre, crazy, silly, unknown holidays & observances" and links for many of them, including National Procrastination Week, celebrated the first week of March, Learn What Your Name Means Day on March 10, or Eeyore's birthday on April 24. You can even print out each month as a calendar.

ACTIVITY:

- Just like Clementine's dad does, kids can compile a list of holidays they'd like to celebrate, either from the list on the website, or by making up their own, and make a plan of how they'd commemorate each one.

WRITING YOUR AUTOBIOGRAPHY

Part of being Friend of the Week is telling the class your life story. When Clementine is summoned to the front of the class on Tuesday to do just that, she begins, "I was born," and then has a hard time thinking of more substantive information. Teacher Mr. D'Matz says, "I'm sure you've done lots of interesting things since you've been born. What do you think a biographer would say in a book about you?" *(page 39)*

ACTIVITY:

- Have students make a timeline of life events they would include in their autobiographies. Then have them flesh out their lists, adding details about their families, friends, and important life events, writing it as a narrative. Have them include photographs of themselves in the finished autobiographies.

ONE INTERESTING FACT

Next, Mr. D'Matz has the class become reporters. Each person is to find out one interesting fact about Clementine. During recess, the kids ask her questions like, "If you were an animal, what would you be?" and "What is your favorite color?" (Clementine's answers: a gorilla and all of them) *(page 44)*

ACTIVITY:

- Brainstorm a list of 10 interesting questions that could be asked in such an interview. Each question should reveal something about the person being interviewed. Write them down on a large chart.

- Have students pair off and interview each other orally or in writing, using the list of 10 questions. If the interview is an oral one, the interviewers can take notes or simply listen carefully and attempt to remember the answers. They can then present their findings to the rest of the group, saying, for example, "This is David. He was born in Chicago, has three older sisters, loves to play soccer, and hates lima beans . . ." David will then introduce his partner in the same way.

- In a slightly different approach, take the 10 questions the children suggested, type them up as a worksheet, with a heading like "WHO AM I?", and run off a copy for each student. Without putting their names on the paper, children can record their answers to each question. Collect their papers and redistribute them randomly. Each person can read aloud the answers for one of the pages while the rest of the class listens carefully for details and tries to deduce the writer's identity. You could have children draw self-portraits and make a bulletin board of the portraits and the "WHO AM I" papers, labeled, GET TO KNOW OUR CLASS.

ABOUT MARGARET AND MITCHELL

When Clementine visits Margaret's apartment after school on Tuesday, hoping to make amends, Margaret's brother, Mitchell, brings her into the living room to see his baseball trophies. Each one is wearing a little diaper made out of paper towels, and that cracks Mitchell up. Who diapered them? Margaret, of course. Clementine says, "Why aren't you mad, Mitchell? You love baseball. You're obsessed with baseball . . . Margaret has three hundred awards. Don't you mind that she's so good at everything? Doesn't it make you feel kind of . . sorry for yourself?"

He replies, "I feel sorry for *her*. I love playing baseball. Margaret just loves winning awards." *(page 54-59)*

Read aloud pages 54-59 for a look into the different personalities of Margaret and her brother, Mitchell.

DISCUSSION POINTS:

- Why do you think Margaret diapered Mitchell's baseball trophies?

- How does Mitchell react?

- Why does Margaret want so many trophies?

- What is the difference between her trophies and those won by her big brother, Mitchell?

- How are the two of them different?

- How do they feel about each other?

THE GOLDEN RULE

Clementine's parents are big believers in the Golden Rule, "Do unto others as they would do unto you." They apply it to all sorts of situations, including Dad's rule: "Be quiet in the movies, as you would have others be quiet in the movies unto you." Mom's is: "Don't interrupt people when they're drawing unless it's an emergency with blood, as you would have them not interrupt you when you're drawing unless it's an emergency with blood." *(page 61)*

WRITING PROMPT:

- What "golden-rule"-like statement would best apply to you? Write and illustrate a new rule.

FREE TATTOOS

At recess on Wednesday, Clementine comes up with a Golden Rule good idea to make her classmates happy with her so they'll write good things about her in her Friend of the Week booklet: "Give tattoos unto others as you would have others give tattoos unto you." She draws free tattoos with markers on the arms of her classmates. Each person tells her what to draw. Charlie gets a naked fish sitting on an anchor, Lilly wants a rainbow with tulips under it, and her twin brother, Willy, wants the usual: a zombie shark with pointy teeth. On the arm of Norris-Boris-Morris-Horace-Brontosaurus, she draws peanuts so when he goes to the park and lies down on the sidewalk, pigeons will land on his arm and peck. *(page 64)*

ACTIVITY:

- If you could have a tattoo (and you can't, so don't ask your parents, though they might not mind one drawn in washable marker, and drawing tattoos on other kids' arms gets Clementine in trouble with the principal, so don't try that either), what would it be and why?

- Design your own personal tattoo, drawing it on paper (not your arm) and describing what it is and why you'd like it on your arm.

PROFESSIONAL DEVELOPMENT DAYS

After recess, Clementine's teacher sends her to see her principal, Mrs. Rice, to talk about her tattoo activity. Clementine shares her great new idea: she thinks students should have professional development days just like the teachers do. She'd like "some extra days off to get better at stuff. So if anybody wants to do a biography about us, they'd have something to write about." She figures they could go someplace like Jack's Joke Shop or a casino, where a kid could learn interesting things. *(page 75)*

ACTIVITY:

- Children can brainstorm and plan their own Professional Development Day. Ask them to work out the schedule for the day, planning where they would you go and what they would do.

WHAT'S SO FUNNY?

About Clementine's idea for a professional development day for students, Mrs. Rice thinks the school board would say, " . . . you students already have professional development days . . . They're called Saturday and Sunday."

"Then Mrs. Rice swiveled her chair away from me and clutched the top of her head, with her shoulders shaking. I knew she was secretly laughing, so I said I was all done visiting her, and I left. One thing they do not teach in principal school: what is funny and what is not." *(page 76)*

DISCUSSION POINT:

- Why does Mrs. Rice think this is funny?

- How does Clementine feel about her principal laughing like that?

- When and why do grownups laugh at kids?

- When and why do kids laugh at grownups?

ACTIVITY:

- What is the difference between what grownups and what kids think is funny? Make a chart like this:

WHAT GROWNUPS THINK IS FUNNY	WHAT KIDS THINK IS FUNNY
1. 2. 3. 4. 5.	1. 2. 3. 4. 5.

TV ROTS YOUR BRAIN FOR LIFE?

Maria's mother never lets her play at Clementine's house because there's a television set there. "Maria's mother thinks watching any television at all, even PBS, rots your brain for life, so there's no TV for Maria." *(page 77)*

DEBATING POINT: OPPOSING VIEWPOINTS

- Break your group into two teams: TV and NO TV. Have them make notes supporting their arguments, and then stage a debate. You could pair them up and have them debate each other, or set up a panel of children, with perhaps 4-6 on a side. Or have the whole group join in on a more freewheeling discussion, citing reasons for their arguments, listening to each other, and not interrupting. Your debating points could be on or more of the following:
  - Does TV rot your brain for life?
  - Should children be allowed to watch TV?
  - Should children be allowed to watch TV on school nights?

WHAT'S IN A NAME?

Clementine names Maria's lizard. "I'm an expert at picking pet names!" she cries. In the bathroom, she sees the perfect word: "...Your lizard's name is Flomax." *(page 80)* (OK, fine, you probably won't want to explain to your students that Flomax is a drug used to treat men with prostate problems. That's TMI—too much information. Just tell them it's a type of pill. They'll still think it's funny.)

ART ACTIVITY:

- What is your pet's name? If you had a new lizard like Maria's, what would you name it?

- Draw a picture of the pet you would most love to have if you could, and label it with the perfect name.

A PERFECT PRESENT

Maria shows Clementine the bike she decorated for the rally, which Clementine doesn't think looks decorated at all. "And that's when it hit me—an idea for an even better present than tattoos to give everybody!" *(page 83)*

MAKING PREDICTIONS:

- What do you think Clementine's idea is this time?

- What idea could you give her for a great present to give to her classmates?

RELATED RESOURCES:

- To see pictures of and information about Boston Common (which is the oldest park in the U.S.) and other landmarks in Boston, where Clementine lives, go to: **www.cityofboston.gov/freedomtrail/**. There you'll find maps, videos, and links to other attractions, like riding the Swan Boats in the Boston Public Garden across the street from the Common, which children may recognize from the classic picture book, *Make Way for Ducklings* by Robert McCloskey (Viking, 1941).

DECORATE YOUR BIKE

Clementine offers to help everyone decorate their bikes right before the bike rally using all the great plastic stuff her dad uses to decorate the lobby for each holiday. *(page 87)*

ART ACTIVITY:

- Design your own best bike decorations.

MISSING MOISTURIZER

When Clementine's beloved kitten, Moisturizer, goes missing on Thursday evening, first she searches the apartment building for him. Then she and her parents canvass the neighborhood, to no avail. Clementine cries, but her father says, "You can't give up hope. Moisturizer is counting on you. Wherever he is, he's not giving up hope . . . He didn't get out because you were careless. He got out because he was curious. Kittens are curious." *(page 103)*

"That reminded me about a certain terrible saying about curiosity and cats, which I am not going to repeat. I saw my dad remembering it."

" 'But satisfaction brought him back.' That's the end of that saying, remember," he said. *(page 105)*

Over the next day, Clementine cries and cries, even while she sleeps. She says, "I did not know one person could hold that much water." *(page 107)* Clementine tells her mom, "You know how Pea Pod says, 'You broke my feelings,' when he means they're hurt? Well. That's how I feel—like all the feelings inside me are broken."

Mom promises her feelings will be fixed again, saying, "You're a human being, right? Human brings have feelings. Everybody feels that sad sometimes. People write stories about it, and poetry; they paint pictures and compose music about it. To share how it feels."

Then her mom reminds her of how the characters in the book *Ginger Pye* felt when their dog was missing. "And do you remember how long it took to find him? And how they never stopped looking, and how finally, they got him back?"

Clementine says, "That was a book. This is real life." *(page 115)*

This is a book too, but we sure grieve with Clementine over her missing cat.

DISCUSSION POINTS:

- What is the saying Clementine does not want to repeat out loud? (Curiosity killed the cat.) What does this saying mean? What does the end of the saying—"But satisfaction brought him back."—mean?

- Have you ever felt the way Clementine did right then? What did you do about it, "to share how it feels"?

- What is the difference between a book and real life?

- What comforting words would you give to Clementine, based on your own experiences?

RELATED RESOURCE:

- Introduce your kids to the oldie-but-goodie Newbery Award book, *Ginger Pye* by Eleanor Estes (Harcourt, 1951).

LETTING EVERYONE DOWN

Early Saturday morning, Margaret comes to the door. Upon seeing Clementine's face, she says, "Hey! Did you go blind? Is that why you weren't in school yesterday?... Your eyes! They're red and all swollen. They look like tomatoes."

Dad counsels Clementine to tell Margaret about Moisturizer, saying, "It might help to talk to a friend . . ." Clementine says, "Margaret isn't my friend. She's mad at me and I don't even know why . . . She'd just tell me it's my fault. She never loses anything. She'd tell me I shouldn't have lost Moisturizer." Dad says, "She might surprise you. Why don't you give her a chance?" *(page 119-123)*

DISCUSSION POINTS:

- Should Clementine tell Margaret about her lost kitten? Why or why not?

- Why does Clementine feel she's let everyone down. Has she? What do you think her classmates are thinking about her right now?

ENEMY OF THE YEAR

When Margaret brings over Clementine's Friend of the Week booklet, Clementine is too distraught to read it, knowing her friends must be thinking of her as their Enemy of the Year for not showing up at the bike rally and helping them decorate their bikes. It's Mitchell, Margaret's older brother, who finally clues Clementine in on why Margaret got so mad at her. He tells her it's because Margaret's own Friend of the Week booklet is practically empty, with only a couple of pages of kids' comments. *(page 125-133)*

DISCUSSION POINTS:

- Why can't Clementine face her schoolmates at the bike rally on Boston Common?

- Why didn't Margaret enter the hula competition?

- Why does Clementine throw her new Friend of the Week booklet into The Black Hole under her bed?

ORANGE KITTEN SERIES

Angry at everyone for not finding or seeming to care about her kitten, Clementine figures the only thing she'll do for the rest of her life is to draw pictures of Moisturizer, " . . . like that famous artist in New Orleans who only paints one thing—a bight blue dog. I always wondered why that artist painted that one dog, but now I knew. He must have missed that dog a lot." *(page 137)*

Missing her kitten, Clementine draws many pictures of him from memory, calling it her "soon-to-be-famous "Orange Kitten" series.

RELATED RESOURCES:

That artist is George Rodrigue. Go to George Rodrigue's website, **www.georgerodrigue.com/rodrigue/** and click on PAINTINGS and then BLUE DOGS to see many examples of this series, all featuring a, well, blue dog.

ART ACTIVITY:

Children can draw a series of portraits of their own pets or animals around them, sketching them from memory or from real life.

UNSUNG HEROINE

But, unbeknownst to Clementine, it's Margaret who takes charge and saves the day, organizing the school's bike rally on Boston Common and having nearly a hundred kids decorate their bikes with copies of Clementine's missing kitten poster. This results in a photo and an article captioned, "STUDENTS USE BIKE RALLY TO HELP FIND MISSING PET" in the Sunday *Boston Globe*, which leads to a phone call from the man who has found what sounds like Moisturizer in Quincy, fifteen miles away. *(page 140-151)*

Clementine says, "I was so happy. I couldn't get over what Margaret had done. Just when I thought she was being the meanest to me, she was being the nicest." *(page 143)*

DISCUSSION POINTS:

- How does Margaret help Clementine?

- How does Clementine figure out that Margaret was responsible for organizing the bike rally?

- Why didn't she tell Clementine about what she had done?

- What Margaret does for Clementine is called a selfless or charitable act, an act of kindness, a mission of mercy, a mitzvah, or just a good deed. Have you ever known someone who did something like that for you or a person you know? What were the circumstances? Why do people do that?

- How did Moisturizer end up in Quincy, so far away?

JUST SMILE

When Clementine and her dad drive home (with Moisturizer draped around Clementine's neck), her dad says, "I wish I'd brought my sunglasses. They might as well shut down the power in Boston—you could light up the whole city tonight with your smile." *(page 151)*

DISCUSSION POINTS:

Why is Clementine smiling?

How does smiling make you feel?

ACTIVITY:

Just smile. Have your kids practice doing it. Everyone will feel better.

RELATED RESOURCES:

Do you know the song "Smile"? The music was written by famed silent movie icon, Charlie Chaplin, in 1936, and more recently recorded by Michael Jackson, the late pop star. If you want your kids to smile and laugh a lot, just show the spectacularful video of the song, sung by Michael Jackson, with clips of the Little Tramp from all of Chaplin's movies. Go to:

www.youtube.com/watch?v=iu-rLA4POkI (Or just look up the key words Smile and Charlie Chaplin.)

THE BEST FRIEND A PERSON COULD EVER HAVE

When Clementine finally reads her Friend of the Week booklet, it is "full of long paragraphs about stuff I hardly remembered doing." When she reads that, because of her, her friend Maria is now allowed to watch TV, she muses, "Which just goes to show that you never know when you're doing a good deed." Reading her classmates' comments gives her "an astoundishing idea" to make pet portraits for every person in her class to thank them for helping her find her kitten. For Margaret, though, she does something even more special, writing in Margaret's Friend of the Week booklet to describe everything she did for her on Saturday. *(page 152)*

DISCUSSION POINTS:

- What is an I.O.U.?

- What is the difference between Clementine's earlier compliments and presents for her classmates and the final good deeds she does for them?

- What kinds of good deeds have you done without realizing it?

- How does Clementine repay Margaret for her help?

- Why does Margaret finally smile at Clementine?

- What have you done for your friends lately to let them know you care?

ACTIVITIES:

- Have kids finish this sentence with an anecdote, either orally or written and illustrated, based on their own experiences: "Friendship is when . . ."

- Play for them one of the many YouTube videos of the song "Friendship," which was written by Cole Porter in 1939. You can find it sung by Ethel Merman to a group of sailors and in a duet with Judy Garland. Look up the key words "Friendship" and "Cole Porter" and you'll find the lyrics, which start with: "If you're ever in a jam, here I am." (You may omit the last of the three verses, as it's a little dicey, but the first two are great to sing with the kids.)

PORTMANTEAUS

Clementine makes up such colorful and fun words, like spectacularful (pages 52 and 85). This word, spectacularful, is what we call a portmanteau (first coined by Lewis Carroll in his classic nonsense poem, "Jabberwocky" in his 1871 book, Through the Looking Glass and What Alice Found There). In a portmanteau (pronounced port-man-toe), two or more words and their meanings are joined together to make a new word. Spectacularful combines spectacular and wonderful. Clementine also coins the word astoundishing on page 154. Ask your listeners what two words make up that one (astounding and astonishing).

ACTIVITY:

- Each student can make up his or her own portmanteau, write a definition of it, and compose an interesting sentence using it. Each can then write his or her word on a chart, and then read the sentence aloud to the rest of the group. Looking at the word and listening to the sentence for content clues, listeners will need to figure out what two words were joined together and what the new word means. (See page 123 of this handbook for worksheet template.)
    Example: NEW WORD: SNOUGH or SNOUGHING.
    SENTENCE: When I had a bad cold, I couldn't stop snoughing.
    DEFINITION: A sneeze and a cough, done at the same time.

FRIEND OF THE WEEK BOOKLETS

Here's how Friend of the week works in Clementine's classroom: "Every Monday, our teacher pulls a name out of a Kleenex box. That person, who is me this week, gets to be the leader of everything and tell about themselves. And everybody else has to say why it's so great to have that person around. The best part is that on Friday, they write it all down in a booklet for me to bring home." *(page 25)*

CULMINATING ACTIVITY:

- Start your own Friend of the Week program, based on Mr. D'Matz's plan. Or, do it in one fell swoop. Make a booklet for each child, and have students write a comment in each one, based on the personality and actions of each different child.

MEET THE AUTHOR, SARA PENNYPACKER

Get to know Sara Pennypacker from these interesting interviews and websites:
www2.scholastic.com/browse/article.jsp?id=3748896
    Scroll down the list of author videos to find an interview of Sara Pennypacker, describing her main character, Clementine
www2.scholastic.com/browse/contributor.jsp?id=2665
    In each of 16 short videos, author Sara Pennypacker answers a question about her writing and her book character, Clementine.
www.sarapennypacker.com
    In the "Ask Sara" feature of her website, the author says, "Do you have questions about writing or being a writer, or about the characters in any of my books? Would you like to know what's coming up? Please fill out the form below. I can't answer every question—pretty busy writing new books these days—but each month I'll answer one or two questions in my blog." In the "Share Your Thoughts" section, kids can write in their comments, and Sara answers some of their questions.

MEET THE ILLUSTRATOR, MARLA FRAZEE

Marla Frazee won a Caldecott Honor (silver medal) in 2009 for her picture book, *A Couple of Boys Have the Best Week Ever* (Harcourt, 2008) and another one in 2010 for her illustrations in *All the World* by Liz Garton Scanlon. (Simon & Schuster/Beach Lane, 2009). Her effusive pen and ink renderings of Clementine have helped make that character iconic for young readers everywhere. Visit her Web site at **www.marlafrazee.com**.

MAKE UP YOUR OWN PORTMANTEAU

In the Clementine books by Sara Pennypacker, Clementine uses many colorful and fun words, including "spectacularful." This word is what we call a portmanteau, a combination of two or more words joined together—in this case "spectacular" and "wonderful."

Make up your own portmanteau, merging together two words.

_____ + _____ = _____

My new word is: _____.

Write a definition of your new word:

_____

_____

_____

Now write an interesting sentence using your new word so people can figure out what it means.

_____

_____

_____

In Lewis Carroll's *Through the Looking Glass*, Humpty Dumpty tells Alice about portmanteaus, two words joined together to make a new one. According to Humpty Dumpty, the new words "mimsy" is a combination of "flimsy and miserable." As he says, "When *I* use a word . . . it means just what I choose it to mean—neither more nor less."

INSTRUCTIONS FOR MAKING ORIGAMI YODA

From the book, *The Strange Case of Origami Yoda* by Tom Angleberger (Amulet, 2010)
Used with permission of Amulet Books/Abrams.

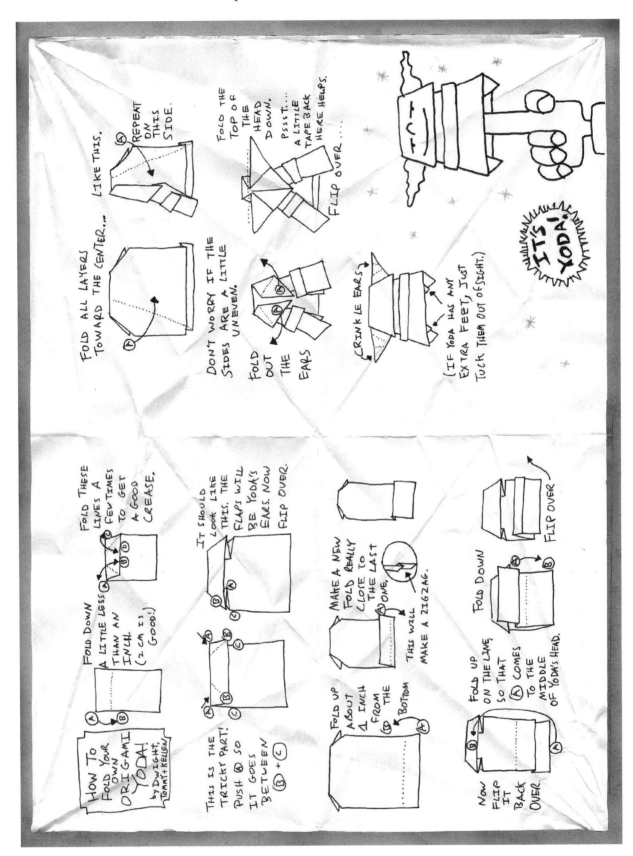

If you liked "The Strange Case of Origami Yoda" you'll love folding this E-Z Origami Yoda! You're ony 5 folds away from having your own Origami Yoda finger puppet to give wise advice with! Use your new power carefully!!

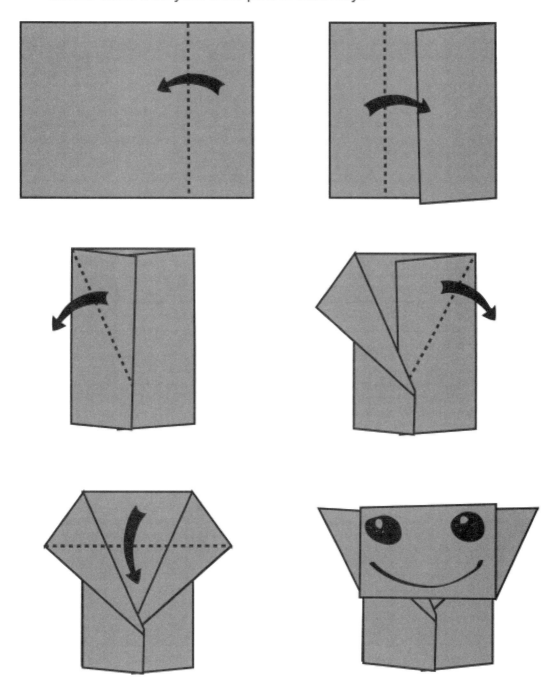

Look for new books coming from Tom Angleberger in 2011!

How to Fake Crack Your Knuckles Like Dwight Does

1. Put your right index finger between your left index and middle fingers.

2. Get it in there tight! The tip of your finger should be on the web between the left-hand fingers.

3. Now push your right finger against your chin. You need to push hard enough to make an airtight seal.

4. Quickly curl your right index finger down. When your finger pops loose it will make a . . .

You may only get a little pop at first, but with practice you should get loud enough to annoy a whole room full of people. Use your new power wisely.

TALK LIKE YODA!

Once you've made an Origami Yoda puppet, here's how to make it

Start with a simple sentence.

Move the last word or phrase to the front.

Now take the main name or noun and move it to the front. Replace it with "he," "she," "it," or "they."

Add a pause and an "erm." Talk slowly.

CHEWBACCA IS FUZZY.

FUZZY CHEWBACCA IS.

PRONOUN

CHEWBACCA FUZZY HE IS

ERM, CHEWBACCA . . . FUZZY HE IS

Note: For a question — like, "do you like Wookies?" — move the last word to the front, remove the "do," and add a "hmmm?"

WOOKIES YOU LIKE. HMMM?

I CAN READ YOUR MIND

Tell your audience, whether it's one person or more than one, "I'm going to ask you a series of questions. Don't say any of your answers out loud. Let's see if I can read your mind."

1. Pick a number between 1 and 9.

2. Multiply that number by 9.

3. Add those two numbers together.

4. Subtract 5. *(Note: their answers will always be 4.)*

5. Pick the letter of the alphabet that corresponds with your number. A is 1, B is 2, and so on. *(Note: their answers will always be D.)*

6. Think of country starting with that letter.

7. Take the second letter of that country and think of an animal starting with that letter.

8. What color is that animal?

9. And how is that gray elephant in Denmark anyhow?

NOTE: OK, they won't all think of a gray elephant from Denmark, but most will and will be astonished that you read their minds! It's up to you whether or not you want to let them in on the trick. In thinking of a country, the only nations, aside from Denmark, that begin with a D are Djibouti, Dominica, and the Dominican Republic—not exactly places that will come to mind. If you're doing this with younger kids, help them think by saying, "Think of a country *in Europe* that starts with that letter." There also aren't all that many animals that start with E. Of the ones we know best, there's earthworm, echidna, eel, egret, elk, emu, ermine, and ewe, so most will come up with elephant as the most ubiquitous of their choices.

I FEEL BETTER WITH A FROG IN MY THROAT:
History's Strangest Cures
by Carlyn Beccia (Houghton Mifflin, 2010)

How well do you know the cures for sickness and other ailments? Before sharing Beccia's book with your children, have them predict which of the following cures actually worked, which ones may have worked, and which ones didn't help one bit. Each cure listed below was actually used (and includes its place and time of origin). Write *Yes* for "Yes, I think it worked," *Maybe* for "Maybe it helped some," and *No* for "This cure either didn't work or it even made things worse." (**NOTE**: Of each trio of cures, at least one is a *Yes* or a *Maybe*.) Then read the book to find out the astonishing (and sometimes sickening) history of each cure.

CURES FOR COUGHS:
1. Caterpillar fungus (Ancient China)   _____
2. Frog Soup (16th century England   _____
3. Cherry bark (Native American)   _____

CURES FOR COLDS:
1. Chicken soup (Medieval Europe)   _____
2. Puke weed (16th century England)   _____
3. Skunk oil (Early 20th century America)   _____

CURES FOR SORE THROATS:
1. A frog down the throat (Medieval Europe)   _____
2. A necklace made from earthworms (Medieval Europe)   _____
3. Dirty sock tied around the neck (Early 20th century America)   _____

CURES FOR WOUNDS:
1. Moldy bread (Ancient Egypt)   _____
2. Puppy kisses (Ancient Greece)   _____
3. Spider webs (First century Rome)   _____

CURES FOR STOMACHACHES:
1. Drinking urine (Medieval Europe)   _____
2. Eating dirt (Ancient Native American)   _____
3. Drinking water with 50 live millipedes (17th century England)   _____

CURES FOR FEVERS:
1. Cut a vein and bleed (Ancient Egypt)   _____
2. Let leeches suck out your blood (Ancient Egypt)   _____
3. Burn the skin with hot cups (Ancient Egypt)   _____

CURES FOR HEADACHES:
1. Make a hole in the head (Prehistoric man)   _____
2. Apply mustard to the head (Ancient Greece)   _____
3. A shock from an electric eel (Ancient Rome)   _____

I FEEL BETTER WITH A FROG IN MY THROAT:
History's Strangest Cures
by Carlyn Beccia (Houghton Mifflin, 2010)

ANSWER KEY

How well do you know the cures for sickness and other ailments? Before sharing Beccia's book with your children, have them predict which of the following cures actually worked, which ones may have worked, and which ones didn't help one bit. Each cure listed below was actually used (and includes its place and time of origin). Write *Yes* for "Yes, I think it worked," *Maybe* for "Maybe it helped some," and *No* for "This cure either didn't work or it even made things worse." (**NOTE**: Of each trio of cures, at least one is a *Yes* or a *Maybe*.) Then read the book to find out the astonishing (and sometimes sickening) history of each cure.

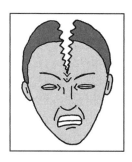

CURES FOR COUGHS:
1. Caterpillar fungus (Ancient China)	MAYBE
2. Frog Soup (16th century England	NO
3. Cherry bark (Native American)	YES

CURES FOR COLDS:
1. Chicken soup (Medieval Europe)	YES
2. Puke weed (16th century England	NO
3. Skunk oil (Early 20th century America)	NO

CURES FOR SORE THROATS:
1. A frog down the throat (Medieval Europe)	MAYBE
2. A necklace made from earthworms (Medieval Europe)	NO
3. Dirty sock tied around the neck (Early 20th century America)	NO

CURES FOR WOUNDS:
1. Moldy bread (Ancient Egypt)	YES
2. Puppy kisses (Ancient Greece)	MAYBE
3. Spider webs (First century Rome)	YES

CURES FOR STOMACHACHES:
1. Drinking urine (Medieval Europe)	NO
2. Eating dirt (Ancient Native American)	YES
3. Drinking water with 50 live millipedes (17th century England)	NO

CURES FOR FEVERS:
1. Cut a vein and bleed (Ancient Egypt)	MAYBE
2. Let leeches suck out your blood (Ancient Egypt)	NO
3. Burn the skin with hot cups (Ancient Egypt)	NO

CURES FOR HEADACHES:
1. Make a hole in the head (Prehistoric man)	NO
2. Apply mustard to the head (Ancient Greece)	NO
3. A shock from an electric eel (Ancient Rome)	MAYBE

BONES!

```
P N M O R T U S N I N E L E L
N A E E U X N W O W H A L E O
W O L C E A O C E R C O U E F
C S T B K R T S R I C O K O X
B R V E R T E B R A T E S N M
T I Y A L T L T R Y N S E N P
W Y M S F E E G A L I T R A C
E U N E E M K R I L O R S M I
X U A N M N S S E E J S L O N
S U I Y U H O W O A S X C R S
K P S M R F X B M J E S E I T
S B I R X O E N R E K S B W L
S B S L H C U C B E U C S E N
F J I S E A E I E O H E E R B
I S U N N M R K T O S M W S Y
```

BONES   VERTEBRATES   NECK
SKELETON   SKULL   SNAKE
FOSSIL   JOINT   FEMUR
RIBS   SYMMETRICAL   EXOSKELETON
FUNNY   SPINE   MARROW
CARTILAGE   WHALE

NOTE: I made this word search at a wonderful free site at **www.armoredpenguin.com**, using vocabulary from the book *Bones: Skeletons and How They Work* by Steve Jenkins (Scholastic, 2010). You can make all kinds of fun puzzles here and save them in PDF or HTML formats, and print them out for your kids to do. What a wonderful way to check if your students have assimilated the vocabulary words from a book or lesson. To add definitions for each word, see the crossword puzzle I made at the same site, on page 121 of this handbook.

BONES!

Across

3 Bones in an animal's body, put together
7 Humans have 206 of these
9 Soft, jelly-like material inside your bones
11 Backbone
13 Both sides of an animal are the same or _____
14 Rock cast of ancient bones
16 The place where bones meet

Down

1 Animals with bony skeletons
2 Human body's longest bone
4 Surprisingly, both giraffes and humans have 7 of these bones
5 Humans have 12 pairs of these
6 Largest animal skeleton, the blue _____
8 What an insect or spider or crab has outside its body
10 This animal can have 400 pairs of ribs
12 What supports a shark's body, instead of bone
14 Just a nerve, but we call it the _____ bone
15 The brain is protected by this

WORDS:

BONES	SKULL	FEMUR	WHALE
SKELETON	JOINT	EXOSKELETON	CARTILAGE
FOSSIL	SYMMETRICAL	FUNNY	
RIBS	NECK	SPINE	
VERTEBRATES	SNAKE	MARROW	

NOTE: This puzzle was composed on the free website, **www.armoredpenguin.com**, using facts and vocabulary from the book *Bones: Skeletons and How They Work* by Steve Jenkins (Scholastic, 2010). I added my own list of words at the bottom, since kids probably won't know how to spell them. Also see the word search on page 120 of this handbook.

BONES! ANSWER KEY

BONES!

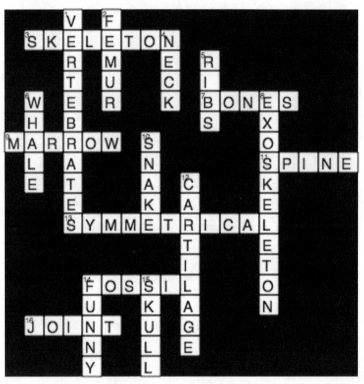

Across

3 Bones in an animal's body, put together
7 Humans have 206 of these
9 Soft, jelly-like material inside your bones
11 Backbone
13 Both sides of an animal are the same or _____
14 Rock cast of ancient bones
16 The place where bones meet

Down

1 Animals with bony skeletons
2 Human body's longest bone
4 Surprisingly, both giraffes and humans have 7 of these bones
5 Humans have 12 pairs of these
6 Largest animal skeleton, the blue _____
8 What an insect or spider or crab has outside its body
10 This animal can have 400 pairs of ribs
12 What supports a shark's body, instead of bone
14 Just a nerve, but we call it the _____ bone
15 The brain is protected by this

DO YOU KNOW LIZARDS?

DIRECTIONS: Write the number of each description next the name of the one lizard it fits. Then look at the boxed letters in each lizard's name. Fill in the letters, in number order, on the lines at the bottom of the page to spell a secret message. (Answers can be found in *Nic Bishop Chameleons* by Nic Bishop (Scholastic, 2010) and on page 124 of this handbook.)

1. Has no legs and looks like a snake
2. Smallest lizard
3. Largest lizard, and the world's largest venomous animal
4. Swims beneath the desert sand like a little shark
5. Its head looks just like its tail
6. Drinks water by rubbing belly on damp sand
7. Can change colors when excited, sleepy, or cold
8. Can run across the surface of water without sinking
9. Can squirt blood from its eyes to foil coyotes
10. Uses flaps of skin like wings to glide from tree to tree

S̲ANDFISH   ___

KOMOD̲O DRAGON   ___

FLY I̲N̲G̲ DRAGON   ___

GL̲ASS LI̲Z̲ARD   ___

THOR̲NY DE̲VIL   ___

BA̲SILISK   ___

CHA̲M̲ELEON   ___

DWA̲R̲F GECKO   ___

SHINGLEBA̲CK SKINK (OR TWO-HEADED SKINK)   ___

HORNED LIZ̲ARD   ___

FILL IN LETTERS BELOW TO SPELL A SECRET MESSAGE:

___ ___ ___ ___ ___ ___ ___ ___   ___ ___ ___   ___ ___ ___ ___ ___ ___ ___!

DO YOU KNOW LIZARDS?

ANSWER KEY

DIRECTIONS: Write the number of each description next the name of the one lizard it fits. Then look at the boxed letters in each lizard's name. Fill in the letters, in number order, on the lines at the bottom of the page to spell a secret message. Answers can also be found in *Nic Bishop Chameleons* by Nic Bishop (Scholastic, 2010).

1. Has no legs and looks like a snake
2. Smallest lizard
3. Largest lizard, and the world's largest venomous animal
4. Swims beneath the desert sand like a little shark
5. Its head looks just like its tail
6. Drinks water by rubbing belly on damp sand
7. Can change colors when excited, sleepy, or cold
8. Can run across the surface of water without sinking
9. Can squirt blood from its eyes to foil coyotes
10. Uses flaps of skin like wings to glide from tree to tree

SANDFISH	<u>4</u>
KOMO**D**O DRAGON	<u>3</u>
FLY**ING** DRAGON	<u>10</u>
G**L**ASS L**IZ**ARD	<u>1</u>
THO**R**NY D**E**VIL	<u>6</u>
B**A**SILISK	<u>8</u>
CH**AM**ELEON	<u>7</u>
DW**AR**F GECKO	<u>2</u>
SHINGLEB**A**CK SKINK (OR TWO-HEADED SKINK)	<u>5</u>
HORNED LI**Z**ARD	<u>9</u>

FILL IN LETTERS BELOW TO SPELL A SECRET MESSAGE:

L I Z A R D S   A R E   A M A Z I N G!

BIOGRAPHY HASH
An updated excerpt from
Books Kids Will Sit Still For 3 by Judy Freeman
(Libraries Unlimited, ©2006)

The biography section is the weakest link in most elementary school libraries. Brilliant, compelling, fascinating biographies are still in short supply, though there are increasingly more notable exceptions, including those by David A. Adler, Don Brown, Marie Ferguson Delano, Candace Fleming, Russell Freedman, Jean Fritz, Barbara Kerley, Kathleen Krull, Meghan McCarthy, Andrea Davis Pinkney, Diane Stanley, Marie Ferguson Delano, Candace Fleming, Barbara Kerley, Susan Goldman Rubin, Judith St. George, and Tanya Lee Stone. After weeding the outdated, inaccurate, unattractive, and downright dull biographies out of your school library collection, the shelves can look pitifully sparse. Bit by bit, we strive to build them up again, adding a handful of treasures each year with which we hope to lure our students to the genre. The Picture Book Biography bibliography on page 128 of this handbook provides a list of 99 unforgettable biographies that you can use to introduce students of all ages to the genre or demonstrate the components of a good biography to go with the following biography lesson.

GOT ANY BIOGRAPHY IDEAS?

Third grade teacher, Julie Kotcho, mentioned to me that her class was about to start a biography unit. "Can you give us a biography intro in the library?" Sure. No problem.

For the first lesson, I usually booktalk a variety of biographies to get kids interested, discussed what makes a person famous, and review how to find them on the shelves. We break down the word into its roots: "BIO" means life, "GRAPHY" means writing, and "AUTO" means self, so children readily put together the meaning for the word "AUTOBIOGRAPHY."

Next we go over our biography chant. Mnemonic devices always help us remember which section of the library is which, and if you add motions, it's a snappy way to get children involved physically as well as vocally.

BIOGRAPHY CHANT (by Judy Freeman)

BI-O-GRA-PHY (swing arms back & snap fingers after each syllable)
They're IN ALPHABETICAL ORDER *(clap clap)*
By the FAMOUS PERSON'S last name (hands on hips)
NOT THE AUTHOR! (point and shake both index fingers at each other)
They're IN ALPHABETICAL ORDER *(clap clap)*
By the FAMOUS PERSON'S last name (hands on hips)
NOT THE AUTHOR! (point and shake both index fingers at each other)

BIOGRAPHY HASH, cont.

Several days before my first scheduled biography lesson, I logged on to my e-mail. I subscribe to LM_NET, the indispensable school librarian's listserv (see page 187 for instructions on how to subscribe), and every day I plow through hundreds of fascinating questions and comments about every possible issue a school librarian can face: censorship, cuts in funding, requests for booklists, computer problems, you name it.

There was an intriguing and lively post about a biography lesson called *Bio Stew* by librarian Patty Melville from Pittsfield, Massachusetts. Patty described how she brings in a big pot, apron, hat, and spoon. Inside the pot, she places colored strips of paper that say "Name," Where lived," "Family members," and so on. The kids pull out the strips and read them. Then, after she reads aloud a book about Martin Luther King, Jr., the children recall a component of the biography and return that strip to the pot.

What a great follow-up idea, I thought. But what if . . . (As teachers, we always need to ask "what if." When we hear a good idea, we try to put our own spin on it.) What if we were to put together a recipe the kids could actually eat? Then we could say we *ate* a biography. Hmm. Why not? I was ready for something new, ever on the lookout for innovative and irresistible ways to bombard my students with books.

A trip to the grocery store helped me put together my "recipe" as follows:

11 BIOGRAPHY HASH INGREDIENTS:

Label—*Ingredient* (Explanation of its connection to a person's life.)

Birth date and place — *Yellow raisins* (We come out wrinkled, and see the sun.)

Family members — *Ritz Bits crackers* (Some family members can be a bit crackers sometimes.) (NOTE: You could use little corn chips, because family members are all "chips" off the old block, or little jellybeans, because family members are "human beans."

Childhood and School Life — *Goldfish crackers* (Fish gather in schools, too.)

Hobbies, Interests, and Activities — *Bugles crackers* (Sometimes we like to blow our own horns.)

Anecdotes — *Pretzels* (All people have interesting stories in their lives, with twists and turns, ups and downs, just like a pretzel.)

Career — *Chocolate chips* (When a person makes a lot of money or has good fortune, we say he or she is "in the chips.")

Reasons for Fame — *Cheerios* (We cheer a famous person's successes.)

Later life / Old age — *M&Ms* (This stands for More Mature.)

Death — *Black raisins* (We become shriveled and the lights go out.)

Photos and likenesses — *Sunflower seeds* (Good biographies let us see how the person looked or looks. Sunflower seeds remind me of sunflowers, which remind me of Vincent Van Gogh's paintings of sunflowers, which remind me of his self portraits . . .)

BIOGRAPHY HASH, cont.

YOU ARE WHAT YOU EAT

Using the computer, I designed, then printed out and laminated, a simple new label for each of the ten bags, boxes, and jars of snack foods I had bought. After affixing each new label to its product, I packed all the ingredients into a large picnic basket and a giant soup pot.

Wearing my white toque and apron, I greeted the class at the door. "Perhaps you've heard of the great chef, Julia Child? She couldn't make it here this week, so today, welcome to Cooking with Freeman. Last week we found out a bit about biographies. This week, let's really sink our teeth into them."

I had set up the library with 24 chairs in rows, audience-style, and two long tables across the front of the room. Children love props. Bring out a magic box or bag with a mysterious object within and they're hooked. Stepping behind the tables, with great flourish I lifted the soup pot and the picnic basket and placed them on the surface. Dramatically, I unpacked a series of measuring cups, a wooden spoon, and a huge mixing bowl.

"Today we prove that old saying, 'You are what you eat.' I need volunteers to help me unpack our ten special ingredients." Every hand went up.

Each child selected to come up to the Cook's Table extracted from the pot or basket one ingredient and read the laminated label aloud to the class. I then explained the connections of each ingredient to a famous person's life. As we lined up the food items in chronological order on our long table, the class began to salivate audibly. When one child drew out the big brown bag of M&Ms, the class let out a collective moan.

"Are there really M&Ms in there? Could we eat them?" they asked. "Hmmm. That's an interesting thought," I replied mysteriously. "We'll have to see about that."

We talked about the ways a biography can be put together. Some are chronological, starting with the subject's birth, and ending with his or her death. Others start in adulthood and flash back to childhood. Others leave out key ingredients that may be unknown or irrelevant to the subject. We discussed how biographies do not necessarily use all ten ingredients (the person may still be alive or information about the person's early life may not be known), and that the order of ingredients can vary depending on how the biographer chooses to tell the story.

GETTING TO KNOW YOU

Next I read aloud a picture book biography. Picture book biographies can be finished in one sitting and give a brief and visually appealing overview of a person's life. (They work well with older readers, too, who still love to view a great story.) One objective was to introduce the class to a biography about a person who had overcome or coped with adversity or dedicated his or her life to a selfless purpose. Children tend to gravitate to the rich and flamboyant as heroes, not realizing that there are often other, better reasons for fame.

"Listen carefully as I read the book aloud. Try to commit to memory the most interesting facts, dates, and anecdotes. Those of you who remember the best details and can connect them to the ingredients we have assembled here may be asked to come up and assist with the mixing of our Biography Hash."

All eyes and ears were riveted to *Snowflake Bentley* by Jacqueline Briggs Martin, the visually stunning 1999 Caldecott Medal winner about the Vermont farmer, born in 1865, who was so infatuated with drawing and photographing snow that he was the first to discover that most snowflakes have six sides or branches, and that no two snowflakes are alike.

Miss Kotcho's third graders were most taken with *Snowflake Bentley* with its striking woodcuts hand tinted with watercolors, especially when they realized that a snow story they had just read for science class coincidentally included photos taken by none other than Wilson Bentley. The group decided that though Bentley died of pneumonia from being out in a blizzard only two weeks after his book was published, it was somehow fitting he died from doing what he loved best—walking in the snow.

BIOGRAPHY HASH, cont.

After our read-aloud session, I called on children to recall one fact that would tie in with one ingredient—for example, education: "Wilson Bentley's mother taught him at home. He read a whole set of encyclopedias." For Later Life, they volunteered: "Willie published a book of his snow crystal photographs when he was 66 years old."

Each child who could volunteer a pertinent fact then came up to the Cook's Table and measured out the corresponding ingredient (1 1/2 cups of bugles; 1/2 cup yellow raisins, 1/4 cup sunflower seeds, etc.) into a huge bowl and stirred the contents with a large wooden spoon. I made up the amounts as we went along. This is a hard recipe to wreck. Pretty much anything goes.

By the time all ten ingredients were mixed together, the results were not only colorful, but tantalizing as well. "Are we going to taste the recipe?" the kids begged, and of course that was my intention all along. Miss Kotcho and I spooned portions for all into small individual paper cups for an all-class munch. The children heartily approved of our new recipe as we snacked on our crunchy, salty, sweet, and altogether satisfying trail mix, made up of all the parts of a famous person's life. I also referred the ever-ravenous class to the cook books in the 641.5's for more swell recipes.

Julie Kotcho, the teacher who got me re-thinking biographies, was elated. Here was a perfect new structure for her follow-up assignment. Children then selected and read a biography from the library, wrote up a report using the ten ingredients as their organizing points, and prepared an oral presentation, which they made in full costume, assuming the identity of their famous person. All in all, it was a most satisfying way to work collaboratively with a teacher to let students meet the rich and famous.

99 EXEMPLARY ONE- OR TWO-SESSION READ-ALOUD PICTURE BOOK BIOGRAPHIES FOR GRADES 2-6

compiled by Judy Freeman

In the past 20 years, the genre of the picture book biography has blossomed. Below is a list of my top 95 read-aloud titles that children of all ages will find fascinating and enlightening.

Adler, David A. *America's Champion Swimmer: Gertrude Ederle.* Illus. by Terry Widener. Harcourt, 2000.

Adler, David A. *A Picture Book of Louis Braille.* Illus. by John and Alexandra Wallner. Holiday House, 1997.

Adler, David A. *Lou Gehrig: The Luckiest Man.* Illus. by Terry Widener. Harcourt, 1997.

Aldrin, Buzz. *Reaching for the Moon.* Illus. by Wendell Minor. HarperCollins, 2005. (Buzz Aldrin)

Aliki. *William Shakespeare & the Globe.* Illus. by the author. HarperCollins, 1999.

Anderson, Laurie Halse. *Thank You, Sarah: The Woman Who Saved Thanksgiving.* Illus. by Matt Faulkner. Simon & Schuster, 2002. (Sarah Hale)

Anderson, M. T. *Handel, Who Knew What He Liked.* Illus. by Kevin Hawkes. Candlewick, 2001.

Anholt, Laurence. *Stone Girl, Bone Girl: The Story of Mary Anning.* Illus. by Sheila Moxley. Orchard, 1999.

Barasch, Lynne. *Hiromi's Hands.* Illus. by the author. Lee & Low, 2007. (Hiromi Suzuki)

Barasch, Lynne. *Knockin' on Wood: Starring Peg Leg Bates.* Illus. by the author. Lee & Low, 2004.

Barton, Chris. *The Day-Glo Brothers: The True Story of Bob and Joe Switzer's Bright Ideas and Brand-New Colors.* Illus. by Tony Persiani. Charlesbridge, 2009.

Brown, Don. *Alice Ramsey's Grand Adventure.* Illus. by the author. Houghton Mifflin, 1997.

Brown, Don. *American Boy: The Adventures of Mark Twain.* Illus. by the author. Houghton Mifflin, 2003.

Brown, Don. *Dolley Madison Saves George Washington.* Illus. by the author. Houghton Mifflin, 2007.

Brown, Don. *Odd Boy Out: Young Albert Einstein.* Illus. by the author. Houghton Mifflin, 2004.

Brown, Don. *Rare Treasure: Mary Anning and Her Remarkable Discoveries.* Illus. by the author. Houghton Mifflin, 1999.

Brown, Don. *Ruth Law Thrills a Nation.* Illus. by the author. Houghton Mifflin, 1993.

Brown, Don. *Teedie: The Story of Young Teddy Roosevelt.* Illus. by the author. Houghton, Mifflin, 2009.

Brown, Don. *A Wizard from the Start: The Incredible Boyhood & Amazing Inventions of Thomas Edison.* Illus. by the author. Houghton Mifflin, 2010.

Brown, Monica. *Pelé, King of Soccer / Pelé, El Rey del Futbol.* Illus. by Rudy Gutierrez. Trans. by Fernando Gayesky. HarperCollins/Rayo, 2009.

Brown, Tami Lewis. *Soar, Elinor!* Illus. by Francois Roca. Farrar, 2010.

Bryant, Jen. *A River of Words: The Story of William Carlos Williams.* Illus. by Melissa Sweet. Eerdmans, 2008.

Burleigh, Robert. *Flight: The Journey of Charles Lindbergh.* Illus. by Mike Wimmer. Philomel, 1991.

Busby, Peter. *First to Fly: How Wilbur and Orville Wright Invented the Airplane.* Illus. by David Craig. Random, 2003.

Byrd, Robert. *Leonardo, Beautiful Dreamer.* Illus. by the author. Dutton, 2003. (Gr. 4-8) (Leonardo da Vinci)

Carlson, Laurie. *Boss of the Plains: The Hat That Won the West.* Illus. by Holly Meade. DK Ink, 1998. (John Stetson)

Chandra, Deborah and Madeline Comora. *George Washington's Teeth.* Illus. by Brock Cole. Farrar, 2003.

Christensen, Bonnie. *The Daring Nellie Bly: America's Star Reporter.* Illus. by the author. Knopf, 2003.

Christensen, Bonnie. *Woody Guthrie: Poet of the People.* Illus. by the author. Knopf, 2001.

Cline-Ransome, Lisa. *Satchel Paige.* Illus. by James E. Ransome. Simon & Schuster, 2000.

Coerr, Eleanor. *Sadako.* Illus. by Ed Young. Putnam, 1993. (Sadako Sasaki)

Cohn, Amy L. and Schmidt, Suzy. *Abraham Lincoln.* Illus. by David A. Johnson. Scholastic, 2002.

Cooney, Barbara. *Eleanor.* Illus. by the author. Viking, 1996. (Eleanor Roosevelt)

Corey, Shana. *Mermaid Queen: The Spectacular True Story of Annette Kellerman, Who Swam Her Way to Fame, Fortune, & Swimsuit History!* Illus. by Edwin Fotheringham. Scholastic, 2009.

Corey, Shana. *You Forgot Your Skirt, Amelia Bloomer!: A Very Improper Story.* Illus. by Chesley McLaren. Scholastic, 2000.

Davies, Jacqueline. *The Boy Who Drew Birds: A Story of John James Audubon.* Illus. by Melissa Sweet. Houghton Mifflin, 2003.

Delano, Marie Ferguson. *Inventing the Future: A Photobiography of Thomas Alva Edison.* Illus. with photos. National Geographic, 2002.

Erdrich, Lise. *Sacagawea.* Illus. by Julie Buffalohead. Carolrhoda, 2003.

Freedman, Russell. *The Adventures of Marco Polo.* Illus. by Bagram Ibatoulline. Scholastic, 2006.

Gerstein, Mordicai. *What Charlie Heard: The Story of the Composer Charles Ives.* Illus. by the author. Farrar, 2002.

Giblin, James Cross. *George Washington: A Picture Book Biography.* Illus. by Michael Dooling. Scholastic, 1992.

Giblin, James Cross. *The Many Rides of Paul Revere.* Illus. with reprods. Scholastic, 2007.

Gilliland, Judith Heide. *Steamboat: The Story of Captain Blanche Leathers.* Illus. by Holly Meade. DK Ink, 2000.

Giovanni, Nikki. *Rosa.* Illus. by Bryan Collier. Henry Holt, 2005. (Rosa Parks)

Hopkinson, Deborah. *Home on the Range: John A. Lomax and His Cowboy Songs.* Illus. by S. D. Schindler. Putnam, 2009.

Houston, Gloria. *My Great Aunt Arizona.* Illus. by Susan Condie Lamb. HarperCollins, 1992. (Arizona Houston Hughes)

Joseph, Lynn. *Fly, Bessie, Fly.* Illus. by Yvonne Buchanan. Simon & Schuster, 1998. (Bessie Coleman)

Kerley, Barbara. *The Dinosaurs of Waterhouse Hawkins.* Illus. by Brian Selznick. Scholastic, 2001. (Benjamin Waterhouse Hawkins)

Kerley, Barbara. *The Extraordinary Mark Twain (According to Susy).* Illus. by Edwin Fotheringham. Scholastic, 2010.

Kerley, Barbara. *What to Do About Alice?: How Alice Roosevelt Broke the Rules, Charmed the World, and Drove Her Father Teddy Crazy!* Illus. by Edwin Fotheringham. Scholastic, 2008.

Krull, Kathleen. *The Boy on Fairfield Street: How Ted Geisel Grew Up to Become Dr. Seuss.* Illus. by Steve Johnson and Lou Fancher. Random, 2004.

Krull, Kathleen. *The Boy Who Invented TV: The Story of Philo Farnsworth.* Illus. by Greg Couch. Knopf, 2009.

Krull, Kathleen. *Harvesting Hope: The Story of Cesar Chavez.* Illus. by Yuyi Morales. Harcourt, 2003.

Krull, Kathleen. *Houdini: World's Greatest Mystery Man and Escape King.* Illus. by Eric Velasquez. Walker, 2005.

Krull, Kathleen. *Kubla Khan.* Illus. by Robert Byrd. Viking, 2010.

Krull, Kathleen. *The Road to Oz: Twists, Turns, Bumps, and Triumphs in the Life of L. Frank Baum.* Illus. by Kevin Hawkes. Knopf, 2008.

Krull, Kathleen. *Wilma Unlimited: How Wilma Rudolph Became the World's Fastest Woman.* Illus. by David Diaz. Harcourt, 1996.

Lasky, Kathryn. *The Librarian Who Measured the Earth.* Illus. by Kevin Hawkes. Little, Brown, 1994. (Eratosthenes)

Lasky, Kathryn. *The Man Who Made Time Travel.* Illus. by Kevin Hawkes. Farrar, 2003. (John Harrison)

Lasky, Kathryn. *A Voice of Her Own: The Story of Phyllis Wheatley, Slave Poet.* Illus. by Paul Lee. Candlewick, 2002.

Lester, Helen. *Author: A True Story.* Illus. by the author. Houghton Mifflin, 1997. (Helen Lester)

Li, Cunxin. *Dancing to Freedom: The True Story of Mao's Last Dancer.* Illus. by Anne Spudvilas. Walker, 2008. (Li Cunxin)

Martin, Jacqueline Briggs. *Snowflake Bentley.* Illus. by Mary Azarian. Houghton Mifflin, 1998. (Wilson Bentley)

McCarthy, Meghan. *Strong Man: The Story of Charles Atlas.* Illus. by the author. Knopf, 2007.

McCully, Emily Arnold. *Marvelous Mattie: How Margaret E. Knight Became an Inventor.* Illus. by the author. Farrar, 2006.

McCully, Emily Arnold. *My Heart Glow: Alice Cogswell, Thomas Gallaudet and the Birth of American Sign Language.* Illus. by the author. Hyperion, 2008.

McGinty, Alice B. *Darwin.* Illus. by Mary Azarian. Houghton Mifflin, 2009. (Charles Darwin)

Millman, Isaac. *Hidden Child.* Illus. by the author. Farrar, 2005. (Isaac Millman)

Mochizuki, Ken. *Passage to Freedom: The Sugihara Story.* Illus. by Dom Lee. Lee & Low, 1997. (Chiune Sugihara)

Nelson, Vaunda Micheaux. *Bad News for Outlaws: The Remarkable Life of Bass Reeves, Deputy U.S. Marshal.* Illus. by R. Gregory Christie. Carolrhoda, 2009.

Old, Wendie. *To Fly: The Story of the Wright Brothers.* Illus. by Robert Andrew Parker. Clarion, 2002. (Gr. 4-8)

Parks, Rosa with Jim Haskins. *I Am Rosa Parks.* Illus. by Wil Clay. Dial, 1997.

Pinkney, Andrea Davis. *Bill Pickett: Rodeo-Ridin' Cowboy.* Illus. by Brian Pinkney. Harcourt/Gulliver, 1996.

Pinkney, Andrea Davis. *Duke Ellington.* Illus. by Brian Pinkney. Hyperion, 1998.

Pinkney, Andrea Davis. Ella Fitzgerald: The Tale of a Vocal Virtuosa. Illus. by Brian Pinkney. Hyperion, 2002.

Pinkney, Andrea Davis. *Sojourner Truth's Step-Stomp Stride.* Illus. by Brian Pinkney. Disney Hyperion/Jump at the Sun, 2009.

Poole, Josephine. *Anne Frank.* Illus. by Angela Barrett. Knopf, 2005.

Rappaport, Doreen. *Eleanor, Quiet No More: The Life of Eleanor Roosevelt.* Illus. by Gary Kelley. Disney/Hyperion, 2009.

Rappaport, Doreen. *Martin's Big Words: The Life of Dr. Martin Luther King, Jr.* Illus. by Bryan Collier. Hyperion, 2001.

Ray, Deborah Kogan. *Down the Colorado: John Wesley Powell, the One-Armed Explorer.* Illus. by the author. Farrar, 2007.

Ray, Deborah Kogan. *Wanda Gág: The Girl Who Lived to Draw.* Illus. by the author. Viking, 2008.

Reich, Susanna. *José!: Born to Dance.* Illus. by Raúl Colón. Simon & Schuster, 2005. (José Limón)

Rumford, James. *Sequoyah: The Man Who Gave His People Writing.* Illus. by the author. Houghton Mifflin, 2004.

Ryan, Pam Muñoz. *When Marian Sang.* Illus. by Brian Selznick. Scholastic, 2002. (Marian Anderson)

Schanzer, Rosalyn. *How Ben Franklin Stole the Lightning.* Illus. by the author. HarperCollins, 2003.

Silverman, Erica. *Sholom's Treasure: How Sholom Aleichem Became a Writer.* Illus. by Mordicai Gerstein. Farrar, 2005.

Silvey, Anita. *Henry Knox: Bookseller, Soldier, Patriot.* Illus. by Wendell Minor. Clarion, 2010.

St. George, Judith. *Stand Tall, Abe Lincoln.* Illus. by Matt Faulkner. Philomel, 2008.

Stamaty, Mark Alan. *Shake, Rattle & Turn that Noise Down!: How Elvis Changed Music, Me, and Mom.* Illus. by the author. Knopf, 2010.

Stauffacher, Sue. *Nothing But Trouble: The Story of Althea Gibson.* Illus. by Greg Couch. Knopf, 2007.

Stone, Tanya Lee. *Elizabeth Leads the Way: Elizabeth Cady Stanton and the Right to Vote.* Illus. by Rebecca Gibbon. Henry Holt, 2008.

Tavares, Matt. Henry Aaron's Dream. Illus. by the author. Candlewick, 2010.

Weatherford, Carole Boston. *I, Matthew Henson: Polar Explorer.* Illus. by Eric Velasquez. Walker, 2008.

White, Linda Arms. *I Could Do That: Esther Morris Gets Women the Vote.* Illus. by Nancy Carpenter. Farrar, 2005.

Winter, Jonah. *Roberto Clemente: Pride of the Pittsburgh Pirates.* Illus. by Raúl Colón. Atheneum, 2005.

Winter, Jonah. *You Never Heard of Sandy Koufax?!* Illus. by Andre Carilho. Schwartz & Wade, 2009.

Yolen, Jane. *Perfect Wizard.* Illus. by Dennis Nolan. Dutton, 2005.

Yoo, Paul. *Sixteen Years in Sixteen Seconds: The Sammy Lee Story.* Illus. by Dom Lee. Lee & Low, 2005.

Younger, Barbara. *Purple Mountain Majesties: The Story of Katherine Lee Bates and "America the Beautiful."* Illus. by Stacey Schuett. Dutton, 1998.

CREATE AN INSTANT TALL TALE

OBJECTIVES:

To reinforce the 5 Ws: Who, What, Where, When, Why

To introduce the concept of absurdity in Tall Tales

SUPPLIES NEEDED:

1 long strip of legal sized paper, cut in half the long way (4 x 14"), for each person
pencil for each person

PROCEDURE:

1. To construct an instant absurd TALL TALE, each person in a group of 7 writes down a response to your first writing prompt (below), folds over a flap of the paper to cover up the writing, and passes it on to the person on the right. On receiving a new paper from the person on the left, each person writes an answer for the second prompt, folds the paper over again, and passes it to the right again.
2. At the end of the exercise, each person will have written one answer to each prompt, but on seven different strips of paper. Each writer unfolds his or her paper and reads aloud the usually hilarious composite sentence to the group or entire class.

LEADER'S PROMPTS:

1. Who (Think of a real or fictional person's name: **The Stinky Cheese Man**)

2. Did What (Describe an activity: **Climbed Mt. Everest**)

3. With Whom (Think of another real or fictional person's name: **with Cinderella**)

4. Where (Think of a place: **On the back of a chicken**)

5. When (Time: **Last Tuesday**)

6. Why (Give a reason: **Because roses are red and violets are blue**)

7. And all the people said: (Think of a quote: **"To be or not to be. That is the question."**)

Final sentence, composed by 7 individual writers:

The Stinky Cheese Man

Climbed Mt. Everest

with Cinderella

On the back of a chicken

Last Tuesday

Because roses are red and violets are blue,

And all the people said,

"To be or not to be. That is the question"

USING READER'S THEATER

Adapted from *Once Upon a Time: Using Storytelling, Creative Drama, and Reader's Theater with Children in Grades PreK-6* by Judy Freeman (Libraries Unlimited, 2007). Reprinted with permission of Libraries Unlimited.

Improvised drama depends on the talents of the actors to make its unscripted production smooth and believable. With Reader's Theater, a more structured drama variation, children are given or write their own scripts to act out a scene. Reader's Theater stresses reading aloud, and as such, is a boon to the children who are less confidant about extemporaneous speaking.

When my very first edition of *Books Kids Will Sit Still For* was published back in 1984, I recall one reviewer who was disappointed because I didn't include any information on or mention of Reader's Theater. "What on earth is Reader's Theater?" I said as I looked it up. I found it means you hand out copies of a script derived from a book or story, and have readers act it out. "Wait, I do that!" I said.

The inspiration for what we now call Reader's Theater had to be old time radio. Before television, people listened to weekly radio shows like "The Lone Ranger" and "Fibber McGee and Molly." In the radio studio, actors would stand in front of their microphones, scripts in hand, and read their parts.

You can find some of these scripts old online, including Abbott and Costello's famous bit, "Who's On First?" (**www.louandbud.com/WOF.htm**), and act them out. There are scripts for 117 different vintage radio series from 1930-1960 at **www.genericradio.com**.

Here's how I got started with Reader's Theater. It was the week before Christmas vacation and I was gearing up to do a week of storytelling for the students in the elementary school where I was the librarian. Then laryngitis struck.

I got to school that morning, and headed straight for the books of plays on the library shelf-the 812's. Finding several cute holiday-related plays with lots of parts, I ran off scripts for each class, rearranged the chairs into a big semicircle, and crossed my fingers. I wrote instructions on the board. Something like: "Can't talk. It's up to you today. Let's put on a play." It was a huge hit. Necessity was the mother of invention, though I had no idea there was a name for what we were doing and that it was an educationally sound and wise process. We were just having fun with drama. A lot of fun. And I've been doing it ever since.

Reader's Theater is not to be confused with round robin reading where one child after another reads paragraphs aloud from a story. Round robin reading can be deadening.

When I was a child in elementary school, my classmates and I spent a fair amount of time reading aloud from our basal readers, Round Robin-style, up and down the rows. I remember, when it was my turn, trying to read aloud with lots of expression. I never could recall any details from the passage I was assigned, focused, as I was, on the written text in lieu of comprehending its meaning. If I made a mistake, I felt humiliated. Kids would laugh at stumblers, stammerers, and mispronouncers, unless they were too busy nervously surveying the upcoming text for their own turns. That type of Round Robin reading has fallen out of fashion.

So how do we help sharpen children's oral reading skills and encourage their response to literature? How do you get them to think deeper, beyond the usual glib happy-sad-mad-glad-bad responses when you read aloud a picture book like *The Trial of Cardigan Jones* by Tim Egan (Houghton Mifflin, 2004). Cardigan, a moose, is accused of stealing Mrs. Brown's freshly baked apple pie. He says he didn't do it.

Write up a Reader's Theater script of the story for children to act act. After your group has acted out their script two or three times, you can ask them, "How did Cardigan Jones feel when the jury finally declared him not guilty?"

Your actors will not just have seen the book and heard the story and read the story. They will have lived the story. They'll know that story from the inside out. Maybe you'll even bring out an apple pie for the cast party. What a fine way to get children invested in literature.

We all know there are no quick fixes in turning children into readers, don't we? Well, there are a few. And Reader's Theater is one of them. If you're searching for a painless, effective way to get your children reading aloud with comprehension, expression, fluency, volume, and, most important, joy, Reader's Theater is a miracle. It allows children to get invested in the plot of a story, to see it unfold and come together.

What is Reader's Theater (or Readers Theatre, another of its many spellings)? It's nothing fancy. And you can do it yourself. After you read a book aloud to your children, you hand out a photocopied play script of the story with a part for each child, and they simply read the script aloud and act it out. You don't need props, costumes, or scenery, unless you want them. Children don't need to memorize their lines, though they will often do so just because they want to. (They have more brain cells than we do. Memorizing lines is child's play to them.) You don't need to perform your play in front of an audience, though actors may decide they want to do that, too. That's it? Pretty much. It's the process that's important here, not a finished product. And then magic happens.

Students have a script to hold and follow, but they also interact with the other readers as the group acts out its playlet. They bond with their fellow actors and respond to them in character, walking, for a short time, in their characters' shoes. By participating in an activity they love, they become more proficient and self-confident as readers and as performers.

If you are looking for a way to enhance presentation and public speaking skills, to get your children working together in harmony, to enunciate when they speak, to listen to what others have to say, to get to the heart of a story, to boost self esteem, and to hone every reading skill, Reader's Theater is your free ticket to change lives and raise contented, fulfilled, and motivated children. Watch your reading scores soar while children think they're just having a great time.

In my many years as a school librarian, I had each class put on at least one Reader's Theater play each year, starting with first grade (spring is best, when their reading skills are coming along), based on books I read aloud to them. Children thrive, even the quiet ones, on the thrill of being a star for a little while.

SOURCES OF READER'S THEATER PLAYS

How do you get going with Reader's Theater? First off, choose a good book and read it aloud to your group. They need to hear your expressive voice in their heads and have a sense of the characters, plot, setting, and sequence. They will be making an important connection between a book and the play that emerges from the book's text.

When you finish reading aloud or sharing a book, tell children you will then be acting out the story as a Reader's Theater play, they will probably cheer.

Where can you get plays? Look in the 812s on your library shelves for books of plays. Check out *Plays: The Drama Magazine for Young People* (and its website at **www.playsmag.com**), an indispensable magazine which comes out monthly, and is filled with good, royalty-free plays for elementary through high school. These are not always connected with children's books, but they're still good plays to read.

There are wonderful books containing Reader's Theater scripts by Suzanne Barchers, Caroline Feller Bauer, Toni Buzzeo, Anthony Fredericks, Aaron Shepard, and Judy Sierra.

Authors are starting to write Reader's Theater scripts for their own books and put them on their websites. See Margie Palatini's site, **www.margiepalatini.com**, and Toni Buzzeo's site, **www.tonibuzzeo.com**, for instance.

Another excellent online source is Rick Swallow's Readers Theater/Language Arts Home Page for Teachers at **www.timelessteacherstuff.com**, with more than eighty scripts, many from well-known children's picture books.

My favorite source for Reader's Theater scripts is the amazing website of author Aaron Shepard, who has retold and published many wonderful folk tales, most of which he has also adapted into Reader's Theater Scripts. Go to **http://aaronshep.com/rt**, where you can easily download his scripts, buy his books, or get in touch with him to have him visit your school to give a workshop.

WRITING YOUR OWN READER'S THEATER SCRIPTS

You can, of course, write up your own scripts, just like Aaron Shepard does, which is far easier than you might think. I write up at least one new Reader's Theater script a year. If you type up just one script each year, pretty soon you'll have a drawerful of interesting plays to use with your kids.

Many books you read aloud or booktalk have scenes or chapters with multiple characters and an emphasis on dialogue. Picture books are a logical starting place, but controlled vocabulary Easy Readers, dialogue-rich scenes or chapters in fiction books, folktales, narrative poems like "Casey at the Bat," picture book biographies, and even science and history books can lend themselves to being turned into plays. Keep an open mind when considering possibilities for drama.

When deciding on a book or excerpt to transform into a script, I consider my own Freeman's Five Essential Ingredients. For the elementary school audience, a story should have:

1. Peppy dialogue
2. A little action
3. Laugh out loud parts
4. Lively narration
5. Enough roles for all

It takes me about an hour to do a good first draft of a picture book, even when typing with my usual two fingers and a thumb. Some of my favorite picture books I've adapted include Matt Novak's *Mouse TV* (Orchard, 1994), Helen Bannerman's *The Story of Little Babaji* (HarperCollins, 1996), Susan Meddaugh's *Martha Walks the Dog* (Houghton Mifflin, 1998), Diane Stanley's *Raising Sweetness* (Putnam, 1999), Doreen Cronin's *Click, Clack, Moo: Cows That Type* (Simon & Schuster, 2000), Shelley Moore Thomas's *Get Well, Good Knight* (Dutton, 2002), Antonio Sacre's *The Barking Mouse* (Albert Whitman, 2003), Tim Egan's *The Trial of Cardigan Jones* (Houghton Mifflin, 2004), Kate DiCamillo's *Mercy Watson to the Rescue* (Candlewick, 2005), and Lane Smith's *John, Paul, George & Ben* (Hyperion, 2006).

SCRIPTWRITING TIPS

If you've ever seen a real script for a play or movie, you'll note that the formatting of a RT script is simpler. It needs to be easy for children to read so they can scan down and find their lines and follow along as the play progresses. Here are some of my script tips:

1. At the top of your script, include a list of all the acting roles, in order of appearance, plus the narrators.
2. Use a good-sized font for your scripts, so students can see and read their lines clearly. I like 14-or 18-point Helvetica or Times, both of which are easy on the eyes.
3. Justify your right margin to give the script a clean look.
4. Add page numbers at the bottom.
5. Always photocopy your scripts single-sided. It's very confusing to try to follow a double-sided script, especially for children. "I can't find the page," they'll wail.
6. Character names, including narrators, are on the left, in caps and in bold. Set up tabs for the dialogue, so actors can scan down the left side of each page to find their names and look to the right for their lines.
7. Single-space each character's lines, but add a double space between lines.
8. Put your stage directions in italics and in parenthesis. *(Explain to children that they don't read these out loud as lines, but that they should follow the stage directions so they know what to do.)*
9. Bold and/or capitalize those lines, phrases, or words you want an actor to say with more **force** or VOLUME or **EXPRESSION**.
10. In writing a script, try to incorporate verbatim as much of the story's actual dialogue and narration as possible, but don't be afraid to change, rearrange, edit, or add, if it will make the play flow better. You don't have to be a word-for-word slave to the book, though you do want to stay true to the author's words.
11. You can condense scenes, or even leave them out, especially if you're doing a long, involved chapter or scene from a fiction book.
12. Try to ensure that everyone will get a good speaking part, both actors and narrators. This means you may need to add lines. You might turn some dialogue into narration, and vice versa
13. Even if you proofread and run your spellcheck, you won't catch all of the typos you made until you run off a script and hand it out. (Then they will jump out at you.)
14. As for problems with the script itself, make notes as you watch your group perform their first reading. Did one character get too many lines? Not enough? Are the stage directions clear? Afterwards, go back to your computer and fix everything that wasn't perfect, and run off a second draft.
15. If you like, you can start with the characters introducing themselves. ("I'm Josh, and I play the Lawyer.") This makes sure the audience knows who's who, and also gives each character an extra line. This isn't necessary, and you don't have to write it in the script if you want your players to do it.

KIDS WRITE SCRIPTS

As a writing exercise, scripting a scene is challenging and fun for children, once you have demonstrated the format and construction. Students in grades two and up can learn to write scripts, adapting published books or their own original stories. Get them started by giving each person a copy of a sample play for reference.

Do your first script together as a class. First hand out copies of a brief story for all to read. With their input, outline the story on the board, chart, or overhead projector. Model how to turn dialogue from a story into play dialogue and how to turn narration into lines for narrators to read. Show them how to write stage directions in italics.

When students are adapting print into a script, photocopy the original story. Have them mark up the copy with highlighters, using a different color for each part. This will make it easier for them to transcribe and keep track of who says what.

The tedious part is copying down or typing the dialogue and narration. Think of it as a good way to practice handwriting or keyboarding.

One excellent source for younger readers is the "I Can Read" genre, those easy-to-read early chapter books like the "Frog and Toad" series by Arnold Lobel or the "Henry and Mudge" and "Poppleton" books by Cynthia Rylant. Short, self-contained chapters which contain snappy dialogue are ideal for small group productions. Break children into small groups to work on their scripts and then act them out.

Students in all grades can also write new dialogue-filled chapters. Just because these stories are easy to read, doesn't mean they're that easy to write. If your students create a couple of new scripts each year, in no time you'll have a lifetime supply of scripts to use.

READER'S THEATER LOGISTICS

How do you give everyone a part? You'll need to do a bit of juggling to make everything come out even. With Reader's Theater scripts, you can expand the number of parts by adding narrators, doubling up on characters, or even splitting a character's part into two or more. When you type up a new script, estimate how many acting parts you have and how many students, and add narrators to make up the difference. If you have 12 narrators and 10 to 12 actors, this usually works fine. If you have more parts than actors, double the lines of the narrators. Have Narrator 11 also read Narrator 10's part as well, for instance.

What about an existing script that has 11 parts when you have 23 kids? You can easily add more parts by doubling or tripling the number of narrators. Tell one child, for example, "You are Narrator 1, pages one to three," and the next one, "And you are Narrator 1, pages four to six." And so on. If necessary, divide the roles of your main characters in the same way.

You can also break the script into three or four smaller scenes, with a separate cast for each. Each group can practice its small scene several times and then put it on for the others.

Or you could have two separate casts, rehearsing on separate sides of the room. Each group can then do the play for each other, giving everyone a chance to be both actors and audience members. You also can have simultaneous rehearsals for two or three separate plays, and then have the casts perform for each other. As long as everyone gets a part, you can make almost any configuration work.

IT'S SHOWTIME!

If you're putting on an all-class production, you'll most likely want to rearrange desks to make space for a makeshift stage or space. In a library, you'll need to move tables, which could be trickier, but certainly not impossible. I like to arrange 24 chairs in a big semicircle or arc so actors can see each other, with open space in the front of the chairs for interaction-a chase scene, for instance-so they can get up and move around. Set up a chair for yourself, facing the actors, so you can be the director, prompter, and appreciative audience all in one.

Once the children are sitting in the chairs, hand out the scripts in order. About half of your group will be narrators. I designate the children who sit on the left side as narrators, and the right side, actors. I hand out the parts sequentially, with Narrator 1 on the left, and then 2, 3, 4, and so on, sitting next to each other. Don't get fancy here. You always want to be able to figure out whose line is next. Someone will always say,"I can't remember which narrator I am." Count over and say, "You're Narrator 5." Easy.

Unless you have a few parts that are particularly difficult to read, don't worry about who gets what role. Some of your shyest kids will shine doing this activity. I do try to make sure the boys get boy parts, as there's usually an outcry if they don't. The girls tend to be a bit more flexible and don't mind as much if they get a boy part.

Give the children a few minutes to go over their lines and practice a bit. When they can't figure out a word or phrase, instruct them to turn to the actors on their left or right for help.

Give a little pep talk as follows:

"This is a first reading, just like real actors do on Broadway or on TV when they start to rehearse a new play or episode. Nobody expects it to be perfect and nobody should care if someone misses a line or stumbles on a word. Never laugh at a fellow actor who makes a mistake. We're all in this together.

"Keep an eye out for your neighbors on either side of you during the play. If you see the person next to you has lost his place, don't say a thing. Just lean over and put your finger on his script to show him where we are.

"I am the prompter for this play. When an actor gets stuck, the prompter helps by giving the correct line or word. Even actors on Broadway look to the prompter if they forget their lines. If you get confused and your neighbors can't help you, then look at me."

Then it's showtime. Each time a child has a line, he or she must stand up to deliver it in a loud, clear, and expressive voice. Prompt them as needed, and laugh with them. That first reading, while exhilarating, can be choppy, but who cares?

Once is not enough with Reader's Theater; try for two or even three readings for it to be truly effective. Even though your group will have heard you read the story aloud, the first time they undertake to plow through the script for themselves, they will stumble and stammer and lose their places. They'll struggle with decoding unfamiliar words, getting a sense of how their parts might sound, and making sense of the plot.

During the second reading, your actors will start to listen to the others' lines, to relax and watch the story unfold, and they'll read with more understanding and expression. If you have time to do it a third time, it will seem like a revelation. Readers will be able to focus on enjoying the performance and their parts in it.

You might want to change parts the third time you run through the script, giving the actors a chance to be narrators, and vice versa. Challenge your actors in a constructive way. Say to them, "How can you make this next reading better? What will you do this time that you didn't do the first time?"

Now when you ask all those lovely interpretive questions to foster higher level thinking and reasoning skills, your children will be brilliantly prepared to discuss a story they have heard, then read, then lived.

Make sure you have extra copies of the script. You want your actors to mark up their parts—they love to use highlighters—and get comfortable with their scripts. If they take them home to read and practice, that's ideal. So don't chew anyone out for leaving her script at home. Just hand out extra copies.

If you expect your students to do well, they probably will. I used my Reader's Theater script of Matt Novak's picture book *Mouse TV* (Orchard 1994) with several classes of first graders in my school library one year. It was the first time these children had ever done RT and I was excited about it. We had read the story the week before.

When the first class entered the library, I had them sit in the chairs I had arranged in a long arc across the room. We talked about the story. I handed out parts and let them find their lines and practice them for a few minutes. Then we started acting. I had written the song "Three Blind Mice" into the script for the whole cast to sing, and when we got to that part in the script, they sang it with great exuberance. They read with expression. They had a ball. Their teacher was amazed. "Wow! I didn't know they could do that!"

The next class came in and I explained what we were going to do. The teacher said, sharply, "They won't be able to read that! This is *much* too hard for first grade!"

Well, guess what. Those children found it much too hard. They whined and said, "I don't know what to do!" and "I can't read this."

Talk about your self-fulfilling prophecy. If I hadn't seen the first class, I would have believed that teacher. Yeah, this is too hard for first grade, I guess. Maybe next year. But I knew they could do it and they did. You will have children and teachers who tell you it's too hard. Don't give up on them. They feel so proud of themselves when they realize they can do it.

In 2002, when Aaron Shepard's book of the West African pourquoi tale, *Master Man: A Tall Tale of Nigeria* (HarperCollins, 2001), was published, I couldn't wait to try out his new script with two classes of third graders at Van Holten School.

In the first production, the boy who played Shadusa, the cocksure man who considers himself the strongest man in the world, was himself a self-assured, brash kid, well-liked for his comic take on the world. He was very funny and brazen in the part.

Then in came the second class eager for their chance to act. I handed out the scripts, giving the lead part of Shadusa to the boy who sat at the end of the semicircle of chairs, on the right. His teacher pulled me aside. "Maybe he's not such a good person to play the main character," she whispered. "He's so shy, he barely talks. We haven't heard him say Boo all year."

"That's OK," I told her. "It doesn't matter if he's not fabulous. The play will still be fun."

And then the miracle happened. The boy playing Shadusa got into his role. And while he wasn't as flamboyant as the first boy had been, he was still plenty expressive and blustery, fitting the part just fine. The other children in the class looked at him in amazement when he started to speak, hearing that quiet boy become a whole new person.

When children finish reading a script, they usually feel pretty good about it. Reinforce that by teaching them how to do their bows, just like on Broadway. I have them face front, join hands, hold their arms up high, and then bow in unison on the count of three. They come up on the count of three, and repeat it three times. They have to watch each other out of the corners of their eyes so they go down and come up together. It looks pretty cool. You keep the count and applaud and cheer like crazy, especially if you are their only audience member.

RT PERFORMANCE TIPS FOR ACTORS

1. Read over your lines so you know where they are in the script and how to pronounce all the words.

2. Hold your script still. If you rattle the paper, the other actors will be distracted. When you need to turn the page of your script, do it quickly and as quietly as you can. [NOTE: Teachers can circumvent the problem by putting the pages of each script in plastic sleeves and in a notebook binder. Children can either hold their binders or place them on music stands in front of them. For everyday RT, this is more work than necessary, but if you're putting on a performance for parents or an audience, it's a nice professional touch.]

3. If the cast is sitting in chairs, stand up when you have a line. Sit down when you finish.

4. When you stand up to deliver a line, hold your script down by your belly button. (I call this, "Belly It Up.") Make sure it stays there so everyone can see and hear you. Don't let your script creep up to cover your face.

5. If you can't see the audience, they can't see you either. In Reader's Theater, you act with your face. Make sure it's visible at all times.

6. Never turn your back on the audience. People need to be able to see your face, not your fanny.

7. Read your lines slowly and clearly so everyone can understand you.

8. Use your playground voice. Imagine your voice bouncing off the back wall like a rubber ball. You may think you are speaking loudly, but chances are no one can hear you.

9. Always read with expression. Concentrate. Think about how your lines should sound or how you can do them better next time.

10. If your line is funny, don't laugh unless the script calls for it. Let the audience will figure out the funny parts.

11. If you're acting for an audience and they laugh, freeze until they stop laughing. If you say your next line while they are still laughing, they won't hear it.

12. Stay in character. When you act out a play, you become someone else. Try to act like that person would.

13. Follow along in your script so you don't lose your place.

14. If you do lose your place, catch the eye of the actor sitting next to you. Point to his or her script, and shrug your shoulders. That person will know you're lost and will put a finger on the correct line of your script. Return the favor when needed.

15. If you mess up a line, don't worry about it. Just keep going.

16. Be considerate of the other actors. If you fool around while they're delivering their lines, they might do the same to you.

17. Take your script home and practice reading it aloud with someone—a friend, your parents, or a brother or sister. If there's no one around, read it to the mirror.

A BEDTIME FOR BEAR

(For grades 1-3)

Reader's Theater adaptation by Judy Freeman (www.JudyReadsBooks.com). Adapted from *A Bedtime for Bear*, written by Bonny Becker and illustrated by Kady MacDonald Denton, published by Candlewick Press, 2010. Reprinted with permission of the publisher, Candlewick Press.

ROLES: Narrator 1, Narrator 2, Narrator 3, Narrator 4, Bear, Mouse

NOTE: This script can be handed out to groups of students to act out together. If you need more parts, have two sets of narrators, one for pages 1-3, and the other for pages 4-6. You can do the same with Mouse and Bear. One prop that might be fun to have for Bear is some sort of simple nightcap, made from cloth and ribbon, or even a paper towel with yarn stapled to it.

HELPFUL ADVICE: When you photocopy this script, be sure to number the pages and run it single-sided. Double-sided scripts are confusing for children to follow. Explain and demonstrate how the actors can make use of the stage directions, which are written in italics and enclosed in parenthesis, even though they do not actually read them aloud during the play.

NARRATOR 1:	Everything had to be just so for Bear's bedtime.
NARRATOR 2:	His glass of water had to sit on the exact right spot on his bedstand.
NARRATOR 3:	His favorite pillow must be nicely fluffed.
NARRATOR 4:	His nightcap needed to be snug.
NARRATORS 1-4:	(*loud whispers*) Most of all, it had to be quiet—very, very quiet.
NARRATOR 1:	One evening, Bear heard a tap, tap, tapping on his front door.
NARRATOR 2:	When he opened the door, there stood Mouse, small and gray and bright-eyed. He clasped a tiny suitcase in his paw.

MOUSE:	*(wiggles with excitement)* I am here to spend the night!
BEAR:	Surely we agreed on next Tuesday.
MOUSE:	No, you most definitely said tonight.
BEAR:	Oh.
NARRATOR 3:	Bear had never had an overnight guest before.
NARRATOR 4:	Guests could quite possibly mess things up and make noise, and Bear needed quiet, absolute quiet, at bedtime.
NARRATOR 1:	Even so, Bear and Mouse enjoyed an evening of checkers and warm cocoa, and soon it was time for bed.
BEAR:	Remember, I must have absolute quiet.
MOUSE:	Oh, indeed.
NARRATOR 2:	Bear set out his glass of water . . .
NARRATOR 3:	Adjusted his nightcap . . .
NARRATOR 4:	Fluffed his favorite pillow . . .
NARRATOR 1:	And climbed into bed.
NARRATORS 1-4 :	*(whispering)* It was very, very quiet.
NARRATOR 2:	He closed his eyes.
NARRATORS 1-4 :	Bristle, bristle, bristle.
NARRATOR 3:	Bear heard a noise. His eyes opened.
NARRATOR 4:	It was Mouse, brushing his teeth.
BEAR:	Ahem!

NARRATOR 1:	Bear cleared his throat in a reminding sort of way.
MOUSE:	Most sorry.
NARRATOR 2:	Bear closed his eyes again.
MOUSE:	*(hums while putting on nightshirt)* Humm, hum-pa-pummmmmm. Pa-pummmmmm.
NARRATOR 3:	Mouse hummed while putting on his nightshirt.
BEAR:	*(patiently)* Absolute quiet. *(sits up in bed and shakes finger at Mouse)*
MOUSE:	Yes, indeed.
NARRATOR 4:	Mouse hopped into bed.
NARRATORS 1-4 :	Creak, squeak, rattle.
NARRATOR 1:	Bear jammed his pillow over his ears, gritted his teeth, and closed his eyes.
NARRATOR 2:	He was just about to drift off when . . .
MOUSE:	*(softly)* Good night, Bear.
NARRATOR 3:	Bear tried to pretend he was asleep.
MOUSE:	*(louder)* Good night.
BEAR:	My ears are highly sensitive!
MOUSE:	How interesting.
NARRATOR 4:	Mouse mumbled into his pillow . . .
MOUSE:	*(softly)* Can you hear this?
BEAR:	**Yes!**

NARRATOR 1: Mouse said, from under his pillow . . .

MOUSE: *(even more softly)* Amazing. How about this?

BEAR: **QUIET!**

NARRATOR 2: Mouse slipped under his blankets, crawled to the bottom of his bed, and whispered.

MOUSE: Can you hear—

BEAR: *(roaring)* **SILENCE!**

NARRATOR 3: Mouse slid from his bed, went into the closet, and said in the tiniest possible voice into the farthest, darkest, teeniest possible corner of the closet . . .

MOUSE: *(very, very quietly)* Surely you can't—

BEAR: **WILL THIS TORMENT NEVER CEASE!**

MOUSE: *(whispering)* Sorry, Bear. Good night, Bear.

NARRATOR 4: Mouse tiptoed back into bed as quiet as a . . . well, you know.

NARRATOR 1: Bear fluffed his favorite pillow, adjusted his nightcap, and waited.

NARRATOR 2: But there was no more sound from Mouse.

NARRATOR 3: At last it was quiet.

NARRATORS 1-4: *(whispering)* Very, very quiet.

NARRATOR 4: Bear heard a shuffling sound.

BEAR: Mouse, is that you?

NARRATORS 1-4: No answer.

NARRATOR 1:	Bear heard a crick, crick, crick on the floorboards.
BEAR:	I know it's you, Mouse.
NARRATORS 1-4:	No answer.
BEAR:	You can't fool me.
NARRATOR 2:	But he didn't sound very certain.
NARRATOR 3:	Bear heard a low moaning noise.
BEAR:	**MOUSE?**
NARRATORS 1-4:	Silence.
NARRATOR 4:	Bear was sure something rustled on the floor.
BEAR:	**MOUSE! WAKE UP!**
NARRATOR 1:	Mouse stumbled out of bed, small and gray and sleepy-eyed.
MOUSE:	What is it?
NARRATOR 2:	But Bear couldn't see any rustly, moany sort of thing in his room.
NARRATOR 3:	His room looked quite like it always looked.
NARRATOR 4:	Bear, still clutching his blanket to his chin, told a little lie.
BEAR:	Nothing. I must have been talking in my sleep. Ha ha ha.
NARRATOR 1:	Bear chuckled. But it was a rather quavery chuckle.
NARRATOR 2:	Mouse glanced at Bear.

MOUSE:	Ahhhh. Could I peek under your bed? Sometimes I like to check for . . . things, you know.
BEAR:	Well, if you insist.
NARRATOR 3:	Mouse went under the bed.
MOUSE:	Nothing.
BEAR:	You'll want to check behind the curtains, I suppose.
NARRATOR 4:	Mouse checked behind the curtains.
MOUSE:	All clear.
BEAR:	You'd better check the closet. Then you won't be the least bit nervous.
NARRATOR 1:	Mouse came out of the closet, dusting his paws.
MOUSE:	Not a thing. Thank you, Bear. Goodnight.
BEAR:	**WAIT!** You'll want a bedtime story, I expect. For your nerves.
MOUSE:	For my nerves? Oh, indeed. I'm quite shaken.
NARRATOR 2:	Then with an eager flick of his tail, he settled on Bear's favorite pillow.
NARRATOR 3:	And Bear told him about the adventures of the Brave Strong Bear and the Very Frightened Little Mouse.
NARRATOR 4:	Soon Bear began to yawn.
NARRATOR 1:	Mouse yawned, too.
MOUSE:	Good night Bear.

BEAR:	*(mumbles, sleepily)* Good night, Mouuuuzzzz.
NARRATOR 2:	Then Bear began to snore. . . LOUDLY.
NARRATOR 3:	But Mouse just smiled.
NARRATOR 4:	And soon Mouse and Bear were fast asleep.
NARRATORS 1-4:	**Shhhhhhhh . . .**

A Reader's Theater Script for
THE 3 LITTLE DASSIES
(For grades 1-3)

Reader's Theater adaptation by Judy Freeman (www.JudyReadsBooks.com). Adapted from *The 3 Little Dassies*, written and illustrated by Jan Brett, copyright © 2010 by Jan Brett. Used by permission of G. P. Putnam's Sons, a division of Penguin Young Readers Group, and an imprint of Penguin Group (USA) Inc.

ROLES: Narrator 1, Narrator 2, Narrator 3, Narrator 4, Narrator 5, Mimbi, Pimbi, Timbi, Agama Man, Eagle

NOTE: If you want everyone in your class to have a role, expand the number of narrators. One child can be Narrator 1 on pages 1 and 2, and another can be Narrator 1 on pages 3 and 4, and so on. You could have 20 narrators this way, if you need to.

NARRATORS 1-5:	Hot, hot, hot!
NARRATOR 1:	The three little dassies were almost grown up and it was time for them to find their own place.
NARRATOR 2:	Mimbi, Pimbi, and Timbi waved good-bye to Mommy, Daddy, aunties, uncles, and all their cousins and set out for the distant mountain.
3 DASSIES:	Good-bye! Come and visit us!
MIMBI:	A place cooler!
PIMBI:	A place less crowded!
TIMBI:	A place safe from big eagles!
NARRATOR 3:	The sisters traveled all day and all night across the Namib Desert, arriving at the foot of the mountain the next morning.
3 DASSIES:	This is where we will live!

NARRATOR 4:	Out from the scree came a handsome smiling lizard with a squeaky voice.
AGAMA MAN:	Welcome! No one has lived here for a long time. Just me and a family of eagles up on the mountain.
3 DASSIES:	Eagles?
NARRATOR 5:	The three little dassies shivered in the hot, hot sun.
NARRATORS 1-2:	Where would they build their houses?
NARRATOR 1:	Mimbi eyed the long grasses that grew there.
MIMBI:	Look at these long grasses. They will make a lovely cool house.
NARRATOR 2:	Mimbi set to work cutting, twisting, braiding, and bundling. She finished in no time.
MIMBI:	Be near and dear sisters.
NARRATORS 3-5:	She crawled into her grass house for a nap.
NARRATOR 3:	Pimbi spotted pieces of driftwood, silver from the sun, lying in the sand of the dry riverbed.
MIMBI:	These will make a fine wooden house.
NARRATOR 4:	She set about collecting as many pieces as she could find.
NARRATOR 5:	When it was finished, Pimbi hung up a hammock.
MIMBI:	Be near and dear, sisters, while I rest my eyes.
NARRATOR 1:	Timbi looked at the rocks around their mountain.
MIMBI:	I will make a stone house, but it won't be as easy to build as one made of grasses or sticks.

NARRATORS 1-5	And it wasn't.
NARRATOR 2:	She had to work all day in the hot sun to get it finished in time to sleep in it that night.
NARRATOR 3:	Agama Man had been watching them.
AGAMA MAN:	I am so happy the three dassie sisters are staying on. I have missed having company.
NARRATOR 4:	The three little dassies slept late into the morning as the sun rose higher and higher in the sky.
NARRATOR 5:	The big old eagle who lived up on the mountain stretched his wings and flew down.
EAGLE:	I need to find a meal for my hungry chicks.
NARRATOR 1:	Mimbi woke up hungry and went outside.
NARRATOR 2:	Suddenly a long-winged shadow passed over her.
MIMBI:	Oh, no! It's the eagle!
NARRATOR 3:	Suddenly a long-winged shadow passed over her.
NARRATOR 4:	Mimbi hurried back into her grass house.
EAGLE:	I see you, dassie! I'll flap and I'll clap and I'll blow your house in.
NARRATOR 5:	The eagle beat the air with his wings until the grass roof sailed off.
NARRATORS 1-5:	The eagle grabbed Mimbi and lifted her up, up, up to his nest.
AGAMA MAN:	Oh, no! The eagle has Mimbi!
NARRATOR 1:	But the eagle was greedy.

NARRATOR 2:	No sooner had he dropped Mimbi into the nest than he spotted Pimbi in front of her stick house far below.
EAGLE:	Two dassies would be double delicious!
NARRATORS 1-5:	Down he went, feathers flying.
NARRATOR 3:	Pimbi looked up and saw him coming.
PIMBI:	Oh, no! It's the eagle!
NARRATOR 4:	She turned and ran back inside.
EAGLE:	I see you, dassie! I'll flap and I'll clap and I'll blow your house in.
NARRATORS 1-2:	Twigs flew, sticks rattled, until Pimbi's stick house fell apart.
NARRATOR 5:	Then, just like Mimbi, Pimbi felt herself being lifted high in the sky and plunked down in the eagle's nest.
AGAMA MAN:	Oh, no! Now the eagle has Pimbi, too! I have to help them!
NARRATOR 1:	Agama Man started climbing the rocks to reach the eagle's nest at the top of the mountain.
NARRATOR 2:	Down below, at the bottom of the mountain, Timbi looked out of her stone house.
TIMBI:	Sisters! Where are you? I'm making tasty seed porridge for your breakfast!
NARRATOR 3:	Instead of a grass house and a stick house, she saw a long shadow streaking across the rocks.
TIMBI:	Oh, help! It's the eagle!
NARRATOR 4:	Timbi darted her head back inside.

EAGLE:	I see you, dassie! I'll flap and I'll clap and I'll blow your house in.
NARRATORS 1-5:	He flapped and clapped and beat his wings.
NARRATOR 5:	Dust and sand blew everywhere.
NARRATORS 1-5:	But the stone house didn't move.
EAGLE:	I'll try harder this time.
NARRATORS 1-5:	He flapped and clapped and beat his wings even harder.
NARRATOR 1:	Dust and sand got in his eyes.
NARRATORS 1-5:	But the stone house didn't budge.
NARRATOR 2:	In the meantime, Agama Man climbed up the rocks of the mountain, higher and higher until he reached the eagle's nest.
NARRATOR 3:	There he found the sisters, Mimbi and Pimbi, in between the eagle's two chicks.
AGAMA MAN:	Sisters, you are safe! Thank goodness!
MIMBI & PIMBI:	Brave Agama Man! You found us!
AGAMA MAN:	Quick, I know the way down. Let me help you out of here.
MIMBI & PIMBI:	We are saved!
NARRATOR 4:	The three raced down the rocks.
NARRATOR 5:	Meanwhile, down below, when the dust settled, the stone house was still standing.
EAGLE:	*(coughing and sneezing)* Just look at my wing feathers! They're bent. That one's broken! Oh, no! I'm missing tail feathers, too!

NARRATOR 1: Knowing when to quit, the eagle hopped his way up to his nest.

EAGLE: *(still coughing and sneezing)* At least I have two dassies waiting for my dinner!

NARRATORS 3-5: When the eagle reached his nest, he could see the dassies were gone.

EAGLE: Where did they go? *(peers down the mountain)* There they are, heading for the stone house. This is my last chance, but I'll catch them now!

NARRATOR 2: The eagle streaked down toward the open chimney of Timbi's stone house as the three dassies raced inside.

NARRATOR 3: Inside the house, the three dassies hugged each other.

3 DASSIES: There's nothing like a stone house when there are eagle abundant!

NARRATOR 4: Just then, the eagle tumbled down the chimney.

EAGLE: I'll flap and I'll clap and I'll . . .

NARRATORS 1-5: **WHOOSHH!**

NARRATOR 5: A hot blast from the fire hit him.

EAGLE: I'll fly home for a nap!

NARRATOR 1: As fast as he could, he squeezed back up the chimney and flew home, all black and singed from the smoky fire.

3 DASSIES: Hooray! He's gone!

NARRATORS 1-5: And Mimbi, Pimbi, and Timbi never saw so much as a tail feather of that eagle ever again.

NARRATOR 2: Mommy, Daddy, aunties, uncles, and all their cousins —

AGAMA MAN: And Agama Man, too!

NARRATOR 3:   . . . came to celebrate.

3 DASSIES: Welcome!

MIMBI: To a place cooler!

PIMBI: To a place less crowded!

TIMBI: To a place safe from big eagles!

NARRATOR 1:   And if you travel to Namibia today, you will see dassies living in stone houses with handsome agama men looking out for them.

NARRATORS 1-5:   As for those pesky eagles, they are easily spotted, for their feathers are as black as soot.

A Reader's Theater Script for
CLEVER JACK TAKES THE CAKE
(For grades 2-4)

Reader's Theater adaptation by Judy Freeman (www.JudyReadsBooks.com) of *Clever Jack Takes the Cake*, written by Candace Fleming, illustrated by G. Brian Karas (Schwartz & Wade, 2010). Adapted from CLEVER JACK TAKES THE CAKE by Candace Fleming, copyright © 2010 by Candace Fleming. Used by permission of Schwartz & Wade Books, an imprint of Random House Children's Books, a division of Random House, Inc.

ROLES: Narrators 1-5, Jack, Mother, Troll, Gypsy Woman, Bear, Guard, Princess, Sound Effects Chorus

NOTE: When you photocopy this script, be sure to number the pages and run it single-sided. Double-sided scripts are confusing for children to follow. If you are acting the story out with a larger class, have two or more sets of narrators.

NARRATOR 1:	One summer morning long ago, a poor boy named Jack found an invitation slipped beneath his cottage door. It read . . .
NARRATORS 1-5:	His Majesty the King cordially invites all the children of the realm to the Princess's Tenth Birthday Party tomorrow afternoon in the castle courtyard.
JACK:	A party! For the princess.
MOTHER:	What a shame you can't go.
JACK:	Why not?
MOTHER:	Because we've nothing fine enough to give her and no money to buy a gift.
NARRATOR 2:	Jack had to admit his mother was right. His pockets were empty except for the matchsticks he always carried.
NARRATOR 3:	As for their few belongings—a spinning wheel, a threadbare quilt, a pitted ax—what princess wanted those?

JACK:	*(thinking)* Then I will make her something! I will make her a cake.
MOTHER:	From what? From the dust in the cupboard? From the dirt on the floor?
JACK:	I have a better idea.
NARRATOR 4:	That same morning, he traded his ax for two bags of sugar and his quilt for a sack of flour.
NARRATOR 5:	He gave the hen an extra handful of the seed in exchange for two fresh eggs, and he kissed the cow on the nose for a pail of her sweetest milk.
NARRATOR 1:	He gathered walnuts. He dipped candles.
NARRATOR 2:	And in the strawberry patch, he searched . . . and searched . . . and searched until he found the reddest, juiciest, and most succulent strawberry in the land.
JACK:	DELICIOUS!
NARRATOR 3:	Said Jack as he plucked it from its stem.
NARRATOR 4:	Then he set to work, churning, chopping, blending, baking.
BAKERS' CHORUS:	Churn, churn, churn. Chop, chop, chop. Blend, blend, blend. Bake, bake, bake.
NARRATOR 5:	That same night, Jack stood back to admire his creation— two layers of golden-sweet cake covered in buttery frosting and ringed with ten tiny candles.
NARRATOR 1:	Across the cake's top, walnuts spelled out "Happy Birthday, Princess." And in the very center—in the place of honor—sat the succulent strawberry.
MOTHER:	What a fine, fine gift.

NARRATOR 2:	Jack grinned.
NARRATOR 3:	Early the next morning, with combed hair and a clean shirt, Jack set off for the castle, holding the cake proudly before him.
NARRATOR 4:	Before long, he came to a bloom-speckled meadow.
JACK:	Perhaps I should pick a bouquet for the princess.
NARRATOR 5:	Just then, four-and-twenty blackbirds rose into the air. Like a sudden summer storm cloud, they swirled around the cake, pecking, nipping, flapping, picking.
BIRD CHORUS:	*(cackling)* Aw-caw-caw-caw-caw!
JACK:	*(hollering)* GET BACK. I'm taking this cake to the princess.
NARRATOR 1:	And as quickly as they had come, they were gone, taking with them the walnuts that spelled "Happy Birthday, Princess."
JACK:	*(looking at his cake)* At least I still have two layers of cake, ten candles, and the succulent strawberry.
NARRATOR 2:	Holding the cake proudly before him, Jack continued on to the castle. Before long he came to a bridge.
TROLL:	**TOLL!**
NARRATOR 3:	Out stepped a wild-haired troll.
TROLL:	No one crosses my bridge without paying.
JACK:	But I haven't any money.
TROLL:	*(licking his lips)* But you do have a cake.
JACK:	I'm taking this to the princess.

TROLL:	*(growling)* And just how will you get it there. You and your cake are on this side of the river. The princess is on that side, and my bridge is the only way across.
NARRATOR 4:	Jack considered the problem.
JACK:	I will make you a deal. If you let me cross, I will give you half this cake.
TROLL:	*(grunting)* Agreed.
NARRATOR 5:	So Jack slid out one layer and, as the troll slobbered and gobbled, crossed the bridge.
NARRATOR 1:	On the other side, he looked down at his gift.
JACK:	At least I still have a layer of cake, ten candles, and the succulent strawberry.
NARRATOR 2:	Holding the cake proudly before him, Jack continued on to the castle.
NARRATOR 3:	Before long he came to the forest. No birds chirped here. No squirrels chattered.
NARRATOR 4:	As if under a spell, the entire wood lay silent, sleeping. Only the wind seemed to whisper . . .
WIND CHORUS:	*(whispering)* Beware! Beware!
NARRATOR 5:	Pulling the cake closer, Jack pressed on. The road grew narrower. The trees grew thicker. The light grew dimmer.
NARRATOR 1:	Soon it was so dark that Jack couldn't see the cake in front of his face.
WIND CHORUS:	*(whispering)* Turn back! Turn back!
JACK:	**I CAN'T!** I'm taking this cake to the princess.

NARRATOR 2:	And he reached into his pocket for a matchstick, struck it on his shoe, and lit one of the ten candles.
NARRATOR 3:	The tiny flame cast a magical circle of light. In its warm glow, Jack carefully made his way forward.
NARRATOR 4:	But the little candle quickly burned down and—
CANDLE CHORUS:	**Pffft!**
NARRATOR 5:	It snuffed out. So Jack lit a second candle.
NARRATOR 1:	But he had not gone much farther before—
CANDLE CHORUS:	**Pffft!**
NARRATOR 2:	It, too, snuffed out.
NARRATOR 3:	So Jack lit a third . . . then a fourth . . . then a fifth . . . until the tenth and final candle flickered, fluttered, sputtered to its end.
NARRATOR 4:	And as it did, the road widened, the trees thinned, and the bright sunlight shone once more.
JACK:	*(looking down at his gift)* At least I still have a layer of cake and the succulent strawberry.
NARRATOR 5:	Holding the cake proudly before him, Jack continued on to the castle.
NARRATOR 1:	Before long he came to a clearing where an old gypsy woman stood with her dancing bear.
GYPSY WOMAN:	Good morning young sir! Have you come to see Samson dance?
NARRATOR 2:	At the sound of his name, the bear beside her rose up on his hind legs.

BEAR:	Growwwl.
JACK:	I don't have time. I'm taking this cake to the princess.
GYPSY WOMAN:	Then we shall make it a quick jig.
NARRATOR 2:	She snatched up her concertina and set the instrument to wheezing.
DANCE CHORUS:	OOMPA-OOMPA! OOMPA-OOMPA!
NARRATOR 4:	The bear began to dance.
BEAR:	*(dances and kicks, side to side)*
DANCE CHORUS:	Shuffle-shuffle-kick. Shuffle-shuffle-kick.
NARRATOR 5:	TAP-TAP-TAP, went Jack's foot, as he set down the cake to dance with his new friends.
BEAR:	**G-U-U-U-L-P!**
JACK:	**HEY,** that bear ate the princess's cake!
BEAR:	**PATOOIE!** *(spits out strawberry)*
GYPSY WOMAN:	But not the strawberry. Samson hates fruit.
NARRATOR 1:	Jack looked down at his gift, and for several seconds he was unable to speak. Finally, he said—
JACK:	At least I still have this—the reddest, juiciest, most succulent strawberry in the land.
NARRATOR 2:	And holding the strawberry proudly before him, Jack continued on to the castle.
NARRATOR 3:	Across the drawbridge . . .
NARRATOR 4:	Through the fortress walls . . .

NARRATOR 5:	Straight into the courtyard.
NARRATOR 1:	What a sight! There, smack in the center of all the festivities, sat the princess on her velvet throne, a long line of guests stretched before her.
NARRATOR 2:	One by one, they presented her with their gifts, each more fabulous than the last.
NARRATOR 3:	But even the most magnificent treasures did not seem to interest Her Highness.
PRINCESS:	*(with a bored yawn)* More rubies? How tiresome. Another tiara? How dull.
NARRATOR 4:	Joining the line, Jack glanced down at his humble gift. A guard noticed him.
GUARD:	And just what have you brought the princess?
JACK:	A strawberry. The reddest, juiciest, most succulent one in the land.
NARRATOR 5:	He held it out for the guard to see.
GUARD:	That is a fine piece of fruit, but I cannot allow you to give it to the princess.
JACK:	Why not?
GUARD:	Because she is allergic to strawberries. One taste and she swells up like a balloon.
JACK:	*(gasps)* NO!
GUARD:	Yes. I'm sorry, but you'll have to give it to me.
NARRATOR 1:	Reluctantly, Jack handed over the strawberry.
GUARD:	Mmmmm!

NARRATOR 2:	Now Jack found himself at the front of the line.
PRINCESS:	*(turning her gaze to Jack)* And what have *you* brought me?
NARRATOR 3:	Jack gulped.
NARRATOR 4:	He blushed.
NARRATOR 5:	He shuffled his feet.
PRINCESS:	Well?
NARRATOR 1:	Jack took a deep breath and knelt down before her.
JACK:	Your Highness, let me explain what happened.
NARRATOR 2:	And he told the princess about trading for the ingredients to bake a golden-sweet cake just for her.
BAKERS' CHORUS:	Churn, churn, churn. Chop, chop, chop. Blend, blend, blend. Bake, bake, bake.
NARRATOR 3:	He told her about the swirling storm of blackbirds, the wild-haired troll, and the dark, dark wood.
BIRD CHORUS:	*(cackling)* Aw-caw-caw-caw-caw!
NARRATOR 4:	He told her about the old gypsy woman and her concertina, and the bear who loved to dance but hated fruit.
DANCE CHORUS:	OOMPA-OOMPA! OOMPA-OOMPA! Shuffle-shuffle-kick. Shuffle-shuffle-kick.
JACK:	And in the end, I still had the succulent strawberry, but . . . *(sighs)* you're allergic to strawberries.
NARRATOR 5:	He waited for her to yawn.
JACK:	So the guard ate it.

NARRATOR 1:   The princess laughed and clapped her hands in delight.

PRINCESS: A STORY! And an adventure story at that! What a fine gift. *(rising from her throne)* Time for a birthday cake. And my new friend Jack shall have the honor of cutting it.

NARRATOR: And so he did, for his new friend, the princess.

A Reader's Theater Script for
ANIMAL CRACKERS FLY THE COOP
(For grades 2-4)

Reader's Theater adaptation by Judy Freeman (www.JudyReadsBooks.com). Adapted from *Animal Crackers Fly the Coop*, written and illustrated by Kevin O'Malley, published by Walker and Company, 2010. Reprinted with permission of the author, Kevin O'Malley. Copyright 2010 by Kevin O'Malley.

ROLES: Narrator 1, Narrator 2, Narrator 3, Narrator 4, Hen, Chickens, Farmer 1, Farmer 2, Farmer 3, Farmer 4, Dog, Cat, Cow, Robber 1, Robber 2, Robber 3

NOTE: If you have a smaller group, you could have the actors who play the three chickens also play the three robbers. Or, if you are acting the story out with a larger class, expand the number of chickens, and have two sets of narrators. One child can be Narrator 1 on pages 1-4, and another can be Narrator 1 on pages 5-7, and so on. You could have 8 narrators this way, if you need to.

When you photocopy this script, be sure to number the pages and run it single-sided. Double-sided scripts are confusing for children to follow. You don't need costumes in Reader's Theater unless you want them, but for this play, it would be fun to have some sort of hat or sign to differentiate between each animals—children with those parts could each make a decorated headband, for instance. If you happen to have a cowbell lying around the room, now's the time to find it.

NARRATOR 1:	Hen loved to tell jokes.
HEN:	Why did the chicken go to the library?
CHICKENS:	I don't know. Why?
HEN:	To check out a *bawk, bawk, bawk.*
CHICKENS:	*(laughing like chickens)* Bawk, bawk, bawk.
HEN:	How do comedians like their eggs?
CHICKENS:	I don't know. How?
HEN:	Funny-side up!
CHICKENS:	*(laughing like chickens)* Bawk, bawk, bawk.
NARRATOR 2:	Hen dreamed of standing on a stage in a comedy club and cracking up the crowd.

HEN:	I simply HAVE to be a comedi-hen!
NARRATOR 3:	The farmer wanted her to lay eggs. But Hen was just too tired of working for chicken feed. Being an egg layer wasn't all it was cracked up to be. Using fowl language, the farmer said . . .
FARMER 1:	So you won't lay eggs, huh? Well come this Fry-day, you'll make a fine chicken dinner.
NARRATOR 4:	That night Hen talked to the other chickens.
HEN:	Where do chickens have the most feathers?
CHICKENS:	I don't know. Where?
HEN:	On the outside! And I plan on keeping it that way!
NARRATOR 1:	So that night Hen flew the coop and headed across the field.
NARRATOR 2:	Early the next morning Hen saw a dog chasing its own tail.
HEN:	What are you doing, Dog?
DOG:	I'm trying to make ends meet.
HEN:	Would you please tell me your sad tale?
DOG:	My sad tail can't talk, but I can tell you my story. One night I was doing a comedy show for the sheep, and a wolf stole a side of beef from the smokehouse. The farmer got mad at me.
FARMER 2:	"Doggone it, Dog, you're all bark and no bite."
DOG:	I figured I better hightail it out of there!
NARRATOR 3:	Hen told Dog about her dream to open a comedy club.
HEN:	Won't you join me, Dog?

DOG: Yes! Can't you see my tail wagging?

HEN: Why do dogs wag their tails?

DOG: Because no one will do it for them.

NARRATOR 4: Dog and Hen were walking down a dusty road when they passed an old shed.

NARRATOR 1: A fat cat was lying on a wall. Mice were jumping all around him.

HEN: You don't see that every day. Clearly that cat isn't any good at claw enforcement.

DOG: So, Cat, can you "hiss and tell" your story to us?

CAT: I want to be a performer. But my master didn't like my *cat*-erwauling. I sing funny songs, like *(singing)* "Have Yourself a Furry Little Christmas" and *(singing)* "Silent Mice." The farmer got mad.

FARMER 3: Quit that noise or I'll throw you in the river!

CAT: So I left.

NARRATOR 2: Hen and Dog told the cat about their idea for a comedy nightclub.

NARRATOR 3: It didn't take much *purr*-suasion to get the cat to go with them.

CAT: *(singing)* I saw Mommy hiss at Santa Claws.

NARRATOR 4: Several hours later the three comedians came to a pasture. Standing outside the fence was a cow.

DOG: You look udderly miserable.

CAT:	*(turns to Hen)* If that cow were a musical note, she'd be a Beef-flat.
HEN:	We herd there was a problem. No use crying over spilled milk. Let's see if we can help you fix it.
COW:	I'm in a real stew. Last night the farmer said . . .
FARMER 4:	No milk again? I'm going to sell you to the butcher!
COW:	See, I completely forgot about making milk. All I do is think about jokes. I guess you'd say I have Milk of Amnesia. So I snuck out of the barn, and now I'm *cow*-culating what my next *moo*ve should be.
NARRATOR 1:	Hen, Dog, and Cat told her of their plan for a comedy nightclub and invited her to join them. Cow said yes and rang her bell.
DOG:	Why did you ring your bell?
COW:	Because my horns don't work.
NARRATOR 2:	The four comedians walked and walked. They were getting tired and hungry.
NARRATOR 3:	Finally, they passed an old house and looked inside.
NARRATOR 4:	Sitting in the kitchen were three robbers.
ROBBER 1:	*(to other robbers)* Don't eat all the food right now. We'll be hungry when we get back from robbing the bank.
ROBBERS 2 & 3:	OK, boss.
NARRATOR 1:	The four comedians hid in the bushes and watched the robbers leave.
NARRATOR 2:	As quickly as they could, they ran into the house and ate every last bit of food they could find.

DOG: What did the mother ghost tell the baby ghost when he ate too fast?

HEN: Stop *goblin* your food.

CAT: Why did the student eat his homework?

COW: The teacher told him it was a piece of cake.

NARRATOR 3: Tired and happy, the four comedians laid down and fell asleep.

NARRATOR 4: Around midnight the robbers returned to the house.

NARRATOR 1: When the first robber stepped inside, he tripped on Cow.

ROBBER 1: **Whoops!**

NARRATOR 2: The second robber tripped on the first.

ROBBER 2: **Hey!**

NARRATOR 3: And the third robber tripped on the second.

ROBBER 3: **Ouch!**

NARRATOR 4: The four comedians awoke with a start. They did the only thing they could think of . . .

NARRATORS 1-4: They told jokes.

COW: Why does a milking stool have only three legs? Because the cow has the udder.

NARRATORS 1 & 2: But the robbers saw just two horns and heard. . .

COW: **Moooooo, moooooooo, mooo!**

ROBBERS 1-3: *(startled)* **AAGGGHHHHH!**

DOG:	My master asked me why I go into a corner when I hear a bell. . . . I said, "Cause I'm a boxer."
NARRATORS 3 & 4:	But the robbers saw only sharp teeth and heard . . .
DOG:	**Growl, woof! Growl, woof!**
ROBBERS 1-3:	*(scared)* **EEEEHHHHH!**
CAT:	*(singing, to the tune of "Over the River and Through the Woods")* Over the counter and into my mouth, the tasty mouse will go!
NARRATORS 1 & 2:	But the robbers felt only sharp claws and heard . . .
CAT:	**Meeeeooooowwwww!**
ROBBERS 1-3:	*(terrified)* **OHHHHH NO!**
NARRATOR 1:	And, of course, Chicken woke up and said . . .
HEN:	The farmer I worked for was so dumb, he plowed his field with a steamroller because he wanted mashed potatoes.
NARRATORS 3 & 4:	The robbers just felt her sharp beak and heard . . .
HEN:	**Bawk, bawk, bawk!**
ROBBERS 1-3:	**Let's get out of here!**
NARRATORS 1-4:	The robbers got so scared, they ran off and never came back.
NARRATOR 2:	Now the four comedians have a comedy club. It's called COW-DOG KIT-HEN.
NARRATOR 3:	Animals come from far and wide. The comedians do two shows a night.
NARRATOR 4:	And every night, just like Hen dreamed . . .

NARRATORS 1-4: They crack them up.

HEN: What was the name of the very intelligent monster?

CAT: Frank Einstein.

DOG: What do cows do for entertainment?

COW: They rent *mooo*vies.

HEN: What do you call a boomerang that doesn't work?

CAT: A stick.

DOG: What do you call cheese that isn't yours?

COW: Nacho cheese.

HEN: Why didn't the skeleton cross the road?

AUDIENCE: Why?

HEN: He didn't have the guts! Thank you everyone! Let's hear it for our comedians! Good night, everyone. You've been a great audience. Thank you! *(comedians bow and hold up arms, fists clenched, "Rocky"-style)*

AUDIENCE: *(wild cheers and applause)*

A Reader's Theater Script for
SPACEHEADZ
(For grades 3-5)

Reader's Theater adaptation by Judy Freeman (www.JudyReadsBooks.com) of "Chapter 1!!: Spaceheadz Attack!" and "Chapter 3!!: Room 501-B" from *Spaceheadz*, written by Jon Scieszka and Francesco Sedita, illustrated by Shane Prigmore, published by Simon & Schuster. *Spaceheadz*, copyright ©2010 by Jon Scieszka, adapted with permission of the author, Jon Scieszka.

ROLES: Narrators 1-4, Michael K., Bob, Jennifer, Hamster, Mrs. Halley

NOTE: This script is based on the first and third chapters of Jon Scieszka's wacky, sci-fi, graphic novel-ish fiction saga, *Spaceheadz*. You can break into groups of 9 and have each group act out the whole script together. Or, if you want to do it as a whole-class activity, you could have two different casts—one for Chapter 1 (with 8 parts, if you include the class hamster, who only has one line) and a separate one for Chapter 3 (with 9 parts, though the hamster's role is still very small). There are many other dialogue-filled in this book that would be perfect for children to act out in small groups. They can write up their own scripts, using this one as their prototype.

NARRATORS 1-4:	Chapter 1: SPACEHEADZ ATTACK.
NARRATOR 1:	Michael K. knew his first day in a new school in a new city was going to be weird.
NARRATOR 2:	How could a first day at someplace in Brooklyn, New York, called P.S. 858 not be weird?
MICHAEL K.:	I just had no idea it could be this weird.
NARRATOR 3:	Michael K. had been in fifth grade for only twenty minutes, and already . . .
NARRATOR 4:	One: Mrs. Halley had stuck him in the slow group with the two strange new kids.
NARRATOR 1:	Two: the new girl had eaten half of his only pencil . . .
JENNIFER:	*(crunches down pencil)* Yum.

MICHAEL K.:	Hey! That's my only pencil!
NARRATOR 2:	Three: the new boy had just told Michael K. that they were Spaceheadz from another planet.
BOB:	Hey! We're Spaceheadz from another planet!
MICHAEL K.:	Uh, yeah. I just moved here too.
NARRATOR 3:	The girl flexed her arm. She said, in a voice like a wrestling announcer:
JENNIFER:	*(flexes her arm to show her muscle)* **SMACKDOWN!**
MICHAEL K.:	*(nods)* Very nice. *(to audience)* Sure, I'm a new kid, too. But these other new kids are seriously creeping me out. I don't want to get stuck with these losers on the first day of school. It could ruin my whole life.
BOB:	*(nods back to Michael K.)* **JUST DO IT.**
NARRATOR 4:	The girl drew the word SPHDZ (Spaceheadz) on her school lunch box.
MICHAEL K.:	This is getting beyond weird.
BOB:	Michael K., **I'M LOVING IT**! We need your help. You must become a Spaceheadz. Save your world. I am Bob.
JENNIFER:	*(in a deep, echoing voice)* Jennifer. *(crunches the rest of pencil)*
NARRATOR 1:	Michael K. watched Jennifer crunch the last of his Dixon Ticonderoga Number 2 pencil.
MICHAEL K.:	*(to audience)* How did this new kid know my name? I never said it. What did he mean, "save your world"? Were they just messing with me? Yeah, that's it. They were just goofing around.
NARRATOR 2:	Michael K. decided he would goof right back . . . and then move his seat as far away from them as possible.
MICHAEL K.:	I get it. You are Spaceheadz from another planet. On a mission to Earth. Here to take over the world. Take me to your leader. Bzzt, bzzt.

BOB: See! I told you, Jennifer! Michael K. can do anything. He is like a rock. **MMM, MMM, GOOD.**

NARRATOR 3: Jennifer burped up the eraser from Michael K.'s only pencil. She spit it out.

JENNIFER: **BURRRPPP. SPACEHEADZ — GET RRRREADY TO RRRRRUMBLE!**

NARRATOR 4: The class hamster said . . .

HAMSTER: Eeek eeek.

NARRATOR 1: Room 501-B went silent except for the sound of Mrs. Halley writing on the chalkboard.

NARRATOR 2: The thought occurred to Michael K. that Bob and Jennifer were not joking.

MICHAEL K.: *(to himself)* Bob and Jennifer are not joking.

NARRATOR 3: The thought occurred to Michael K. that they really were Spaceheadz from another planet.

MICHAEL K.: *(to himself)* They really are Spaceheadz from another planet.

NARRATOR 4 The thought exploded in Michael K.'s head that those thoughts were ridiculous.

MICHAEL K.: *(to himself)* That's right! Ridiculous! Aliens don't invade fifth grade classrooms. They don't look like fifth graders. And they don't talk like commercials and pro wrestlers.

NARRATORS 1-4: Bob and Jennifer were probably just from somewhere else.

MICHAEL K.: *(nods)* Just from somewhere else.

NARRATORS 1-4: And kind of confused.

MICHAEL K.: And kind of confused.

NARRATORS 1-4: Right.

MICHAEL K.: *(looking confused)* Right?

NARRATORS 1-4: Chapter 3: ROOM 501-B.

MRS. HALLEY: *(writing on chalkboard)* P.S. 858, room 501-B. Your new home for this year. I like to say you are all Mrs. Halley's comets—out of this world!

NARRATOR 1: Bob and Jennifer jumped up and started hooting and cheering like a Nickelodeon awards-show audience.

BOB & JENNIFER: *(cheer loudly and jump up and down)*

NARRATOR 2: The class hamster did three flips, then conked his head on the side of his food bowl.

HAMSTER: Eeek eeek.

NARRATORS 1-4: **BONK!**

HAMSTER: Eeek eeek, owwwk.

MRS. HALLEY: Oh, my.

NARRATOR 3: Mrs. Halley had been teaching at P.S. 858 for thirty-seven years.

NARRATOR 4: Thirty-six of those years she had taught fifth grade.

NARRATORS 1-4: But she had never seen anything quite like this.

MRS. HALLEY: Thank you for your excitement.

NARRATOR 1: She adjusted her tiny glasses to scan her class list.

NARRATOR 2: She couldn't seem to find the names of these new students anywhere.

NARRATOR 3: Maybe that other new student in their group knew them.

MRS. HALLEY: Michael K.? Could you explain to your friends that in this country we show our enthusiasm by remaining seated and clapping our hands.

MICHAEL K.: What? Huh? Me? Oh, no, I'm not Bob and Jennifer's friend. I don't even know them.

MRS. HALLEY: Thank you, Michael K. Very helpful of you to tell me your friends' names.

NARRATOR 4:	Mrs. Halley wrote "Bob" and "Jennifer" on the class list in her perfect handwriting.
MRS. HALLEY:	And do you mind if I call you Michael K.? We have several Michaels this year, and your last name is such a long one. You may speak to your friends in your own language if you wish.
NARRATOR 1:	Bob and Jennifer hooted some more.
BOB & JENNIFER:	*(jumping up and down)* Yahoo! Hee-haw! Wacka wacka wacka!
NARRATOR 2:	Now everyone in class was staring at Michael K. He had to do something.
MICHAEL K.:	Sure, that's fine. But see, I don't really know—
BOB & JENNIFER:	*(jumping up and down)* Wacka wacka wacka! Hee-haw! Yahoo!
MICHAEL K.:	Bob and Jennifer, be quiet! Sit down!
NARRATORS 1&2:	Bob and Jennifer sat down on the floor.
MICHAEL K.:	No! Sit in your seats!
NARRATORS 3&4:	Bob and Jennifer sat in their seats.
NARRATOR 3:	Mrs. Halley continued her beginning-of-the-year introduction like nothing had happened.
MRS. HALLEY:	And this year, room 501-B will be on the World Wide Internet. Our new computer teacher, Mr. Boolean, helped me build our class website.
NARRATOR 4:	The girl behind Jennifer smiled at Michael K.
NARRATOR 1:	The kid next to her stopped drawing his comic to stare.
NARRATOR 2:	Mrs. Halley kept talking, more to herself than to the class.
MRS. HALLEY:	*(types on her computer keyboard)* Here we type in **www.mrshalleyscomets.com**. And there it is. Our class schedule. Your list of supplies. Class calendar. Assignments. and look—we can even see the weather. And lunch.
NARRATOR 3:	Bob made a face, showing his teeth to Michael K.

BOB:	*(shows teeth in a weird smile)* I am making a smile. I am happy Mission Spaceheadz has begun. **THINK OUTSIDE THE BUN!**
JENNIFER:	Be Spaceheadz!
HAMSTER:	Eeek eee ee we weeee!
BOB:	*(to hamster)* Yes, he can. Michael K. can do anything.
NARRATOR 4:	Michael K. was afraid to ask, but he knew he had to.
MICHAEL K.:	And what's with the hamster?
NARRATOR 1:	He tried to keep his voice down, but the other kids were starting to look over.
BOB:	Major Fluffy? Oh, he is the mission leader.
HAMSTER:	*(smiles at Michael K., showing his teeth)* Eeek eeek!
BOB:	**WE TRY HARDER!** Spaceheadz wants you.
NARRATOR 2:	The big kid in the back of the class twirled his finger around next to his big head in the universal sign for "Cuckoo!"
NARRATORS 1-4:	This was bad. Very bad.
MICHAEL K.:	*(to Bob and Jennifer)* Don't talk to me.
NARRATORS 1&2:	Are Bob and Jennifer really Spaceheadz from another planet?
NARRATORS 3&4:	Will Michael K. join their cause?
EVERYONE:	Read *Spaceheadz* by Jon Scieszka, rhymes with Fresco, to find out.

JUDY FREEMAN'S SONGBOOK

THE BIGGEST BOOK

(by Judy Freeman, ©1989; To the tune of "The Darby Ram")

As I went to the library, it was on library day,
I spied the biggest book, sir, just standing on display.

CHORUS:
Well it's true, my lad, it's true, my lad, I never was known to lie.
And if you go to the library, you'll see the same as I.

The pages in this book, sir, they reached up to the moon;
I started it in January, didn't finish till June.

The print inside this book, sir, was tiny beyond hope;
To read a single page, sir, you'd need a microscope.

The cover of this book, sir, it reached up to the sky;
The eagles built a nest in it, you could hear the young ones cry.

The text inside this book, sir, was wild beyond belief;
I wiped my brow a thousand times with a nine-foot handkerchief.

The pictures in this book, sir, they leaped right off the page;
I caught them as they came to life and stuffed them in a cage.

The author of this book, sir, was mighty rich and fine,
But not so much a liar as the singer of these lines.

LOOK FOR 398.2

If you want a good story, let me tell you what to do—
LOOK FOR 398.2, LOOK FOR 398.2!

Prince or princess in hot water, trouble with a witch's brew—
LOOK FOR 398.2, LOOK FOR 398.2!

Fierce and fire-breathing dragons, shiny scales of green and blue—
LOOK FOR 398.2, LOOK FOR 398.2!

Ogres, leprechauns, and goblins all are waiting just for you—
LOOK FOR 398.2, LOOK FOR 398.2!

Find a tale from every country, from Australia to Peru—
LOOK FOR 398.2, LOOK FOR 398.2!
That's all you've got to do!

ROCKABYE BABY
(First verse traditional; second verse by Sarah Vesuvio's grandfather; third verse by Judy Freeman)

Rockabye baby, on the treetop;
When the bough bends, the cradle will rock;
When the bough breaks, the cradle will fall,
And down will come baby cradle and all.

Rockabye baby, upon the moon,
Eating her cornflakes with a big spoon;
When the wind blows, the moon it will break,
And down will come baby on a cornflake.

Rockabye baby, up in the stars,
Waving to Earth and waving to Mars;
When the stars shine, the sky will be bright,
And down will come baby with a night light.

HEY, COUSIN JENNY

Hey, cousin Jenny *(cup hands to mouth)*
Look at Uncle Benny *(make glasses with hands)*
Down by the seashore *(thumb over shoulder)*
Learning how to swim *(stroke, stroke)*
First he does the sidestroke *(pantomime sidestroke on each side)*
Then he does the backstroke *(pantomime backstroke, one arm after another)*
Then he goes and beats against the tide, 1, 2. *(2 slaps on thighs, 2 claps, 2 slaps on thighs, 1 clap)*

BABY JAWS
(Learned from Loreli Stochaj)

Baby jaws (chew chew chew chew chew) (2X)
Mama jaws (chew chew chew chew chew) (2X)
Daddy jaws (chew chew chew chew chew) (2X)
Grandma jaws (gum gum gum gum gum)
Grandpa jaws (gum gum gum gum gum)
Lady swim (swim swim swim swim swim) (2X)
Shark attack (doo doo doo AUUUGHH!) (2X)
Swim away (swim swim swim swim swim) (2X)

176

JOHNNY HAS A HEAD LIKE A PING PONG BALL
(To the tune of the William Tell Overture)

Johnny has a head like a ping-pong ball
Johnny has a head like a ping-pong ball
Johnny has a head like a ping-pong ball
Like a ping, like a ping-pong ball
Johnny has a head like a ping-pong, ping-pong, ping-pong, ping-pong, ping-pong ball
Johnny has a head like a ping-pong, ping-pong, ping-pong, ping-pong ball
Ping, ping, ping, ping, ping, ping, ping, ping, ping
Pong, pong, pong, pong, pong, pong, pong, pong, pong
Hey!

*NOTE: To see the coolest ping pong thing ever, go to **www.YouTube.com** and look up "hofersymphoniker" and the concert pianist, Joja Wendt, playing "The Ping Pong Song."*

APPLES AND BANANAS

I like to eat, eat, eat, apples and bananas;
I like to eat, eat, eat apples and bananas;

I like to ate, ate, ate, apples and banaynays (2X)
I like to eat, eat, eat, eepples and baneenees (2X)
I like to ite, ite, ite, ipples and baninis (2X)
I like to ote, ote, ote, opples and banonos (2X)
I like to ute, ute, ute, upples and banunus (2X)

Now we're through, through, through
With apples and bananas;
Now we're through through, through,
With A-E-I-O-U, U , U.

BANANAS, COCONUTS AND GRAPES
(To the tune of "The Battle Hymn of the Republic")

I like bananas, coconuts and grapes
I like bananas, coconuts and grapes
I like bananas, coconuts and grapes
That's why they call me: TARZAN OF THE APES!

NOTE: Sing three or four times: the first time yelling, the second time loudly; the third time softly (except for the "Tarzan" part); the third time, whisper all but the "Tarzan" part; the last time, no one makes a sound until all shout in unison, 'TARZAN OF THE APES'

GO BANANAS

If you look up this yell on YouTube or Google, you will find a zillion versions. Of all I've heard and watched and participated in, this one's my favorite. Do this with kids for a bit of controlled frenzy. If your group doesn't know this yet, get someone to say the word "bananas." You could prompt them by saying, "What kind of fruit has a yellow peel you can't eat, but it could make you slip?" Many will call out, "Bananas!"

"Bananas?" you yell. "Did somebody say bananas?" Stand up straight and yell, "Bananas of the world unite!" and motion for everyone to stand up. This is a call-and-response chant, so your group needs to repeat everything you say and do. Ready? Here we go.

Bananas of the world unite!" *(clasp hands over head)*
Form banana, form form banana *(pull one arm up over your head)*
Form banana, form form banana *(pull other arm up over your head, with hands in a point)*
And you peel banana, peel peel banana *(lower one arm to side, like you're peeling it)*
Peel banana, peel peel banana *(lower other arm to side, like you're peeling it)*
Then you go bananas, go go bananas *(wave arms, go a little crazy)*
And you go bananas, go go bananas

OTHER VERSES, IN THE SAME FORMAT:

Form the corn . . . shuck the corn . . . pop the corn *(pop up and down)*
Form the apple . . . peel the apple . . . chop the apple *(make chopping motions with hands)*
Form the orange . . . peel the orange . . . squeeze the orange *(hug self or person beside you)*
Form potato . . . peel potato . . . mash potato *(mash with feet, like the dance, "The Mashed Potato")*

OTHER VERSES:

Form the avocado . . . peel the avocado. *(Lower other arm.)*
Guacamole, gua-gua-camole, guacamole, gua-gua-camole

Build the house, build, build the house. *(Arms form roof over head.)*
Paint the house, paint, paint the house. *('paint' your neighbor.)*
Rock the house, rock, rock the house. *(dance)*

MAKE UP NEW VERSES UNTIL YOU'RE EXHAUSTED

BLACK SOCKS

Black socks, they never get dirty;
The longer you wear them the blacker they
get.
Sometimes I think I should wash them,
But something inside me keeps saying not
yet.

Not yet, not yet, not yet, not yet

Black socks, they never get dirty;
The longer you wear them the stronger they get.
Sometimes I think I should wash them,
But something inside me keeps saying not yet.

Not yet, not yet, not yet, not yet

Black socks, they never get dirty;
The longer you wear 'em, the stiffer they get.
Sometimes, I think of the laundry,
But something inside me says "Don't send them yet."

Not yet, not yet, not yet, not yet

NOTE: Reading the first chapter of Kate DiCamillo and Alison McGhee's *Bink and Gollie* (Candlewick, 2010) about Gollie's love of garish striped socks? You'll want to follow up with this song, which can be sung as a round. For the tune, go to **YouTube.com.** One adorable version, done as a round, is sung by the Leland and Gray Middle School Chorus at: **www.youtube.com/watch?v=ZHq7ksnvPcM.**

GOD BLESS MY UNDERWEAR
(To the tune of "God Bless America,"
with apologies to Kate Smith)

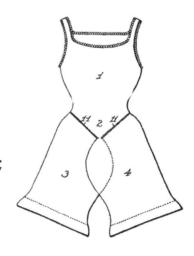

God bless my underwear, my only pair;
Stand beside them, and guide them,
Through the rips, through the holes, through the tears.
From the washer, to the dryer, to the clothesline in the air;
God bless my underwear, my only pair.

CHEWING GUM

(To hear Teresa Brewer's version of this 1950's novelty song,
go to YouTube: **www.youtube.com/watch?v=a18sZGr8lIE**)

My mom gave me a nickel to buy a pickle;
I didn't want a pickle, so I bought chewing gum.
Chew chew chew chew chew chewing gum, how I love chewing gum,
I'm crazy over chewing gum, I chew, chew, chew.

My mom gave me a dime to buy a lime;
I didn't want a lime, so I bought chewing gum.
Chew chew chew chew chew chewing gum, how I love chewing gum,
I'm crazy over chewing gum, I chew, chew, chew.

I chew the day away, it seems; I'm even blowin' bubbles in my dreams.

My aunt gave me a quarter for soda water;
I didn't buy the water, I bought some chewing gum.
Chew chew chew chew chew chewing gum, how I love chewing gum,
I'm crazy over chewing gum, what can I do?

I chew the day away, it seems; I'm even blowin' bubbles in my dreams.

My pop gave me a dollar to buy a collar;
You should have heard him holler when I bought chewing gum.
Chew chew chew chew chew chewing gum, how I love chewing gum,
I'm crazy over chewing gum, I chew, chew, chew.

NOTE: In addition to being recorded as "Choo'n Gum" by Teresa Brewer, it was covered by such musical icons as Dean Martin, The Andrews Sisters, and Ella Fitzgerald. This little ditty is ridiculously fun to sing, especially when you read the nonfiction picture book *Pop!: The Invention of Bubble Gum* by Meghan McCarthy (Simon & Schuster/Paula Wiseman, 2010), on page 52 of this handbook and pair it with *Trouble Gum* by Matthew Cordell (Feiwel & Friends, 2009), the crazy funny picture book about two piglet brothers who break all of their mother's rules about chewing gum. You can also sing it to kick off a math lesson about money, along with the classic Shel Silverstein poem, "Smart" from *Where the Sidewalk Ends* (HarperCollins, 1974).

JUDY FREEMAN'S STORYBOOK

HA HA HA!
HEARD ANY GOOD JOKES LATELY?

What does a pig use for a sore throat?
Oinkment.

What did the walls say to each other?
Meet you at the corner.

What goes Ho Ho Ho, Thump?
Santa Claus laughing his head off.

What did the judge say when the skunk came into the court?
Odor in the court.

What gets wetter and wetter the more it dries?
A towel.

What walks on four legs in the morning, two legs in the afternoon, and three legs at night?
Man. As a baby he crawls on all fours. As a young man he walks on two legs. As an old man he walks with a cane. (Riddle of the Sphinx)

What gets bigger the more you take away?
A hole.

What is the difference between an elephant and peanut butter?
An elephant doesn't stick to the roof of your mouth.

What did Tarzan say when he saw the elephant wearing sunglasses?
Nothing. He didn't recognize him.

Where were the first doughnuts fried?
In Greece.

What did the grapes say when the elephant stepped on them?
They let out a little wine.

Why was 6 so nervous?
Because 7 8 9.

What did the zero say to the 8?
Nice belt.

What time is it when you go to the dentist with a bad cavity?
2:30.

YOUR TURN! WRITE YOUR JOKE OR RIDDLE HERE:

THE CHICKEN IN THE LIBRARY

(Retold by Caroline Feller Bauer and Judy Freeman)

One day, a chicken came into the library, walked up to the librarian at the circulation desk, flapped her wings and clucked, "Bok, bok."

The librarian said, "You want a book? Okay. Here you go"

She handed a book to the chicken, who tucked it under her wing and went outside. Two minutes later, the chicken returned to the library, dropped the book on the desk, and said, "Bok, bok, bok, bok."

The librarian said, "You want more books? Okay. Here you go."

She handed two books to the chicken, who tucked them under her wing and went outside. Two minutes later, the chicken returned to the library, dropped the books on the desk, and said, "Bok, bok, bok, bok, bok, bok."

The librarian said, "You want more books? Here you go," and handed three books to the chicken, who tucked them under her wing and went outside.

By now, the librarian was curious. "What is going on with this chicken?" she said. So she followed the chicken outside and over to the little pond nearby. There she saw a large bullfrog, sitting on a lily pad in the water. The chicken held up the books, one at a time, for him to see, but the bullfrog just said, "Read it! Read it! Read it!"

CECIL WAS A CATERPILLAR

(Thanks to Cynthia Prince, third grade teacher in Cairo, Georgia, who heard this told at a workshop presented by several educators from England and then passed it on to me.)

Cecil was a caterpillar. Cecil was MY friend. The first time I saw Cecil he was THIS BIG.
I said, "Cecil! What have you done?"
He said, "I ate all the cabbages in *Maplewood*."

Cecil was a caterpillar. Cecil was MY friend. The next time I saw Cecil he was THIS BIG.
I said, "Cecil! What have you done?"
He said, "I ate all the cabbages in *Essex County*."

Cecil was a caterpillar. Cecil was MY friend. The next time I saw Cecil he was THIS BIG.
I said, "Cecil! What have you done?"
He said, "I ate all the cabbages in New Jersey."

Cecil was a caterpillar. Cecil was MY friend. The next time I saw Cecil he was THIS BIG.
I said, "Cecil! What have you done?"
He said, "I ate all the cabbages in the *United States*."

Cecil was a caterpillar. Cecil was MY friend. The next time I saw Cecil he was THIS BIG.
I said, "Cecil! What have you done?"
He said, "I ate all the cabbages in *North America*."

Cecil was a caterpillar. Cecil was MY friend. The next time I saw Cecil he was THIS BIG.
I said, "Cecil! What have you done?"
He said, "I ate all the cabbages in the *Northern Hemisphere*."

Cecil was a caterpillar. Cecil was MY friend. The next time I saw Cecil he was THIS BIG.
I said, "Cecil! What have you done?"
He said, "I ate all the cabbages on *Earth*."

Cecil was a caterpillar. Cecil was my friend. The last time I saw Cecil he was THIS BIG.
I said, "Cecil! What have you done?"
He said, "HICCUP!"

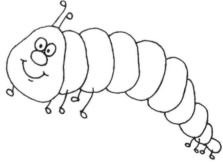

THE BREMEN TOWN MUSICIANS

From *Household Tales* by Jacob and Wilhelm Grimm; translated by Margaret Hunt. London: George Bell, 1884.

A certain man had a donkey, which had carried the corn-sacks to the mill indefatigably for many a long year; but his strength was going, and he was growing more and more unfit for work. Then his master began to consider how he might best save his keep; but the donkey, seeing that no good wind was blowing, ran away and set out on the road to Bremen. "There," he thought, "I can surely be town-musician." When he had walked some distance, he found a hound lying on the road, gasping like one who had run till he was tired. "What are you gasping so for, you big fellow?" asked the donkey.

"Ah," replied the hound, "as I am old, and daily grow weaker, and no longer can hunt, my master wanted to kill me, so I took to flight; but now how am I to earn my bread?"

"I tell you what," said the donkey, "I am going to Bremen, and shall be town-musician there; go with me and engage yourself also as a musician. I will play the lute, and you shall beat the kettledrum."

The hound agreed, and on they went.

Before long they came to a cat, sitting on the path, with a face like three rainy days! "Now then, old shaver, what has gone askew with you?" asked the donkey.

"Who can be merry when his neck is in danger?" answered the cat. "Because I am now getting old, and my teeth are worn to stumps, and I prefer to sit by the fire and spin, rather than hunt about after mice, my mistress wanted to drown me, so I ran away. But now good advice is scarce. Where am I to go?"

"Go with us to Bremen. You understand night-music, you can be a town-musician."

The cat thought well of it, and went with them. After this the three fugitives came to a farm-yard, where the cock was sitting upon the gate, crowing with all his might. "Your crow goes through and through one," said the donkey. "What is the matter?"

"I have been foretelling fine weather, because it is the day on which Our Lady washes the Christ-child's little shirts, and wants to dry them," said the cock; "but guests are coming for Sunday, so the housewife has no pity, and has told the cook that she intends to eat me in the soup to-morrow, and this evening I am to have my head cut off. Now I am crowing at full pitch while I can."

"Ah, but red-comb," said the donkey, "you had better come away with us. We are going to Bremen; you can find something better than death everywhere: you have a good voice, and if we make music together it must have some quality!"

The cock agreed to this plan, and all four went on together. They could not, however, reach the city of Bremen in one day, and in the evening they came to a forest where they meant to pass the night. The donkey and the hound laid themselves down under a large tree, the cat and the cock settled themselves in the branches; but the cock flew right to the top, where he was most safe. Before he went to sleep he looked round on all four sides, and thought he saw in the distance a little spark burning; so he called out to his companions that there must be a house not far off, for he saw a light.

The donkey said, "If so, we had better get up and go on, for the shelter here is bad." The hound thought that a few bones with some meat on would do him good too!

So they made their way to the place where the light was, and soon saw it shine brighter and grow larger, until they came to a well-lighted robber's house. The donkey, as the biggest, went to the window and looked in.

THE BREMEN TOWN MUSICIANS, cont.

"What do you see, my grey-horse?" asked the cock. "What do I see?" answered the donkey; "a table covered with good things to eat and drink, and robbers sitting at it enjoying themselves." "That would be the sort of thing for us," said the cock. "Yes, yes; ah, how I wish we were there!" said the donkey.

Then the animals took counsel together how they should manage to drive away the robbers, and at last they thought of a plan. The donkey was to place himself with his fore-feet upon the window-ledge, the hound was to jump on the donkey's back, the cat was to climb upon the dog, and lastly the cock was to fly up and perch upon the head of the cat.

When this was done, at a given signal, they began to perform their music together: the donkey brayed, the hound barked, the cat mewed, and the cock crowed; then they burst through the window into the room, so that the glass clattered! At this horrible din, the robbers sprang up, thinking no otherwise than that a ghost had come in, and fled in a great fright out into the forest. The four companions now sat down at the table, well content with what was left, and ate as if they were going to fast for a month.

As soon as the four minstrels had done, they put out the light, and each sought for himself a sleeping-place according to his nature and to what suited him. The donkey laid himself down upon some straw in the yard, the hound behind the door, the cat upon the hearth near the warm ashes, and the cock perched himself upon a beam of the roof; and being tired from their long walk, they soon went to sleep.

When it was past midnight, and the robbers saw from afar that the light was no longer burning in their house, and all appeared quiet, the captain said, "We ought not to have let ourselves be frightened out of our wits," and ordered one of them to go and examine the house.

The messenger finding all still, went into the kitchen to light a candle, and, taking the glistening fiery eyes of the cat for live coals, he held a lucifer-match to them to light it. But the cat did not understand the joke, and flew in his face, spitting and scratching. He was dreadfully frightened, and ran to the back-door, but the dog, who lay there sprang up and bit his leg; and as he ran across the yard by the straw-heap, the donkey gave him a smart kick with its hind foot. The cock, too, who had been awakened by the noise, and had become lively, cried down from the beam, "Cock-a-doodle-doo!"

Then the robber ran back as fast as he could to his captain, and said, "Ah, there is a horrible witch sitting in the house, who spat on me and scratched my face with her long claws; and by the door stands a man with a knife, who stabbed me in the leg; and in the yard there lies a black monster, who beat me with a wooden club; and above, upon the roof, sits the judge, who called out, 'Bring the rogue here to me!' so I got away as well as I could."

After this the robbers did not trust themselves in the house again; but it suited the four musicians of Bremen so well that they did not care to leave it any more. And the mouth of him who last told this story is still warm.

SURFING THE NET

A GUIDE TO USEFUL AND SCINTILLATING WEBSITES AND LISTSERVS AND BLOGS FOR KIDS AND GROWNUPS

compiled and updated by Judy Freeman,
with much input from posts on LM_NET and from
Carol Shields, Stevens Institute of Technology

Edited by Jane Scherer

Revised and Updated, Spring, 2011

NOTE: If you have a great site to recommend, or
find a dead link on this list or information that needs
updating, please let me know.
E-mail me at: BKWSSF@aol.com.

In the years since my book *More Books Kids Will Sit Still For* (Libraries Unlimited, 1995) was published, the Internet has bloomed. It has changed the way we access information. In writing *Books Kids Will Sit Still For 3* (Libraries Unlimited, 2006), I was grateful to be be able to sit at my desk and look up definitions, book reviews, details about authors and illustrators, magazine and newspaper articles, publishing info, video clips, and almost anything else I had a burning desire to know. And then there's the e-mail that we now check several times a day, for making further contacts with sources or simply to stay in touch with family and friends. It is my lifeline when I am holed up in the attic, writing.

Our computers, as we moved from dial-up to speedy cable connections, have revolutionized the way we look at the world and what we know about the world. As new developments spring forth at a dramatic pace, in a few years, we'll look back to today's Internet and it will seem quaint and primitive. Children nowadays have never not known computers, and think of ancient history as being the days before we had a cell phone in every pocket.

I've been accumulating interesting and useful websites related to children's literature and education, and offer them here to provide you with some helpful links, which will in turn lead you to even more links.

LISTSERVS

Stay current in your field, make new friends, and learn something new every single day. That's what you get when you join a free listserv. I couldn't cope without my daily reading of messages on **LM_NET**, the school librarian's listserv. It's better than a second Masters degree, and a whole lot more fun.

LM_NET

LM_NET is a school librarian's listserv with more than 17,000 members worldwide. To subscribe:
1. Send an e-mail message to: **listserv@listserv.syr.edu**
2. In the first line of the message, type: SUBSCRIBE LM_NET Firstname Lastname

Example: SUBSCRIBE LM_NET Judy Freeman

Requests for membership in LM_NET are handled automatically by the Syracuse University listserv computer and software. The LM_NET listserv computer will respond with an informative message, which will ask you for a confirmation. You will then be added if you properly follow the directions (which are easy), and you'll then receive further instructions on how to use LM_NET, one of the most valuable resources you'll ever find.

HELPFUL AND ESSENTIAL TIP: When you subscribe to LM_NET, or any high volume listserv, check the instructions and be sure you ask for your messages in the much-easier-to-handle **DIGEST** form. This means 8 to 10 messages come together in the body of a single message, with a table of contents at the top for easy perusal. Instead of finding 100+ messages in your box every day, you will get, instead, a far more manageable 5 to 10 digests.

If you want to see what's been said on any library-related topic imaginable, search the LM_NET Archives: **www.eduref.org/lm_net/archive/.**

PUBYAC

According to its mission statement, "PUBYAC is an Internet discussion list concerned with the practical aspects of Children and Young Adult Services in Public Libraries, focusing on programming ideas, outreach and literacy programs for children and caregivers, censorship and policy issues, collection development, administrative considerations, puppetry, job openings, professional development, and other pertinent services and issues.

The name PUBYAC amalgamates the most important aspects of the discussion: **PUB**lic libraries, **Y**oung **A**dults, and **C**hildren.

PUBYAC's home page, with more instructions and links, is at: **www.PUBYAC.org**

To join the list and receive the mailings from PUBYAC, send an e-mail message (no subject line necessary) to: **listproc@prairienet.org**

In the body of the e-mail, type this message: **subscribe pubyac**

CHILD_LIT

This unmoderated discussion group examines the theory and criticism of literature for children and young adults. Home page with all info: **www.rci.rutgers.edu/~mjoseph/childlit/about.html**

TO SUBSCRIBE: Send an e-mail to: **<listserv@email.rutgers.edu**

Leave the subject heading blank. In the body of the e-mail, type: **SUB child_lit** [your full name]

Example: **SUB child_lit Judy Freeman**

KIDLIT-L

For teachers, librarians, students, and others interested in the field of children's literature, this discussion list deals with teaching strategies and current research.

TO SUBSCRIBE: Send an e-mail to: **<listserv@bingvmb.cc.binghamton.edu**

Leave the subject heading blank. In the body of the e-mail, type:
    subscribe KIDLIT-L [your full name]

Example: **subscribe KIDLIT-L Judy Freeman**

PUBLISHERS' WEBSITES

These days, you don't need to keep a zillion book catalogs filed away. Most of the information about forthcoming and backlist titles is available on the publishers' websites. Here are the major ones.

ABRAMS (Harry N. Abrams): www.abramsbooks.com
ALBERT WHITMAN: www.awhitmanco.com
AMERICAN LIBRARY ASSOCIATION: www.ala.org
ANNICK PRESS: www.annickpress.com
ATHENEUM: www.SimonSaysKids.com (A division of Simon & Schuster)
AUGUST HOUSE: www.augusthouse.com
BAREFOOT BOOKS: www.barefoot-books.com/us
BLOOMSBURY: kids.bloomsburyusa.com
BOYDS MILLS PRESS: www.boydsmillspress.com
CANDLEWICK PRESS: www.candlewick.com
CAROLRHODA: www.lernerbooks.com
CHARLESBRIDGE: www. charlesbridge.com
CHILDREN'S BOOK COUNCIL: www.cbcbooks.org
CHILDREN'S BOOK PRESS: www.childrensbookpress.org
CHRONICLE BOOKS: www.chroniclekids.com
CLARION: www.hmhbooks.com (now part of Houghton Mifflin Harcourt)
DELACORTE: www.randomhouse.com/kids
DIAL: www.penguin.com/youngreaders (A division of Penguin)
DK: us.dk.com
DOUBLEDAY: www.randomhouse.com/kids
DUTTON: www.penguin.com/youngreaders (A division of Penguin)
FARRAR, STRAUS AND GIROUX: www.fsgkidsbooks.com (now part of Macmillan; can also be accessed through: us.macmillan.com/FSGYoungReaders.aspx)
FEIWEL & FRIENDS: (part of Macmillan; can also be accessed through: us.macmillan.com/FeiwelAndFriends.aspx)
FIREFLY BOOKS: www.fireflybooks.com
FITZHENRY & WHITESIDE: www.fitzhenry.ca
    (Includes: Fitzhenry Kids and Stoddart Kids)
FRONT STREET: www.frontstreetbooks.com
GALE: www.gale.com
GODINE: www.godine.com
GREENWILLOW: www.harperchildrens.com (A division of HarperCollins)
GROUNDWOOD: www.groundwoodbooks.com
HANDPRINT BOOKS: www.handprintbooks.com
HARCOURT: www.hmhbooks.com (now part of Houghton Mifflin Harcourt)
HARPERCOLLINS: www.harperchildrens.com (Includes Greenwillow, HarperCollins)
HEINEMANN: www.heinemann.com
HENRY HOLT: www.henryholtchildrensbooks.com (now part of Macmillan; can also be accessed through: us.macmillan.com/HoltYoungReaders.aspx)
HIGHSMITH PRESS: www.accessola.com
HOLIDAY HOUSE: www.holidayhouse.com
HOUGHTON MIFFLIN HARCOURT: www.hmhbooks.com
    (Includes: Clarion, Harcourt, Houghton Mifflin)
HYPERION: www.hyperionbooksforchildren.com (Includes Jump at the Sun)

KANE/MILLER: www.kanemiller.com

KIDS CAN: www.kidscanpress.com

KINGFISHER: us.macmillan.com/Kingfisher.aspx (now part of Macmillan)

KNOPF: www.randomhouse.com/kids

LEE & LOW: www.leeandlow.com

LERNER: www.lernerbooks.com

LIBRARIES UNLIMITED: www.lu.com
    (Includes: Libraries Unlimited and Teacher Ideas Press)

LINWORTH: www.linworth.com

LITTLE, BROWN: www.lb-kids.com

MACMILLAN: us.macmillan.com (Includes Farrar, Straus & Giroux; Feiwel & Friends; First
    Second, Henry Holt; Kingfisher; and Roaring Brook)

MARSHALL CAVENDISH: www.marshallcavendish.com

MCELDERRY: www.SimonSaysKids.com (Part of Simon & Schuster)

MILKWEED EDITIONS: www.milkweed.org

MONDO: www.mondopub.com

NATIONAL GEOGRAPHIC: www.nationalgeographic.com/books

OXFORD UNIVERSITY PRESS: www.oup.co.uk/oxed/children

PEACHTREE: www.peachtree-online.com

PENGUIN GROUP: www.penguin.com/youngreaders
    (Includes: Dial, Dutton, Firebird, Frederick Warne, Philomel, Putnam, Price Sloan Stern,
    Puffin, Viking)

PHILOMEL: www.penguin.com/youngreaders (A division of Penguin)

PLEASANT COMPANY/AMERICAN GIRL: www.americangirl.com

PUTNAM: www.penguin.com/youngreaders (A division of Penguin)

RANDOM HOUSE: www.randomhouse.com/kids
    (Includes: Bantam, David Fickling, Delacorte, Disney, Doubleday, Dragonfly, Golden, Knopf,
    Laurel Leaf, Random House, Schwartz & Wade, Wendy Lamb, Yearling)

ROARING BROOK: www.roaringbrookpress.com (now part of Macmillan; can also be accessed
    through: us.macmillan.com/RoaringBrook.aspx)

SCARECROW: www.scarecrowpress.com

SCHOLASTIC: www.scholastic.com (Includes Arthur A. Levine Books, Chicken House, Graphix,
    Michael di Capua Books, Orchard Books, Scholastic, and Blue Sky Press)

SIMON & SCHUSTER: www.SimonSaysKids.com
    (Includes: Atheneum, Little Simon, Margaret K. McElderry, Scribner, Simon & Schuster)

STENHOUSE: www.stenhouse.com

STERLING: www.sterlingpub.com

TILBURY HOUSE: www.tilburyhouse.com

TRICYCLE: www.tenspeedpress.com

TUNDRA: www.tundrabooks.com

VIKING: www.penguin.com/youngreaders (A division of Penguin)

WALKER & COMPANY: www.walkeryoungreaders.com
    (A division of Bloomsbury)

WORKMAN: www.workman.com

EDUCATION AND LIBRARY PUBLICATIONS

AMERICAN LIBRARIES: www.ala.org/alonline
BOOK LINKS: www.ala.org/booklinks
BOOKLIST: www.ala.org/booklist
EDUCATION WEEK ON THE WEB: www.edweek.org
HORN BOOK MAGAZINE: www.hbook.com
INSTRUCTOR: www.scholastic.com/instructor
KNOWLEDGE QUEST: www.ala.org/aasl/kqweb
LIBRARY MEDIA CONNECTION: www.linworth.com/lmc/
LIBRARY SPARKS: www.librarysparks.com
NEA TODAY: www.nea.org/neatoday
NEW YORK TIMES BOOK REVIEW: www.nytimes.com/books
PUBLISHERS WEEKLY ONLINE: www.publishersweekly.com
SCHOOL LIBRARIAN'S WORKSHOP: www.school-librarians-workshop.com
SCHOOL LIBRARY JOURNAL ONLINE: www.schoollibraryjournal.com
SCHOOL LIBRARY MONTHLY: www.schoollibrarymonthly.com
TEACHER LIBRARIAN: www.teacherlibrarian.com

POETRY WEBSITES

DOUGLAS FLORIAN'S BLOG
(With poems, pictures, and more from one of our leading children's poets): **floriancafe.blogspot.com/**

GIGGLEPOETRY.COM
(Poetry site for kids with funny poems, poetry contests, teaching ideas, and more): **www.gigglepoetry.com/index.cfm**

POETRY FOR CHILDREN
(Fabulous blog written by Slyvia Vardell, professor at Texas Woman's University, about finding and sharing poetry with young people; filled with poems, children's poetry book reviews, pictures, and links): **poetryforchildren.blogspot.com**

POETRY FOR KIDS BY KENN NESBITT
(Funny poems by Kenn Nesbitt, as well as games, contests, lessons, and a rhyming dictionary): **www.poetry4kids.com**

POETRY TEACHERS
(Great links and ideas for teaching poetry with kids): **www.poetryteachers.com**

POETRY ZONE
(For children and teenagers to publish their own poetry and reviews online): **www.poetryzone.ndirect.co.uk/index2.htm**

WRITER'S WORKSHOP WITH JACK PRELUTSKY
(In an online tutorial, beloved children's poet Jack Prelutsky takes children through the steps of writing their own poems. This site will also lead you to Writer's Workshop with Karla Kuskin and Writing *I Spy* Riddles with Jean Marzollo.): **teacher.scholastic.com/writewit/poetry/jack_home.htm**
Also don't miss his own website: **www.jackprelutsky.com**

CREATIVE DRAMA AND READER'S THEATER WEBSITES

Look online and find ideas, techniques, lesson plans, scripts, and guidelines for writing, acting, and staging. Try these for starters.

AARON SHEPARD
(Check out author Aaron Shepard's amazing website, download one of his many fine Reader's Theater scripts, or get in touch with him to book him for a workshop at your school.): **http://aaronshep.com/rt**

AUTHORS' WEBSITES
(A few children's book authors are providing Reader's Theater scripts for their books on their websites, which is a wonderful service for all of us.)

Toni Buzzeo:	**www.tonibuzzeo.com**
Katie Davis:	**www.katiedavis.com**
Suzy Kline:	**www.suzykline.com**
Margie Palatini:	**www.margiepalatini.com**

BAD WOLF PRESS
(More than 30 clever, melodious, and entertaining shows for children to perform, all available at very reasonable prices. The Bad Wolf folks advertise their scripts as "Musical plays for musically timid teachers." Each play comes with a spiral bound script and practical guide for the teacher, with permission to make copies of the script for the whole class, and a CD with a recording of each song.): **www.badwolfpress.com**

CREATIVE DRAMA AND THEATRE EDUCATION RESOURCE SITE
(Information and concrete ideas, sectioned into Reader's Theater, classroom ideas, theater games, and an extensive booklist.): **www.creativedrama.com**

CHILDDRAMA
(Matt Buchanan, playwright and drama teacher, has packed his website with resources for drama teachers, including his original plays, lesson plans, detailed curriculum outlines, and a bibliography of professional books.): **www.childdrama.com**

FICTIONTEACHERS.COM
(Bruce Lansky and Meadowbrook Press's wonderful website contains Classroom Theater scripts based on stories from *Girls to the Rescue,* featuring clever, courageous girls and *Newfangled Fairy Tales,* featuring fairy tales with humorous twists; and links to Poetry Theater poems from **www.gigglepoetry**.com.): **www.fictionteachers.com**

JUDY FREEMAN'S READER'S THEATER SCRIPTS ONLINE INCLUDE:

John, Paul, George & Ben by Lane Smith (www.hyperionbooksforchildren.com)
Emmy and the Incredible Shrinking Rat by Lynne Jonelle (www.lynnejonelle.com)
The Fabled Fourth Graders of Aesop Elementary School (**"The Boy Who Cried Lunch Monitor"**) **by** Candace Fleming (www.candacefleming.com)
The Cheese by Margbie Palatini (www.margiepalatini.com)
The Miraculous Journey of Edward Tulane by Kate DiCamillo (www.edwardtulane.com)

For links to all of the above and to new ones, as they are posted, go to **www.JudyReadBooks.com** and click on **Related Websites**.

CREATIVE DRAMA AND READER'S THEATER WEBSITES, cont.

LITERACY CONNECTIONS
("Promoting literacy and a love of reading" is the banner for this useful site which has many annotated links to other Reader's Theater sites.): **www.literacyconnections.com/ReadersTheater.php**

LOIS WALKER
(Canadian RT maven, Lois Walker, provides a step-by-step teacher's guide to get you started using RT in the classroom. This site links to her site, **www.scriptsforschools.com**, where you'll find more than 250 of her scripts for sale and a few free ones, too**.): www.loiswalker.com/catalog/teach.html**

PLAYS MAGAZINE
(Plays: The Drama Magazine for Young People is an indispensable magazine that comes out monthly, and is filled with good, royalty-free plays for elementary through high school. Find subscription information and a few sample plays you can download for free on their website.): **www.playsmag.com**

TIMELESS TEACHER STUFF
(Teacher Rick Swallow's language arts materials and Reader's Theater activities, plus many scripts you can download.): **www.timelessteacherstuff.com**

WEB ENGLISH TEACHER
("Web English Teacher presents the best of K-12 English / Language Arts teaching resources: lesson plans, WebQuests, videos, biography, e-texts, criticism, jokes, puzzles, and classroom activities," including RT.): **www.webenglishteacher.com/rt.html**

FOLKLORE AND STORYTELLING WEBSITES

New Jersey storyteller, Carol Titus, who provided some of the links on this list, says, "These sites shift and change like the sands and this is in no way a definitive list. Put 'storytelling' in as a subject on your favorite search engine and the sea of story will wash over you. Surfing them will turn up lots of shiny pebbles, interesting shells and some buried treasure. Happy hunting and when you find a good story, catch it and cast it adrift again for others to hear and ponder."

AARON SHEPARD.COM (Check out author Aaron Shepard's amazing website, download one of his many fine Reader's Theater scripts, or get in touch with him to book him for a workshop at your school.): **http://aaronshep.com/**

AESOP'S FABLES (Contains all 655 of Aesop's fables—indexed in table format—with morals listed, illustrations, lesson plan links, and Real Audio narrations): **www.aesopfables.com**

ANDREW LANG'S FAIRY BOOKS (Find the text of every story in Andrew Lang's 13 colors of Fairy Books, first published in the late 19th century. Access the stories by book, title, or place of origin.): **www.mythfolklore.net/andrewlang/**

FOLKLORE AND MYTHOLOGY ELECTRONIC TEXTS (Texts and commentary on thousands of stories, arranged by themes, motifs, and, story titles; compiled by D. L. Ashliman, a retired professor from the University of Pittsburgh): **www.pitt.edu/~dash/folktexts.html**

INTERNATIONAL STORYTELLING CENTER (Website of the International Storytelling Center in Jonesboro, TN, "dedicated to building a better world through the power of storytelling," and a sponsor of the National Storytelling Festival in Jonesboro every October): **www.storytellingfoundation.net**

LEGENDS (Links to texts of King Arthur, Robin Hood, Grimm, and Andrew Lang's Fairy Books series): **bestoflegends.org**

STORYARTS (Useful site from Heather Forest, the well-known storyteller and writer, with loads of stories to download, as well as telling techniques, ideas, lesson plans, and activities): **www.storyarts.org**

THE STORY CONNECTION (Storyteller and author Dianne de Las Casas includes book activities, games, and the full text of more than 50 of her retold folktales.): **www.storyconnection.net**

STORY LOVERS WORLD (Comprehensive free archival library for finding stories, sources and advice from professional storytellers, teachers, librarians, parents and grandparents; SOS: Searching Out Stories feature): **www.story-lovers.com**

STORYNET (Website of the National Storytelling Association (NSA); provides a U.S. calendar of events and links to resources for storytelling): **www.storynet.org**

SURLALUNE FAIRY TALE PAGES
(Annotated texts of 35 well-known fairy tales, with detailed analysis of illustrations, history, variants, and modern interpretations of each): **www.surlalunefairytales.com**

JUDY FREEMAN'S FAVORITE
CHILDREN'S LITERATURE BLOGS

I check in to each of these blogs several times a week to see what Esmé Codell and Elizabeth Bird and others are reading and writing. I appreciate their good taste in children's books, and admire their stimulating, well-written book reviews. Check out the following:

PLANET ESME: THE PLANET ESME BOOK-A-DAY PLAN: THE BEST NEW CHILDREN'S BOOKS FROM ESME'S SHELF: http://planetesme.blogspot.com/
Esmé Raji Codell, proprietress of this remarkable blog, is the author of several books I consider essential. For adults, there's *How to Get Your Child to Love Reading: For Ravenous and Reluctant Readers Alike* (Algonquin Books, 2003) and *Educating Esmé: Diary of a Teacher's First Year* (Algonquin Books, 2003). She's also written a batch of terrific children's books, my favorite of which is *Sahara Special* (Hyperion, 2003). And then there's her fabulous blog, about which she says: "This blog is a supporting page to sister site, **www.PlanetEsme.com**, where you will find a silly amount of additional reviews, thematic lists, links, and much more...everything you need to become an expert in children's literature . . . I'm a professional readiologist who thinks children's trade literature is our best hope for equalizing education in America . . . I'm a woman on a mission. Let me rock your pedagogical world."

SCHOOL LIBRARY JOURNAL BLOGS:
Go to **www.schoollibraryjournal.com** and pull down **BLOGS** at the top of the page. There are nine of them and all are extraordinary, covering every aspect of the library world.

A FUSE # 8 PRODUCTION
Elizabeth (Betsy) Bird, children's librarian at the Central Children's Room of the New York Public Library, keeps up a most remarkable blog, writing long, meaty, conversational, honest, and compelling reviews of new children's books—at least one a week. (As "Ramseelbird," she has written more than 1,000 children's book reviews on Amazon.com.) She reports on what's new in the field, does wonderful podcasts, and generates excitement about all things kid-lit-ish. If you're in a blog-gy mood, she has links to some of her favorite children's lit-related blogs—more than 70 of them!

NONFICTION MATTERS
Nonfiction children's book author Mark Aronson's blog about all things factual.

PRACTICALLY PARADISE
Middle school librarian, the effervescent and indefatigable Diane Chen from Nashville, lays it on the line with observations about books, lids, and life in the trenches.

HEAVY MEDAL: A MOCK NEWBERY BLOG
A discussion of prospective award-winners with, Nina Lindsay, former Newbery Chair; book reviewer and public children's librarian at the Oakland Public Library, California; and Jonathan Hunt, a teacher, reviewer, and presenter from Modesto, California.

MORE CHILDREN'S LITERATURE-BASED
WEBSITES & BLOGS

THE BOOK WHISPERER (Donalyn Miller, 6th grade language arts teacher in Texas and author of *The Book Whisperer: Awakening the Inner Reader in Every Child*, blogs for *Teacher Magazine* about turning kids into readers.): **blogs.edweek.org/teachers/book_whisperer/**

CYNTHIA LEITICH SMITH'S CHILDREN'S LITERATURE RESOURCES: (Named one of the Top 10 Writers' Sites by *Writer's Digest* and selected as one of the "Great Web Sites for Kids" by ALA/ALSC, this site contains info on books, stories, articles, teacher/reader guides, links to multicultural booklists, and articles for concerned educators): **www.cynthialeitichsmith.com**

CYNSATIONS: (Children's book author Cynthia Leitich Smith provides, in her excellent blog, "Interviews, reading recommendations, publishing information, literacy advocacy, writer resources, and breaking news in children's and young adult literature.): **cynthialeitichsmith.blogspot.com**

FOLLETT LIBRARY RESOURCES (If you're a teacher or librarian, go to Follett's indispensable site and sign up, for free, for **TitleWave**. Search for books and audiovisual materials by author, title, subject, or key word; work on library collection development; build and store lists; and order online. Find full cataloguing info, reading levels and lexiles, the book cover in color, and full text book reviews from *Booklist*, *Hornbook*, *Kirkus*, *Publishers Weekly*, and *School Library Journal*.): **www.titlewave.com**

GUYSREAD (Jon Scieszka's push for getting boys to read): **www.guysread.com**

I.N.K.: INTERESTING NONFICTION FOR KIDS
 "Here we will meet the writers whose words are presenting nonfiction in a whole new way . . . Rethink nonfiction for kids." Posters include Jennifer Armstrong, Steve Jenkins, Vicki Cobb, Katherine Krull, Sneed B. Collard III, Susanna Reich, Tanya Stone, Sue Macy, April Pulley Sayre, Susan E. Goodman, David Schwartz, Linda Salzman, Jan Greenberg, and Loreen Leedy. Quite an impressive line-up of some of our most outstanding nonfiction writers for children. (Also see Marc Aronson's splendid blog, "**Nonfiction Matters**" at **www.schoollibraryjournal.com**.) **http://inkrethink.blogspot.com/**

JEN ROBINSON'S BOOK PAGE (A blog "promoting the love of books by children, and the continued reading of children's books by adults"): **Jjkrbooks.typepad.com**

JENNY BROWN'S TWENTY BY JENNY
("The 20 best books for your child" plus reviews, interviews with children's book authors, and a free monthly online newsletter): **www.twentybyjenny.com**

JIM TRELEASE (America's Reading Guru includes thoughtful commentary on reading, censorship, AR, and getting children to read.): **www.trelease-on-reading.com**

LINDA'S LINKS TO LITERATURE: (Subscribe for $24.95 a year to access 25,000+ links to book units, lesson plans, activities, booktalks, book quizzes, puzzles, games and more. Subscribe **for free** to Linda Bendall's monthly newsletter, *The Bookmark*, for practical classroom ideas related to children's and young adult literature and information on favorite books and authors.): **www.lindaslinkstoliterature.com**

LISA VON DRASEK'S BLOG FOR EARLY WORD: EARLY WORD KIDS (Brief reviews and heads-ups on new books for children and young adults): **www.earlyword.com/category/childrens-and-ya/**

MORE CHILDREN'S LITERATURE-BASED WEBSITES AND BLOGS,
cont.

MIMI'S MOTIFS (Fabulous source for storytelling dolls and puppets that can be tied into a variety of children's books): **www.mimismotifs.com**

MOTHER READER: REAL BOOKS FOR REAL READERS: (A blog from Virginia library assistant and mom, who pegs herself: "The heart of a Mother. The soul of a Reader. The mouth of a smartass."): **www.motherreader.com**

NANCY KEANE'S BOOKTALKS (Booktalks, quick and simple. Includes indexes by author, title, subject, and interest level as well as general booktalking tips and student written talks): **nancykeane.com/booktalks**

NANCY POLETTE (Ideas for using the best of the best picture books, fiction, and nonfiction. Features a monthly sample literature guide): **www.nancypolette.com**

NOFLYINGNOTIGHTS (Comprehensive graphic novel review site for teens, including a blog and a link to their sister site, **Sidekicks for Kids**): **www.noflyingnotights.com**

PURPLE CRAYON (Well-known children's editor Harold Underdown shares his knowledge about writing, illustrating, and publishing children's books.): **www.underdown.org**

READKIDDOREAD (Author James Patterson's terrific new website for parents, grandparents, teachers, librarians, to help them find unforgettable titles to turn kids on to books. Most titles are chosen and extensively annotated by Judy Freeman, with links, related titles, ideas, and then some. Join the free Community for its blog, discussions, and podcasts with well-known children's book authors and illustrators.): **www.readkiddoread.com**

READING ROCKETS (Reading Rockets, an educational initiative of WETA, the public TV and radio station in Washington, D.C., is "a national multimedia project offering information and resources on how young kids learn to read, why so many struggle, and how caring adults can help." You'll find podcasts, videos, webcasts, blogs, articles, reading research, and free reading guides.): **www.readingrockets.org**

SOCIETY OF CHILDREN'S BOOK WRITERS & ILLUSTRATORS (SCBWI) (For professional and aspiring writers and illustrators of children's books): **www.scbwi.org**

STORYLINEONLINE: (Screen Actors Guild site presents more than 20 picture books read aloud by actors; includes activity guides for each book): **www.storylineonline.net**

TEACHINGBOOKS.NET (A WOW! of a website, started by Nick Glass, a guy with a mission. "From one easy-to-use website, TeachingBooks makes instantly available original, in-studio movies of authors and illustrators, audio excerpts of professional book readings, guides to thousands of titles and a wealth of multimedia resources on children's and young adult literature. Our hope is that by utilizing TeachingBooks' multimedia resources, educators will better understand the spirit and personality behind books and discover exciting ways to share these insights with children and teens."): **www.teachingbooks.net**

A YEAR OF READING ("Two teachers who read. A lot." A blog of reviews and observations by Franki Sibberson, author of *Beyond Leveled Books* and *Still Learning to Read*, and Mary Lee Hahn, author of *Reconsidering Read-Aloud*.): **readingyear.blogspot.com**

69 EXEMPLARY CHILDREN'S BOOK
AUTHOR AND ILLUSTRATOR WEBSITES

Of the hundreds of author and illustrator websites I have visited in the past few years, there are some that really stand out. When it comes to innovative design, the illustrators have the edge, of course, as they can beautify their sites with their own gorgeous artwork. Some folks have obviously spent a fortune on their websites, with sound, color, graphics, interactive home pages, games, and video clips. Others are much more print-based. A good author or illustrator website will include a biography, a personal message, photographs, descriptions and pictures of published books, teacher's guides, activities for children, working links to other good sites, and contact information.

When compiling my list of exemplary sites, I was looking for ones that went beyond the everyday and provided surprises and some heart. That doesn't necessarily mean visual hoopla, although that is certainly welcome. Some sites included a series of questions from children and the author's thoughtful, personal responses. Others included revealing essays; a series of well-thought-out teacher's guides for each of an author's books; Reader's Theater scripts; an illustrator's description of how he or she created the art; or useful ways to bring children and adults to reading. When we finish wending our way through one of these sites, we should feel as if we've gotten to know that author or illustrator a bit as a person. I love a website with personality and passion.

Children are using author websites to do research into authors' and illustrators' lives, find out information about their books, and get motivated to read them. Teachers and librarians use them to plan author visits to schools and libraries and to find teaching guides to books they plan to read aloud or use with students. The possibilities are growing as authors and illustrators grapple with just how much they want to reveal on the now ubiquitous sites. Can they afford to be left behind?

Adler, David A.	**www.davidaadler.com**
Anderson, Laurie Halse	**www.writerlady.com**
Armstrong, Jennifer	**www.jennifer-armstrong.com**
Arnold, Tedd	**www.teddarnoldbooks.com**
Arnosky, Jim	**www.jimarnosky.com**
Asch, Frank	**www.frankasch.com**
Barron, T. A.	**www.tabarron.com**
Blume, Judy	**www.judyblume.com**
Brett, Jan	**www.janbrett.com**
Buzzeo, Toni	**www.tonibuzzeo.com**
Carle, Eric	**www.eric-carle.com**
Carlson, Nancy	**www.nancycarlson.com**
Choldenko, Gennifer	**www.choldenko.com**
Christelow, Eileen	**www.eileenchristelow.com**
Cleary, Beverly	**www.beverlycleary.com**
Codell, Esmé Raji	**www.planetesme.com**
Coville, Bruce	**www.brucecoville.com**
Creech, Sharon	**www.sharoncreech.com**
Davis, Katie	**www.katiedavis.com**
DePaola, Tomie	**www.tomie.com**
DiPucchio, Kelly	**www.kellydipucchio.com**
DiTerlizzi, Tony	**www.diterlizzi.com**
Fleming, Denise	**www.denisefleming.com**
Fox, Mem	**www.memfox.net**
Frasier, Debra	**www.debrafrasier.com**

Gaiman, Neil	www.mousecircus.com
George, Kristine O'Connell	www.kristinegeorge.com
Grimes, Nikki	www.nikkigrimes.com
Gutman, Dan	www.dangutman.com
Henkes, Kevin	www.kevinhenkes.com
Keller, Laurie	www.lauriekeller.com
Kinney, Jeff	www.wimpykid.com
Kirk, Daniel	www.danielkirk.com
Krosoczka, Jarrett J.	www.studiojjk.com
Krull, Kathleen	www.kathleenkrull.com
Leedy, Loreen	www.loreenleedy.com
MacDonald, Suse	www.susemacdonald.com
Martin, Jacqueline Briggs	www.jacquelinebriggsmartin.com
Meghan McCarthy	www.meghan-mccarthy.com
McDonald, Megan	www.meganmcdonald.net
Munsch, Robert	www.robertmunsch.com
Myracle, Lauren	www.laurenmyracle.com
Numeroff, Laura	www.lauranumeroff.com
Palatini, Margie	www.margiepalatini.com
Park, Barbara	www.randomhouse.com/kids/junieb
Patterson, James	www.max-dan-wiz.com
Pilkey, Dav	www.pilkey.com
Prelutsky, Jack	www.jackprelutsky.com
Pulver, Robin	www.robinpulver.com
Rex, Adam	www.adamrex.com
Reynolds, Peter H.	www.peterhreynolds.com
Riordan, Rick	www.rickriordan.com
Rowling, J. K.	www.jkrowling.com
	www.scholastic.com/harrypotter
Sabuda, Robert	www.robertsabuda.com
Sayre, April Pulley	www.aprilsayre.com
Shepard, Aaron	www.aaronshep.com
Silverstein, Shel	www.shelsilverstein.com
Smith, Cynthia Leitich	www.cynthialeitichsmith.com
Snicket, Lemony	www.lemonysnicket.com
Spinelli, Jerry	www.jerryspinelli.com
Stevens, Janet	www.janetstevens.com
Van Allsburg, Chris	www.chrisvanallsburg.com
Willems, Mo	www.mowillems.com
	www.pigeonpresents.com
Wood, Audrey	www.audreywood.com
Woodson, Jacqueline	www.jacquelinewoodson.com
Yolen, Jane	www.janeyolen.com
Zelinsky, Paul O.	www.paulzelinsky.com

The 100+ Top-Rated Children's Books of 2010

AUTHOR AND TITLE INDEX

AUTHOR AND TITLE INDEX

AUTHOR AND TITLE INDEX

AUTHOR AND TITLE INDEX

AUTHOR AND TITLE INDEX

AUTHOR AND TITLE INDEX

AUTHOR AND TITLE INDEX

AUTHOR AND TITLE INDEX

SUBJECT INDEX

SUBJECT INDEX

SUBJECT INDEX

AUTOBIOGRAPHY
Hobbie, Holly. *Everything But the Horse.* E (Gr. K-4) *12*
Stamaty, Mark Alan. *Shake, Rattle & Turn that Noise Down!: How Elvis Changed Music, Me, and Mom.* 782.4 (Gr. 2-6) *53*
Telgemeier, Raina. *Smile!* FIC (Gr. 5-8) *38*

B

BABIES
Burningham, John. *There's Going to Be a Baby.* E (Gr. PreK-1) *23*
Frazee, Marla. *The Boss Baby.* E (Gr. PreK-2) *5*
Willems, Mo. *Knuffle Bunny Free: An Unexpected Diversion.* E (Gr. PreK-2) *14*

BABYSITTERS
Spratt, R. A. *The Adventures of Nanny Piggins.* FIC (Gr. 3-7) *25*

BALLET
Greenberg, Jan, and Sandra Jordan. *Ballet for Martha: Making Appalachian Spring.* 780 (Gr. 2-6) *42*

BANANAS
Vere, Ed. *Banana!* E (Gr. PreK-1) *3*

BANNING, JAMES HERMAN
Bildner, Phil. *The Hallelujah Flight.* E (Gr. 1-6) *46*

BARBERSHOPS
McElligott, Matthew. *Even Monsters Need Haircuts.* E (Gr. PreK-2) *12*

BASEBALL PLAYERS
Tavares, Matt. *Henry Aaron's Dream.* 796.357 (Gr. 2-6) *47*

BEARS
Becker, Bonny. *A Bedtime for Bear.* E (Gr. PreK-2) *3*
Browne, Anthony. *Me and You.* E (Gr. PreK-2) *16*
Elya, Susan Middleton. *Rubia and the Three Osos.* E (Gr. PreK-2) *20*
Spratt, R. A. *The Adventures of Nanny Piggins.* FIC (Gr. 3-7) *25*

BEDTIME
Becker, Bonny. *A Bedtime for Bear.* E (Gr. PreK-2) *3*
Stein, David Ezra. *Interrupting Chicken.* E (Gr. PreK-2) *14*
Willems, Mo. *Time to Sleep, Sheep the Sheep.* **(Cat the Cat series)** E (Gr. PreK-1) *8*

BEDTIME—POETRY
Yolen, Jane, ed. *Switching on the Moon: A Very First Book of Bedtime Poems.* 398.8 (Gr. PreK-1) *61*

BEDTIME STORIES
Stein, David Ezra. *Interrupting Chicken.* E (Gr. PreK-2) *14*

BEHAVIOR
Angleberger, Tom. *The Strange Case of Origami Yoda.* FIC (Gr. 3-6) *39*
Khan, Rukhsana. *Big Red Lollipop.* E (Gr. K-4) *4*
Peirce, Lincoln. *Big Nate: In a Class by Himself.* FIC (Gr. 3-6) *26*

BEST FRIENDS
DiCamillo, Kate, and Alison McGhee. *Bink and Gollie.* E (Gr. PreK-2) *4*
Pennypacker, Sara. *Clementine, Friend of the Week.* FIC (Gr. 1-4) *26*
Willems, Mo. *Can I Play, Too?* **(Elephant & Piggie series)** E (Gr. PreK-1) *11*
Willems, Mo. *I Am Going!* **(Elephant & Piggie series)** E (Gr. PreK-1) *11*

BICYCLES
Hobbie, Holly. *Everything But the Horse.* E (Gr. K-4) *12*

SUBJECT INDEX

SUBJECT INDEX

BOYS—POETRY
Raczka, Bob. *Guyku: A Year of Haiku for Boys.* 811 (Gr. PreK-4) *58*

BRACES
Telgemeier, Raina. *Smile!* FIC (Gr. 5-8) *38*

BROOKLYN (NEW YORK, N.Y.)
Scieszka, Jon, and Francesco Sedita. *Spaceheadz.* (SPHDZ, Book #1!) FIC (Gr. 3-5) *38*

BROTHERS AND SISTERS
Burningham, John. *There's Going to Be a Baby.* E (Gr. PreK-1) *23*
Erskine, Kathryn. *Mockingbird: (Mok'ing-bûrd).* FIC (Gr. 4-7) *32*
Gidwitz, Adam. *A Tale Dark & Grimm.* FIC (Gr. 5-7) *40*
Riordan, Rick. *The Red Pyramid.* FIC (Gr. 5-9) *36*
Spratt, R. A. *The Adventures of Nanny Piggins.* FIC (Gr. 3-7) *25*

BUBBLE GUM
McCarthy, Meghan. *Pop!: The Invention of Bubble Gum.* 664 (Gr. K-4) *52*

BULLIES
Polacco, Patricia. *The Junkyard Wonders.* FIC (Gr. 2-6) *32*

BUSES
McMullan, Kate. *School!: Adventures at the Harvey N. Trouble Elementary School.* FIC (Gr. 2-5) *37*

BUTTERFLIES
Engle, Margarita. *Summer Birds: The Butterflies of Maria Merian.* 595.78 (Gr. 1-4) *55*

C

CAKES
Fleming, Candace. *Clever Jack Takes the Cake.* E (Gr. PreK-3) *10*

CALDECOTT MEDAL
Stead, Philip C. *A Sick Day for Amos McGee.* E (Gr. PreK-1) *21*

CALIFORNIA
Williams-Garcia, Rita. *One Crazy Summer.* FIC (Gr. 5-8) *35*

CARTOONS AND COMICS
Peirce, Lincoln. *Big Nate: In a Class by Himself.* FIC (Gr. 3-6) *26*
Spires, Ashley. *Binky to the Rescue.* 741.5 (Gr. PreK-3) *5*
Stamaty, Mark Alan. *Shake, Rattle & Turn that Noise Down!: How Elvis Changed Music, Me, and Mom.* 782.4 (Gr. 2-6) *53*
Telgemeier, Raina. *Smile!* FIC (Gr. 5-8) *38*

CATERPILLARS
Engle, Margarita. *Summer Birds: The Butterflies of Maria Merian.* 595.78 (Gr. 1-4) *55*

CATS
Epstein, Adam Jay, and Andrew Jacobson. *The Familiars.* FIC (Gr. 4-7) *29*
Litwin, Eric. *Pete the Cat: I Love My White Shoes.* E (Gr. PreK-1) *19*
O'Malley, Kevin. *Animal Crackers Fly the Coop.* E (Gr. 1-4) *1*
Pennypacker, Sara. *Clementine, Friend of the Week.* FIC (Gr. 1-4) *26*
Spires, Ashley. *Binky to the Rescue.* 741.5 (Gr. PreK-3) *5*
Willems, Mo. *Cat the Cat, Who Is That?* (Cat the Cat series) E (Gr. PreK-1) *7*
Willems, Mo. *Let's Say Hi to Friends Who Fly!* (Cat the Cat series) E (Gr. PreK-1) *7*
Willems, Mo. *Time to Sleep, Sheep the Sheep.* (Cat the Cat series) E (Gr. PreK-1) *8*
Willems, Mo. *What's Your Sound, Hound the Hound?* (Cat the Cat series) E (Gr. PreK-1) *8*

SUBJECT INDEX

SUBJECT INDEX

COMEDIANS
O'Malley, Kevin. *Animal Crackers Fly the Coop.* E (Gr. 1-4) *1*

COMMUNICATION
Draper, Sharon M. *Out of My Mind.* FIC (Gr. 4-8) *36*

COMPASSION
Stead, Philip C. *A Sick Day for Amos McGee.* E (Gr. PreK-1) *21*
Winter, Jeanette. *Biblioburro: A True Story from Columbia.* 020 (Gr. K-6) *43*

COMPETITION
Barton, Chris. *Shark Vs. Train.* E (Gr. PreK-2) *21*

COMPOSERS—BIOGRAPHY
Greenberg, Jan, and Sandra Jordan. *Ballet for Martha: Making Appalachian Spring.* 780 (Gr. 2-6) *42*

CONDUCT OF LIFE
Khan, Rukhsana. *Big Red Lollipop.* E (Gr. K-4) *4*
Peet, Mal, and Elspeth Graham. *Cloud Tea Monkeys.* FIC (Gr. 1-4) *27*

CONFLICT RESOLUTION
Pennypacker, Sara. *Clementine, Friend of the Week.* FIC (Gr. 1-4) *26*

CONFORMITY
Lairamore, Dawn. *Ivy's Ever After.* FIC (Gr. 4-7) *31*

COOPERATION
Walton, Rick. *Mr. President Goes to School.* E (Gr. K-5) *17*

COPLAND, AARON, 1900-1990
Greenberg, Jan, and Sandra Jordan. *Ballet for Martha: Making Appalachian Spring.* 780 (Gr. 2-6) *42*

COUNTING BOOKS
LaRochelle, David. *1+1=5: And Other Unlikely Additions.* 513.2 (Gr. PreK-2) *51*

COUNTRY LIFE
Hobbie, Holly. *Everything But the Horse.* E (Gr. K-4) *12*

COUSINS
Holm, Jennifer L. *Turtle in Paradise.* FIC (Gr. 3-6) *40*

CREATIVE DRAMA
Baker, Keith. *LMNO Peas.* E (Gr. PreK-2) *15*
Emberley, Rebecca, and Ed Emberley. *The Red Hen.* 398.2 (Gr. PreK-1) *60*
Litwin, Eric. *Pete the Cat: I Love My White Shoes.* E (Gr. PreK-1) *19*
Thomson, Bill. *Chalk.* E (Gr. PreK-3) *9*
Vere, Ed. *Banana!* E (Gr. PreK-1) *3*

D

DANCE
Greenberg, Jan, and Sandra Jordan. *Ballet for Martha: Making Appalachian Spring.* 780 (Gr. 2-6) *42*

DANCERS
Greenberg, Jan, and Sandra Jordan. *Ballet for Martha: Making Appalachian Spring.* 780 (Gr. 2-6) *42*

DASSIES
Brett, Jan. *The 3 Little Dassies.* E (Gr. PreK-2) *62*

SUBJECT INDEX

DAVE THE POTTER, 1801?-1870?
Hill, Laban Carrick. *Dave the Potter: Artist, Poet, Slave.* 738 (Gr. 2-8) *45*

DEATH
Erskine, Kathryn. *Mockingbird: (Mok'ing-bûrd).* FIC (Gr. 4-7) *32*
Polacco, Patricia. *The Junkyard Wonders.* FIC (Gr. 2-6) *32*
Tashjian, Janet. *My Life As a Book.* FIC (Gr. 4-7) *34*
Willems, Mo. *City Dog, Country Frog.* E (Gr. PreK-1) *9*

DEPRESSIONS—1929—U.S.
Holm, Jennifer L. *Turtle in Paradise.* FIC (Gr. 3-6) *40*
Vanderpool, Clare. *Moon Over Manifest.* FIC (Gr. 5-8) *33*

DIARIES
Kerley, Barbara. *The Extraordinary Mark Twain (According to Susy).* FIC (Gr. 3-6) *45*

DINOSAURS
Thomson, Bill. *Chalk.* E (Gr. PreK-3) *9*

DIVORCE
Alvarez, Julia. *How Tía Lola Learned to Teach.* FIC (Gr. 3-6) *31*

DOGS
Hills, Tad. *How Rocket Learned to Read.* E (Gr. PreK-1) *13*
Nelson, Marilyn. *Snook Alone.* E (Gr. 2-6) *22*
O'Malley, Kevin. *Animal Crackers Fly the Coop.* E (Gr. 1-4) *1*
Tashjian, Janet. *My Life As a Book.* FIC (Gr. 4-7) *34*
Willems, Mo. *City Dog, Country Frog.* E (Gr. PreK-1) *9*

DOGS—FOLKLORE
Huling, Jan. *Ol' Bloo's Boogie-Woogie Band and Blues Ensemble.* 398.2 (Gr. 1-5) *59*

DOMINICAN AMERICANS
Alvarez, Julia. *How Tía Lola Learned to Teach.* FIC (Gr. 3-6) *31*

DONKEYS—FOLKLORE
Huling, Jan. *Ol' Bloo's Boogie-Woogie Band and Blues Ensemble.* 398.2 (Gr. 1-5) *59*

DRAGONS
Lairamore, Dawn. *Ivy's Ever After.* FIC (Gr. 4-7) *31*
Vernon, Ursula. *Dragonbreath: Curse of the Were-wiener.* FIC (Gr. 3-5) *28*

DRAWING
Lichtenheld, Tom. *Bridget's Beret.* E (Gr. PreK-2) *6*
Thomson, Bill. *Chalk.* E (Gr. PreK-3) *9*

E

EARTHQUAKES
Telgemeier, Raina. *Smile!* FIC (Gr. 5-8) *38*

EASY READERS
Lin, Grace. *Ling & Ting: Not Exactly the Same!* E (Gr. PreK-2) *15*
Vere, Ed. *Banana!* E (Gr. PreK-1) *3*
Willems, Mo. *Can I Play, Too?* **(Elephant & Piggie series)** E (Gr. PreK-1) *11*
Willems, Mo. *Cat the Cat, Who Is That?* **(Cat the Cat series)** E (Gr. PreK-1) *7*
Willems, Mo. *I Am Going!* **(Elephant & Piggie series)** E (Gr. PreK-1) *11*
Willems, Mo. *Let's Say Hi to Friends Who Fly!* **(Cat the Cat series)** E (Gr. PreK-1) *7*
Willems, Mo. *Time to Sleep, Sheep the Sheep.* **(Cat the Cat series)** E (Gr. PreK-1) *8*
Willems, Mo. *What's Your Sound, Hound the Hound?* **(Cat the Cat series)** E (Gr. PreK-1) *8*

SUBJECT INDEX

SUBJECT INDEX

SUBJECT INDEX

SUBJECT INDEX

SUBJECT INDEX

HUMOROUS FICTION
Angleberger, Tom. *The Strange Case of Origami Yoda.* FIC (Gr. 3-6) *39*
Barnett, Mac. *Oh No!, or, How My Science Project Destroyed the World.* E (Gr. PreK-3) *18*
Barton, Chris. *Shark Vs. Train.* E (Gr. PreK-2) *21*
Boyce, Frank Cottrell. *Cosmic.* FIC (Gr. 5-8) *27*
DiCamillo, Kate, and Alison McGhee. *Bink and Gollie.* E (Gr. PreK-2) *4*
Frazee, Marla. *The Boss Baby.* E (Gr. PreK-2) *5*
Holm, Jennifer L. *Turtle in Paradise.* FIC (Gr. 3-6) *40*
Isaacs, Anne. *Dust Devil.* E (Gr. K-4) *10*
McElligott, Matthew. *Even Monsters Need Haircuts.* E (Gr. PreK-2) *12*
McMullan, Kate. *School!: Adventures at the Harvey N. Trouble Elementary School.* FIC (Gr. 2-5) *37*
O'Malley, Kevin. *Animal Crackers Fly the Coop.* E (Gr. 1-4) *1*
Peirce, Lincoln. *Big Nate: In a Class by Himself.* FIC (Gr. 3-6) *26*
Pennypacker, Sara. *Clementine, Friend of the Week.* FIC (Gr. 1-4) *26*
Scieszka, Jon, and Francesco Sedita. *Spaceheadz.* (SPHDZ, Book #1!) FIC (Gr. 3-5) *38*
Spires, Ashley. *Binky to the Rescue.* 741.5 (Gr. PreK-3) *5*
Spratt, R. A. *The Adventures of Nanny Piggins.* FIC (Gr. 3-7) *25*
Stein, David Ezra. *Interrupting Chicken.* E (Gr. PreK-2) *14*
Vernon, Ursula. *Dragonbreath: Curse of the Were-wiener.* FIC (Gr. 3-5) *28*

HUMOROUS FOLKLORE
Emberley, Rebecca, and Ed Emberley. *The Red Hen.* 398.2 (Gr. PreK-1) *60*

HURRICANES
Holm, Jennifer L. *Turtle in Paradise.* FIC (Gr. 3-6) *40*

I

IGUANAS
Vernon, Ursula. *Dragonbreath: Curse of the Were-wiener.* FIC (Gr. 3-5) *28*

IMAGINATION
Barton, Chris. *Shark Vs. Train.* E (Gr. PreK-2) *21*
Burningham, John. *There's Going to Be a Baby.* E (Gr. PreK-1) *23*
DiCamillo, Kate, and Alison McGhee. *Bink and Gollie.* E (Gr. PreK-2) *4*
Henkes, Kevin. *My Garden.* E (Gr. PreK-1) *17*
Spires, Ashley. *Binky to the Rescue.* 741.5 (Gr. PreK-3) *5*
Thomson, Bill. *Chalk.* E (Gr. PreK-3) *9*

IMMIGRATION AND EMIGRATION
Alvarez, Julia. *How Tía Lola Learned to Teach.* FIC (Gr. 3-6) *31*
Khan, Rukhsana. *Big Red Lollipop.* E (Gr. K-4) *4*

INDIVIDUALITY
Lin, Grace. *Ling & Ting: Not Exactly the Same!* E (Gr. PreK-2) *15*

INSECTS
Engle, Margarita. *Summer Birds: The Butterflies of Maria Merian.* 595.78 (Gr. 1-4) *55*
Spires, Ashley. *Binky to the Rescue.* 741.5 (Gr. PreK-3) *5*
Voake, Steve. *Insect Detective.* 595.7 (Gr. PreK-2) *65*

INTERPERSONAL RELATIONS
Angleberger, Tom. *The Strange Case of Origami Yoda.* FIC (Gr. 3-6) *39*
Draper, Sharon M. *Out of My Mind.* FIC (Gr. 4-8) *36*
Polacco, Patricia. *The Junkyard Wonders.* FIC (Gr. 2-6) *32*

INTERPLANETARY VOYAGES
Boyce, Frank Cottrell. *Cosmic.* FIC (Gr. 5-8) *27*

SUBJECT INDEX

SUBJECT INDEX

SUBJECT INDEX

M

MAGIC
Epstein, Adam Jay, and Andrew Jacobson. *The Familiars.* FIC (Gr. 4-7) *29*
Riordan, Rick. *The Red Pyramid.* FIC (Gr. 5-9) *36*

MANNERS
Vere, Ed. *Banana!* E (Gr. PreK-1) *3*

MARTHA'S VINEYARD (MASS.)
Tashjian, Janet. *My Life As a Book.* FIC (Gr. 4-7) *34*

MASON, JOSEPH, 1807-1883
Cole, Henry. *A Nest for Celeste: A Story About Art, Inspiration, and the Meaning of Home.* FIC (Gr. 3-6) *34*

MATHEMATICS
LaRochelle, David. *1+1=5: And Other Unlikely Additions.* 513.2 (Gr. PreK-2) *51*

MEDICINE
Beccia, Carlyn. *I Feel Better with a Frog in My Throat: History's Strangest Cures.* 610 (Gr. 3-6) *48*

MERIAN, MARIA SIBYLLA, 1647-1717
Engle, Margarita. *Summer Birds: The Butterflies of Maria Merian.* 595.78 (Gr. 1-4) *55*

METAMORPHOSIS
Engle, Margarita. *Summer Birds: The Butterflies of Maria Merian.* 595.78 (Gr. 1-4) *55*

MICE
Becker, Bonny. *A Bedtime for Bear.* E (Gr. PreK-2) *3*
Cole, Henry. *A Nest for Celeste: A Story About Art, Inspiration, and the Meaning of Home.* FIC (Gr. 3-6) *34*

MIDDLE SCHOOLS
Angleberger, Tom. *The Strange Case of Origami Yoda.* FIC (Gr. 3-6) *39*
Peirce, Lincoln. *Big Nate: In a Class by Himself.* FIC (Gr. 3-6) *26*

MONGOLS—BIOGRAPHY
Krull, Kathleen. *Kubla Khan: The Emperor of Everything.* B (Gr. 3-6) *49*

MONKEYS
Peet, Mal, and Elspeth Graham. *Cloud Tea Monkeys.* FIC (Gr. 1-4) *27*
Vere, Ed. *Banana!* E (Gr. PreK-1) *3*

MONKS
Nelson, Marilyn. *Snook Alone.* E (Gr. 2-6) *22*

MONSTERS
McElligott, Matthew. *Even Monsters Need Haircuts.* E (Gr. PreK-2) *12*

MONTANA
Isaacs, Anne. *Dust Devil.* E (Gr. K-4) *10*

MOSQUITOES
Isaacs, Anne. *Dust Devil.* E (Gr. K-4) *10*

MOTHER GOOSE
Mavor, Sally. *Pocketful of Posies: A Treasury of Nursery Rhymes.* 398.8 (Gr. PreK-1) *60*

MOTHERS
Bottner, Barbara. *Miss Brooks Loves Books! (And I Don't).* E (Gr. PreK-2) *16*
Burningham, John. *There's Going to Be a Baby.* E (Gr. PreK-1) *23*
Holm, Jennifer L. *Turtle in Paradise.* FIC (Gr. 3-6) *40*

SUBJECT INDEX

SUBJECT INDEX

PARODIES
Brett, Jan. *The 3 Little Dassies.* E (Gr. PreK-2) *62*
Browne, Anthony. *Me and You.* E (Gr. PreK-2) *16*
O'Malley, Kevin. *Animal Crackers Fly the Coop.* E (Gr. 1-4) *1*
Sylvester, Kevin. *Splinters.* E (Gr. 1-4) *22*

PARROTS
Montgomery, Sy. *Kakapo Rescue: Saving the World's Strangest Parrot.* (Scientists in the Field series) 639.9 (Gr. 4-8) *49*

PARTIES
Khan, Rukhsana. *Big Red Lollipop.* E (Gr. K-4) *4*

PEAS
Baker, Keith. *LMNO Peas.* E (Gr. PreK-2) *15*

PEOPLE WITH DISABILITIES
Draper, Sharon M. *Out of My Mind.* FIC (Gr. 4-8) *36*
Lyon, George Ella. *The Pirate of Kindergarten.* E (Gr. PreK-1) *19*
Polacco, Patricia. *The Junkyard Wonders.* FIC (Gr. 2-6) *32*

PERSEVERANCE
Hills, Tad. *How Rocket Learned to Read.* E (Gr. PreK-1) *13*

PERSONAL NARRATIVES
Angleberger, Tom. *The Strange Case of Origami Yoda.* FIC (Gr. 3-6) *39*
Barnett, Mac. *Oh No!, or, How My Science Project Destroyed the World.* E (Gr. PreK-3) *18*
Bottner, Barbara. *Miss Brooks Loves Books! (And I Don't).* E (Gr. PreK-2) *16*
Boyce, Frank Cottrell. *Cosmic.* FIC (Gr. 5-8) *27*
Draper, Sharon M. *Out of My Mind.* FIC (Gr. 4-8) *36*
Erskine, Kathryn. *Mockingbird: (Mok'ing-bûrd).* FIC (Gr. 4-7) *32*
Henkes, Kevin. *My Garden.* E (Gr. PreK-1) *17*
Hobbie, Holly. *Everything But the Horse.* E (Gr. K-4) *12*
Holm, Jennifer L. *Turtle in Paradise.* FIC (Gr. 3-6) *40*
McElligott, Matthew. *Even Monsters Need Haircuts.* E (Gr. PreK-2) *12*
Peirce, Lincoln. *Big Nate: In a Class by Himself.* FIC (Gr. 3-6) *26*
Pennypacker, Sara. *Clementine, Friend of the Week.* FIC (Gr. 1-4) *26*
Riordan, Rick. *The Red Pyramid.* FIC (Gr. 5-9) *36*
Stamaty, Mark Alan. *Shake, Rattle & Turn that Noise Down!: How Elvis Changed Music, Me, and Mom.* 782.4 (Gr. 2-6) *53*
Tashjian, Janet. *My Life As a Book.* FIC (Gr. 4-7) *34*
Telgemeier, Raina. *Smile!* FIC (Gr. 5-8) *38*
Vanderpool, Clare. *Moon Over Manifest.* FIC (Gr. 5-8) *33*
Williams-Garcia, Rita. *One Crazy Summer.* FIC (Gr. 5-8) *35*

PERSONIFICATION
Baker, Keith. *LMNO Peas.* E (Gr. PreK-2) *15*
Barton, Chris. *Shark Vs. Train.* E (Gr. PreK-2) *21*

PETS
DiCamillo, Kate, and Alison McGhee. *Bink and Gollie.* E (Gr. PreK-2) *4*

PICTURE BOOKS FOR ALL AGES
Barnett, Mac. *Oh No!, or, How My Science Project Destroyed the World.* E (Gr. PreK-3) *18*
Frazee, Marla. *The Boss Baby.* E (Gr. PreK-2) *5*
Isaacs, Anne. *Dust Devil.* E (Gr. K-4) *10*
Sylvester, Kevin. *Splinters.* E (Gr. 1-4) *22*
Walton, Rick. *Mr. President Goes to School.* E (Gr. K-5) *17*
Willems, Mo. *City Dog, Country Frog.* E (Gr. PreK-1) *9*
Winter, Jeanette. *Biblioburro: A True Story from Columbia.* 020 (Gr. K-6) *43*

PICTURE BOOKS FOR OLDER READERS
Bildner, Phil. *The Hallelujah Flight.* E (Gr. 1-6) *46*
Hill, Laban Carrick. *Dave the Potter: Artist, Poet, Slave.* 738 (Gr. 2-8) *45*

SUBJECT INDEX

Q

QUIETUDE
Underwood, Deborah. *The Quiet Book.* E (Gr. PreK-2) *20*

R

RACE RELATIONS
Pinkney, Andrea Davis. *Sit-In: How Four Friends Stood Up by Sitting Down.* 323.1196 (Gr. 2-6) *54*
Smith, Charles R. *Black Jack: The Ballad of Jack Johnson.* B (Gr. 2-5) *43*
Tavares, Matt. *Henry Aaron's Dream.* 796.357 (Gr. 2-6) *47*

RAIN AND RAINFALL
Thomson, Bill. *Chalk.* E (Gr. PreK-3) *9*

RATS—FOLKLORE
Emberley, Rebecca, and Ed Emberley. *The Red Hen.* 398.2 (Gr. PreK-1) *60*

READER'S THEATER
Becker, Bonny. *A Bedtime for Bear.* E (Gr. PreK-2) *3*
Emberley, Rebecca, and Ed Emberley. *The Red Hen.* 398.2 (Gr. PreK-1) *60*
Fleming, Candace. *Clever Jack Takes the Cake.* E (Gr. PreK-3) *10*
Hoberman, Mary Ann. *You Read to Me, I'll Read to You Very Short Fables to Read Together.* 811 (Gr. PreK-3) *63*
O'Malley, Kevin. *Animal Crackers Fly the Coop.* E (Gr. 1-4) *1*
Scieszka, Jon, and Francesco Sedita. *Spaceheadz.* (SPHDZ, Book #1!) FIC (Gr. 3-5) *38*

REPTILES AND AMPHIBIANS
Bishop, Nic. *Nic Bishop Lizards.* 596 (Gr. PreK-4) *50*
Brett, Jan. *The 3 Little Dassies.* E (Gr. PreK-2) *62*

RESPONSIBILITY
Graham, Bob. *April and Esme, Tooth Fairies.* E (Gr. PreK-2) *2*

RIDDLES
O'Malley, Kevin. *Animal Crackers Fly the Coop.* E (Gr. 1-4) *1*

ROBBERS AND OUTLAWS
Isaacs, Anne. *Dust Devil.* E (Gr. K-4) *10*
O'Malley, Kevin. *Animal Crackers Fly the Coop.* E (Gr. 1-4) *1*
Huling, Jan. *Ol' Bloo's Boogie-Woogie Band and Blues Ensemble.* 398.2 (Gr. 1-5) *59*

ROBOTS
Barnett, Mac. *Oh No!, or, How My Science Project Destroyed the World.* E (Gr. PreK-3) *18*

ROCK HYDRAXES
Brett, Jan. *The 3 Little Dassies.* E (Gr. PreK-2) *62*

ROCK MUSIC
Stamaty, Mark Alan. *Shake, Rattle & Turn that Noise Down!: How Elvis Changed Music, Me, and Mom.* 782.4 (Gr. 2-6) *53*

ROOSTERS—FOLKLORE
Huling, Jan. *Ol' Bloo's Boogie-Woogie Band and Blues Ensemble.* 398.2 (Gr. 1-5) *59*

S

SAN FRANCISCO
Telgemeier, Raina. *Smile!* FIC (Gr. 5-8) *38*
Williams-Garcia, Rita. *One Crazy Summer.* FIC (Gr. 5-8) *35*

SUBJECT INDEX

SCHNEIDER FAMILY AWARD
Lyon, George Ella. *The Pirate of Kindergarten.* E (Gr. PreK-1) *19*

SCHOOL LUNCHROOMS, CAFETERIAS, ETC.
Vernon, Ursula. *Dragonbreath: Curse of the Were-wiener.* FIC (Gr. 3-5) *28*

SCHOOL SHOOTINGS
Erskine, Kathryn. *Mockingbird: (Mok'ing-bûrd).* FIC (Gr. 4-7) *32*

SCHOOLS
Alvarez, Julia. *How Tía Lola Learned to Teach.* FIC (Gr. 3-6) *31*
Angleberger, Tom. *The Strange Case of Origami Yoda.* FIC (Gr. 3-6) *39*
Bottner, Barbara. *Miss Brooks Loves Books! (And I Don't).* E (Gr. PreK-2) *16*
Draper, Sharon M. *Out of My Mind.* FIC (Gr. 4-8) *36*
Erskine, Kathryn. *Mockingbird: (Mok'ing-bûrd).* FIC (Gr. 4-7) *32*
Lyon, George Ella. *The Pirate of Kindergarten.* E (Gr. PreK-1) *19*
McMullan, Kate. *School!: Adventures at the Harvey N. Trouble Elementary School.* FIC (Gr. 2-5) *37*
Peirce, Lincoln. *Big Nate: In a Class by Himself.* FIC (Gr. 3-6) *26*
Pennypacker, Sara. *Clementine, Friend of the Week.* FIC (Gr. 1-4) *26*
Polacco, Patricia. *The Junkyard Wonders.* FIC (Gr. 2-6) *32*
Scieszka, Jon, and Francesco Sedita. *Spaceheadz.* (SPHDZ, Book #1!) FIC (Gr. 3-5) *38*
Vernon, Ursula. *Dragonbreath: Curse of the Were-wiener.* FIC (Gr. 3-5) *28*

SCIENCE
Angleberger, Tom. *The Strange Case of Origami Yoda.* FIC (Gr. 3-6) *39*
Barnett, Mac. *Oh No!, or, How My Science Project Destroyed the World.* E (Gr. PreK-3) *18*
Beccia, Carlyn. *I Feel Better with a Frog in My Throat: History's Strangest Cures.* 610 (Gr. 3-6) *48*
Bildner, Phil. *The Hallelujah Flight.* E (Gr. 1-6) *46*
Bishop, Nic. *Nic Bishop Lizards.* 596 (Gr. PreK-4) *50*
Boyce, Frank Cottrell. *Cosmic.* FIC (Gr. 5-8) *27*
Brown, Don. *A Wizard from the Start: The Incredible Boyhood & Amazing Inventions of Thomas Edison.* B (Gr. 1-4) *56*
Brown, Tami Lewis. *Soar, Elinor!* B (Gr. 2-6) *54*
Cole, Henry. *A Nest for Celeste: A Story About Art, Inspiration, and the Meaning of Home.* FIC (Gr. 3-6) *34*
Henkes, Kevin. *My Garden.* E (Gr. PreK-1) *17*
Isaacs, Anne. *Dust Devil.* E (Gr. K-4) *10*
Jenkins, Steve. *Bones: Skeletons and How They Work.* 573.7 (Gr. K-5) *44*
McCarthy, Meghan. *Pop!: The Invention of Bubble Gum.* 664 (Gr. K-4) *52*
McCully, Emily Arnold. *The Secret Cave: Discovering Lascaux.* 944 (Gr. 2-6) *52*
Montgomery, Sy. *Kakapo Rescue: Saving the World's Strangest Parrot.* (Scientists in the Field series) 639.9 (Gr. 4-8) *49*
Willems, Mo. *City Dog, Country Frog.* E (Gr. PreK-1) *9*

SCIENCE EXPERIMENTS
Barnett, Mac. *Oh No!, or, How My Science Project Destroyed the World.* E (Gr. PreK-3) *18*

SCIENCE FAIRS
Barnett, Mac. *Oh No!, or, How My Science Project Destroyed the World.* E (Gr. PreK-3) *18*

SCIENCE FICTION
Barnett, Mac. *Oh No!, or, How My Science Project Destroyed the World.* E (Gr. PreK-3) *18*
Boyce, Frank Cottrell. *Cosmic.* FIC (Gr. 5-8) *27*
Scieszka, Jon, and Francesco Sedita. *Spaceheadz.* (SPHDZ, Book #1!) FIC (Gr. 3-5) *38*

SCIENCE—POETRY
Elliott, David. *In the Wild.* 811 (Gr. PreK-1) *58*
Hopkins, Lee Bennett, comp. *Sharing the Seasons: A Book of Poems.* 811 (Gr. 2-6) *61*
Sidman, Joyce. *Dark Emperor & Other Poems of the Night.* 811 (Gr. 3-6) *57*
Sidman, Joyce. *Ubiquitous: Celebrating Nature's Survivors.* 811 (Gr. 3-6) *62*
Yolen, Jane, ed. *Switching on the Moon: A Very First Book of Bedtime Poems.* 398.8 (Gr. PreK-1) *61*

SCIENCE PROJECTS
Barnett, Mac. *Oh No!, or, How My Science Project Destroyed the World.* E (Gr. PreK-3) *18*

SUBJECT INDEX

SCIENTISTS
Brown, Don. *A Wizard from the Start: The Incredible Boyhood & Amazing Inventions of Thomas Edison.* B (Gr. 1-4) *56*
Engle, Margarita. *Summer Birds: The Butterflies of Maria Merian.* 595.78 (Gr. 1-4) *55*
Montgomery, Sy. *Kakapo Rescue: Saving the World's Strangest Parrot.* (Scientists in the Field series) 639.9 (Gr. 4-8) *49*

SEASHORE
Nelson, Marilyn. *Snook Alone.* E (Gr. 2-6) *22*

SEASONS
Willems, Mo. *City Dog, Country Frog.* E (Gr. PreK-1) *9*

SEASONS—POETRY
Hopkins, Lee Bennett, comp. *Sharing the Seasons: A Book of Poems.* 811 (Gr. 2-6) *61*
Raczka, Bob. *Guyku: A Year of Haiku for Boys.* 811 (Gr. PreK-4) *58*

SECRETS
Riordan, Rick. *The Red Pyramid.* FIC (Gr. 5-9) *36*
Tashjian, Janet. *My Life As a Book.* FIC (Gr. 4-7) *34*
Vanderpool, Clare. *Moon Over Manifest.* FIC (Gr. 5-8) *33*

SELF-CONFIDENCE
Lichtenheld, Tom. *Bridget's Beret.* E (Gr. PreK-2) *6*

SELF-ESTEEM
Polacco, Patricia. *The Junkyard Wonders.* FIC (Gr. 2-6) *32*
Telgemeier, Raina. *Smile!* FIC (Gr. 5-8) *38*

SELFLESSNESS
Pennypacker, Sara. *Clementine, Friend of the Week.* FIC (Gr. 1-4) *26*
Winter, Jeanette. *Biblioburro: A True Story from Columbia.* 020 (Gr. K-6) *43*

SHARING
Vere, Ed. *Banana!* E (Gr. PreK-1) *3*

SHARKS
Barton, Chris. *Shark Vs. Train.* E (Gr. PreK-2) *21*

SHIPS
Preus, Margi. *Heart of a Samurai: Based on the True Story of Nakahama Manjiro.* FIC (Gr. 5-8) *30*

SHIPWRECKS
Preus, Margi. *Heart of a Samurai: Based on the True Story of Nakahama Manjiro.* FIC (Gr. 5-8) *30*

SHOES
Litwin, Eric. *Pete the Cat: I Love My White Shoes.* E (Gr. PreK-1) *19*

SIBLING RIVALRY
Khan, Rukhsana. *Big Red Lollipop.* E (Gr. K-4) *4*

SICK
Beccia, Carlyn. *I Feel Better with a Frog in My Throat: History's Strangest Cures.* 610 (Gr. 3-6) *48*
Peet, Mal, and Elspeth Graham. *Cloud Tea Monkeys.* FIC (Gr. 1-4) *27*
Stead, Philip C. *A Sick Day for Amos McGee.* E (Gr. PreK-1) *21*

SINGERS—FOLKLORE
Huling, Jan. *Ol' Bloo's Boogie-Woogie Band and Blues Ensemble.* 398.2 (Gr. 1-5) *59*

SINGING
Litwin, Eric. *Pete the Cat: I Love My White Shoes.* E (Gr. PreK-1) *19*

SUBJECT INDEX

SUBJECT INDEX

SUBJECT INDEX

Polacco, Patricia. *The Junkyard Wonders.* FIC (Gr. 2-6) *32*
Scieszka, Jon, and Francesco Sedita. *Spaceheadz.* (SPHDZ, Book #1!) FIC (Gr. 3-5) *38*
Walton, Rick. *Mr. President Goes to School.* E (Gr. K-5) *17*

TEETH
Graham, Bob. *April and Esme, Tooth Fairies.* E (Gr. PreK-2) *2*
Telgemeier, Raina. *Smile!* FIC (Gr. 5-8) *38*

THREE LITTLE PIGS
Brett, Jan. *The 3 Little Dassies.* E (Gr. PreK-2) *62*

TOOTH FAIRY
Graham, Bob. *April and Esme, Tooth Fairies.* E (Gr. PreK-2) *2*

TOYS
Barton, Chris. *Shark Vs. Train.* E (Gr. PreK-2) *21*
Willems, Mo. *Knuffle Bunny Free: An Unexpected Diversion.* E (Gr. PreK-2) *14*

TRAINS
Barton, Chris. *Shark Vs. Train.* E (Gr. PreK-2) *21*

TRANSCONTINENTAL FLIGHTS
Bildner, Phil. *The Hallelujah Flight.* E (Gr. 1-6) *46*

TRAVELING LIBRARIES
Winter, Jeanette. *Biblioburro: A True Story from Columbia.* 020 (Gr. K-6) *43*

TURTLES
Nelson, Marilyn. *Snook Alone.* E (Gr. 2-6) *22*

TWAIN, MARK, 1835-1910
Kerley, Barbara. *The Extraordinary Mark Twain (According to Susy).* FIC (Gr. 3-6) *45*

TWINS
Lin, Grace. *Ling & Ting: Not Exactly the Same!* E (Gr. PreK-2) *15*

U

U.S.—HISTORY—REVOLUTION, 1775-1783
Freedman, Russell. *Lafayette and the American Revolution.* B (Gr. 6-9) *50*
Silvey, Anita. *Henry Knox: Bookseller, Soldier, Patriot.* B (Gr. 3-6) *47*

U.S.—HISTORY—TWENTIETH CENTURY
Pinkney, Andrea Davis. *Sit-In: How Four Friends Stood Up by Sitting Down.* 323.1196 (Gr. 2-6) *54*

V

VACATIONS
Williams-Garcia, Rita. *One Crazy Summer.* FIC (Gr. 5-8) *35*

VAMPIRES
McElligott, Matthew. *Even Monsters Need Haircuts.* E (Gr. PreK-2) *12*

VERMONT
Alvarez, Julia. *How Tía Lola Learned to Teach.* FIC (Gr. 3-6) *31*

VISION
Lyon, George Ella. *The Pirate of Kindergarten.* E (Gr. PreK-1) *19*

SUBJECT INDEX

235

We've been listening
—a new

NoveList® K-8

is here!

You told us that you're looking for quick and easy ways to lead readers to the books they will love — and we listened. The enhanced version of NoveList® K-8 is designed to make searching more intuitive and reading recommendations easier to obtain, and allows for quicker access to more curricular-based content than ever.

▶ We know that searching is important, so the search box will stay at the top of every page.

▶ A new Teaching with Books page is dedicated to connecting books to the curriculum and engaging readers to promote reading success.

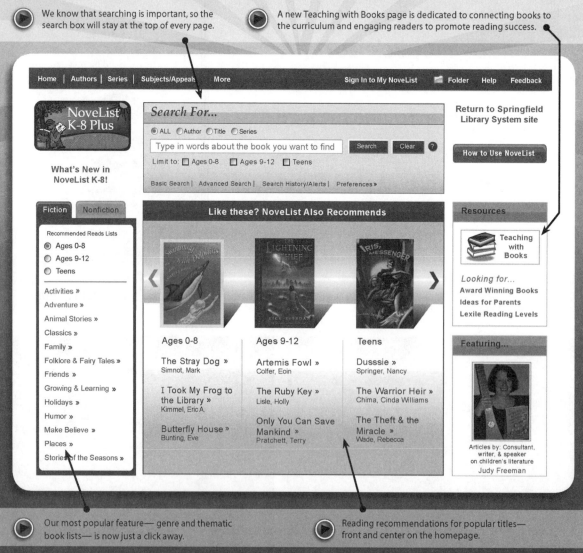

▶ Our most popular feature— genre and thematic book lists— is now just a click away.

▶ Reading recommendations for popular titles— front and center on the homepage.

Be sure to check out **http://support.ebsco.com/novelist** for the latest information.

Teaching with Books

Another great new feature of NoveList K-8

Here you'll find curriculum-related articles arranged by grades covering school subjects such as:

- Language Arts
- Math
- Science

Not only that, you'll quickly and easily be able to view Curriculum Standards and get to Lexile information.

The **Teaching with Books** page is a wonderful resource for librarians, teachers, and parents alike.

TO FIND JUDY FREEMAN'S BER & WINNERS!
BOOKLISTS FROM THE PAST 2 YEARS:

1. Log in to Follett Library Resources at **www.titlewave.com**

2. Click on **ESSENTIALS** at the top of the page.

3. Scroll down to **EXPERT PICKS** and click on: **Judy Freeman**.

4. Near the top of the page, click on the name **Judy Freeman** again and you'll see links to the booklists for her past and present workshops. Sort by author, title, or subject; find reviews, full-color book covers, and even levels and lexiles, if you need them. Save your own lists on the site, and print them out with or without annotations.

JAMES PATTERSON, FIRST BOOK, & Judy Freeman present . . .

The 2008 Kids and Family Reading Report by Yankelovich and Scholastic found that **82% of parents want their child to read more books for fun** and employ many tactics—from buying books as gifts to using their kids' interest in TV shows and movies—to encourage reading. Also, almost **50% of parents admit to needing help finding information about books for their children**.

America's #1 storyteller, James Patterson, has joined forces with First Book (an organization that works to get kids their first book) and acclaimed children's literature expert Judy Freeman to start **ReadKiddoRead.com**—a website designed to help parents, teachers, and librarians ignite the next generation's excitement about reading by recommending books carefully chosen for their ability to make kids' mouths water—books kids can really sink their teeth into.

Complete with age designations, thoughtful book descriptions, author and celebrity interviews, and more, **ReadKiddoRead.com** will help make finding a book for a young person easy and, ultimately, rewarding. The site features:

- Book selections in appropriate age categories and extensive reviews by children's literature expert Judy Freeman
- Thoughtful descriptions of each recommended book with easily accessed links to online retailers where books can be purchased
- A lively community network which will promote helpful discussions about personal experiences with books found on the site—or off of the site—that are great for kids (Click on COMMUNITY at the top of the home page.)
- Personal input and messages from James Patterson about the importance of getting kids excited about reading and his own experience as a father of a ten-year-old son
- Contributions from other authors and celebrities who believe in the importance of getting kids excited about reading

With promotional support from Scholastic Book Fairs, *People* magazine, and others, word about **ReadKiddoRead.com** is spreading fast and wide. The site was mentioned in a feature story on James Patterson in the current issue of *American Way* magazine, and launched in September of 2008. Since then, it has won the first annual Foundations in Reading Prize from the National Book Foundation in 2009 and been named an ALA Great Site. Our goal? To help your kids become readers for life!

WWW.READKIDDOREAD.COM

Books Kids Will Sit Still For 3: A Read-Aloud Guide

By Judy Freeman

This excellent resource will be a favorite with teachers who need assistance finding quality children's literature, and it will also aid librarians and media specialists . . . She encourages educators to create lifelong learners, library users, and book lovers.—School Library Journal

Every school library must have a copy of this book, and every teacher needs to know about it to freshen his or her own use of literature in the classroom. There has never been a time in education when better children's literature--fiction and nonfiction--existed, and this book will lead you to the best blooms in the garden of print. Essential as a book selection tool and a source to feature, booktalk, read aloud, and tantalize elementary school children.—Teacher Librarian

Elementary school teachers, librarians, and parents rejoice! *Books Kids Will Sit Still For 3* by librarian and children's literature troubadour Judy Freeman is here at last. It's an all-new treasure trove of 1,700 all-new, tried-and-true, child-tested favorite read-aloud titles, published since 1995, and a comprehensive source of thousands of inspirational literature-based ideas.

Books Kids Will Sit Still For 3 is the definitive source for the best recent picture books, fiction, poetry, folklore, and nonfiction books to share with children from preschool through sixth grade. Along with the extensively annotated bibliography of 1,705 outstanding recent children's books to read aloud, it incorporates thousands of new and practical ideas for booktalking, creative drama, storytelling, poetry, creative writing, library skills, and other literature-based teaching. There is also a completely new bibliography of professional books.

Extensive all-new chapters offer entertaining, informative, and instantly useful approaches to reading aloud, storytelling, creative drama, Reader's Theater, and nonstop classroom and library activities across the curriculum. Find out "17 Things You Need to Know to Be a Great School Librarian." Learn how to evaluate a new book. See what it's like to be on the Newbery Committee. Each entry in the bibliography now contains five parts: bibliographic information; a lively descriptive annotation; a series of brief follow-up ideas called "Germs"; related titles list; and subjects list. You'll find *Books Kids Will Sit Still For 3* to be a goldmine and a godsend!

Children's and Young Adult Literature Reference Series
Libraries Unlimited, 2006
ISBN: 1-59158-163-X; 936 pgs; $70.00 hardcover
ISBN: 1-59158-164-8; 936 pgs; $55.00 paper
For a 20% Conference Discount, use Code #091FLA4

JUDY FREEMAN (www.JudyReadsBooks.com) is a well-known speaker, consultant, and writer on all aspects of children's literature, storytelling, booktalking, and school librarianship. A former elementary school librarian, she gives workshops, speeches, and performances throughout the U.S. and the world for teachers, librarians, parents, and children, and is a national seminar presenter for BER (Bureau of Education and Research). Judy writes several children's book review columns, including "Desperate Librarians" for the online fiction database *NoveList,* and "What's New" for *School Library Journal*'s *Curriculum Connections*, and writes the reviews and content for author James Patterson's new website for parents, **www.ReadKiddoRead.com.**

More Books Kids Will Sit Still For
By Judy Freeman

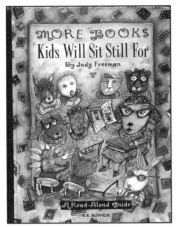

"Liberally sprinkled with titles, chock full of ideas and supplemented with high-quality bibliographies ... librarians will find helpful and few children will be able to resist."—**Booklist**

"Drawing on her years of experience as librarian and storyteller, Freeman offers practical suggestions for numerous literature-based activities to enrich the language arts curriculum."—**School Library Journal**

Based on the author's longtime experience as a school librarian and storyteller, this book offers 1,400 titles—including picture books, folk tales, poetry, and nonfiction—guaranteed to engage children. Annotated entries include brief plot summaries, subject designations, related titles, and curriculum tie-ins. **Libraries Unlimited, 1995**

0-8352-3731-1; 868 pages; 1995; $32.95 (paper)
0-8352-3520-3; 868 pages; 1995; $55.00 (hardcover)

Books Kids Will Sit Still For
By Judy Freeman

"The book talk, creative dramatics, storytelling and book-celebrating activities should be a part of every reading and language arts program."— **The Reading Teacher**

". . . detailed annotations of over 2,000 kid-tested titles, curriculum tie-ins and classroom activities, grade-level suggestions, and a comprehensive subject index that alone is worth the cost of the book."—**Library Talk**

Libraries Unlimited, 1990
0-8352-3010-4; 660 pages; 1990; $55.00 hardcover

Quantity	ISBN	AUTHOR/TITLE	PRICE	TOTAL
	1-59158-163-X	**Books Kids Will Sit Still For 3 (hardcover)**		
	1-59158-164-X	**Books Kids Will Sit Still For 3 (paper)**		
	0-8352-3731-1	**More Books Kids Will Sit Still For (paper)**		
	0-8352-3520-3	**More Books Kids Will Sit Still for (hardcover)**		
	0-8352-3010-4	**Books Kids Will Sit Still For (hardcover)**		
Send order to address below Or call: 1-800-368-6868; Or fax: 1-805-685-9685 Or Online: www.lu.com Orders by email: orders@abc-clio.com For a 20% Conference Discount, use Code #091FLA4		Subtotal:		
		Shipping: (add 10% or $8.00 Minimum)		
		Sales Tax: (IL, MA, CO, CT, PA, MD, SD, MO, NJ) Canada residents add GST Tax Or include Tax Exempt #		
		Total:		

If using a purchase order please attach it to this form.

Send order to: Libraries Unlimited
            ABC-CLIO Customer Service
            P.O. Box 1911
            Santa Barbara, CA 93116-1911

LIBRARIES UNLIMITED

AN IMPRINT OF ABC-CLIO, LLC
Santa Barbara, California • Denver, Colorado • Oxford, England

The WINNERS! Handbook
A Closer Look at Judy Freeman's
Top-Rated Children's Books

By Judy Freeman

 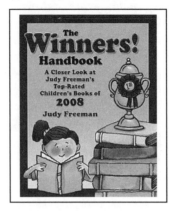 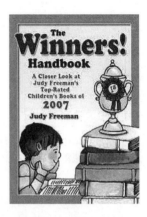

Libraries Unlimited; approx. 200 pages each; $35.00; Grades K-6.
FOR A 20% CONFERENCE DISCOUNT, USE CODE #091FLA4

Each year's *The WINNERS! Handbook* contains Judy Freeman's extensively annotated list of her 100+ best books of the past year for grades K-6, including the Newbery, Caldecott, Sibert, and Geisel Medal winners. Each entry includes:

- a meaty and thoughtful annotation; most of the books are fabulous read-alouds, read-alones, and natural choices for Guided Reading, Literature Circles, or Book Clubs;
- a "Germ" (If you're looking for a good idea or two or three to try out with your children, a Germ is a series of practical, do-able, useful, pithy ideas for reading, writing, and illustrating prompts and other activities across the curriculum. From story hour to school curriculum tie-ins, the many connections include strategies for comprehension, critical thinking skills, research and problem-solving, songs, games, crafts, poetry, creative drama and Reader's Theater, storytelling, booktalking, and book discussion.);
- a Related Titles list of exemplary books to use for thematic units, follow-ups, read-alouds, and to recommend to readers; and
- a list of subjects to give you a quick idea of the book's genre and themes to ascertain where the book might fit thematically into your curricular plan or program.

If you own Judy's *Books Kids Will Sit Still For 3*, the book reviews follows the same format. (Indeed, you can consider each year's new *WINNERS! Handbook* an update to that book.) In addition to the booklists, you'll find scores of useful and fun ideas, activities, lessons, and ways you can incorporate literature into every aspect of your day and your life. Included are numerous Reader's Theater scripts; articles; lots of lesson plans, worksheets, activities, and book tie-ins; teacher's guides; a collection of songs and stories; and a chapter chock full of children's literature-based websites called "Surfing the Net." The author and title, and extensive subject indexes will help you locate everything. What new books do you need to buy and why? Judy's choices are books she thinks no teacher, librarian, or child can live without. She's tested scores of them with children, and says, with gusto, "These books work!"

The WINNERS! Handbook is based on Judy Freeman's popular Annual WINNERS! Workshops she presents each Spring, sponsored by Libraries Unlimited. For information on the workshop, go to **www.LU.com/winners**.

JUDY FREEMAN (**www.JudyReadsBooks.com**) is a well-known speaker, consultant, book reviewer, columnist, and writer on all aspects of children's literature, storytelling, booktalking, and school librarianship. A former elementary school librarian, she gives workshops, speeches, and performances throughout the U.S. and the world for teachers, librarians, parents, and children. Read her reviews and articles at **www.ReadKiddoRead.com**.

For more information or to order, visit **www.lu.com**. Or call: 1-800-368-6868; or fax: 1-805-685-9685; or email: orders@abc-clio.com. Send purchase orders to:
Libraries Unlimited, ABC-CLIO Customer Service, P.O. Box 1911, Santa Barbara, CA 93116-1911